BRITISH SECRET PROJECTS

BRITISH SECRET PROJECTS 3

Fighters 1935 to 1950
Second Edition

TONY BUTTLER MA AMRAeS

First published in 2004 by Midland Publishing
Second edition published in 2018 by Crécy Publishing

All rights reserved. No part of this book may be reproduced or transmitted in any form or by any means electronic or mechanical, including photocopying, recording or by any information storage without permission from the Publisher in writing. All enquiries should be directed to the Publisher.

© Tony Buttler 2018

A CIP record for this book is available from the British Library

Printed in Printed in Bulgaria by Multiprint

ISBN 9781910809174

Crécy Publishing Limited
1a Ringway Trading Estate, Shadowmoss Road, Manchester M22 5LH
www.crecy.co.uk

FRONT COVER Front cover image is a specially commissioned artwork by Daniel Uhr showing the Hawker P.1030 fight project.

FRONT FLAP
TOP A Hurricane Mk.I about to enter a dive.

MIDDLE The Bristol F.18/37 with 'Centaurus' powerplant (2.5.38). *Duncan Greenman Bristol AirChive*

BOTTOM Spitfire Mk.IX MH880 at the Empire Central Flying School (ECFS) at Hullavington in about 1946. *Peter Arnold collection*

REAR COVER
TOP An artist's impression of the P.103B. *Les Whitehouse*

MIDDLE INSET A model of the Type 391. *Joe Cherrie*

BOTTOM On 20 September 1945 EE227 made its first flight fitted with experimental Rolls-Royce Trent turboprop engines, for which it required small additional finlets.

Contents

Introduction 6
Acknowledgements 7

Chapter One - Pre-War Single-Engine Fixed-Gun Fighters...8
Chapter Two - Wartime Single-Engine Fixed-Gun Fighters..29
Chapter Three - Pre-War Twin-Engine Fixed-Gun Fighters..52
Chapter Four - Wartime Twin-Engine Fixed-Gun Fighters...67
Chapter Five - Turret Fighters and Night Fighters 85
Chapter Six - Naval Fighters Part One 105
Chapter Seven - Naval Fighters Part Two including Strike Fighters 120
Chapter Eight - Advances in Technology..143
Chapter Nine - Stand Alone Projects..151
Chapter Ten - Jet Fighters from Gloster...162
Chapter Eleven - Jet Fighters from Other Manufacturers 187

Appendix One - British WW2 Fighter Aircraft Project Summary..202
Appendix Two - British Fighter Project Specifications 215
Appendix Three - British Fighter Prototype Contracts 217
Bibliography and Source Notes 219
Glossary 220
Index 222

Introduction to the Second Edition

This volume is the third in a series of complete updates of the author's *British Secret Projects* titles for Crécy Publishing and covers the design and development of British fighters from approximately the end of the biplane era to the start of the new millennium. The original edition included both fighters and bombers developed for or during the Second World War, but that substantial work has now been split into two. This title will take in just the fighters, with Volume Four, to follow soon, devoted to bombers and attack aircraft. Both titles will include all of the new designs and information uncovered by the author since the original was published in 2004, plus a large selection of new photos, and they are complementary to his *British Experimental Combat Aircraft of World War II* published by Crécy/Hikoki in 2012. It is difficult to believe that the original work appeared some fourteen years ago!

The subtitle dates, 1935 to 1950, embrace the rearmament period right through to the last first flights of types developed during the war. In other words, the book begins with projects prepared in the knowledge that war was probably coming and closes with some aircraft that were essentially wartime designs, such as the Venom and Sea Hawk, but did not get airborne until after the conflict had ended. In fact, the Venom did not fly until 1949 but, as a development of the Vampire, it is fully representative of wartime aerodynamics, structure and technology. Perhaps the Hawker Sea Hawk, with its bifurcated intake and jet pipes developed specifically to solve the problems of jet propulsion, represents the last word in Second World War fighter technology, and as such connects this volume to the post-1950 books.

Finding a demarcation line has been difficult and I am sure some readers will disagree with the decision to omit, or discuss only briefly, some designs from the 1933/34 period. But I feel that a more thorough coverage of such aeroplanes really belongs to a review of 1920s and early-1930s fighter developments. Once war had broken out some of the pre-war ideas, such as the turret fighter, were found to be flawed, but they still form an important part of this story.

Like all of the titles in the Secret Projects series, extensive use has been made again of previously unpublished primary source material held in museums and record offices and in company and private collections. Much of this had in fact been declassified for twenty or thirty years before the original book came out, but for whatever reason had been rarely accessed by researchers (though in many cases because it had previously been inaccessible). To keep in line with the earlier volumes, particular emphasis is placed yet again on the design competitions between projects from different companies; however, the war did witness a good number of types put into the air with little or no competition, and jet aircraft are perhaps the best example of this.

Sadly, unlike the overall situation for post-war British projects, many designs from the Second World War and before are now lost forever. In some cases archives stored 'for safe keeping' during the war were ruined while in store but, quite understandably, it also appears that some companies soon destroyed some of their piston aircraft archives because they had been made obsolete by the advent of the jet. Nevertheless, many designs have survived and a high percentage of those reproduced here had never been published before the arrival of the first edition. A few 'new' designs can now be added to fill some of the gaps, and as a consequence they form the most complete record yet written of British post-1935 fighter development. Project data throughout are the manufacturer's estimates; if submitted to the Ministry, the figures would normally be reassessed by specialists and often updated or changed (weights in particular would regularly increase), but using company data as much as possible provides a common factor to present the figures.

I hope readers will find much to enjoy in this book. Those who have the original will, I hope, find a reasonable amount of new material to make this new publication worthwhile. For those readers who have not seen the original, I hope you will find this maze of fascinating designs as interesting and inspiring as I have since I first began my research more than 25 years ago. Thank you for taking the time to have a look.

Tony Buttler MA AMRAeS
BRETFORTON, APRIL 2018

Acknowledgements

Once again I am greatly indebted to an enormous number of people who have helped me to put this work together. As before, the lists of unbuilt projects in the Putnam series of books on British Aircraft Manufacturers, and selected other titles listed in the Bibliography, gave the framework from which to begin my own research. After that I must thank the following for allowing me to raid their archives for information, drawings and photographs, and for permission to publish material. Sadly, since the first edition was released some well-known names below have passed away and they are all much missed. I hope I've not forgotten anyone.

Peter Amos; the late Fred Ballam (Westland archive), the late David Birch (Rolls-Royce Heritage, Derby); Alec Brew (Boulton Paul Association); Sir George Cox; Gordon Leith and Simon Moody (RAF Museum archive); Ken Ellis; Paul Lawson and the staff of the BAe Brough Heritage Centre; the late Harry Fraser-Mitchell (Handley Page Association); Bruce Gordon; the late Peter Green; Duncan Greenman (Bristol AirChive); Barry Guess (BAe Farnborough archive); Bill Harrison; the late Derek James; George Jenks (Avro Heritage); Tim Kershaw (Jet Age Museum); Brian Kervell; Roger Lindsay; Paul McMaster (Ulster Aviation Society); Museum of Berkshire Aviation; the National Archives at Kew; the late Jim Oughton; Barry Pegram; Ralph Pegram; Brian Riddle (Royal Aeronautical Society); Solent Sky Museum; Chris Stainer; the late Ray Sturtivant (Air-Britain); Chris Farara and Albert Kitchenside (Brooklands Museum); Barry Wheeler; and Ray Williams.

In addition I am particularly grateful to Joe Cherrie and John Hall for making models that filled gaps in my illustrations, to Peter Arnold for the use of some splendid mid-1940s colour images, and to Phil Butler for the contracts list and for various photographs and other materials. Special thanks also go to Les Whitehouse and the late Eric Morgan for making available their archives, and to Clive Richards (then of MoD Air Historical Branch) for alerting me to details and sources that I had missed.

And of course last but not least I must also thank the team at Crécy for asking me to produce this work and for their marvellous support throughout, and also Daniel Uhr for the fabulous front cover (one of my favourites). Once again it has been a pleasure to work with you all.

Chapter One
Pre-War Single-Engine Fixed-Gun Fighters

ABOVE Hawker Typhoon Mk.1B R7700 pictured on 5 September 1942. *Phil Butler*

The most famous British fighter of the Second World War has to be the Supermarine Spitfire; in fact, ahead of the Hurricane wartime fighter, Harrier jump jet and Concorde supersonic airliner, this is probably the most famous British aircraft of all time. The Spitfire's configuration, a single-seat high-performance aircraft with fixed machine guns or cannon all firing forward, is also the classic arrangement for a fighter, which has survived more or less to the present day. There were other types that were conceived before the Spitfire and Hurricane that served their country well throughout the war years, but a survey of the unbuilt 'wartime' projects produced by the British aircraft industry has to begin somewhere and there is nowhere better than these two fighters, which did so much to win the Battle of Britain, and by doing so began the long haul that led to the defeat of Hitler's forces by the Allies.

In November 1934 the Air Staff produced Specification F.5/34, which called for a single-seat fighter capable of 275mph (442km/h) at 15,000ft (4,572m) and armed with six or eight 0.303in (7.7mm) Browning machine guns. The heavy gun armament represented a big increase over previous fighters, a move stimulated by the studies of Squadron Leader Ralph Sorley, who had calculated that, with the speeds of the latest bombers approaching or exceeding that of current fighters, the chances of making more than one attacking pass were small. Consequently a much greater weight of fire was desirable for the short period that the fighter would be in contact with its target. By using eight 0.303in Browning machine guns a density of 256 rounds per second should be possible and a ground trial was staged with these guns that proved convincing enough for the eight-gun theory to be accepted. In addition the new fighter would be a monoplane

LEFT Britain's last biplane fighter was the Gloster Gladiator, first flown in 1934. This view shows serial K6132.

MIDDLE The Bristol Type 146 prototype K5119 was built to F.5/34. It first flew on 11 February 1938 and had a maximum speed of 287mph (462km/h) at 15,000ft (4,572m). However, it was damaged when taxiing on 28 May 1938 and never repaired. *Duncan Greenman*

BELOW Gloster F.5/34 prototype K5604. The correct date of this aircraft's first flight is still uncertain, but almost certainly took place in either May or June 1937. The fighter had a top speed of 315mph (507km/h) at 16,000ft (4,875m).

that would bring to a close the great line of biplane fighters that had served the RAF for so long.

Sorley, in a paper written after the war, noted many of the factors that would be needed to make the new fighter work – the variable-pitch propeller, a much higher all-up weight (which some saw as a restriction after the biplane's usually exceptional manoeuvrability) and a considerable increase in landing speed over the biplane. These apparently simple steps were the results of a period of great discussion within the RAF and many officers were opposed to the new ideas. In the light of this and other controversial steps described in the following chapters, many aviation books and articles have suggested that the RAF and Air Staff were very slow in adopting new developments in military aircraft; in fact, standard procedure has been to describe how the Air Staff was full of old men full of old ideas, all of whom were incapable of taking on anything new.

There is neither time nor space here to show how untrue this is, but the reader is advised to read Colin Sinnott's book *The Royal Air Force and Aircraft Design 1923-1939* to learn how the Air Staff was actually well acquainted with current advances in aviation and quickly worked them into a wide variety of new specifications and operational requirements. An example is the revelation that the three senior officers with the greatest influence on RAF aircraft procurement, Lord Trenchard, Cyril Newell and Sir John Higgins, were in favour of increasing fighter armament to at least four guns, or even six, as early as 1927. By 1934 the Air Staff and its various technical departments were very concerned by the growing superiority of fighters being developed abroad and they did not want the inferiority of contemporary British aircraft to persist during the period of rearmament. In July of that year the whole question of British fighter design against superior foreign products came under review and the development of the resulting ideas was reflected in the Air Staff's

RIGHT Vickers Type 279 Venom fighter to F.5/34. This small aircraft first flew on 17 June 1936 and achieved a top speed of around 325mph (523km/h) at 15,000ft (4,572m). It was scrapped in 1939.

BELOW Another fighter built to F.5/34 was the Martin-Baker MB.2, first flown on 3 August 1938. This machine's best speed was 305mph (491km/h) at 9,250ft (2,819m).

new fighter specifications, which demanded a much higher performance and technical superiority than their predecessors.

Returning to F.5/34, the first attempt to put heavily armed fighters with high performance into production actually proved unsuccessful. Vickers, Hawker, Bristol, Gloster and Westland were all invited to tender on 2 January 1935 and prototypes were ordered for the Bristol 146, Gloster's design and Vickers 279 Venom, but by the time these entered flight test they had been overtaken by some potentially superior products from Hawker and Supermarine. Another specification, F.10/35, also included eight machine guns and high performance (310mph [499km/h] at 15,000ft [4,572m]) but, despite being circulated to industry and discussed in depth, this was never issued officially.

Hawker Hurricane

During the first half of the 1930s Hawker Aircraft was fully occupied with the design and production of a highly successful family of biplane fighters and light bombers. This included the Fury fighter, the first production example of which flew on 26 March 1931. In August 1933 Hawker's Chief Designer, Sydney Camm, discussed with the Deputy Director of Technical Development (DDTD), Major Buchanan, the possibility of building a new type then known as the 'Fury Monoplane'. This would be armed with four machine guns, two in the fuselage and two in the wings, and powered by a Rolls-Royce Goshawk engine. Ahead of any official Ministry specification, a general layout drawing was completed on 5 December and on the 18th of that month it was discussed in detail with the Air Ministry's Capt Liptrot.

In January 1934 the design was altered to take the new Rolls-Royce PV.12 engine (later called the Merlin), which promised to outstrip contemporary engines from a power point of view, a feature that made it particularly suitable for fighters. Stressing of the 'Interceptor Monoplane', as it was now called, commenced in March and two months later working drawings were begun by the Experimental Drawing Office. At this stage the project was still a company private venture, but the configuration had been refined and in July Buchanan was able to report that the preliminary design had been completed and Hawker was on the point of building a prototype. On 4 September the full design was submitted to the Air Ministry, which now assumed responsibility for its development as an experimental type.

On 10 January 1935 a Mock-Up Conference with Air Ministry staff was held at Kingston, and by the 21st the estimated maximum speed was 330mph (531km/h) at 15,000ft, based on a normal loaded weight of 4,900lb

Hawker Hurricane Mk.1 (flown)	
Span:	40ft 0in (12.19m)
Length:	32ft 3in (9.83m)
Wing Area:	258sq.ft (23.99sq.m)
All-Up-Weight:	6,793lb (3,081kg)
Powerplant:	1 x RR Merlin III 1,030hp (768kW)
Max Speed / Height:	320mph (515km/h) at 17,500ft (5,334m)
Armament:	8 x 0.303in (7.7mm) machine guns

(2,223kg). An Air Ministry contract to purchase a prototype of the design submitted the previous September, against a new official specification F.36/34, was placed on 21 February, and in April provision was to be made for two Vickers Mk.V guns housed in the fuselage with one Browning machine gun in each wing. Investigations into the construction of metal stressed-skin outer wings began on 10 July (early Hurricanes had fabric-covered outer wings) and the contract was amended on 20 August to include another set of wings with eight guns (either Vickers or Brownings).

The prototype Hurricane, K5083, made its maiden flight on 6 November 1935 and official documents acknowledge the value of Hawker's private venture work on this aircraft as an important part of the Ministry's plans. Originally the company had hoped to fly K5083 in the spring of 1935, but some of the delay was caused by the Air Staff's desire to fit eight guns. Sorley had pointed out that that the mock-up F.36/34 and F.37/34 (the Spitfire) required few alterations to conform to F.10/35 and both Hawker and Supermarine were anxious to incorporate them.

However, certain technical problems needed to be solved, the biggest being how to mount the eight guns. To enable a fighter to obtain the best possible speed it was necessary to keep it as slim as possible, which made the fuselage size vitally important. Mounting the guns in the fuselage tended to increase the cross-sectional area, but the relatively thick monoplane wing offered a space where the guns might be mounted. A battery of four in each wing demanded a rigid structure, and since the Hurricane wing was relatively thick this installation was somewhat easier than for the Spitfire's thinner example. However, the Hurricane prototype was far too advanced for its wings to be modified and this was the reason why an alternative pair had to be built, which were delivered in June 1936.

ABOVE A well-known photograph of the Hawker Hurricane prototype K5083 taken in October 1935.

The first production Hurricane, L1547, flew on 12 October 1937 and the aircraft proved to be a most versatile machine. Many Merlin-powered variants were developed including a low-level attack version with two 40mm Vickers guns under the wings. The Hurricane also had the distinction of being the first monoplane fighter in the RAF and the first of the new types developed under the early expansion programme to be delivered to the service. More than 14,500 were eventually built, and there were proposals to fit an example with the more powerful Rolls-Royce Griffon. A prototype was begun but never completed, and on 27 February 1941 Roderic Hill, DGRD, reported that 'the Hurricane with Griffon is not considered worthwhile'.

Supermarine Type 300 Spitfire

The Chief Designer at Supermarine, Reginald Mitchell, acquired a great deal of experience of high-speed flight from his series of racing seaplanes built for the Schneider Trophy competition in the 1920s and early 1930s. His first real essay into fighter design was a machine called the Type 224, which was designed to a key specification of the early 1930s called F.7/30. The 224 had an inverted gull wing and a Rolls-Royce Goshawk engine, but did not become airborne until 19 February 1934 (on 20 December 1933 Supermarine asked the Air Ministry's H. Grinstead to reserve the name Spitfire for this aircraft). Because of the long delays, the company was denied a production order but by the time the machine was delivered to A&AEE Martlesham Heath Mitchell was discussing with the Air Ministry a number of drastic changes to increase its performance.

The arrival of the new Rolls-Royce PV.12 allowed Mitchell to move on to a new layout. In a letter to Buchanan dated July 1934 he outlined a specification and drawings for a modified F.7/30 that incorporated new smaller-area wings, a retractable chassis, new fuel tanks and airscrew, new tailplane and a combined oil tank and cooler under the engine. It was estimated that the modified aircraft could fly in early 1935 and would offer a speed of 265mph (426km/h). The Ministry fell in with Mitchell's proposals but Buchanan now pointed out the likely need to fit eight guns (rather than the project's four) and recommended asking Supermarine to build a completely new prototype rather than modify the old one.

ABOVE A Hurricane Mk.I about to enter a dive.

BELOW Hurricane Mk.IIa Z2521.

In December 1934 a contract was placed for a prototype to be delivered by October 1935, although a few days later it was decided to fit a PV.12 rather than retain the Goshawk, thereby improving the performance still further (it was the Air Ministry that pressed Supermarine to use this engine). A new specification, F.37/34, was allocated to the project and the Mock-Up Conference was held on 26 April 1935, during which Mitchell was shown the new F.10/35 document. He expressed a desire to bring his aircraft (now called the Type 300) into line with this specification, and on 29 April he notified the Air Ministry of the modifications that could be incorporated to affect this.

The new thin elliptical wings of the Type 300, which were its special feature, presented many problems for installing the guns, but prototype K5054 made its maiden flight on 5 April 1936. A large production order was placed in June 1936 and the first machine was delivered in July 1938. The Spitfire was to be built in huge numbers (more than 20,000, with another 2,500 Seafires – see Chapter 6), and right through the war its makers achieved a near constant and progressive series of modifications, regularly signposted by the introduction of new marks. There were changes in armament through the introduction of cannon and changes to the cockpit, but above all a continuous improvement to the Rolls-Royce powerplant, which included the introduction of the Griffon.

It was the need to keep a satisfactory margin of performance over enemy fighters that prompted the need to fit the Griffon, the first variant to reach production being the Mk.XII. Supermarine's first proposals for a Griffon Spitfire were in fact made towards the end of 1939, and on 4 December a brochure was completed that suggested a top speed of 423mph (681km/h) at 18,500ft (5,639m), compared to 367mph (591km/h) for the standard Spitfire with the Merlin II. Difficulties with the development

CHAPTER ONE

Supermarine Spitfire Mk.1 (flown)

Span:	36ft 10in (11.23m)
Length:	29ft 11in (9.12m)
Wing Area:	242sq.ft (22.51sq.m)
All-Up-Weight:	6,256lb (2,838kg)
Powerplant:	1 x Merlin III 1,030hp (768kW)
Max Speed / Height:	355mph (571km/h) at 19,000ft (5,791m)
Armament:	8 x 0.303in (7.7mm) machine guns

Supermarine Spitfire Mk.XIV (flown)

Span:	36ft 10in (11.23m)
Length:	32ft 8in (9.96m)
Wing Area:	242sq.ft (22.51sq.m)
All-Up-Weight:	8,488lb (3,850kg)
Powerplant:	1 x RR Griffon 65 2,050hp (1,529kW)
Max Speed / Height:	448mph (721km/h) at 26,000ft (7,925m)
Armament:	2 x 20mm cannon, 4 x 0.303in (7.7mm) machine guns

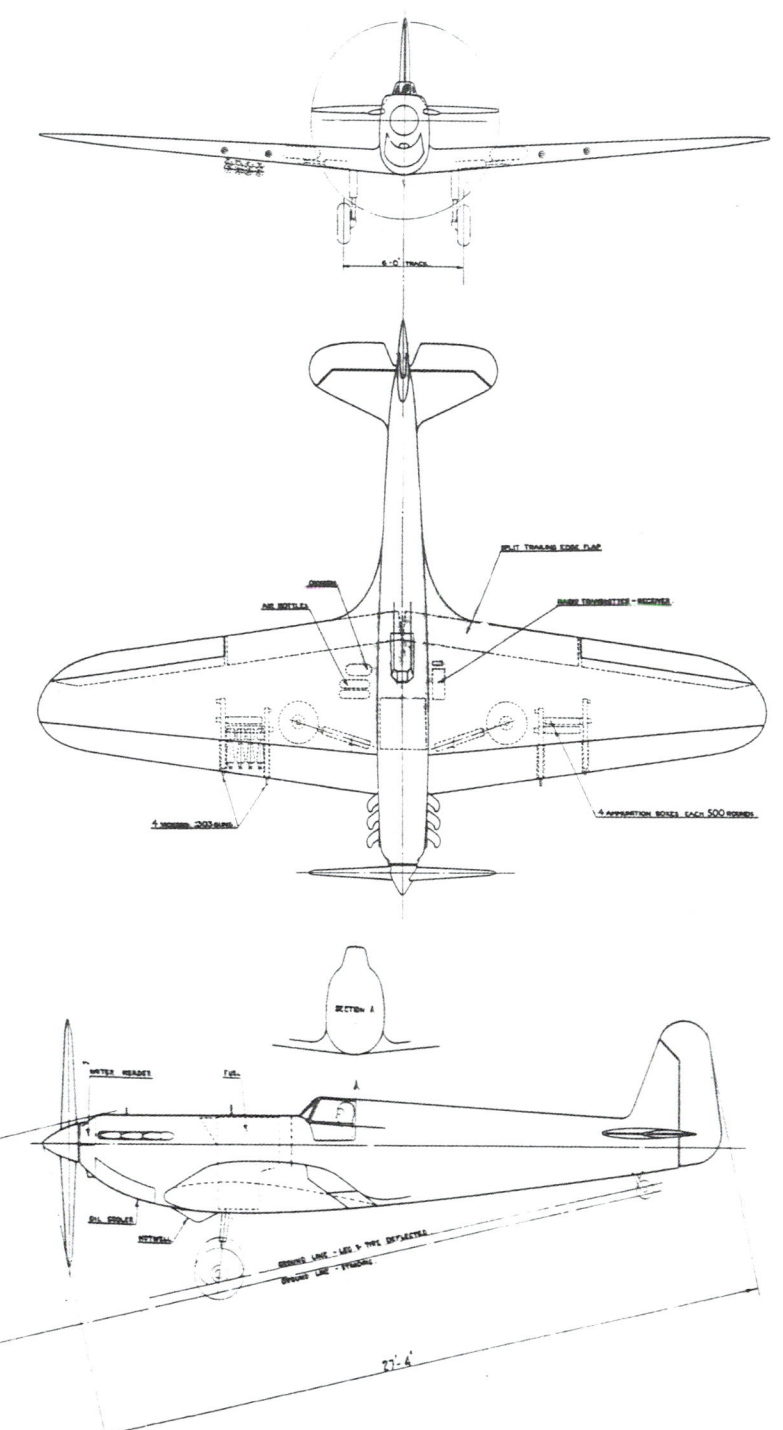

of the Griffon itself brought long delays to this type's service entry, the project often becoming rather static when each new version of the Merlin appeared. It was not until August 1942 that a decision was taken to proceed with a production Spitfire fitted with the alternative engine. A subsequent proposal for a Griffon Spitfire F.Mk.21 development with a reprofiled wing leading edge, the Type 372 or F.Mk.23, was overtaken and pushed out by the 371 Spiteful, described in the next chapter. The Griffon Spitfire should perhaps have received a new name to reflect the great changes made to the original design, but any choice would have struggled to match the charisma of 'Spitfire'.

Specification F.18/37 Hawker Tornado and Typhoon

The description of the Spitfire, outlining as it does the gradual but constant development of the type throughout the war, offers a marked contrast to the method of fighter development adopted by Hawker during this period. In fact, the philosophies of the two companies contrast and complement each other superbly. Reginald Mitchell tragically died in 1937, but was replaced by Joe Smith, who did a wonderful job in keeping his fighter competitive. On the other hand Sydney Camm produced a series of all-new designs, Typhoon,

ABOVE One of the best-known of British unbuilt aircraft designs is this early precursor to the Spitfire, the original Supermarine Type 300 powered by a Rolls-Royce Goshawk engine and carrying four machine guns (24.1.34).

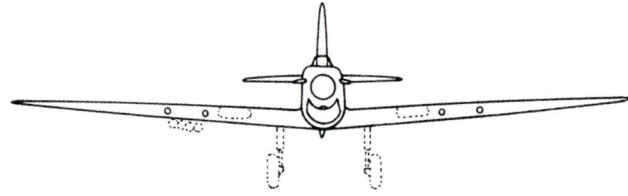
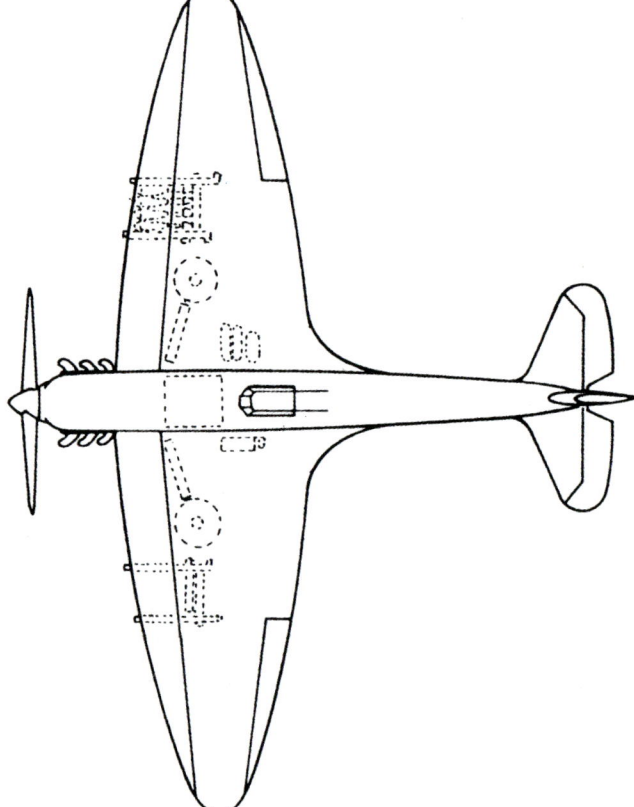
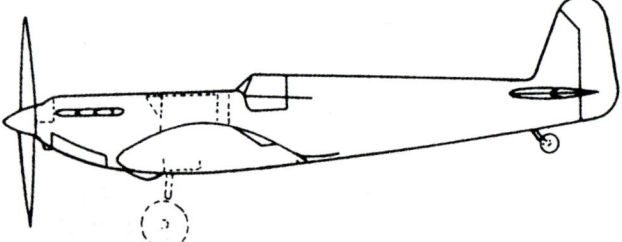
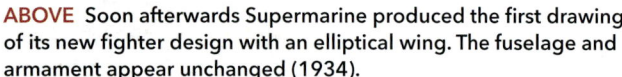

ABOVE Soon afterwards Supermarine produced the first drawing of its new fighter design with an elliptical wing. The fuselage and armament appear unchanged (1934).

TOP RIGHT A view of the Spitfire prototype K5054 with its twin-blade propeller.

MIDDLE RIGHT P9450 was a Spitfire Mk.I.

BOTTOM RIGHT (2) Griffon Spitfire F.Mk.22 PK312 pictured in March 1945.

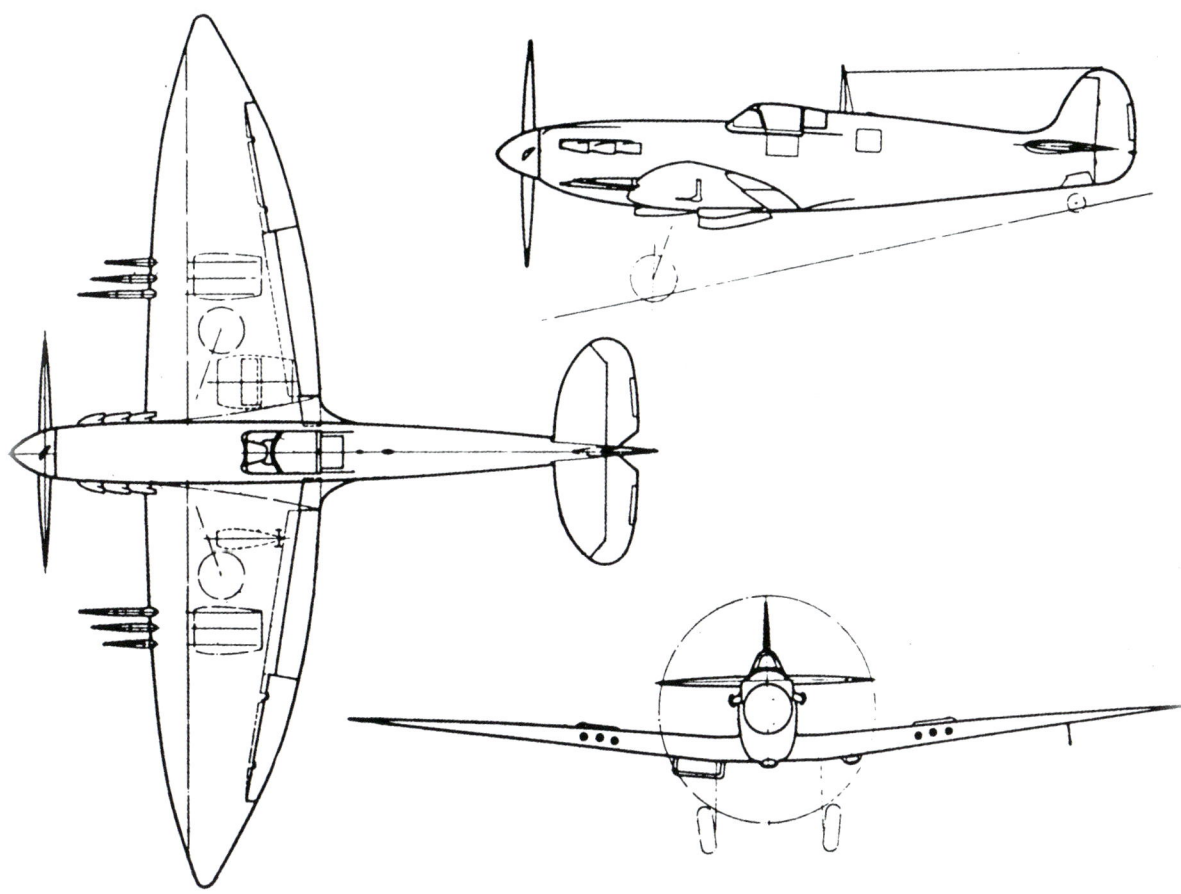

ABOVE As early as 1938 consideration was given to fitting the Rolls-Royce Griffon engine into the Spitfire, and the first brochure was dated 4 December 1939, but it was some time before the idea came to fruition. For a period the Griffon Spitfire was known as the Mk.IV, and Specification F.4/41 was allocated to it in February 1941. This is one of the Mk.IV proposal drawings, thought to be dated April 1941. It is armed with six 20mm cannon (note the rectangular gun blisters on the upper wing surfaces) and has the extended wing tips used later by high-altitude Spitfires. Maximum speed was estimated to be 433mph (697km/h) at 23,500ft (7,163m).

BELOW Spitfire Mk.IX MH880 at the Empire Central Flying School (ECFS) at Hullavington in about 1946. *Peter Arnold collection*

ABOVE Another ECFS Hullavington colour photo, this time showing Spitfire F.Mk.24 VN317 in about 1946. *Peter Arnold collection*

Tempest and Fury, which were, however, closely related since each new layout showed important similarities to its predecessor. Camm's hand was also forced by the lack of development potential in the Hurricane, but the first of these follow-on aeroplanes, the Typhoon, would result from a tender design competition.

Specification F.18/37, officially dated March 1938, called for a high-speed single-seat fighter to replace the Spitfire and Hurricane (for many years it was Air Staff practice to begin looking for a replacement almost as soon as a new type had entered service). A speed of at least 400mph (644km/h) at 15,000ft (4,572m) was requested, armament was increased to twelve 0.303in (7.7mm) Browning machine guns, and the service ceiling was not to be below 35,000ft (10.668m). The designs tendered to the specification are detailed below. (Note: although this chapter describes RAF single-engined fighter development, the need to put the F.18/37 tenders together means that some twin-engine designs have to be considered here.)

Bristol F.18/37

One basic design or airframe was proposed by Bristol to F.18/37, which then had three alternative engine choices, Bristol Centaurus, Napier Sabre or Rolls-Royce Vulture. For the Centaurus the overall drag of the engine body combination was kept low in two ways. First, the external shape was kept as free as possible from all protuberances, and for this reason all of the air necessary for cooling the engine and supplying the carburettor intakes was taken in through the annular opening around the airscrew spinner. As such no scoops of any kind would project through the surface of the body, thereby reducing the overall drag. Second, a method of cowling and cooling was used that avoided all leaks and discontinuities of contour and increased the cooling efficiency. The exhaust tail pipe was taken beneath the wing where it gave the greatest

BELOW Side views of the Bristol F.18/37 fitted with Sabre and Vulture engines (2.5.38). *Duncan Greenman Bristol AirChive*

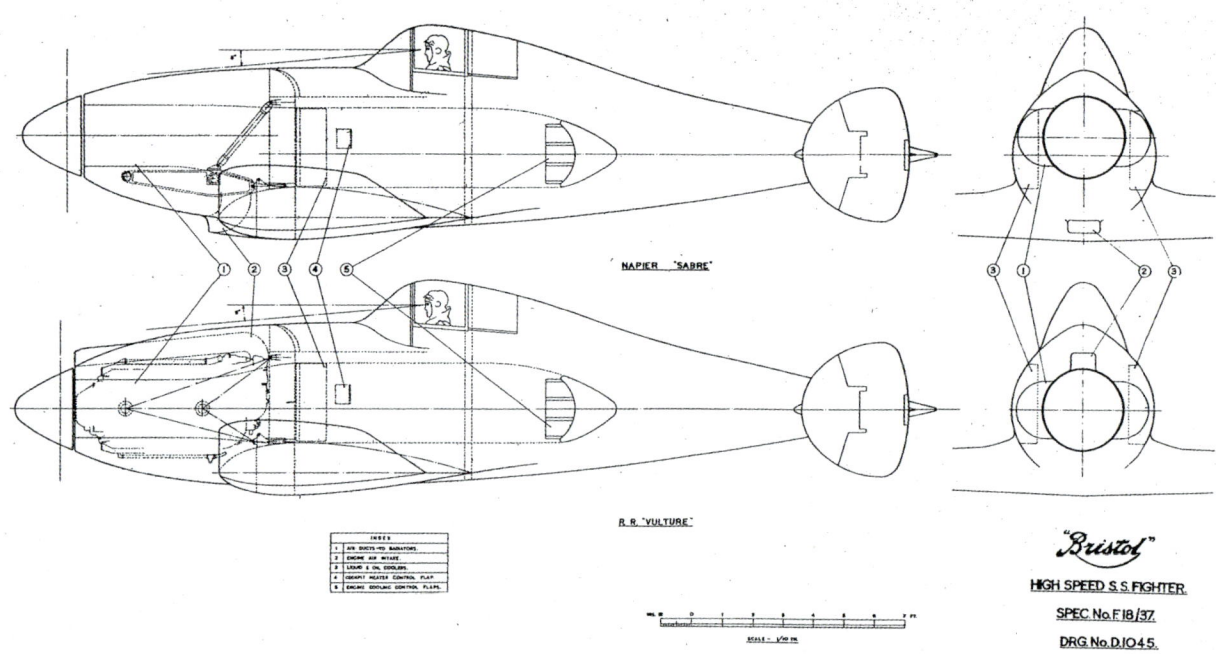

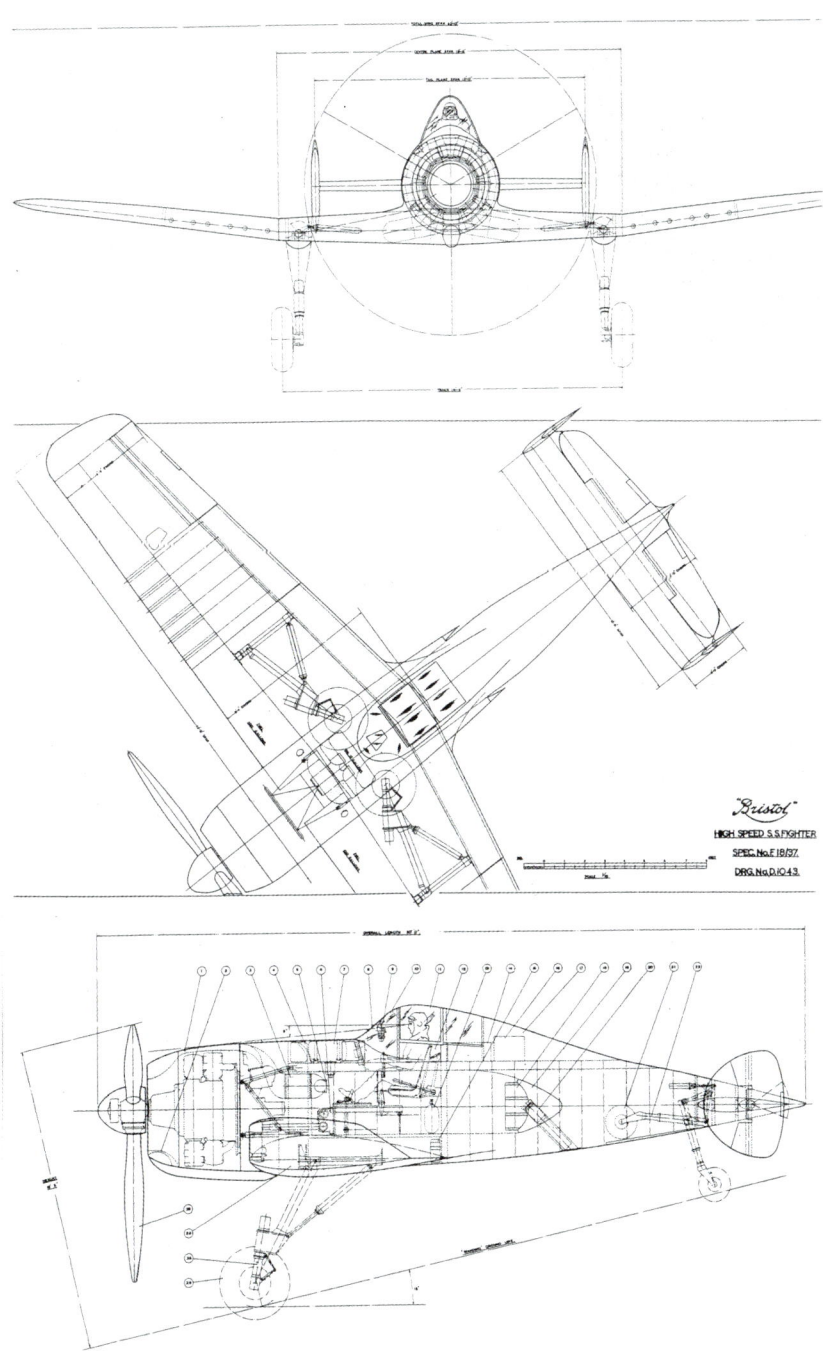

ABOVE The Bristol F.18/37 with 'Centaurus' powerplant (2.5.38). *Duncan Greenman Bristol AirChive*

flame damping and noise insulation, and the end of the pipe was reduced in diameter to offer the greatest possible benefit from exhaust reaction.

The tail had twin fins and rudders mounted on the extremities of the horizontal tailplane. This reduced the overall drag, and the reduction of torque on the body would bring a general reduction of weight and would enable the large tail wheel to be retracted completely without a serious local increase in structure weight. Another benefit was the better spinning qualities obtainable from this type of tail unit. With regard to the wings, to keep the frictional drag as low as possible it was necessary that the installation of the guns, fuel tanks, undercarriage, etc, should interfere as little as possible with the wing's smooth surface. For this reason the forward part of the wing was made as a combined spar and fuel tank. Also, to counteract the propeller torque when taking off, use was made of the Bristol patent differential flap. With this device the normal landing and take-off flaps were moved down to different angles on opposite sides of the machine. Then as the speed increased and torque decreased the difference in angles was automatically reduced. This could be achieved by interconnection with an airspeed or engine revolution device, or could be regulated mechanically by twisting the flap operation lever.

The wing structure consisted of a single tubular spar that formed the leading portion of the wing up to 0.3 of the chord, then ribs extending backwards from this spar were fastened to a large tube that formed the hinge attachment for the flaps and ailerons. The inner portion of the spar was used as the fuel tank, and tubes inserted through the spar formed blast tubes for the guns and also served as a reinforcement to the spar itself. Each inner wing fuel tank had a capacity of 100 gallons (455 litres). The outer wing spars spigot to the centre-section spars were attached by a ring of bolts around the spar contour; the folding undercarriage occupied a large part of the centre plane. Six machine guns were mounted in each wing outside the main wheels, but a separate combination of eight Browning guns was also offered. The fuselage body had an inner shell forming the structure proper and an outer fairing that continued the lines of the engine cowling and formed the side ducts for the engine cooling air. Then, in the region of the duct outlets, the inner shell merged into the rear half of the body where it became the outer skin.

The primary engine choice was the Centaurus, but the Napier Sabre and Rolls-Royce Vulture were available as

Bristol F.18/37 (2.5.38)

Span (all versions):	42ft 0in (12.80m)
Length:	Centaurus 30ft 0in (9.14m), Sabre 30ft 4in (9.24m). Vulture 30ft 8in (9.35m)
Wing Area:	265sq.ft (24.65sq.m) All-Up-Weight (148gal/673lit fuel): 8,765lb (3,976kg)
Powerplant:	1 x Bristol Centaurus CE-ISM, Napier Sabre or Rolls-Royce Vulture
Max Speed / Height	(Centaurus): 352mph (566km/h) at sea level, 410mph (660km/h) at 15,000ft (4,572m)
Armament:	12 x 0.303in (7.7mm) Browning machine guns

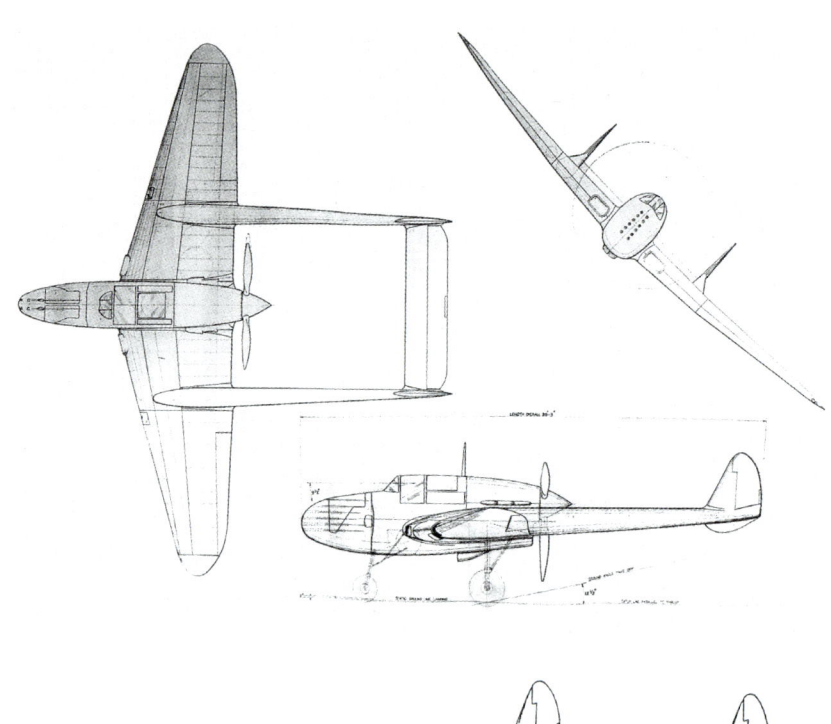

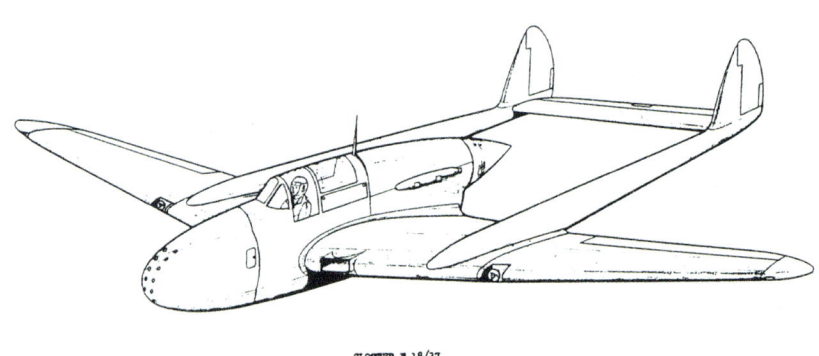

alternatives. In mounting these liquid-cooled engines in the same airframe, it was found advantageous to use the same principle of cooling, with side ducts, as for the Centaurus version. Here, however, the side ducts that formed the conduit for the cooling air that had passed through the engine were used to house the radiators; the radiator came in two units, one situated in each duct. In the case of the Vulture engine the air intake was in the top of the nose, while for the Sabre it was at the bottom. Structurally, the airframe remained the same for each engine up to the special front former, which carried a fireproof bulkhead, its curved front acting as a guide for the cooling air. The Centaurus version would have a three-blade variable-pitch propeller 14ft (4.27m) in diameter, and at its all-up weight the estimated maximum rate of climb was 3,900ft/min (1,189m/min) at 5,000ft (1,524m), sea level rate of climb 3,710ft/min (1,131m/min), service ceiling 37,500ft (11,430m), and absolute ceiling 38,000ft (11,582m). The aircraft would take 4.15 minutes to reach 15,000ft (4,572m).

Gloster F.18/37

Against F.18/37 Gloster proposed two designs, an all-new single-engine twin-boom layout and also a twin-engine aircraft converted and modified from its F9/37 prototype (see Chapter 3) to suit the specification requirements. In fact, it is the former, powered by a single Napier Sabre or Rolls-Royce Vulture liquid-cooled pusher engine

TOP The original Gloster twin-boom F.18/37 design (27.4.38). *Jet Age Museum*

ABOVE An artist's sketch of the Gloster F.18/37.

Gloster F.18/37 (27.4.38)

Span:	46ft 0in (14.02m)
Length Overall:	39ft 3in (11.96m)
Wing Area:	290sq.ft (26.97sq.m)
All-Up-Weight:	10,375lb (4,706kg)
Powerplant:	1 x Napier Sabre 2,100hp (1,566kW) (alternative RR Vulture)
Max Speed / Height	(Sabre): 418mph (673km/h) at 17,500ft (5,334m)
Armament:	12 x 0.303in (7.7mm) machine guns

and first drawn on 27 April 1938, that features most in the Gloster archives. This had radiators placed in the inner wing leading edges and a nose full of guns – twelve Browning machine guns in all, mounted in pairs side by side on a central support. There was

Gloster F.18/37 (14.5.38)

Span:	c50ft (15.24m)
Length:	c40ft (12.19m)
Wing Area:	Unknown
All-Up-Weight:	Unknown
Powerplant:	2 x Bristol Taurus 1,050hp (783kW)
Max Speed / Height:	Unknown
Armament: 1	2 x 0.303in (7.7mm) machine guns

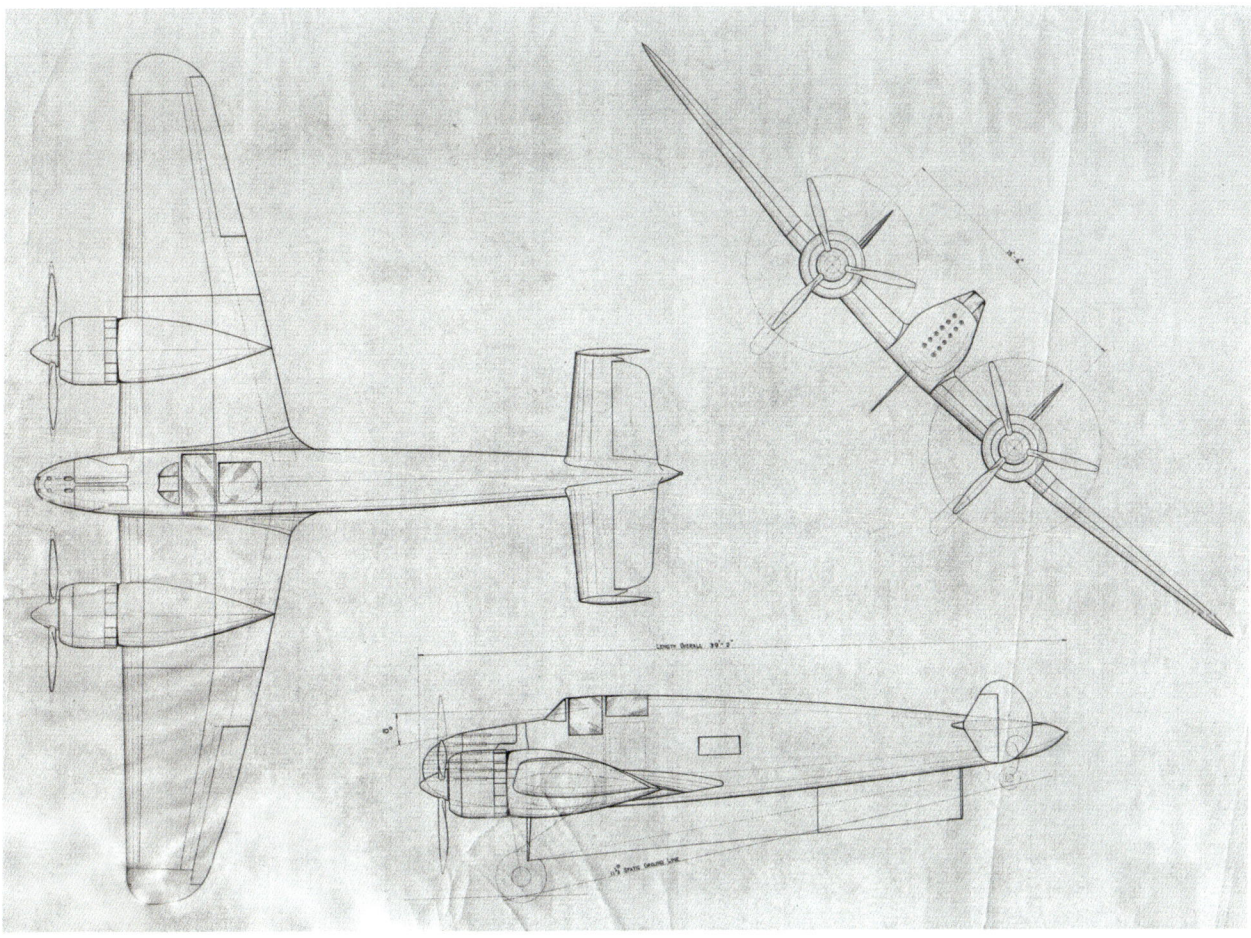

ABOVE The Gloster F.18/37 with twin-Taurus powerplant (14.5.38). *Jet Age Museum*

also a tricycle undercarriage that at the time was still a quite new feature, and the cockpit and engine (with its three-blade propeller) were housed in a small fuselage pod or nacelle. Service ceiling for the Sabre version was given as 38,000ft (11,582m) and the aircraft was expected to take 4.1 minutes to reach 15,000ft (4,572m). It is believed that this project, or a version of it, progressed to the mock-up stage.

The twin-engined design was more conventional and based as stated on the company's F.9/37 fighter, to the point that the wings, engine nacelles, Bristol Taurus radials, tailplane and tailwheel undercarriage employed on the Taurus-powered F.9/37 were carried over to this new proposal. They were married to a new deep fuselage based on the twin-boomer's design, which again had twelve Brownings in its nose in an installation similar to the first design. The drawing is dated 14 May 1938 but data is lacking for this project. In the event Gloster would build the great majority of Hawker Typhoons, the design that entered production following the F.18/37 competition.

Hawker F.18/37

On 12 March 1937 Sydney Camm wrote to the Ministry's Director of Technical Development (DTD), Air Commodore R. H. Verney, to ask what he considered to be the most suitable new project on which his design staff should now concentrate; the reply included a new specification programme that mentioned a dive bomber at the top of the list and a single-seat fighter next. On 5 April design work commenced on a high-speed single-seat fighter fitted with a Napier Sabre and twelve Browning machine guns. Its span was 40ft (12.1m), fuel capacity 200 gallons (909 litres), and consideration was also given to fitting the Rolls-Royce Vulture engine.

Drawings and data for the Sabre fighter were sent to the Ministry on 16 July and Verney replied on 27 August noting that the project had been carefully considered but

'…in view of the fact that the Air Staff are about to issue the requirements for a new type of fighter on the same lines as the one you propose, I think it best to defer any action on your design as you will no doubt submit it again under the new specification [F.18/37], with any alteration you may think necessary. Generally speaking we like the design very much but are doubtful if the construction would provide the stiffness necessary for the speed without a fully stressed-skin wing.'

In October 1937 Hawker began layout drawings for what it called the 'R' type fighter (Vulture engine), while on the 5th mock-up drawings of the 'N' type fighter (Napier Sabre) were issued to the Experimental Shop.

Part of the new specification arrived at Hawker on 14 January 1938 after Camm had made repeated requests to the Air Ministry that it might be issued 'without further delay'. However, the full document was not received until 4 April, together with an invitation to tender; later that month construction of a 'R' type mock-up began and the tender for both fighters was despatched on 30 April.

Supermarine 324

Various alternative arrangements were investigated by Supermarine to fulfil F.18/37 and two versions of

BELOW The Supermarine Type 324 with Merlin engines (21.4.38). *The late Eric Morgan*

BOTTOM The Supermarine Type 324 with Bristol Taurus engines (21.4.38). *The late Eric Morgan*

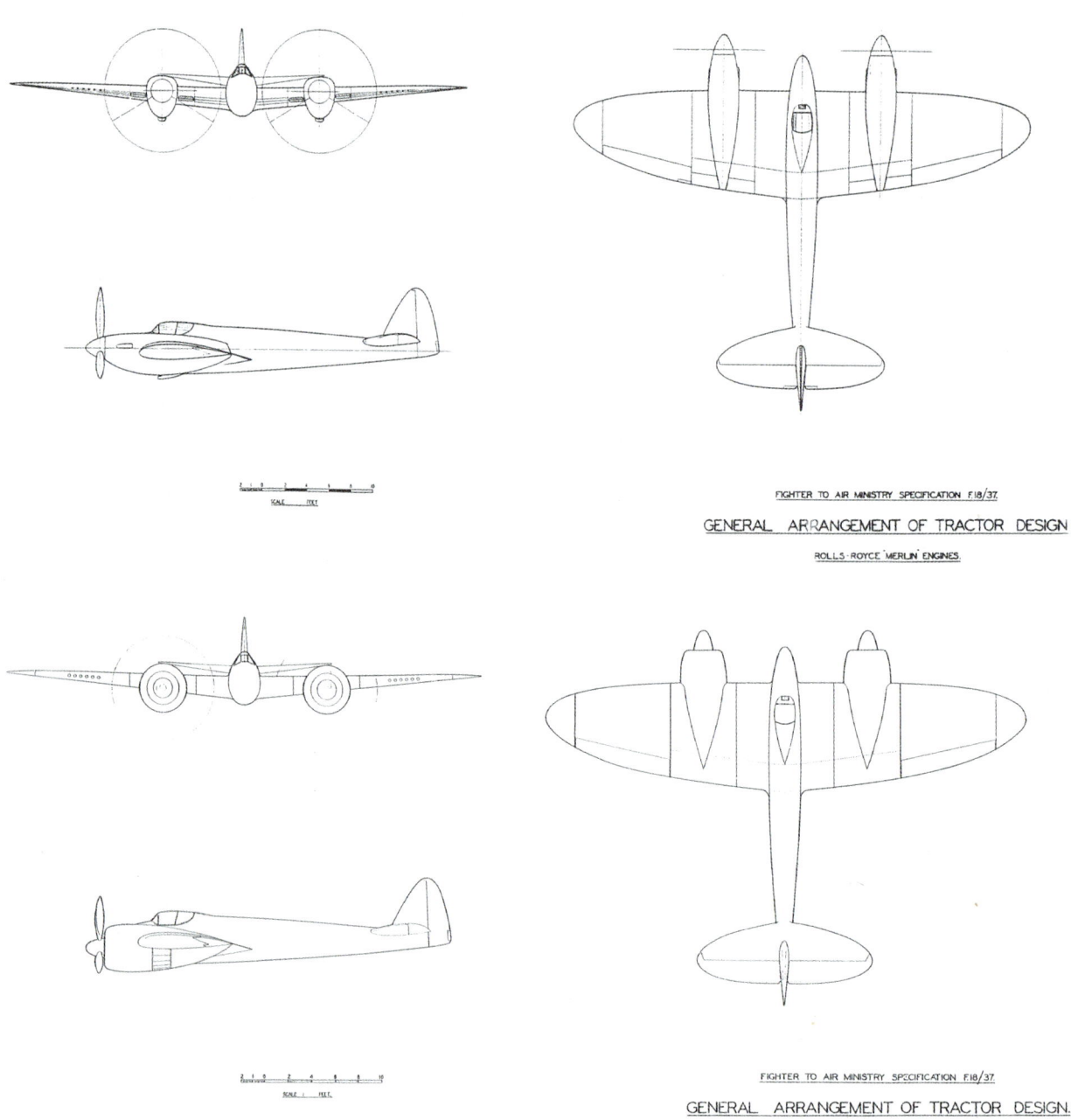

Supermarine 324 (21.4.38) - Merlin

Span:	41ft 0in (12.50m)
Length:	31ft 10in (9.70m)
Wing Area:	290sq.ft (26.97sq.m)
All-Up-Weight:	10,766lb (4,883kg)
Powerplant:	2 x Merlin 2.SM 1,265hp (943kW)
Max Speed / Height:	450mph (724km/h) at 18,250ft (5,563m)
Armament:	12 x 0.303in (7.7mm) machine guns

Supermarine 324 (21.4.38) - Taurus

Span:	46ft 0in (14.02m)
Span:	41ft 0in (12.50m)
Length:	31ft 6in (9.60m)
Wing Area:	290sq.ft (26.97sq.m)
All-Up-Weight:	10,000lb (4,536kg)
Powerplant:	2 x Taurus 3.SM 1,250hp (932kW)
Max Speed / Height:	421mph (677km/h) at 16,500ft (5,029m)
Armament:	12 x 0.303in (7.7mm) machine guns

essentially the same project, each with alternative engines, were described in brochures completed in April 1938. The company judged that twin-engined aeroplanes offered the best performance and produced a smaller machine than a single-engined type. The slightly increased complication from the duplication of engine controls and mountings was, in Supermarine's opinion, more than compensated for by the advantages, which included opposite-rotating airscrews to prevent swing when taking off in formation, a greatly improved pilot's view and a tricycle chassis for easier landing. Supermarine concluded that the twin was a much more efficient fighting aeroplane costing very little more to build or maintain.

The 324 was a tractor type while the alternative 325 described below had pusher engines. Their compact arrangement, made possible largely by the use of Fowler flaps and the tricycle chassis, gave a wing area only 20% greater than that of the Spitfire and a fuselage of the same length. The Fowler flap offered at least 10% more maximum lift over any other type, while the undercarriage (supported by long-travel oleos of 10in [25.4cm] stroke) allowed the aircraft to be flown to the ground, without float, and gave freedom from the danger of ground looping.

A monocoque fuselage and single-spar metal-covered wing, developed by Supermarine over several years, were both well tried and efficient methods of construction, which the company felt was well suited to high speeds. The use of smooth flush-riveted Alclad sheet enabled a perfectly smooth skin surface to be achieved, which would give good aerodynamic efficiency, while careful attention had also been given to simplifying the methods of construction, the latter making full use of the experience gained on the Spitfire and the earlier B.12/36 bomber project. An example in this direction was a reduction in the number of rivets, in certain cases to a third of the number previously thought necessary.

The wing followed the lines of the Supermarine F.7/30 and Spitfire fighters and was to be built of light alloy, chiefly Alclad, which formed the entire covering except for the control surfaces. A single spar was provided at the maximum depth of the wing, and two very robust fuel tanks, made in thick-gauge light alloy, were incorporated in the wing nose forward of the spar. Although detachable, these tanks formed part of the structure and contributed to the structural strength and stiffness; as fuel containers, they imposed very little weight penalty. Further, the weight of fuel relieved the bending loads during flight. A third tank formed the top portion of the fuselage aft of the main spar, and fuel capacity was 163 gallons (741 litres) for the Merlin, 169 gallons (768 litres) for the Taurus. The radiators, main undercarriage and guns were all housed in the wing, and no fabric was used except on the control surfaces. The Fowler flaps, enabling the wing area to be increased for landing and take-off, were of such proportions that they could be supported at the engine nacelle and fuselage only, without external drag-producing supports or complicated linkages.

The guns, twelve 0.303in (7.7mm) Brownings, were grouped in units of six in each wing, which, complete with ammunition, could be quickly removed to allow swift reloading. For this purpose the wing aft of the spar and the torsion box in the way of the guns were hinged on both upper and lower surfaces. The fuselage was a shell structure of Alclad sheet into which was built a short wing centre section, while the tailplane was of similar construction to the mainplane with a single spar and Alclad covering. Trimming was by tab and the elevator had a small horn, mainly to hold the mass balance weight, the aerodynamic balance being part inset and part by tab. A single fin was built into the fuselage rear and the rudder balance and trimming arrangements repeated that for the elevator. All of the fin and the tail were Alclad covered except the rudder and elevator, which used fabric on light alloy spars and ribs.

This aeroplane could use an alternative Bristol Taurus radial engine installation rather than its Merlins. The provision of joints in the wing on each side of the engine nacelle enabled the water-cooled nacelle, complete with the portion of the wing containing the radiators, to be removed and the air-cooled unit, with cooling ducts, to be substituted. The balance was not appreciably affected by the change of engine and the Taurus reduced weight. To cool the Merlins, two interchangeable radiators were provided in each wing with leading edge intakes and trailing-edge outlets, which Supermarine felt gave less drag than any other system known at the time. For the Taurus, short ducts, as used on the B.12/36 bomber, were fitted in the nacelle.

The pilot was seated near the fuselage nose and had an exceptionally good field of view; in addition, he could see the wingtips and so judge the

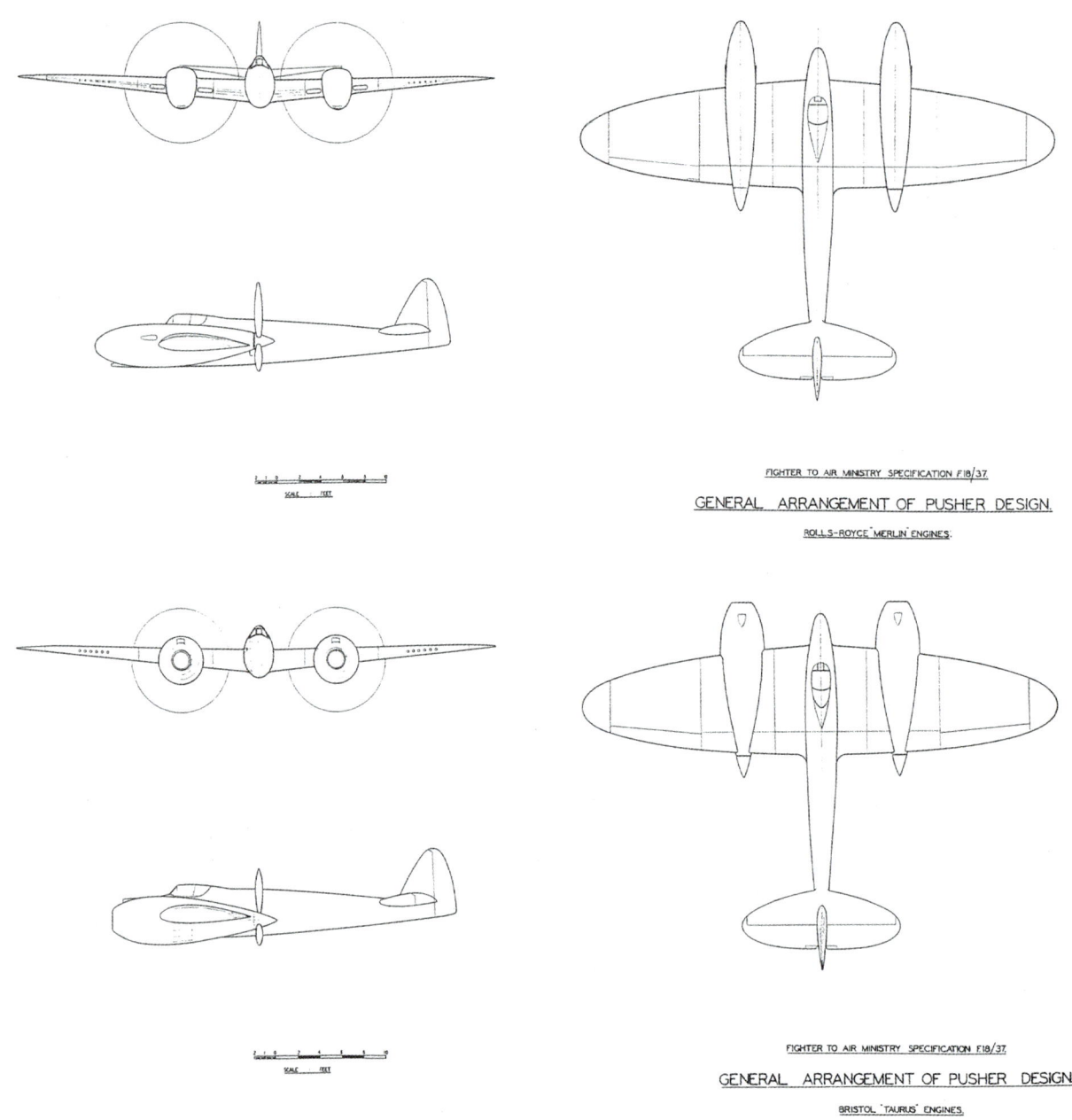

TOP The Supermarine Type 325 with Merlin pusher engines (26.4.38). *The late Eric Morgan*

ABOVE The Supermarine Type 325 with Taurus pusher engines (26.4.38). *The late Eric Morgan*

aircraft's span when this was needed during taxiing or formation flying. With two 1,145bhp (854kW) Merlins, sea level rate of climb was estimated to be 4,900ft/min (1,494m/min) and service ceiling 42,000ft (12,802m); the alternative 1,265bhp (943kW) Taurus units gave equivalent figures of 3,800ft/min (1,158m/min) and 37,900ft (11,552m).

Supermarine 325

This sister project was essentially the same fighter with the same features, although here the Merlin or Taurus power units operated as pusher engines. After an investigation and consultations with Rolls-Royce, which had considerable experience of the transmission of aero engine power by shaft drive, it was decided that a pusher arrangement with an extended shaft to the airscrew was quite practicable for this design. This arrangement resulted in much less drag from the wing (which was removed from the slipstream) and increased the efficiency of the airscrews, and consequently the estimated maximum speed was 8mph (13km/h) higher. To give the pilot the best chance of escaping by parachute

Supermarine 325 (26.4.38) - Merlin

Span:	43ft 0in (13.11m)
Length:	32ft 2in (9.81m)
Wing Area:	306sq.ft (28.46sq.m)
All-Up-Weight:	11,166lb (5,065kg)
Powerplant:	2 x Merlin 2.SM 1,265hp (943kW)
Max Speed / Height:	458mph (737km/h) at 18,250ft (5,563m)
Armament:	12 x 0.303in (7.7mm) machine guns

Supermarine 325 (26.4.38) - Taurus

Span:	43ft 0in (13.11m)
Length:	31ft 0in (9.45m)
Wing Area:	306sq.ft (28.46sq.m)
All-Up-Weight:	10,511lb (4,768kg)
Powerplant:	2 x Taurus 3.SM 1,250hp (932kW)
Max Speed / Height:	429mph (690km/h) at 16,500ft (5,029m)
Armament:	12 x 0.303in (7.7mm) machine guns

BOTH ABOVE Hawker Tornado prototype P5219 with its original ventral radiator position. These pictures were taken in October 1939.

in an emergency, a special brake was provided on each airscrew shaft, which was capable of stopping the airscrew in about 10 seconds.

As before, the engine mountings were braced tubular structures built off the main spar, and to the rear of the spar the nacelles were made of a shell structure that contained strong bulkheads to support the main chassis hinge. Housed at the tail of the nacelle was a rear bearing for the airscrew shaft together with the brake for stopping the airscrews in preparation for a parachute departure. Sea level rate of climb with two Merlins would be 4,950ft/min (1,509m/min) and service ceiling 43,500ft (13,259m); the alternative Taurus powerplant gave figures of 3,850ft/min (1,173m/min) and 38,500ft (11,735m). Fuel capacity was 158 gallons (718 litres) for Merlin, 168 gallons (764 litres) for Taurus. Merlin airscrew diameter was 9ft 8.5in (2.96m), Taurus 8ft 9in (2.67m).

The designs selected for construction and flight test were the Sabre- and Vulture-engined proposals from Hawker. Two prototypes of each had been ordered by 30 August 1938 and the Mock-Up Conference for both was held at Kingston on 16 December. The Vulture flight test engine arrived on 23 December, but delays with the Sabre meant that a flight test engine was not delivered until 30 December 1939. On 10 July 1939 the Air Ministry placed an order for 500 Vulture and 500 Sabre F.18/37s and in August the 'R' type Vulture version was officially named Tornado. Prototype P5219 made its first flight on 6 October, while in December the 'N' type was officially named Typhoon. Typhoon prototype

Hawker Tornado (flown)

Span:	42ft 0in (12.80m)
Length:	32ft 6.5in (9.92m)
Wing Area:	283sq.ft (26.32sq.m)
All-Up-Weight:	10,600lb (4,808kg)
Powerplant:	1 x Vulture 5 1,800hp (1,342kW)
Max Speed / Height:	425mph (684km/h)
Armament:	12 x 0.303in (7.7mm) machine guns

Hawker Typhoon Mk.IB (flown)

Span:	41ft 7in (12.76m)
Length:	31ft 11in (9.73m)
Wing Area:	279sq.ft (25.95sq.m)
All-Up-Weight:	11,400lb (5,171kg)
Powerplant:	1 x Sabre II 2,180hp (1,626kW)
Max Speed / Height:	374mph (602km/h) at sea level, 405mph (652km/h) at 18,000ft (5,486m)
Armament:	4 x 20mm cannon, 8 rocket projectiles

ABOVE LEFT & RIGHT The second Tornado P5224 had the radiator moved forward. *Phil Butler*

ABOVE For comparison this side view shows Typhoon R7579, a Mk.IA with the original canopy. It was built by Gloster Aircraft.

RIGHT Typhoon R8809, pictured on 15 May 1943, has the later sliding hood. *Phil Butler*

BELOW Typhoon IB EK183 of No 56 Squadron at RAF Matlask on 21 April 1943. *RAF Museum*

ABOVE Another Typhoon Mk.IB, JR371, was on the strength of No 198 Squadron when it was photographed at Manston, possibly in January 1944.

P5212 made its maiden flight on 24 February 1940, while the second Tornado, P5224, flew on 5 December with the engine radiator moved to the forward position, local flow reversals having occurred around the rear part of the original ventral arrangement. An Air Staff memo dated 4 January 1939 noted that the 'Vulture is ahead of the Sabre, but the Sabre does promise advantages in horsepower, a better shape and therefore a better engine, and therefore a better aeroplane,' and it recommended continuing with the Sabre installation.

In the event, thanks to problems with the Vulture's design, the Tornado-Vulture programme was stopped on 15 October 1941, although a prototype was later flown with a 2,500hp (1,864kW) Bristol Centaurus 5 radial engine. This latter project was first discussed in January 1940 but a contract to convert one prototype was not placed until 22 February 1941. In October of that year the Ministry renamed the project the 'Centaurus-Typhoon' (because the Tornado had been dropped), but this was not agreed to by Hawker because its fuselage was similar to the Tornado. The prototype, HG641, made its first flight on 23 October 1941 and later achieved a top speed of 402mph (647km/h) at 18,000ft (5,486m). In early 1942 converting the Typhoon to take the Centaurus became an urgent requirement and later plans made in June to fit the engine to the Typhoon II (Tempest) were given the highest priority. At one stage it was intended that, prior to the Sabre (which was suffering many teething problems), production Typhoons would use Centaurus, but none of the later Centaurus proposals ever became hardware.

The first Typhoon prototype was armed with twelve Browning machine guns, but when the second, P5216, became airborne on 3 May 1941 it carried four cannon. In mid-1938 consideration was given to fitting cannon instead of machine guns into the F.18/37s, although work was also ongoing on the Westland F.37/35 (Whirlwind) cannon-armed fighter (see Chapter 3). However, the Air Staff noted that progress on the Westland, and Boulton Paul's F.11/37 twin-engined P.92 turret fighter (Chapter 5), had been slow, possibly because neither company had any competition to fear, and as a result the F.18/37 tenders were revised to carry cannon. Supermarine therefore tendered a new brochure in

BELOW The Supermarine Type 327 with Rolls-Royce Merlins (26.8.38). Note the six-cannon armament positioned in the wing roots just inboard of the propeller arc. *The late Eric Morgan*

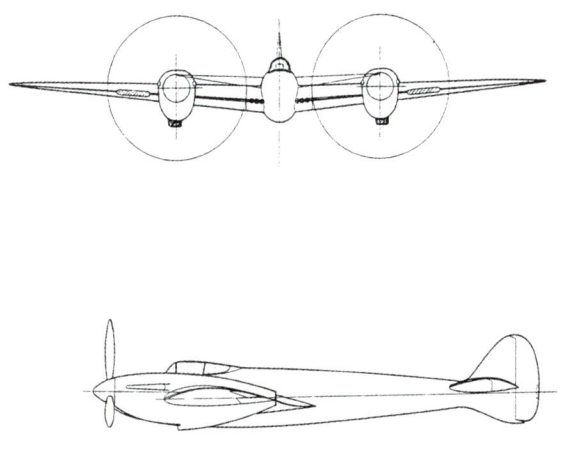
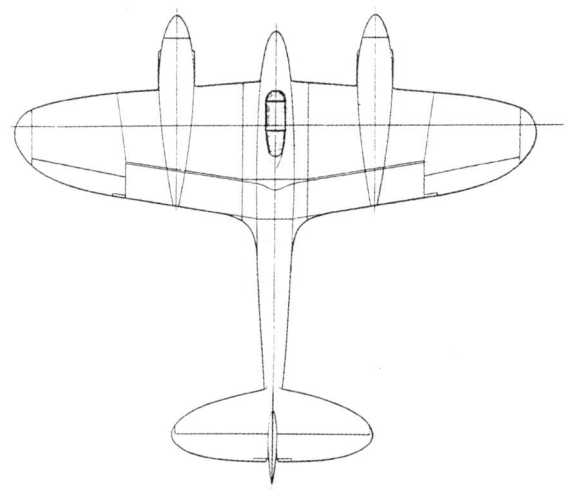

August 1938 after having abandoned its pusher designs. Gloster also continued its twin-boom studies.

Supermarine 327

The main change from the earlier projects was the fitting of three 20mm cannon in each of the wing roots instead of the six machine guns in each outer wing, although by fitting alternative outer wings the Brownings could replace the cannon for ground strafing if so desired. The primary powerplant was the Merlin, but the Taurus was still an option, and the structure was essentially unchanged although the pilot was now protected by armour. Service ceiling was calculated to be 40,000ft (12,192m) with the Merlin and 35,500ft (10,820m) with the Taurus, with rate of climb 4,550ft/min (1,387m/min) and 3,450ft/min (1,052m/min) respectively. The Merlin's fuel capacity was 170 gallons (773 litres) and a mock-up of the 327 was built. Type 327's Merlin airscrew diameter was 10ft 3½in (3.14m), and for the Taurus the diameter was 8ft 9in (2.67m), figures that were exactly the same as the earlier Type 324.

Previously, on 29 July, W. Sholto Douglas, the Assistant Chief of the Air Staff (ACAS), had noted that

'...the Ministry had no interest in machine gun fighters but was anxious to see the development of fighters capable of carrying 20mm Hispanos. Sir Robert McClean [of Vickers] made the point in his Type 327 covering letter that Supermarine "had great experience of high-speed work culminating in the Spitfire". However, after assessing the project, R. N. Liptrot wrote on 16th September that "McClean was naive when he presents a rehash of an earlier tender design as a new conception already considered and found unacceptable." I see no reason for recommending action [on the 327].'

RIGHT A model of the Supermarine 327.
Joe Cherrie

BOTH ABOVE Supermarine must have rated its Type 327 design very highly because in 1938 the firm went to the trouble of building a full-size mock-up of the fuselage and starboard wing and tail at Southampton, complete with tricycle undercarriage.

However, on 24 November an Air Staff meeting chaired by Air Commodore Roderic Hill, the new DTD, discussed the project. H. Grinstead began by saying that the possible adoption of the 327 was one of policy – there was an urgent need for a 20mm gun fighter and the question was whether the need was so urgent that they should 'plunge' on Supermarine's revised design, when the earlier machine gun versions had been turned down in favour of Hawker's proposals because they showed very little advantage over the latter's single-engined layout. Supermarine had pushed for the cannon 327 because Westland's F.37/35 was the only cannon fighter in view, and it contained a number of experimental features, so a back-up was required.

There was at this time a further proposal to redesign the Bristol Beaufort bomber with four 20mm guns (a project that became the Beaufighter – see Chapter 3]), while the Gloster F.9/37 twin-engined fighter (also Chapter 3) had recently been converted into a fixed-gun fighter by deleting a requirement for a four 0.303in (7.7mm) dorsal turret. The latter was to receive forward-firing guns only, while the Boulton Paul P.92 was considered to be a long development job. Grinstead felt that Supermarine was usually slow in producing a prototype and, judging from the Spitfire, in production also. W. S. Farren could see no advantage in the 327 that was not offered by the Gloster F.9/37, while Major H. S. V. Thompson reported that his department (RD Arm) was not impressed with the 327's gun layout; the feed arrangements were thought to be impracticable and there did not appear to be room for three guns in each wing.

The advantages of the 327 were a superior performance over the Bristol,

Supermarine 327 (26.8.38)	
Span:	40ft 0in (12.19m)
Length:	Merlin 33ft 6in (10.22m), Taurus 33ft 2.5in (10.12m)
Wing Area:	304sq.ft (28.27sq.m)
All-Up-Weight:	11,312lb (5,131kg)
Powerplant:	2 x Merlin 2.SM 1,265hp (943kW)
Max Speed / Height:	465mph (748km/h) at 22,000ft (6,706m)
Armament:	6 x 20mm cannon

Gloster and Westland designs, and its tricycle undercarriage. However, the Air Staff felt that the nearest projects for a cannon fighter were the redesigned Beaufort and the Westland F.37/35, and the general consensus of the meeting appeared to be that it could not recommend expending energy in developing the 327, and it would rather concentrate on the three twin-engined designs already in hand. There was also the desirability of avoiding a multiplicity of types, so the meeting recommended that the 327 should not be taken up.

In due course, as noted already, the Hawker Typhoon was adapted to take cannon. In fact, the first modification was proposed in August 1938 and by mid-December of that year discussions between Camm and the Ministry were well advanced. The Typhoon entered service in September 1941 and more than 3,300 were built. In the event, thanks to a poor rate of climb and altitude performance, it did not prove particularly successful as an interceptor fighter but, with four wing-mounted cannon, it became one of the best ground attack aircraft used by any nation during the war.

Gloster Twin-Boom Studies

During October and November 1938 Gloster revised its twin-boom studies with three further versions. The first, dated 15 October, was still armed with twelve machine guns but the fuselage nacelle was of sleeker profile and the engine drove two three-blade contra-rotating propellers. The radiators for engine cooling remained in the leading edges of the wing roots, the design's span was 41ft 0in (12.50m) and overall length 39ft 3in (11.96m). On 7 November 1938 a drawing was completed for a very similar design but in which the nose-mounted machine guns had been replaced by a battery of five 20mm Hispano cannon. Both of these projects still used either a Sabre or Vulture power unit and this cannon version once more showed coolant radiators in the wing roots, but it had a single four-blade propeller. Span was 41ft 0in (12.50m) and length 40ft 5in (12.32m). However, a second drawing of this cannon version had its radiators positioned in the front of the tail booms and the overall length here was about 1ft (0.30m) less. No data is available for any of these designs, but when all of the cannon-armed F.18/37 projects were assessed by the Air Ministry later in the year the Gloster pusher was not included because it was felt to be 'highly experimental'.

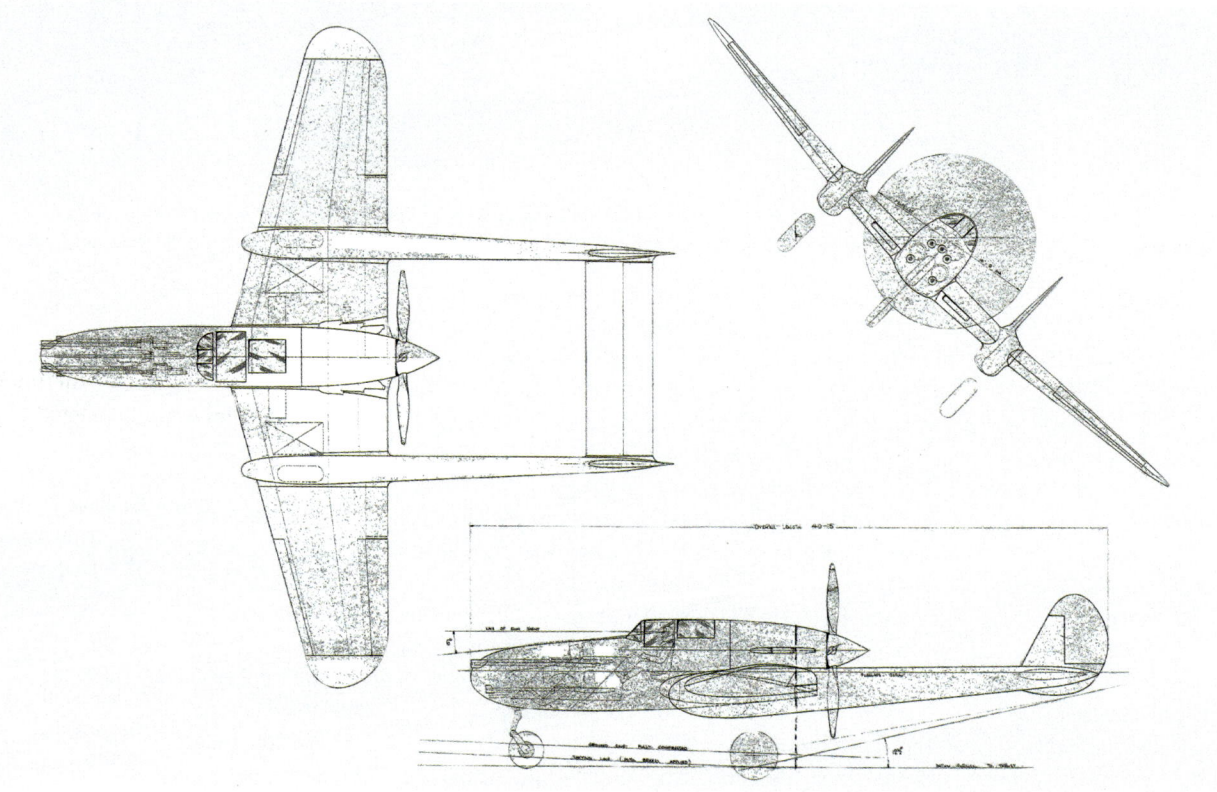

BELOW Gloster's twin boom F.18/37 project further developed, and now armed with cannon (7.11.38). *Jet Age Museum*

Chapter Two
Wartime Single Engine Fixed-Gun Fighters

ABOVE The Hawker Fury prototype LA610 fitted with a Napier Sabre engine was one of the most beautiful piston fighters ever to fly.

Once the Second World War had begun the speed of development of single-engine fighters seemed to accelerate. Chapter 1 referred briefly to the Spitfire development line, but in contrast Hawker's new fighters, although closely related and linked, were essentially all-new designs and the firm's Tempest and Fury form the main subjects of this chapter.

Hawker Tempest

Sydney Camm quickly turned his attention to improving the Typhoon and a redesign was treated virtually as a new type under project number P.1012; it was called the Typhoon II. The first Typhoon II discussions took place on 24 April 1941 when DTD, now N. E. Rowe, visited Sydney Camm at Claremont; the development embraced a Sabre E.107C engine (later the Sabre IV), a four-blade propeller, six cannon wings, extended wingtips to increase the span and a cleaned-up tail. Compared to the original Typhoon I, the new project had completely redesigned thinner wings of elliptical planform and an improved profile, a 42ft (12.8m) span and a wing area of 300sq ft (27.9sq m). The engine was moved forward relative to the wing, which made room for more fuel in the body in front of the pilot, and the nose radiator was deleted and replaced by wing radiators, but the rear fuselage was unchanged. Hawker sent a performance summary and general arrangement drawing of the new design to the Ministry of Aircraft Production (MAP) on 9 September 1941. The elliptical wing had first been investigated in 1940 but was delayed by the demand for Hurricanes.

At a weight of 11,300lb (5,126kg)

the Sabre IV offered 455mph (732km/h) at 26,000ft (7,925m) and a ceiling of 35,300ft (10,759m). Rowe liked the fighter and on 17 September 1941 Camm was notified of a decision to convert two Typhoons to the new design; a formal contract for two prototypes followed on 18 November. Specification F.10/41 was written to cover the aircraft and it was recognised very quickly that this could be a fast aeroplane. In January 1942 Camm suggested to MAP that the modifications to the original Typhoon were so drastic that the Typhoon II should be renamed, and on 6 August it was officially retitled Tempest. It was eventually decided that just the one prototype should be completed, parts for the second being held back in case of damage to the original.

Back in 1941 the halt to the Hawker Tornado production run mentioned in Chapter 1 had meant that the Centaurus programme henceforth became related to the Typhoon, and on 15 October Camm was informed that a strong request should be expected for a 'Centaurus Typhoon'. Six prototypes of this version, what was to become the Tempest II, were ordered in February 1942, Rowe stating on the 3rd that the mark's development was a matter of urgency. The first prototype, LA602, first flew on 28 June 1943, and by 29 August had achieved a top speed of 461mph (742km/h) at 21,000ft (6,401m).

Some six months late, the original Sabre Tempest's first flight date was 2 September 1942. The aircraft, HM595, was in fact fitted with a Sabre II and the standard Typhoon cooling system complete with chin radiator. Delays in developing the Sabre IV had slowed things down and prompted the decision to install this alternative, but, since the airframe had been prepared for the IV, considerable redesign was necessary and the radiator was moved back under the nose to avoid any problems of compressibility. As a solution Rowe recommended more prototypes and the Aircraft Supply Council approved

BOTH ABOVE An excellent series of air-to-air photographs was taken of the Hawker Tempest I during a trials flight. With the later bubble canopy fitted, this aircraft was also very attractive.

six on 27 May. A formal contract was placed on 17 June for two prototypes fitted with Sabres, two with the Bristol Centaurus (down from six) and the last pair with Rolls-Royce Griffons. The Sabre IV prototype with wing leading edge radiators became the Tempest I, while HM595, with the Sabre II,

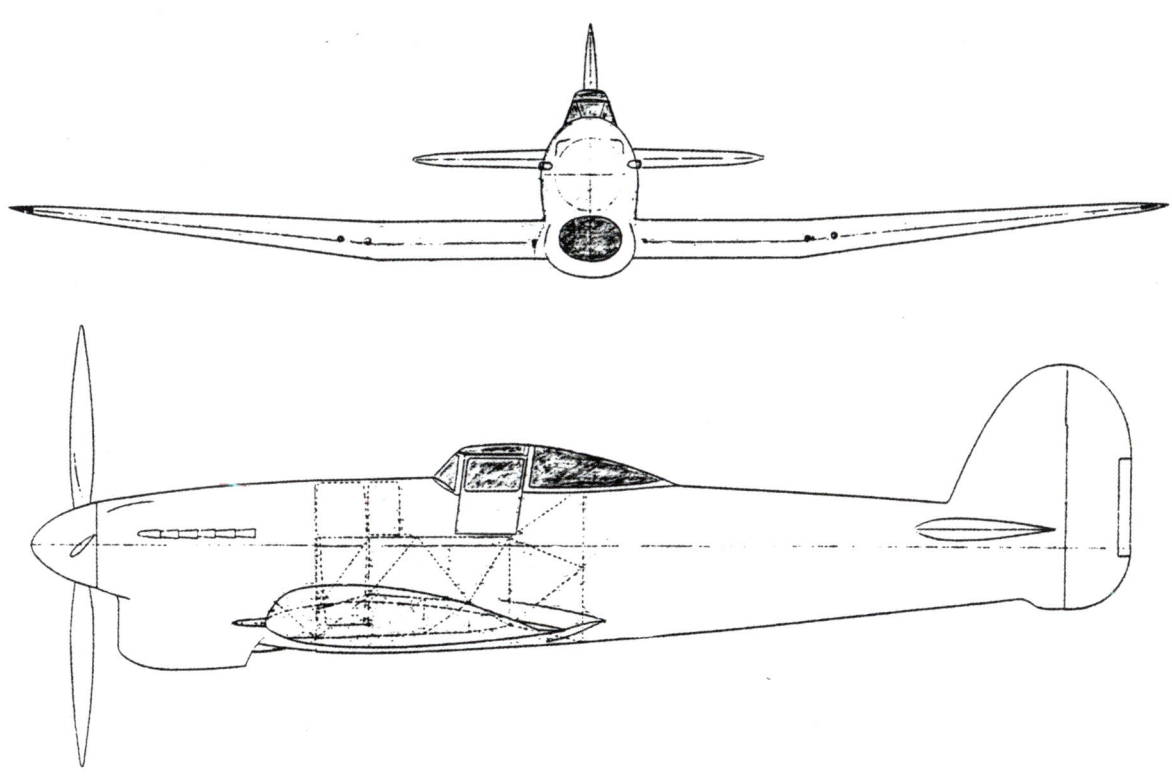

ABOVE A partial general arrangement of the Hawker P.1016, the Tempest III with a modified nose to accommodate a Rolls-Royce Griffon (2.4.42). Note the smaller radiator compared to the Sabre-powered Mk.V. *Adapted from National Archives AVIA 15/1667*

was called the Tempest V prototype. The Centaurus version became the Tempest II and the Griffon-powered aircraft the III and IV.

Work on the Tempest I, the old second prototype, restarted when the Sabre II was fitted to HM595. It was serialled HM599 and first flew on 24 February 1943, and its wing radiators became a source of much discussion. In August 1942 Hawker had proposed a change over to leading edge radiators on the Tempest I after the first few aircraft to cut drag and give better protection to the radiator from fire from the rear, but problems with their manufacture caused delay and the final radiator arrangement chosen for the Tempest was affected by the production situation. As late as 12 November 1942 Camm told the Ministry that 'if the Tempest is delayed we may have time to develop the leading edge position, which is probably the best arrangement.'

The Tempest III and IV were never built. The Griffon version was begun as the P.1016 and a drawing showing a Tempest V with the nose altered accordingly was attached to a letter from Camm to Rowe dated 10 April 1942. Camm explained that Hawker had for some time been considering an alternative engine for the Tempest and he felt that this combination was a good one, particularly since they could use a Griffon 61 when it arrived without structural changes. The Griffon was lighter than the Sabre but slightly longer, which left the balance of the aircraft practically unchanged. Camm felt this project had great possibilities and made the firm feel altogether happier about the Tempest. The Tempest III with the Griffon IIB and Tempest IV with the Griffon 61 carried 140 gallons (637 litres) and 145 gallons (659 litres) of fuel respectively and offered times to 20,000ft (6,096m) of 9.0 and 8.3 minutes, while their ceilings were 31,500ft and 40,000ft (9,601m and 12,192m). The Air Ministry became interested and when Rowe visited Kingston on 6 May he requested that work should begin as soon as possible on a Griffon 61 prototype.

The Controller of Research and Development (CRD), Air Marshal F. J. Linnell, felt that the new aeroplane had a worthwhile performance with the Griffon 61, but was not acceptable with the IIB, although that showed a marked improvement over the Hurricane; it was, however, heavier than an aeroplane specifically designed for the 61. The real merit of the proposal was that it could provide a replacement for the Hurricane and was capable of being produced in the large numbers that this would imply. He felt that the aeroplane could easily be made to carry 'the paraphernalia for low attack work' and the narrower engine automatically improved the view for low-level flying.

ABOVE Tempest V prototype HM595 pictured in September 1942 with its original canopy and fin. *Phil Butler*

ABOVE This is HM595 after the introduction of a fully faired fin and a bubble canopy. This aircraft eventually served as the Tempest Mk.VI prototype.

ABOVE Two views of Hawker Tempest Mk.Vs, the first version of the fighter to fly. The underside photo was taken on 12 March 1943. *Phil Butler*

R. S. Sorley made reference to the time element, where Tempest production would not start until mid-1943, when large numbers of Typhoons would be on the line. The introduction of the Griffon Tempest had to come, but the Typhoon was regarded as the first step in a conversion from the Hurricane in the low attack role; in the event the Typhoon fitted that role perfectly and the Tempest III was never built. The two Tempest III prototypes were to be serialled LA610 and LA614, and the former eventually flew as a Griffon Fury prototype; the latter was cancelled. (There had also been plans for a Griffon Typhoon I, which dragged on for quite a while, but these were dropped when it was realised that this effort would be better spent on a new aircraft.)

The Tempest immediately demonstrated far superior performance, rolling and handling over the Typhoon, while HM599's early flights revealed even better directional stability than the Tempest V and it was unbeatable in the dive or zoom climb. The maximum true airspeed achieved by HM599 appears to have been 472mph (759km/h), well above the original estimate. It remains one of the fastest piston fighters ever to have flown.

The initial plans made in February 1942 called for 100 Tempest Is and a contract was placed on the 24th; five days later this figure was increased to 400. The Mk.I Tempest was intended to be the production version, and the chin-radiator Mk.V to remain as a test bed, but eventually the latter was chosen for manufacture. Another 700 Mk.V and I aircraft were ordered on 12 February 1944, but this was amended two months later to 1,300 Tempest V and 300 Tempest I. The 300 Mk.Is were changed in May to Mk.VI aircraft with chin radiators, and any chance for production of the wing-radiator Mk.I finally disappeared. The Tempest VI was really a Mk.V fitted with a Sabre V, and the original Tempest, HM595, was the first to receive it, flying in this form on 9 May 1944. In June 1943 a comparison of level speeds was completed between the Mks.I and V and the increase in speed using the wing leading edge radiators was found to be between 7mph and 10mph (11km/h and 16km/h) in FS gear, but not measurable in MS gear.

The reason for abandoning the Tempest I, as given by the official historian at MAP, was that by December 1942 the Sabre IV had

LEFT Tempest Mk.VI NX180.

MIDDLE LEFT The prototype Tempest II was LA602, seen here in original condition with bubble canopy and no fin fairing.

BOTTOM LEFT Tempest II MW764 photographed during a publicity flight on 22 March 1945. *RAF Museum via Adrian Balch.*

Hawker Tempest Mk.I (flown)

Span:	41ft 0in (12.50m)
Length:	34ft 2in (10.42m)
Wing Area:	302sq.ft (28.09sq.m)
All-Up-Weight:	11,300lb (5,126kg)
Powerplant:	1 x Sabre IV 2,500hp (1,864kW)
Max Speed / Height:	466mph (750km/h) at 24,500ft (7,468m)
Armament:	4 x 20mm cannon

Hawker Tempest Mk.III (10.4.42)

Span:	43ft 0in (13.11m)
Length:	34ft 3in (10.44m)
Wing Area:	307sq.ft (28.55sq.m)
All-Up-Weight:	10,400lb (4,717kg)
Powerplant:	1 x Griffon IIB
Max Speed / Height:	400mph (644km/h) at 22,000ft (6,706m)
Armament:	4 x 20mm cannon

Hawker Tempest Mk.IV (c4.42)

Span:	43ft 0in (13.11m)
Length:	34ft 3in (10.44m)
Wing Area:	307sq.ft (28.55sq.m)
All-Up-Weight:	10,700lb (4,854kg)
Powerplant:	1 x Griffon 61
Max Speed / Height:	430mph (692km/h) at 31,500ft (9,601m)
Armament:	4 x 20mm cannon

Hawker Tempest Mk.V (flown)

Span:	41ft 0in (12.50m)
Length:	33ft 8in (10.26m)
Wing Area:	302sq.ft (28.09sq.m)
All-Up-Weight:	11,510lb (5,221kg)
Powerplant:	1 x Sabre IIB 2,420hp (1,805kW)
Max Speed / Height:	435mph (700km/h) at 17,500ft (5,334m)
Armament:	4 x 20mm cannon

ABOVE Tempest Mk.V NV768 pictured on 12 July 1946 serving as a test bed for Napier's fan-cooled annular radiator.

Hawker Tempest Mk.II (flown)	
Span:	41ft 0in (12.50m)
Length:	34ft 5in (10.49m)
Wing Area:	303.7sq.ft (28.24sq.m)
All-Up-Weight:	11,900lb (5,398kg)
Powerplant:	1 x Centaurus V 2,590hp (1,931kW)
Max Speed / Height:	450mph (724km/h) at 18,500ft (5,639m)
Armament:	4 x 20mm cannon

failed type testing three times and, when reviewed by the Ministry, was expected to be an unreliable engine. As a result, large-scale production was dropped. However, the staff at Langley understood that the wing leading edge radiators were unpopular with the Air Ministry. Just the one Mk.I Tempest flew, but 452 Mk.IIs (which served with the RAF post-war), 800 Mk.Vs and 142 Mk.VIs were completed.

Specification F.6/42

By the middle of the war, aircraft such as the Typhoon had become rather large for a single-seat fighter. The Typhoon's successor, the Tempest, had a thinner wing that offered improved aerodynamics but was still larger and heavier than, for example, the Spitfire. To further increase performance it was felt that a single-seat light fighter was desirable and to this aim F.6/42 was raised in September 1942, which called for a speed of 450mph (724km/h) at 20,000ft (6,096m), a sea level rate of climb of 4,500ft/min (1,372m/min) and four 20mm cannon. The type was intended to be a medium-altitude high-performance fighter and superior in climb, speed and manoeuvrability to any German fighter that might be developed from the Focke-Wulf Fw 190; the document stressed the importance of rolling manoeuvrability. Five prototypes and eight production aircraft were to be flying by December 1944, and nearly 4,000 by mid-1946, if the war was still ongoing.

In August 1942 the outline requirements were sent to Boulton Paul, Hawker, Vickers-Armstrong, Supermarine and Westland, which prompted Camm to reply that 'the time is long overdue when intensive attention should be given to all weights other than the aircraft structure and the bare military load.' Meanwhile, during July and August 1942 discussions between Folland and Sir Roy Fedden of Bristol Engines led them to think that they could rapidly bring a new design of fighter to fruition. Airspeed also showed interest in the specification, but Boulton Paul felt that it would not be possible to achieve the desired performance with the specified engines, the Griffon 61, Sabre NS.43.SM and Centaurus

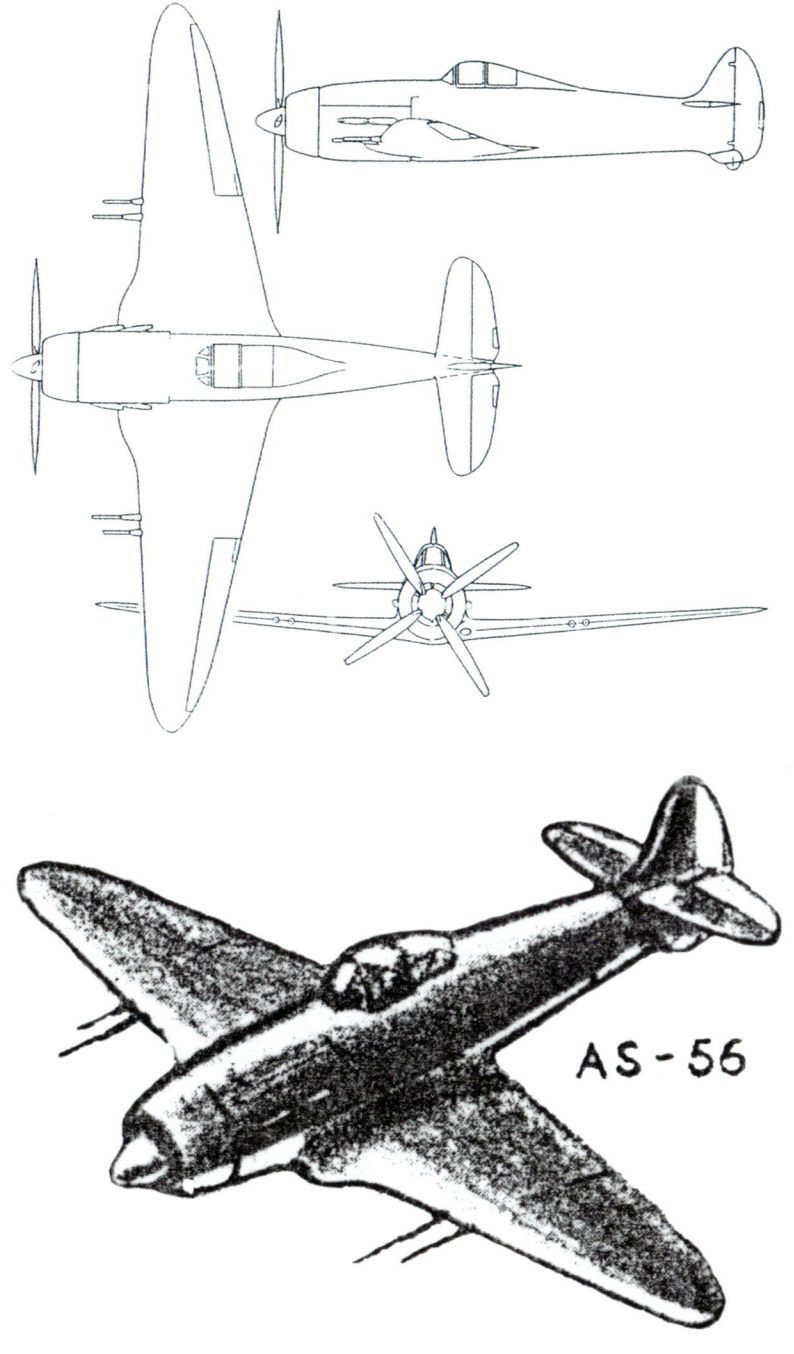

TOP **Airspeed AS.56 (8.9.42).** *Bob Beard*

ABOVE An artist's impression of the AS.56.

Airspeed AS.56

The AS.56 had a Napier Sabre IV with a fan-cooled annular radiator in the nose to reduce drag, and a four-blade propeller 12ft 3in (3.73m) in diameter. There were four 20mm cannon in the wings and the maximum rate of climb was estimated to be 4,675ft/min (1,425m/min) at 6,500ft (1,981m) and 4,020ft/min (1,225m/min) at 18,600ft (5,669m). Design work on this project was quickly abandoned, but work on the radiator arrangement was continued by Napier to try and solve the Sabre's overheating problems, and this was subsequently test-flown on examples of both the Typhoon and Tempest.

Airspeed AS.56 (8.9.42)	
Span:	40ft 0in (12.19m)
Length:	30ft 0in (9.14m)
Wing Area:	237sq.ft (22.04sq.m)
All-Up-Weight:	9,856lb (4,471kg)
Powerplant:	1 x Sabre IV
Max Speed / Height:	492mph (792km/h) at 23,400ft (7,132m)
Armament:	4 x 20mm cannon

Boulton Paul P.98

Boulton Paul's P.98 design featured a tail-first layout and either a Griffon or Sabre pusher engine driving contra-rotating propellers. To date no drawings have ever been traced for the P.98, but it is understood that the designation was first raised long before the specification itself was ready. There were three schemed variations, P.98A, B and C, and at least one canard layout looked something like a short-span version of the manufacturer's P.100 project. On receipt of the document, Boulton Paul first suggested a Sabre powerplant before switching to the Griffon and, as submitted to the Ministry, the mean maximum rate of climb up to 20,000ft (6,096m) was given as 4,640ft/

CE.12.SM. The first half of September saw designs tendered from seven companies; Folland's brochure and model was submitted on the 4th, but a day later Bristol, which was expected to provide testing and laboratory facilities including wind tunnels, withdrew from working with Folland.

The project documents for the M.42, M.43 and M.44 designs from Miles Aircraft apparently also refer to F.6/42, but these studies do not appear in the Ministry appraisal papers. In fact, they were designed for low attack fighter duties and other low-level attack roles and are discussed in

Boulton Paul P.98 Sabre (5.9.42)	
Span:	34ft 6in (10.52m)
Length:	?
Wing Area:	247sq.ft (22.97sq.m)
All-Up-Weight:	9,892lb (4,487kg)
Powerplant:	1 x Sabre
Max Speed / Height:	446mph (718km/h) at 20,000ft (6,096m)
Armament:	4 x 20mm cannon

Boulton Paul P.98 Griffon (5.9.42)	
Span:	33ft 0in (10.06m)
Length:	?
Wing Area:	225ft (20.93sq.m)
All-Up-Weight:	8,861lb (4,019kg)
Powerplant:	1 x Griffon
Max Speed / Height:	440mph (708km/h) at 20,000ft (6,096m)
Armament:	4 x 20mm cannon

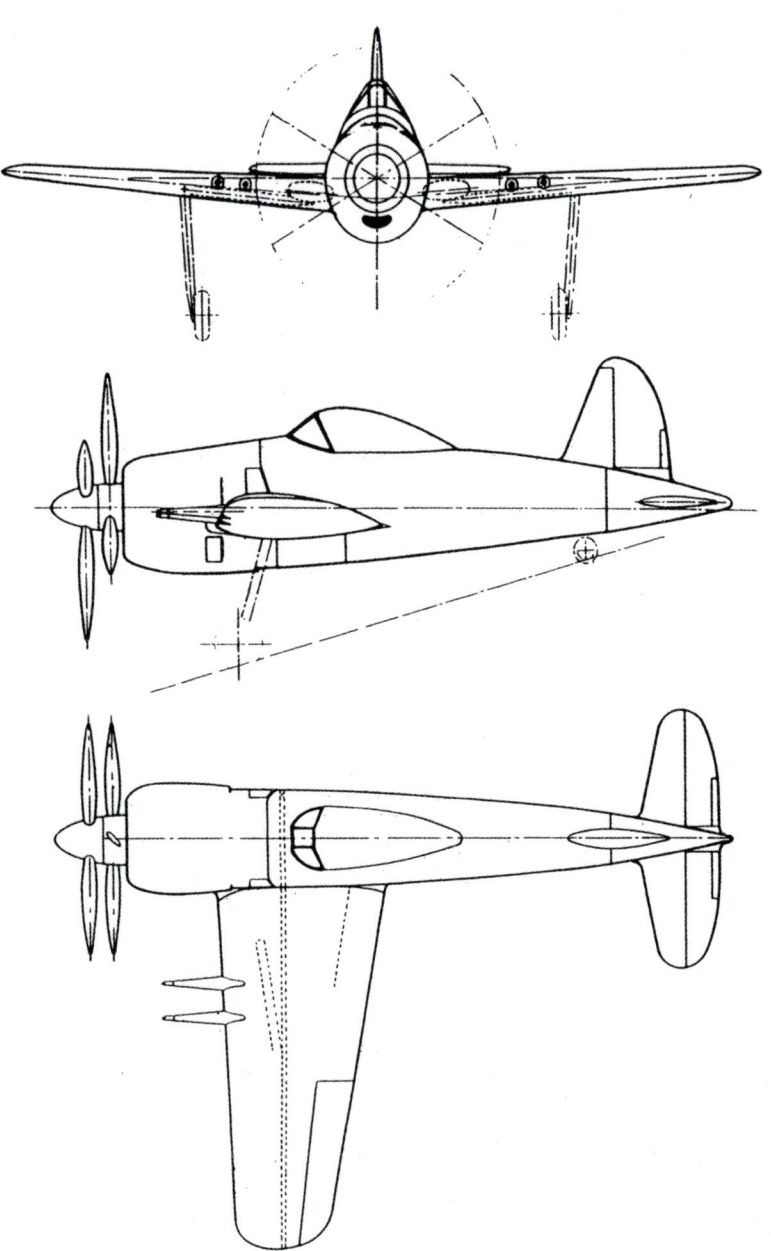

min (1,414m/min) for the Griffon and 4,900ft/min (1,494m/min) for the Sabre. The Sabre version's contra-rotating propellers had a diameter of 12ft 6in (3.81m) while the equivalent on the Griffon was 11ft 6in (3.51m) in diameter. The designers apparently then moved on to a conventional aircraft similar to the firm's P.96 or P.103 studies powered by either a Bristol Centaurus or Napier Sabre with contraprops.

Folland Fo.117

Special attention had been paid in Folland's Fo.117 submission to climb, speed and manoeuvrability, all at medium altitudes, and in fact the fighter was to be superior in these elements to any German fighter that might be developed from the Focke-Wulf Fw 190. Henry Folland's earlier work for Gloster Aircraft had included the Grebe, Gamecock, Gauntlet, Gladiator and F.5/34, aircraft that

Folland Fo.117 (4.9.42)	
Span:	36ft 0in (10.97m)
Length:	31ft 6in (9.60m)
Wing Area:	224sq.ft (20.83sq.m)
All-Up-Weight:	9,749lb (4,422kg)
Powerplant:	1 x Centaurus
Max Speed / Height:	467mph (751km/h) at 20,000ft (6,096m)
Armament:	4 x 20mm cannon

ABOVE The Folland Fo.117 (4.9.42). *Phil Butler*

were all characterised by lightness of control, exceptionally good manoeuvrability for aerobatics, and an extremely low structure weight. In fact, the F.5/34 (see Chapter 1) had been utilised as a basis for the Fo.117 since a considerable amount of wind tunnel data was available and because certain features found in this earlier design had proved good in practice.

The wing and fuselage were to be built in light alloy throughout, the former consisting of one main spar with solid booms and a single shear-web. Additional auxiliary spars would be utilised for transferring torque to the fuselage, and the front portion of the skin was to be made in stout-gauge light alloy to enable an aerodynamically smooth contour to be preserved. Thickness/chord ratio was 18% at the root and 14% at the wingtip. A split trailing edge flap was hinged about the rear auxiliary spar and the main undercarriage retracted inwards. The fuselage skin was supported by stringers and the body contained the main fuel tank with a capacity of 100 gallons (455 litres), while the tail unit, also in light alloy, would have a two-spar structure with a smooth flush-riveted skin covering; the elevators were to be metal covered. Four 20mm cannon were mounted in the wings outboard of the six-blade contra-rotating airscrew disc that was 11ft 6in (3.51m) in diameter. The estimated maximum rate of climb was 4,950ft/min (1,509m/min) at sea level, 4,660ft/min (1,420m/min) at 10,000ft (3,048m), and 3,690ft/min (1,128m/min) at 20,000ft (6,096m). Service ceiling was 37,200ft (11,339m) and absolute ceiling 39,800ft (12,131m). Folland claimed that this project could replace obsolete types still in production.

Hawker P.1018, P.1019 and P.1020

These were essentially the same aircraft but with Sabre 43, Griffon 61 and Centaurus IV engines installed respectively. The Sabre version would have a radiator in a duct in the rear fuselage and a much slimmer fuselage than the Typhoon. The shorter Centaurus variant would allow the pilot to be placed well forward with the fuel stored behind him close to the CofG; armour could then be put behind the tank, thus protecting both pilot and fuel at the same time and saving weight on tank protection. Estimated maximum rates of climb for the Griffon were 5,100ft/min (1,554m/min) at 7,000ft (2,134m) and 4,180ft/min (1,274m/min) at 19,500ft (5,944m); respective figures for the Sabre were 5,500ft/min (1,676m/min) and 4,200ft/min (1,280m/min,) and for the Centaurus 5,700ft/min (1,737m/min) (at 6,500ft [1,981m]) and 4,000ft/min (1,219m/min). All three designs had four-blade propellers for both the Griffon and Sabre versions these were 13ft 0in (3.96m) in diameter while for the Sabre they were 13ft 3in (4.04m).

Hawker P.1018 (14.9.42)

Span:	37ft 0in (11.28m)
Length:	?
Wing Area: 2	45sq.ft (22.79sq.m)
All-Up-Weight:	9,859lb (4,472kg)
Powerplant:	1 x Sabre 43
Max Speed / Height:	465mph (748km/h) at 22,000ft (6,707m)
Armament:	4 x 20mm cannon

Hawker P.1019 (14.9.42)

Span:	36ft 0in (10.97m)
Length:	?
Wing Area:	235sq.ft (21.86sq.m)
All-Up-Weight:	9,019lb (4,091kg)
Powerplant:	1 x Griffon 61
Max Speed / Height:	445mph (716km/h) at 22,000ft (6,707m)
Armament:	4 x 20mm cannon

Hawker P.1020 (14.9.42)

Span:	36ft 0in (10.97m)
Length:	?
Wing Area:	235sq.ft (21.86sq.m)
All-Up-Weight:	9,443lb (4,283kg)
Powerplant:	1 x Centaurus
Max Speed / Height:	450mph (724km/h) at 22,000ft (6,707m)
Armament:	4 x 20mm cannon

Supermarine F.6/42

This was substantially the Spitfire Mk.XXI with a re-rated Griffon 61 and a six-blade propeller with a diameter of 11ft 0in (3.35m). Maximum rate of climb was 5,040ft/min (1,536m/min) at 10,000ft (3,048m) and 4,400ft/min (1,341m/min) at 19,000ft (5,791m).

Supermarine F.6/42 (10.9.42)

Span:	40ft 2.5in (12.26m)
Length:	?
Wing Area:	248sq.ft (23.06sq.m)
All-Up-Weight:	8,750lb (3,969kg)
Powerplant:	1 x Griffon 61
Max Speed / Height:	450mph (724km/h) at 21,000ft (6,401m)
Armament:	4 x 20mm cannon

Vickers F.6/42

On 11 September 1942 Vickers-Armstrong submitted a folder to F.6/42 but the available Ministry documents make little reference to it and no data (apart from a maximum weight of 9,500lb [4,309kg]) or a drawing have been traced. However, Vickers did claim an 'excellent climb rate'.

BELOW A rough sketch of the Westland F.6/42 design (2.9.42). *Westland Archive*

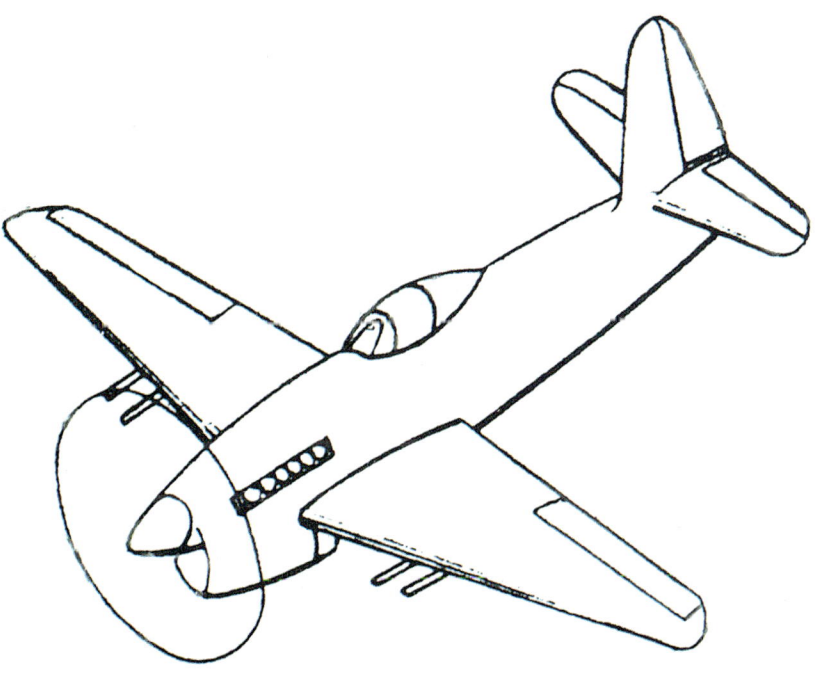

RIGHT Although of poor quality, these original Westland pictures of an unidentified piston fighter model show a design that looks similar to the manufacturer's F.6/42 sketch, so it is assumed that this model is the F.6/42 fighter proposal.

Westland F.6/42

This had a Griffon 61 and a Gallay ('horse collar') radiator slung in a duct beneath the engine. Westland proposed air instead of liquid cooling for the intercooler and claimed that this reduced the final weight by 85lb (39kg), while the Griffon was selected because its production position appeared to be better than the alternatives. There was a four-blade single-rotation propeller of 12ft 6in (3.81m) diameter. Maximum rate of climb was expected to be 4,650ft/min (1,417m/min) at 6,500ft (1,981m) and 4,150ft/min (1,265m/min) at 19,600ft (5,974m); service ceiling was 40,000ft (12,192m). This project was also developed as a naval fighter, possibly to N.7/43.

In mid-September MAP's Capt R. N. Liptrot completed a brief assessment of the contenders. He felt that Westland's suggestions with regard to the power unit, and the cooling system proposed by Airspeed, were probably worth further investigation. Airscrew design was a compromise between top speed and climb; larger diameters would give further improvements in rate of climb but only with serious losses in efficiency at top speed. Westland's rather big propeller diameter would give a rather high tip speed under

Westland F.6/42 (2.9.42)	
Span:	35ft 6in (10.82m)
Length:	?
Wing Area:	206sq.ft (19.16sq.m)
All-Up-Weight:	8,255lb (3,744kg)
Powerplant:	1 x Griffon 61
Max Speed / Height:	443mph (713km/h) at 22,500ft (6,858m)
Armament:	4 x 20mm cannon

ABOVE This artwork, showing an unidentified fighter project, came from a wartime Westland Aircraft magazine advertisement. It appears that the design may have come from the F.6/42/Hawker Fury development period.

top-speed conditions, which would introduce some uncertainty about the airscrew efficiency. Liptrot had spoken to Rolls-Royce about Westland's radiator proposals and was told that Rolls had already tried this arrangement and abandoned it because they considered that there was nothing to gain from it.

For Liptrot, the only real point of interest in the Folland Fo.117 was the use of small-diameter contra-rotating airscrews, while Boulton Paul's layout did not look attractive for a fighter. The AS.56's annular radiator was considered enterprising but necessitated an elongated airscrew shaft and fan drive, which was hardly the sort of thing to contemplate if the F.6/42 was really required in service as quickly as possible. He felt Airspeed could not possibly substantiate the high top speed given in the brochure, which was postulated from an estimated 420hp (313kW) from ejector exhausts and a further 200hp (149kW) from 'alleged heat regeneration made possible by the proposed cooling system'.

RAE Farnborough was also asked to appraise these designs and gave a rough order of merit – 1. Vickers-Armstrong and Folland, 2. Hawker and Airspeed, and 3. Supermarine and Westland – but noted that the Vickers project was completely lacking in detail and 'further detail might make it less satisfactory'. In due course RAE favoured the Fo.117. N. E. Rowe suggested that Folland would have difficulty designing the aircraft quickly enough, and by 13 November 1942 Folland's experience and organisation at Cheltenham had been thoroughly investigated to assess its ability to carry the fighter through to production. The conclusion was that the company was not yet ready, but Folland was prepared to work with another firm. Eventually Rowe contacted all of the companies except Folland and Hawker to say that their designs had been turned down. By 29 December, following several minor modifications, Folland had improved its performance figures and the all-up weight was now stated to be 9,170lb (4,160kg). In February 1943, to simplify the situation, a new specification F.2/43 was allocated to the Hawker proposals.

Support began to grow for Hawker's design, but in some quarters it was seen as a 're-hashed Tempest' (the discussions relating to F.6/42, for Folland or Hawker, appear to have been very heated). Air Chief Marshal Sir Charles Portal, CAS, thought that the Fo.117 was particularly good in control and manoeuvrability, especially in the rolling plane. Also the air-cooled engine was of considerable value to the Air Staff, and he could not see how they could drop the type. Sir Wilfrid Freeman wrote to Portal on 19 December 1942 saying there was little to choose between the Fo.117 and the Tempest II (above), but Folland's was just an estimate of what might be achieved where the Tempest II estimates were based on a fair amount of established evidence with little doubt of attainment. The latter was also at an advanced stage of development when the Fo.117 was just an outline drawing with details and jigging still required. Freeman could not see the Folland in production before the summer of 1945. Six days later, on Christmas Day, Portal asked that the Fo.117 be built, but Freeman maintained his support of the Tempest II.

In March 1943 the decision was taken to drop the Fo.117, a move that made Portal particularly angry. On the 25th Air Marshal Linnell told Portal that he was still quite unconvinced as to the wisdom of starting Folland's design at this time. He felt that Folland was 'much too weak to undertake unaided the design and production of even prototypes in any reasonable time.' At this point, with very heavy civil aviation commitments as well as wartime work, the country's design capacity was absolutely overstretched and Linnell did not wish to 'squander even the slightest bit of it on a job which does not show an absolute clear advantage over anything else we have in hand.' Of the two projects, Folland and Hawker, he expected the latter would be months if not years earlier than the Folland prototype, so the Folland F.6/42 would not affect the war effort by the end of 1944. Had there not been the shortage in design capacity, Linnell would have agreed to letting Folland 'have a try', but at the moment he thought it was quite wrong to squander resources on the Fo.117.

What probably killed the Fo.117, which seemed to offer a superior speed and rate of climb over its Hawker competitor, was that the data

RIGHT Hawker Fury LA610 was photographed at Langley in late 1944 or early 1945 in its original configuration with a Rolls-Royce Griffon engine and contra-rotating propellers.

figures were estimates (experience had shown that these were often over-optimistic), and the Folland company was a relatively new and inexperienced player in fighter design. Folland was told to proceed with its E.28/40 naval project (the Fo.116 torpedo carrier). Later in the year there was an attempt to revive the fighter as the Fo.117A with a laminar flow wing, a 2,500hp (1,864kW) Centaurus 12 and a contra-rotating propeller, with production to be undertaken by English Electric. Six prototypes were ordered on 10 September 1943 to Specification F.19/43, but they were never built.

Hawker Fury

On 3 February 1943 a meeting attended by Linnell, ACAS, Rowe, together with Frank Spriggs and Sydney Camm of Hawker, was held at IC House. The Tempest II programme had slipped badly and a decision was needed regarding whether to cut out the II and go full out for the F.2/43. In the event it was decided that both the Tempest I and Tempest II programmes should continue; the F.2/43 was, however, to be pursued with all speed.

Thanks to Camm's excellent track record with the Hurricane, Typhoon and Tempest, the 'Improved Tempest' or 'Tempest Light Fighter' received strong support. The earliest discussions had centred on lightening the Tempest and included a one-piece wing using Tempest wings brought together on the centre line of the aircraft to reduce the span. Figures suggested a drop in structure weight from the Tempest of around 600lb (272kg), though soon afterwards the span had to be increased again slightly to allow the inboard guns to clear the propeller disc. A layout with a Sabre engine was completed on 2 November 1942 and a version with a Centaurus was finished on 4 December, but work

LEFT Hawker Fury prototype NX798.

BELOW & BOTTOM These views of the Centaurus Fury prototype NX802 were taken in 1945 and 1946.

on the Griffon variant fell behind and its drawings were not ready until 18 September 1943.

Due to the Air Staff's demand for an air-cooled fighter, N. E. Rowe was particularly interested in the Centaurus radial and the promise being shown by Camm's Centaurus-powered Tempest II. The predicted combat power of the CE.12.SM (Centaurus XII) of 2,000hp (1,491kW) at 18,500ft (5,639m) was practically ideal for the low/medium-altitude fighter the Air Staff had in mind where the objective was a maximum rate of climb between ground level and 20,000ft (6,096m). Discussions held at the Air Ministry on 17 January 1943 brought agreement that Bristol would be responsible for the Centaurus XII power egg, while Hawker would provide the airframe. Specification F.2/43 was raised in February 1943 to cover the construction of two Bristol Centaurus prototypes, NX798 and NX802, and an order arrived at Kingston on 9 April. Contra-rotating propellers were requested for production aircraft, but Bristol was informed in May that they were not required on these prototypes. By now the type had been named Fury.

In April 1943 Camm proposed that a new naval fighter specification, N.7/43, could be met by an adapted F.2/43 using a Centaurus XII with extra power. The suggestion was welcomed by Rowe and drawings, weight and performance estimates of this, the P.1022, were forwarded on 22 April. On 12 July it was agreed with J. D. North of Boulton Paul that his firm would modify a Tempest for a trial installation of the wing folding, strengthened undercarriage and arrester gear that would turn the F.2/43 into N.7/43. Boulton Paul was then requested to build two naval Fury prototypes (with those parts standard to both versions being made by Hawker). Production of both versions side by side was to be undertaken by Hawker, which stressed the importance of having contraprops on the Navy aircraft. This type, eventually to become the Sea Fury, really should be described in the naval fighter chapters, but its background is so tied in with RAF developments that it is much more appropriate to cover it here. Specification N.22/43 was duly raised for the Sea Fury.

The need for contra-rotating propellers reflected a growing problem in that the steep gradient of power output that was being obtained with developments of the piston engine necessitated a much bigger airscrew to absorb it all. Keeping a single propeller called for ever larger diameters and consequently a taller undercarriage, which, when retracted, had to be accommodated within the machine's structure, thus forcing the overall size of the conventional fighter to grow. By adopting a contraprop, it became possible to increase the number of blades to six and utilise the extra power while keeping the diameter, and hence aircraft size, within bounds. However, a single five-bladed airscrew did in fact prove suitable for the Sea Fury.

The Griffon prototypes were not ordered until November 1943. By 14 June 1944 the prototype programme had become two F.2/43s with the Centaurus XII, two F.2/43s with the Griffon, one F.22/43 (land-based) prototype to be built by Hawker, only one N.22/43 now to be built by Boulton Paul, and two more N.22/43s to come from Hawker. Development had also continued with numerous versions of the Tempest so, when Rowe suggested in late January 1944 that a Sabre V should be fitted by Napier to a Tempest V to accelerate that engine's air testing, Camm replied that 'in view of the large number of test beds we are already committed to and the necessity for getting the maximum number of machines to the squadrons, we are scarcely able to keep pace with the prototype demand.'

TOP Fury Mk.I LA610 is pictured at Farnborough at the end of June 1946, now with a Sabre engine installed.

ABOVE LA610 poses for an air-to-air publicity photograph.

Plans to build a Fury with a Sabre did not really get going until 1 October 1944 when MAP's J. E. Serby wrote suggesting that two prototype aircraft with the Sabre E.122 could be ready in about a year's time. A trial installation of a Sabre V in one F.2/43 was requested by MAP on 15 November, and on 6 March 1945 Rowe declared that three Sabre prototypes would be needed. Prototype LA610 was to be converted from its Griffon configuration while the others would be new aircraft (VP207 and VP213).

The first Hawker F.2/43, NX798 with a Centaurus XII, left the Experimental Shop on 4 July 1944 and flew for the first time on 1 September. On Monday 4 September Camm reported to the Ministry that 'Lucas [the pilot] was extremely pleased with it, particularly with the feel of the controls which he said were like flying a Snipe' [the biplane Sopwith Snipe had been the RAF's first standard post-First World War fighter and was renowned for its excellent handling]. Camm added that the ailerons were

Hawker Fury Mk.I (flown)

Span:	38ft 4.5in (11.70m)
Length:	34ft 8in (10.57m)
Wing Area:	284.5sq.ft (26.46sq.m)
All-Up-Weight:	12,231lb (5,548kg)
Powerplant:	1 x Sabre VII 3,055hp (2,278kW)
Max Speed / Height:	483mph (777km/h) at 18,500ft (5,639m)
Armament:	4 x 20mm cannon, 2 x 1,000lb (454kg) bombs

Hawker Fury Centaurus Prototype (flown)

Span:	38ft 4.5in (11.70m)
Length:	34ft 7in (10.54m)
Wing Area:	280sq.ft (26.04sq.m)
All-Up-Weight:	11,254lb (5,105kg)
Powerplant:	1 x Centaurus 12 2,440hp (1,820kW)
Max Speed / Height:	455mph (732km/h) at 24,000ft (7,315m)
Armament:	4 x 20mm cannon, bombs, RPs

considered better than the spring tab Tempest ailerons and concluded that 'it looks as though we have achieved something'. The aircraft showed considerable promise and had obviously superior qualities as a fighter over the Tempest on control, stability and view. By 4 October it was possible to compare the F.2/43's top speed to the level speeds of production Tempest Vs, the F.2/43 having already reached 453mph (729km/h) at 26,350ft (8,031m) compared to the Tempest V's 432mph (695km/h) at 18,500ft (5,639m).

The final line-up of Fury and Sea Fury prototypes is quite complex, and most of them later received different engines and propellers.

i. NX798 with Centaurus XII, first flown 1 September 1944.
ii. LA610 with Griffon 85, first flown 27 November 1944. Little information has been traced relating to LA610's performance with the Griffon, and the machine appears to have been flown relatively little with the Rolls-Royce engine. It was later fitted with a Centaurus, then a Sabre VII, making its first flight with the Sabre on 3 April 1946. It was to show a rate of climb at sea level of 5,240ft/min (1,597m/min) and took 9½ minutes to get to 30,000ft (9,144m); equivalent figures for the Centaurus Sea Fury were 4,400ft/min (1,341m/min) at sea level and 8.65 minutes to 30,000ft.
iii. NX802 with Centaurus XV, flown 25 July 1945.
iv. SR661, the Sea Fury semi-navalised prototype. In view of the urgency required, this was adapted from the standard Fury with a Centaurus XII and a four-blade propeller, but had an arrester hook; the wings could not be folded. First flew 21 February 1945.
v. SR666, the fully navalised Sea Fury prototype with a Centaurus XV and a five-blade propeller, folding wings and hook. First flew 12 October 1945.
vi. VB857, the fully navalised Sea Fury prototype with Centaurus XV, manufactured by Boulton Paul but assembly completed by Hawker. Flown 31 January 1946.
vii. VP207, the second Sabre VII prototype (VP213 was not built).

In April 1944 the Admiralty requested 100 N.22/43 aircraft a month. On 29 April Hawker received a contract from the Ministry for 200 F.2/43s and 200 N.22/43s, and in November was advised that the F.2/43 would be named the Fury Mk.1 and the N.22/43 the Sea Fury Mk.10. Production was close and by April 1945 it was decided that all Fury production aircraft were to have the Sabre NS.83.SM (the Sabre VII) and all Sea Furies the Centaurus. In fact, the Sabre would not be ready in time because of work on its Methanol/water injection, so the Sea Fury received total priority over the Fury with deliveries to commence in January 1946; Fury deliveries were to start in August of that year.

However, on 29 January 1946, after a production contract with Boulton Paul had been cancelled, the Sea Fury order was cut from 200 to 100. Already, in February 1945, the Fury order had been cut by 50, and again in September to 120; in February 1946 the number was reduced to 60. In mid-December 1945 it was agreed that the primary role of the Fury I was to be ground support, the first official intimation of such a change, the consequent requirements for low attack armour and additional rear fuel having important implications on its design. These changes were to prove difficult to achieve and Hawker was advised in late February 1946 that if the Fury I could not be used for ground attack purposes it was very unlikely that the Air Staff would have any need for it. On 14 August Hawker was told that the Fury I contract was

BELOW This Supermarine Spiteful Mk.XIV was shown at the post-war exhibition of British and German aircraft held at Farnborough in October and November 1945.

cancelled. However, Centaurus 'land' Fury development was continued by Hawker as a private venture and was duly rewarded with production orders from overseas. Then, during 1946, the number of Sea Furies on order was increased again to help fill a gap in capability, and eventually more than 660 were built for the Fleet Air Arm and overseas customers.

Supermarine Spiteful and Seafang

The final development of the Spitfire was to feature a new wing and receive a new name, Spiteful. In order to improve the Spitfire's rolling characteristics the designers were asked by the Ministry in 1942 to produce a new wing. At the same time it was also considered advantageous to introduce a laminar flow section on this wing, and the result was known as the laminar flow wing or, sometimes, as the 'thin wing', although its t/c ratio was actually greater than the Spitfire's wing. Theoretically the laminar flow wing was designed to move the boundary layer transition point further aft on the wing surface so that the point at which the airflow over the wing became turbulent was delayed and drag was thus reduced. The new wing was considered in relation to aerodynamics, strength and operational requirements, and the main benefits were expected to be an increased performance from the laminar flow, the avoidance of compressibility effects, and improved rolling manoeuvrability from the smaller span. Compressibility was a growing problem caused by flying at speeds ever nearer to the speed of sound, and increasingly more powerful engines meant that the aerodynamics needed to cater for this.

Supermarine's brochure describing a Spitfire with a laminar flow wing was completed in November 1942. The 210sq ft (19.5sq m) wing area was 38.5sq ft (3.6sq m) less than on the Spitfire 21, estimated weight was 200lb (91kg) less, and the predicted

TOP Spiteful RB515 banks away from the camera aircraft.

ABOVE Supermarine Spiteful RB520 had a sting-type arrestor hook fitted to enable it to be used as an interim prototype for the Seafang naval version.

increase in speed 55mph (88km/h). Three aircraft were ordered under specification F.1/43, which defined the new wing and called for a contra-rotating propeller. Initially this document was seen purely as an experimental specification to try out the wing and propellers as soon as possible, and a maximum of four prototypes would be built. In addition the fuselage was to be a converted Mk.VIII Spitfire airframe, but the choice of engine, Merlin or Griffon, was left to Supermarine's discretion.

ABOVE Supermarine Seafang F.Mk.32 prototype VB895, pictured on 13 December 1946.

It was eventually decided that the first two prototypes should have Griffons and the third a Merlin, all with contra-rotating propellers. On 29 December 1942 the first pair of wings was expected to be ready in about eight months.

Among the requirements was that the new wing should be applicable to Spitfire Mk.VIII or Mk.21 airframes and would be applied to production machines of both marks towards the end of 1944. However, the laminar wing's design resulted in a major structural modification (a change to the spacing of the wing spars through the fuselage), which removed any hope of the new wing being directly applicable to the Mk.VIII or 21. In addition, Supermarine was asked to provide a view for the pilot over the nose that was much superior to any previous Spitfire, and the company decided that when the laminar wing was fitted to production aeroplanes it would be associated with a fuselage that allowed the installation of either a Griffon or Merlin with a contra- or single-rotating propeller. Supermarine referred to the new aircraft as the Type 371, although this project number was originally allocated just to the new wing.

A revised prototype programme now requested:
i. A Spitfire Mk.VIII fuselage with a contra-rotating Griffon altered to accommodate the laminar flow wing,
ii. One Type 371 with a contra-rotating Griffon.
iii. One 371 with a single-rotating Merlin (the last was specified because there was no production programme for Merlin contra-rotating gears).

There were discussions for a new name for the 371, which the Air Staff felt was certainly applicable to the contra-rotating Griffon, and by 1 September 1943 the Spitfire Mk.21 with the standard wing was being referred to as the 'Victor I', while Service aircraft with the laminar wing were to be called 'Victor IIs'. By March 1944 production 371s were being called 'Valiant' by the Ministry, but the new aircraft was eventually named Spiteful.

The first aircraft to fly with the new wing, Spitfire Mk.XIV NN660 converted as a hybrid Spiteful prototype, made its first flight on 30 June 1944. The first true prototype, NN664, completed to full F.1/43 production standards, flew on 8 January 1945, but subsequent flight trials indicated that the hoped-for advances over the Spitfire had not been achieved. Tests on the modified Spitfire allowed a direct performance comparison to be made and the laminar wing did produce an increase in speed over the standard Spitfire wing, but it was disappointingly below the excess expected. Any slight degree of surface roughness, even from an impacted insect, could markedly reduce the speed. In addition the new version displayed poor stalling characteristics and more adverse compressibility characteristics than the old Spitfire wing.

Nevertheless extensive flight testing showed that the wing would be suitable for jet aircraft, and it was eventually fitted to the Supermarine 392 jet fighter, which later served with the Fleet Air Arm as the Attacker (see Chapter 11). Due to cutbacks brought about by the end of the war, only seventeen Spitefuls were completed from a planned run of 650, but several were used to improve the laminar wing's aerodynamics or to test alternative powerplants. One, RB518, recorded a speed of 494mph (795km/h) at 27,500ft (8,382m), the

Supermarine Spiteful Mk.XIV (flown)	
Span:	35ft 6in (10.82m)
Length:	32ft 11in (10.03m)
Wing Area:	210sq.ft (19.53sq.m)
All-Up-Weight (no external fuel or bombs):	9,950lb (4,513kg)
Powerplant:	1 x Griffon 101 2,375hp (1,771kW)
Max Speed / Height:	437mph (703km/h) at 5,500ft (1,676m) MS Gear, 483mph (777km/h) at 21,000ft (6,401m) FS Gear
Armament:	4 x 20mm cannon, 2 x 1,000lb (454kg) bombs, 4 x 300lb (136kg) rockets

Supermarine Seafang (flown)	
Span:	35ft 0in (10.67m)
Length:	34ft 1in (10.34m)
Wing Area:	210sq.ft (19.53sq.m)
All-Up-Weight (no external fuel):	10,450lb (4,740kg)
Powerplant:	1 x Griffon 89 c2,400hp (1,790kW)
Max Speed / Height:	428mph (689km/h) at 5,500ft (1,676m), 475mph (764km/h) at 21,000ft (6,401m)
Armament:	4 x 20mm cannon, bombs, RPs

highest speed ever achieved by a British piston-powered aeroplane.

In October 1943 Supermarine began to consider fitting the laminar wing to the Seafire (see Chapter 6) and proposed this as the private venture Type 382 with a Merlin 61. Initially this was not taken up, but interest from the Admiralty began to grow and eventually Specification N.5/45 was written to cover a naval version of the Spiteful, called the Seafang. Spiteful RB520 was fitted with a hook and flew in early 1945 as an interim Seafang prototype, but the first true prototype was VB895. A total of 150 Seafangs were ordered, but just eight were completed and only two of these were flown.

Eagle fighters

The ultimate development in British piston engines was to be the 3,500hp (2,610kW) Rolls-Royce 46H Eagle, a 24-cylinder sleeve-valve H-shaped engine. The initial design project for what became the Eagle was begun in late 1942, but the engine was only ever flown in a Westland Wyvern Mk.I (see Chapter 7); however, Eagle-powered fighter designs were prepared by Hawker and by Supermarine. The 'rivalry' between these two companies is well known, beginning with the Spitfire and Hurricane and leading through to the Spiteful and Fury, then into the jet age with the Attacker and Sea Hawk, and Swift and Hunter. Because of the different dates, the following projects do not appear to have been in competition with one another, but they do represent the ultimate in piston fighter design from these two famous British aircraft manufacturers.

Hawker P.1027

In 1943 Hawker completed a drawing for its P.1027 project that was essentially a Tempest development fitted with a Rolls-Royce 46H Eagle engine. It had four 20mm cannon in the wings, contra-rotating propellers and a radiator placed beneath the fuselage about halfway back directly under the pilot (rather like the Merlin-powered North American P-51 Mustang). This design was not officially tendered, but a preliminary estimate of the Eagle Tempest's performance was prepared by Rolls-Royce at Hucknall and provides the performance information given here.

The P.1027's aerodynamic characteristics had been derived from an analysis of wind tunnel data, from the results of trials with the Tempest, which had flown with a Sabre II installed, and from Hawker's own estimates for a Tempest fitted with a Griffon RG.20.SM. The all-up weight was set at 13,000lb (5,897kg), quite a rise over the Griffon installation's 10,650lb (4,831kg) and due directly to the greater engine weight, and it was assumed that a six-blade contra-rotating propeller 13ft 0in (3.96m) in diameter would be fitted; the internal

Hawker P.1027 (1.7.43)	
Span:	41ft 0in (12.50m)
Length:	37ft 3in (11.35m)
Wing Area:	301.5sq.ft (28.04sq.m)
All-Up-Weight:	13,000lb (5,897kg)
Powerplant:	1 x RR Eagle RH.1.SM
Max Level Speed / Height:	421mph (677km/h) at sea level, 455mph (732km/h) at 7,200ft (2,195m) at MS gear full throttle height, 498mph (801km/h) at 31,100ft (9,479m) at FS gear full throttle height.
Armament:	4 x 20mm cannon

BELOW The only known copy of an original manufacturer's drawing of the Hawker P.1027 (1.7.43). *Chris Farara*

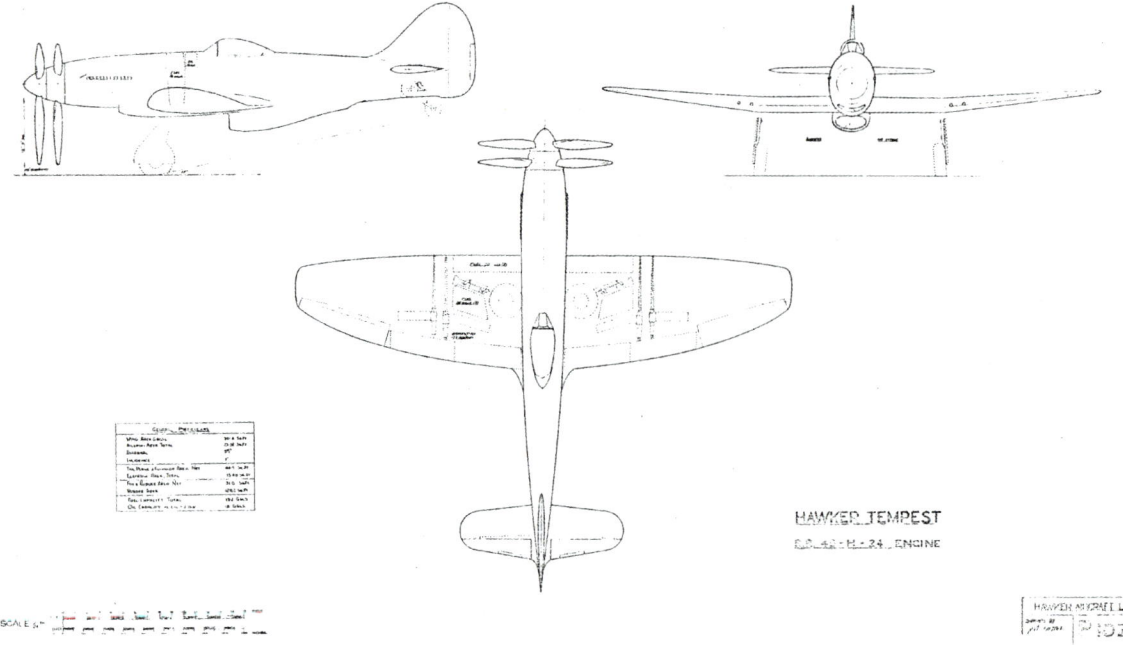

fuel load came to 192 gallons (873 litres). The quoted data was very basic but included a combat rate of climb of 5,850ft/min (1,783m/min) at sea level in MS gear, an operational ceiling of 42,100ft (12,832m), and an absolute ceiling of 44,000ft (13,411m), but this was still enough to suggest that the P.1027's speed performance would have been quite a formidable.

Hawker P.1030

The P.1030 of September 1943 was very similar to the P.1027, but larger and with its radiators moved to the wing leading edges (the arrangement tried earlier on the Tempest I). P.1030 was not tendered and does not appear to have been produced as a full brochure, but a four-page report describing the results of wind tunnel testing and weight assessment was completed.

The project was designed when the 46H was still a paper engine but, using estimates based on Rolls-Royce figures for the Merlin and Griffon, Hawker expected it to give 4,020hp (2,998kW). The wings would be built in one piece and 252gal (1,146lit) of internal fuel would be carried in tanks placed in the inner wings and in the fuselage between the engine and cockpit. The diameter of the two four-blade contra-rotating propellers (13ft 6in [4.1m]) had been chosen to give a level balance between climb and maximum speed efficiency but it was emphasized that very much better efficiencies, both in climb and level speed, could be obtained if a two-speed propeller gearing was fitted. The document stressed that this propeller development should be pressed forward if engines of the 46H's power were to be put into production. P.1030's maximum level speed was calculated to be 509mph (819km/h) at 20,000ft (6,096m), rate of climb 6,400ft/min (1,951m/min) at sea level and 4,680ft/min (1,426m/min) at 20,000ft, time to 20,000ft 4 minutes and 30,000ft (9,144m) just

LEFT A model of the P.1030. *Joe Cherrie*

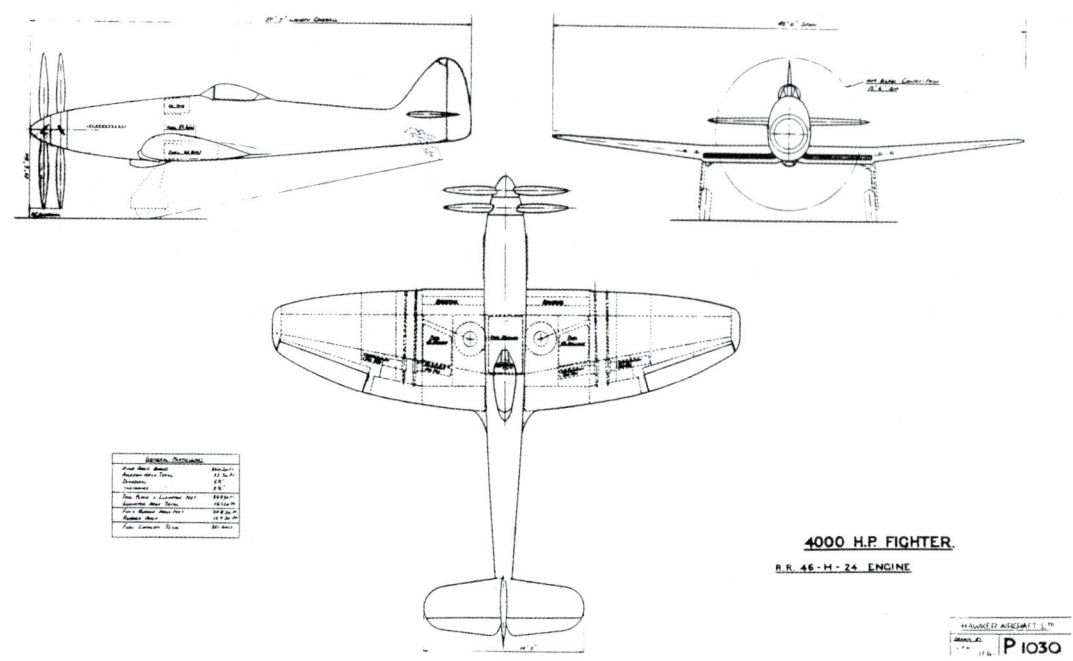

ABOVE The Hawker P.1030 (11.9.43). *Chris Farara*

Hawker P.1030 (11.9.43)	
Span:	42ft 0in (12.80m)
Length:	39ft 9in (12.12m)
Wing Area:	350sq.ft (32.55sq.m)
All-Up-Weight:	14,200lb (6,441kg)
Powerplant:	1 x 46H.24 4,020hp (2,998kW)
Max Speed / Height:	509mph (819km/h) at 20,000ft (6,096m)
Armament:	4 x 20mm cannon

under 7 minutes, and ceiling in excess of 42,000ft (12,802m). Later, in 1944, Hawker proposed a Fury development fitted with an Eagle called the P.1032, but to date no drawing of this has been traced

Supermarine 391

The Type 391 project appeared some time after the P.1030, but did have a full brochure written around it, albeit quite a slim one. It was actually designed as a 'High-Performance Aeroplane for the Royal Navy' capable of operating from a carrier, so should really belong in the naval fighter chapters, but it is better placed alongside the P.1030 (it is not known if the 391 was designed to compete with the Westland Wyvern). The 391 had the Spiteful/Seafang's laminar flow wing (which could be folded to a width of 21ft [6.4m]) and, though primarily a fighter, the aircraft could be converted to carry bombs, rocket projectiles or one 18in (45.7cm) Mk.XV torpedo. The basic aeroplane had four 20mm cannon in the wings, but two would be taken out when carrying the torpedo. Internal fuel totalled 330 gallons (1,500 litres).

The engine was a 46H.24 (RH.2.SM) with contra-rotating propellers of 12ft 0in (3.66m) diameter, and more mature performance figures had by now become available for this unit – combat power would be 3,550bhp (2,647kW) up to 6,000ft (1,829m) in MS gear and 3,260bhp (2,431kW) in FS gear up to 18,000ft

RIGHT The Supermarine Type 391 (20.3.44). *The late Eric Morgan*

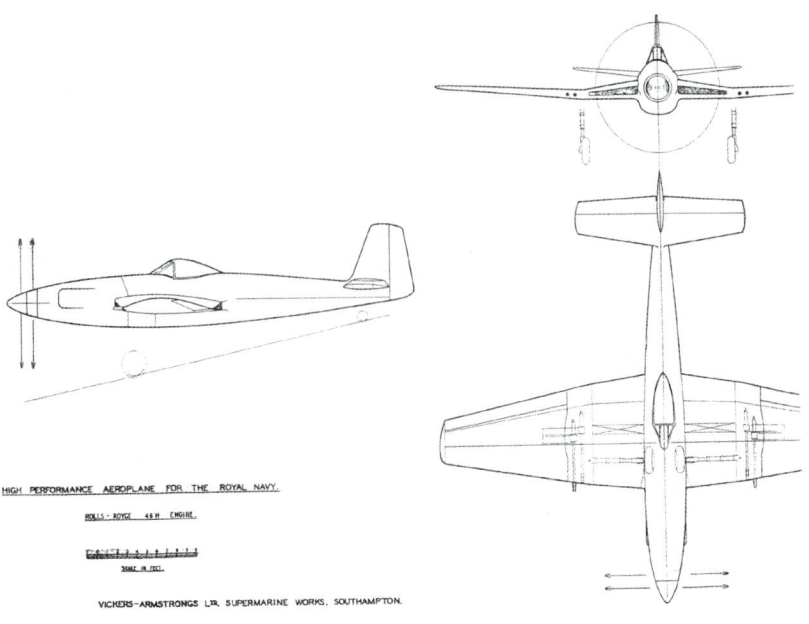

LEFT A model of the Type 391. *Joe Cherrie*

Supermarine 391 (20.3.44)	
Span:	43ft 6in (13.26m)
Length:	39ft 9in (12.12m)
Wing Area:	335sq.ft (31.16sq.m)
All-Up-Weight:	15,750lb (7,144kg), 17,250lb (7,825kg) with torpedo
Powerplant:	1 x 46H.24 3,550hp (2,647kW)
Max Speed / Height:	546mph (879km/h) at 25,000ft (7,620m)
Armament:	4 x 20mm cannon, 1 x 18in (45.7cm) torpedo, bombs, rocket projectiles

(5,486m). As a fighter with a weight of 15,750lb (7,144kg) the 391 showed an initial rate of climb of 4,800ft/min (1,463m/min), time to 20,000ft (6,096m) of 4.35 minutes, service ceiling 41,100ft (12,527), and still air range 765nm (1,417km); equivalent figures when carrying the torpedo at 17,250lb (7,825kg) all-up weight were 4,200ft/min (1,280m/min), 5.0 minutes, 39,300ft (11,979m) and 895nm (1,658km). Sadly, none of these very exciting Eagle-powered designs ever came close to being built.

Martin-Baker MB.3, MB.4 and MB.5

To close this chapter we must take a look at the designs of a company that was really an outsider in the aircraft industry, yet whose final product was one of the most outstanding of British piston fighters. The story of James Martin and Capt Val Baker forming the small Martin-Baker Aircraft company belongs elsewhere, but on 3 August 1938 the team flew a single-seat fighter called the MB.2, powered by a Napier Dagger engine (see Chapter 1). This was followed by the private venture MB.3, of which three were ordered against Specification F.18/39, written around the type in May 1939. The MB.3 had six wing-mounted 20mm cannon and, when flown, was fitted with a Napier Sabre II. It was expected to achieve at least 400mph (644km/h)

LEFT The Martin-Baker MB.3. *Martin-Baker*

TOP MIDDLE This unusual manufacturer's 'cut-out' photo of the MB.3 provides good fuselage detail for this short-lived fighter prototype.

BOTTOM MIDDLE The MB.3 is seen during ground running of its Napier Sabre engine. *Martin-Baker*

BOTTOM The spectacular Martin-Baker MB.5. *Martin-Baker*

at 15,000ft (4,572m), and the only example to be built, R2492, flew on 3 August 1942; sadly it crashed just over a month later, killing Capt Baker.

By this time constant delays and late delivery with the MB.3 had ensured that the type would not receive a production order (the Ministry considered that the fighter was outdated before it flew). However, James Martin had always wanted to use a Rolls-Royce Griffon on his fighters and finally got the chance to fit one in the much-redesigned MB.5. The Bristol Centaurus was considered as an alternative and preliminary drawings of an MB.4 project with this engine were completed, but once the

Martin-Baker MB.3 (flown)	
Span:	36ft 0in (10.97m)
Length:	35ft 4in (10.77m)
Wing Area:	262.5sq.ft (24.41sq.m)
Take-Off Weight:	Unknown but c12,000lb (5,443kg)
Powerplant:	1 x Napier Sabre II 2,020hp (1,506kW)
Max Speed / Height:	430mph (692km/h) at 20,000ft (6,096m)
Armament:	6 x 20mm Hispano cannon

Martin-Baker MB.5 (flown)	
Span:	35ft 0in (10.67m)
Length:	37ft 9in (11.51m)
Wing Area:	263sq.ft (244.59sq.m)
All-Up-Weight:	12,090lb (5,484kg)
Powerplant:	1 x Griffon 83 2,305hp (1,719kW)
Max Speed / Height:	460mph (740km/h) at 20,000ft (6,096m)
Armament:	4 x 20mm cannon

ABOVE The MB.5 on the runway. The aircraft's flaps, nose shape and contra-rotating propellers show up well.

ABOVE Martin-Baker's MB.5 was also displayed at the October/November 1945 Farnborough exhibition.

Griffon was available the MB.4 and all other alternatives were dropped (the only known drawing of what might be the MB.4 shows the aircraft also with a Griffon). The MB.5 was also re-engineered with a four-cannon wing, teardrop canopy and rear fuselage radiator.

The first and only MB.5, R2496, was built under the same F.18/39 contract and made its maiden flight on 23 May 1944; it proved to be a very fine aeroplane and few piston fighters would beat its top speed of 460mph (740km/h) at 20,000ft (6,096m). A&AEE Boscombe Down's assessment noted that the general layout of the MB.5 was 'excellent and infinitely better, from the engineering and maintenance point of view, than any other similar type of aircraft.' It was highly rated by all of the pilots who flew it and made a very good gun platform and a spectacular aerobatic display aircraft, but the end of the war and the slow progress made by the company in getting the machine ready (partly through a lack of facilities) ensured that it, too, remained a prototype. After the MB.5 Martin produced one or two jet fighter designs before concentrating on ejection seats for military aircraft, a product that would make his company world famous.

Conclusion

These first two chapters have described the extraordinary progress made in British piston fighter design before and during the war. With the Fury/Sea Fury and Martin-Baker MB.5 (and the de Havilland Hornet in Chapter 4), these aircraft represented the pinnacle of development for this category because in fact the end of the line had been reached for the piston fighter. Just around the corner was the jet engine, the first jet fighters were already flying, and piston power could never compete with the speed and climb performance offered by the jet once it began to mature. Nevertheless, for a short period these splendid aeroplanes had their moment in the limelight.

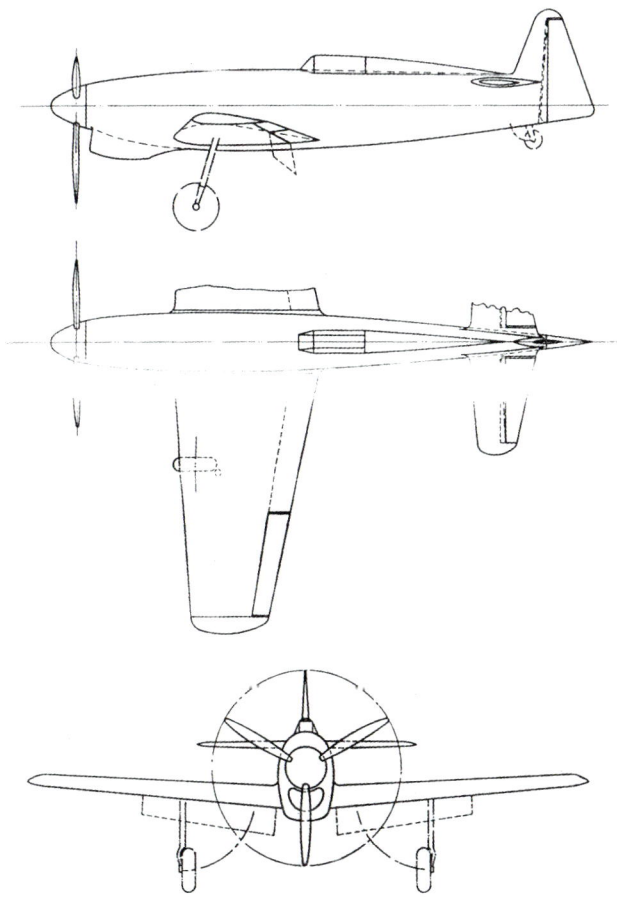

LEFT This is thought to be the Martin-Baker MB.4, but it shows a Griffon powerplant rather than a Bristol Centaurus, so may in fact be an early form of MB.5.

Chapter Three
Pre-War Twin-Engine Fixed-Gun Fighters

ABOVE Westland Whirlwind P6997 photographed on 31 August 1942 with bombs under its wings. *Phil Butler*

The development of the RAF's twin-engined fighters ran concurrently with the single-engined types described in the previous chapters. Once again there is some crossover between single- and twin-engine types because a few of the tenders to the following specifications had just the one engine and they need to be described under the correct requirement.

Specification F.37/35 Westland Whirlwind

As noted in Chapter 1, it was acknowledged during the mid-1930s that for a fighter to be fully effective it needed a very heavy armament of up to eight machine guns, but even more hitting power was offered in the form of four French Hispano-Suiza 20mm cannon with explosive bullets. The arrival of this impressive weapon was to bring about a complete revolution in fighter armament once metal structures were strong enough to absorb the heavy recoil. At the time much attention was being given to the weapon overseas and the Air Staff felt that the need for a British experimental aircraft fitted with the 20mm was now very urgent. F.37/35 requested a top speed at least 40mph (64km/h) in excess of contemporary bombers, giving a minimum of at least 330mph (531km/h) at 15,000ft (4,572m). The Deputy Chief of the Air Staff wrote that 'if the type were successful it would provide ... the most powerful fighter likely to be produced for some time.' It would be a radical departure from any existing types, and five companies responded with eight designs.

Boulton Paul P.88

Two similar designs were proposed powered by either a single Bristol Hercules HE.1.SM (P.88A) or Rolls-Royce Vulture (P.88B). These had two

CHAPTER THREE

PRE-WAR TWIN-ENGINE FIXED-GUN FIGHTERS

LEFT The Boulton Paul P.88 (5.36). *Les Whitehouse, Boulton Paul Archive*

MIDDLE & BOTTOM A model of the Boulton Paul P.88B version fitted with the Vulture engine. *Les Whitehouse, Boulton Paul Archive*

20mm cannon in each wing, mounted on their sides on either side of a beam fitted between the wing spars. P.88A carried 104 gallons (473 litres) of fuel and was expected to show a maximum rate of climb of 3,500ft/min (1,067m/min) at 5,000ft (1,524m), and a service ceiling of 39,500ft (12,040m); the larger P.88B's figures were 133 gallons (605 litres), 3,400ft/min (1,036m/min) at 15,000ft (4,572m) and 38,000ft (11,582m) respectively. A contract for two aeroplanes, L6591 and L6592, was placed in December 1936, but was cancelled on 6 January 1937.

Boulton Paul P.88A (5.36)	
Span:	39ft 6in (12.04m)
Length:	32ft 8in (9.96m)
Wing Area:	260sq.ft (24.18sq.m)
All-Up-Weight:	6,573lb (2,982kg)
Powerplant:	1 x Bristol Hercules I c1,500hp (1,119kW)
Max Speed / Height:	337mph (542km/h) at 15,000ft (4,572m)
Armament:	4 x 20mm cannon

Boulton Paul P.88B (5.36)	
Span:	44ft 0in (13.41m)
Length:	36ft 3in (11.05m)
Wing Area:	320sq.ft (29.76sq.m)
All-Up-Weight:	8,100lb (3,674kg)
Powerplant:	1 x RR Vulture 1,750hp (1,305kW)
Max Speed / Height:	358mph (576km/h) at 15,000ft (4,572m)
Armament:	4 x 20mm cannon

Bristol Type 153

Bristol also produced two designs to F.37/35, one called the Type 153, which had a single Bristol Hercules engine, then the twin-engine 153A below. The 153 was a development of the experimental Type 151 high-speed research aircraft proposed to 35/35

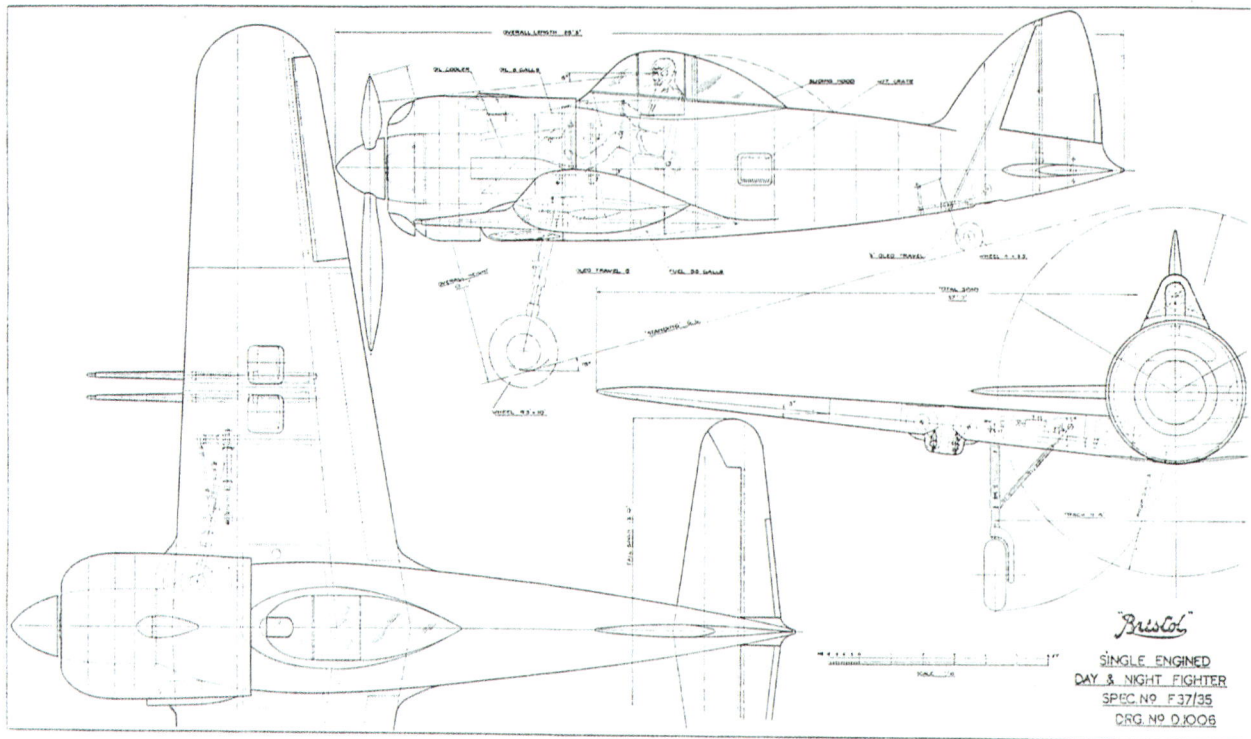

ABOVE The Bristol Type 153 (30.4.36).

in early 1936, and it had the same fuselage and tail unit but with larger wings and the necessary modifications to carry four Hispano-Suiza 20mm cannon. This reduced the estimated top speed to 357mph (574km/h) from the 151's 440mph (708km/h). To provide the room necessary to mount the cannons on the wings a low wing arrangement was adopted, instead of the middle wing on the previous design. This gave a shorter undercarriage, which, being retracted ahead of the front spar, left room for an 85-gallon (386-litre) fuel tank between the spars. The pilot was seated well forward with a good view downwards over the nose and wing. The cannons were carried on the wings, two on each side, just outside the airscrew disc, but it was the worry of stowing such large weapons in cantilever wings outboard of the propeller that prompted Bristol's designers, Frank Barnwell and Leslie Frise, to produce the alternative 153A. The Type 153 had a metal three-blade variable-pitch airscrew 11ft 3in (3.43m) in diameter. The initial rate of climb was 3,580ft/min (1,091m/min), service ceiling 33,200ft (10,119m) and absolute ceiling 34,000ft (10,363m).

From many points of view Bristol considered that it was much more satisfactory to mount the guns on the centreline with two smaller engines set on the wings. The 153A had two Bristol Aquila engines, twin end plate fins and rudders, and a slim fuselage; its wingspan was the same as the 153, but the wing area and weight had increased. The cannon armament was fitted in the lower fuselage nose, which itself was level with the centre-wing leading edge (and gave a strikingly similar appearance to the Grumman XF5F-1 Skyrocket, a contemporary project from America that flew in April 1940).

By adopting a twin-engine arrangement for a single-seater carrying four 20mm cannon, it had proved possible to combine excellent performance with a very practical layout from the viewpoint of fighting efficiency. For instance, the designers considered that the pilot's view was so good that it would be difficult to visualise anything better for considerations of searching, attacking, formation flying and landing. Owing to the relatively small wing, compared with the size of two engine nacelles and body, a special arrangement had been adopted to interfere as little as possible with the wing's efficiency. The engine nacelles were carried beneath the wing, leaving the top surface undisturbed over the semi span. Similarly, the body was mounted wholly on top of the wing, leaving the bottom surface of the wing clean between the engine nacelles. It was considered that this arrangement would give the lowest drag, and also

Bristol 153 (30.4.36)	
Span:	37ft 0in (11.28m)
Length:	25ft 3in (7.70m)
Wing Area:	204sq.ft (18.97sq.m)
Fully Loaded Weight:	6,092lb (2,763kg)
Powerplant:	1 x Hercules HE.IS 1,295hp (966kW)
Max Speed / Height:	300mph (483km/h) at sea level, 357mph (574km/h) at 12,500ft (3,810m)
Armament:	4 x 20mm cannon

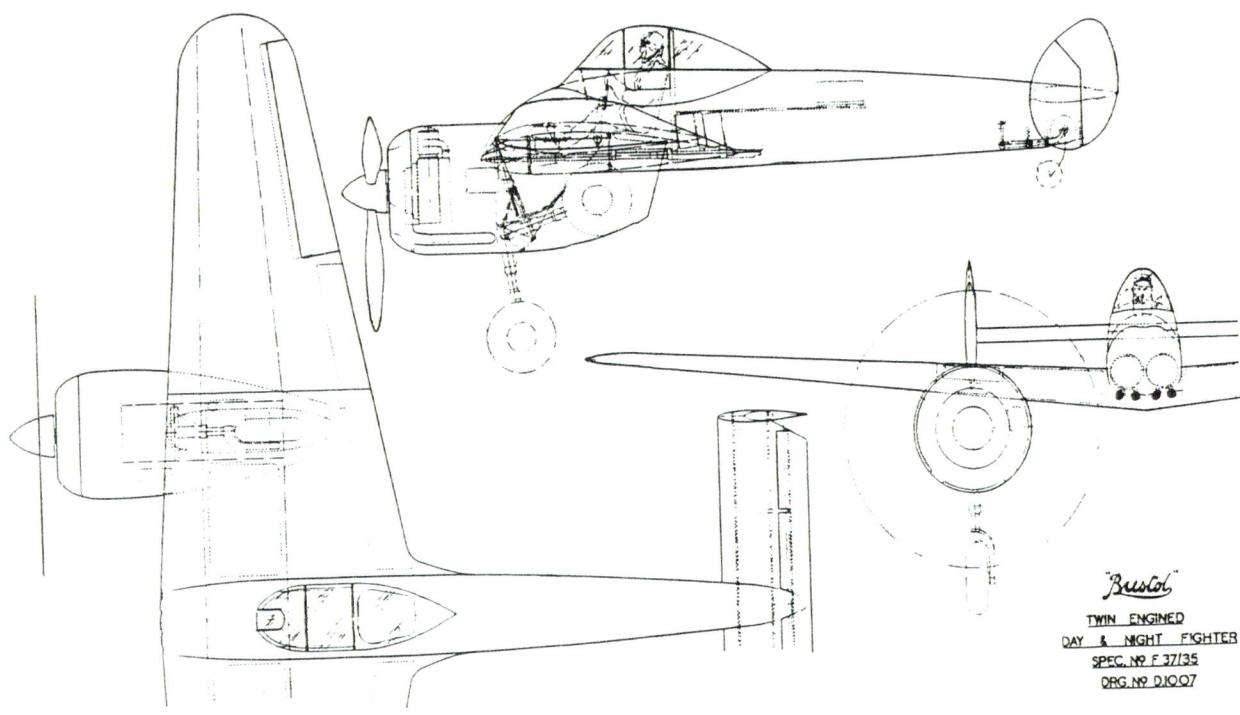

ABOVE The Bristol Type 153A (5.36). *Duncan Greenman Bristol AirChive*

the best layout for providing lift using the flaps. Further, advantage had been taken of the dropped nacelle position to introduce engine cooling arrangements that would give lower drag and save weight. Cooling was by means of a drum cooler mounted inside the nacelle cowling, air being led to the cooler by pipes between the cylinders, the exhaust air escaping through the rear end of the nacelle.

The body was made as small as possible to maintain performance, but with the scheme adopted it had also proved possible to accommodate the four long cannons without added cross

Bristol 153A (30.4.36)	
Span:	37ft 0in (11.28m)
Length:	25ft 6in (7.77m)
Wing Area:	213sq.ft (19.81sq.m)
Fully Loaded Weight:	6,480lb (2,939kg)
Powerplant:	2 x Aquila AE.3S 650hp (488kW)
Max Speed / Height:	302mph (486km/h) at sea level, 370mph (595km/h) at 15,000ft (4,572m)
Armament:	4 x 20mm cannon

section or giving extra drag. These guns were carried in the centre of mass of the aeroplane where the greatest rigidity was obtained, and where no possible deflections of the aircraft in flight could affect the accuracy of fire. And it was possible to remove the cannons from the body without having to cut large openings, a feature that would have reduced the stiffness unduly since the body was already small compared with the size of the cannons. The guns were staggered in side elevation, two lying further aft than the others, to accommodate the large ammunition boxes. Also, to keep the width of the body down to a minimum, the guns were slightly canted towards each other.

It was partly to keep down the torque that the body had to take, and also to provide excellent control and manoeuvring power, with good spin recovery, that a twin fin and rudder arrangement had been adopted. The fins were directly in line with the three-blade variable pitch airscrews, which were made in metal and had a diameter of 8ft 6in (2.59m). A 42.5-gallon (193-litre) fuel tank was placed in each wing between the fuselage and engine nacelle. Sea level rate of climb was 3,800ft/min (1,158m/min), service ceiling 34,600ft (10,546m) and absolute ceiling 35,500ft (10,820m).

Hawker F.37/35

This was a version of the Hurricane with four 20mm Oerlikon cannon mounted in the wing outer panels; the type's general shape was unchanged.

Hawker F.37/35 (23.4.36)	
Span:	40ft 0in (12.19m)
Length:	32ft 3in (9.83m)
Wing Area:	258sq.ft (23.99sq.m)
All-Up-Weight:	c7,000lb (3,175kg)
Powerplant:	1 x Merlin
Max Speed / Height:	c320mph (515km/h)
Armament:	4 x 20mm cannon

Supermarine 312

Spitfire designer R. J. Mitchell's last fighter design, this was an adapted Spitfire with four 20mm Oerlikon

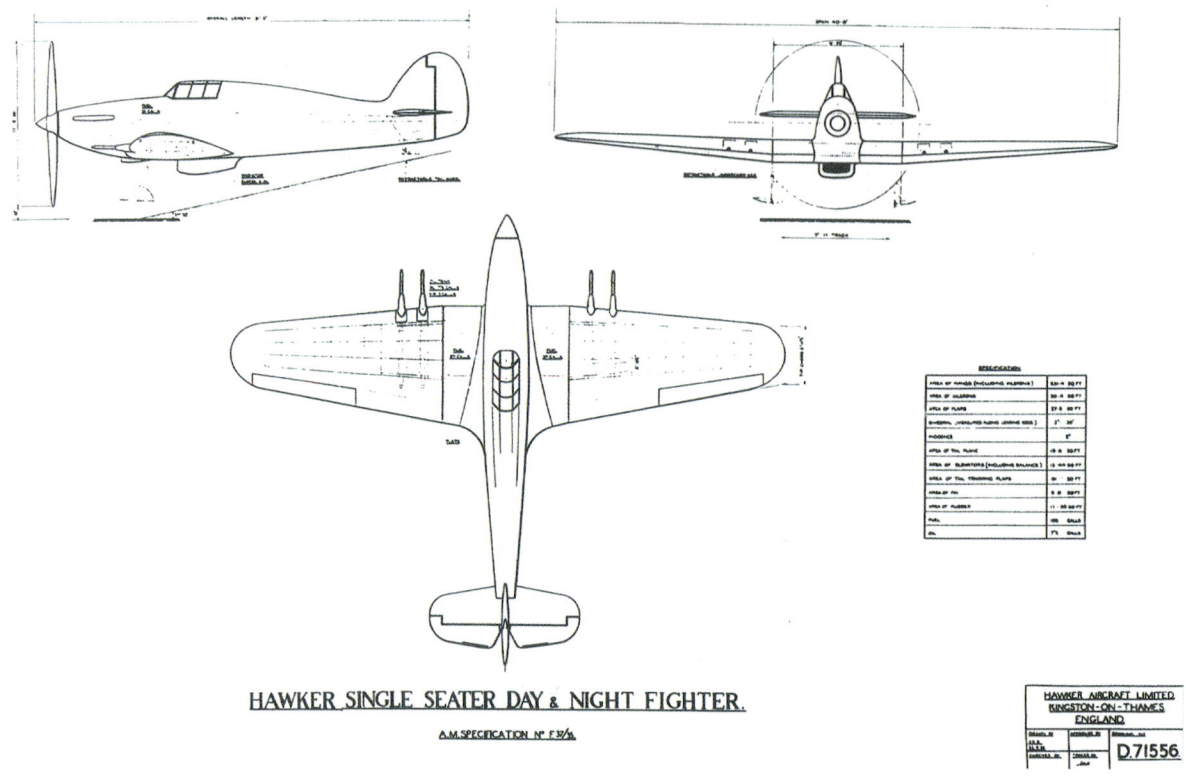

ABOVE Hawker Hurricane variant to F.37/35 (23.4.36). *Chris Farara*

cannon mounted in modified wings and positioned well outside the airscrew disc. The Spitfire's radiator was replaced by an inlet under the fuselage, but the fuselage, engine installation, tail unit and chassis were unaltered. When the project was proposed, the then experimental F.37/34 (Spitfire) had almost completed its contractor's

BELOW The Supermarine Type 313 (25.4.36). *The late Eric Morgan*

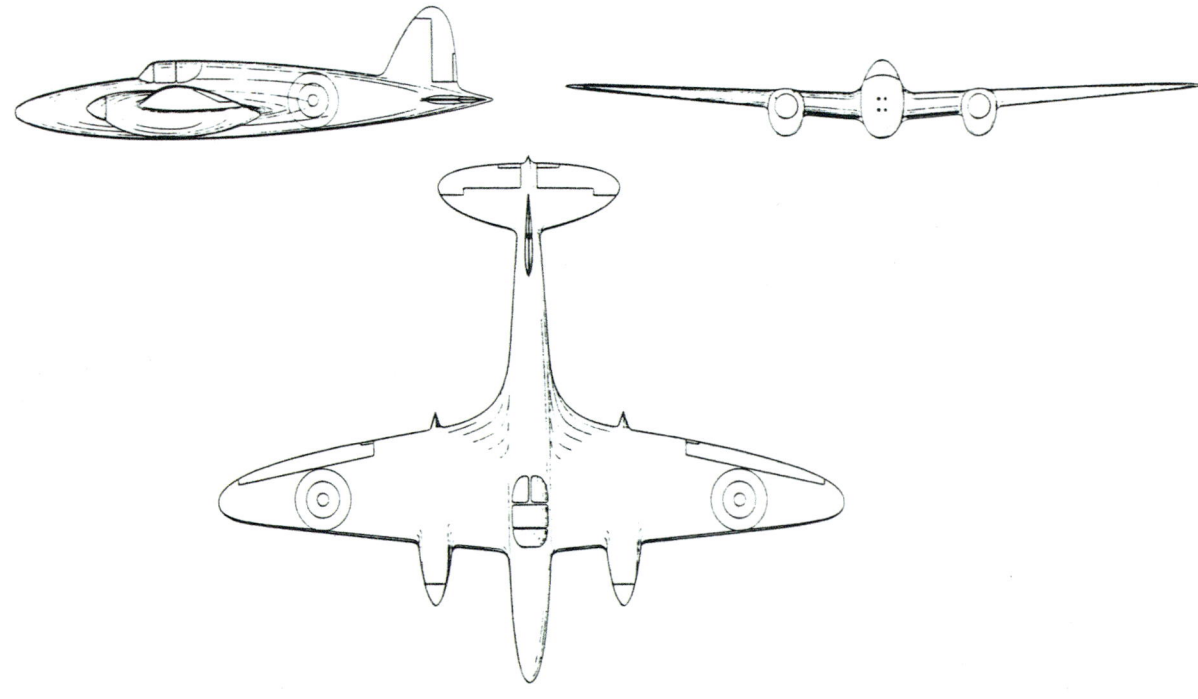

Supermarine 312 (23.4.36)	
Span:	37ft 0in (11.28m)
Length:	29ft 11in (9.12m)
Wing Area:	242sq.ft (22.51sq.m)
All-Up-Weight:	5,800lb (2,631kg)
Powerplant:	1 x Merlin 1,010hp (753kW)
Max Speed / Height:	355mph (571km/h) at 15,000ft (4,572m)
Armament:	4 x 20mm cannon

flight trials and shown itself to be a very satisfactory aeroplane of high performance and no vices. Supermarine felt that if a production order was placed for the F.37/34, the provision of an alternative set of wings would enable one machine to fulfil F.37/35. If hopper-type ammunition boxes were available, the guns could be housed completely inside the wings (except for the outer barrels); if not, then a slight excrescence on each bottom wing surface would be necessary to fair in the ammunition drums, but this would add minimal drag. Apart from the gun mountings the wing would be unaltered. Estimated time to 20,000ft (6,096m) was 9½ minutes and service ceiling 31,000ft (9,449m).

Supermarine 313

This twin-engine project was to be powered by Rolls-Royce Goshawks or, as an alternative, Aero Engines Ltd (Hispano) 12Y glycol-cooled units. The radiators were buried in the inner wing and fed by small-profile inlets under the leading edges, while structurally the design was similar to the Supermarine F.7/30 (Type 224) and F.37/34. It was intended to use the well-tried Supermarine single-spar cantilever wing with a 'D'-shaped nose torsion box. The single spar was very favourable for the engine installation, chassis retraction (into the engine nacelles) and fuel tank location, and the whole wing was metal covered with the smooth leading edge flush-riveted to present an ideally smooth surface to the airstream. Supermarine noted that this type of wing was very favourable in terms of flutter, aileron reversal and

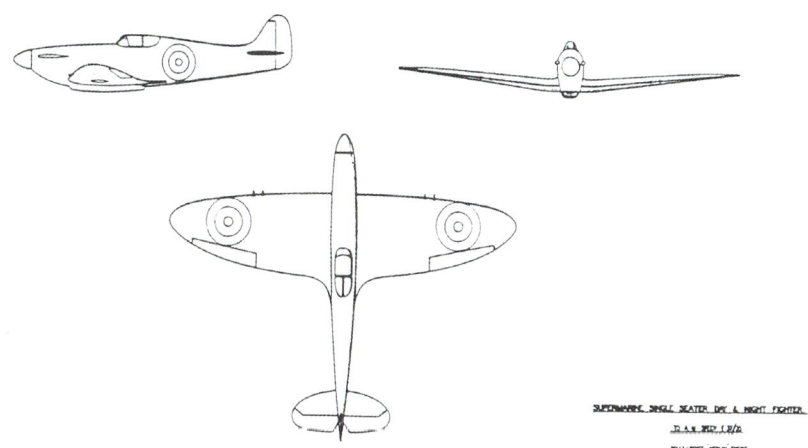

ABOVE **The Supermarine Type 312 (23.4.36).** *The late Eric Morgan*

other flexibility problems.

A battery of four 20mm cannon was grouped and completely enclosed in the nose (if 12T engines were used, two additional cannon could be fitted to fire through the airscrew hubs), and the front section of the fuselage was hinged to allow the guns to be removed. The fuselage itself was metal monocoque, which combined a smooth surface, high torsional rigidity and light weight. Particular care had been taken to make the design as clean as possible and as small as possible with a span only slightly greater than the Type 224. The 313 would take 7½ minutes to get to 20,000ft (6,096m) and its service ceiling was 34,000ft (10,363m). Fitting 12Y engines would add an extra 500lb (227kg) to the maximum weight and give a performance approximately equal to that quoted for the Goshawk, except that the rate of climb below 15,000ft (4,572m) would be slightly better due to the different supercharger height, while the ceiling was slightly lower.

The brochure also noted that the 313 could also be used as a light bomber since space was available in the fuselage behind the pilot to house four 500lb (227kg) bombs. Another crewman would be added, two cannon would be taken out and the all-up weight would reach 10,700lb (4,854kg). One prototype Supermarine F.37/35, L6593 (actually thought to be a Type 312

Supermarine 313 (25.4.36)	
Span:	48ft 0in (14.63m)
Length:	37ft 0in (11.28m)
Wing Area:	325sq.ft (30.225sq.m)
All-Up-Weight:	8,200lb (3,720kg)
Powerplant:	2 x Goshawk 855hp (638kW)
Max Speed / Height:	390mph (628km/h) at 15,000ft (4,572m)
Armament:	4 x 20mm cannon

rather than a 313), was provisionally ordered in December 1936 but was cancelled on 28 January 1937.

Westland P.9

The P.9 was a twin Rolls-Royce Kestrel K.26 project closely resembling the eventual Whirlwind as built, but with a low tail and twin fins instead of the high horizontal surface and single fin (the final tail arrangement was selected in March 1938). The guns were housed in the nose in two pairs one above the other and the fuselage was very thin. The K.26, the ultimate development of Rolls-Royce's successful Kestrel, was later called the Peregrine and embraced some early Merlin features and experience. The original intention (in 1936) had been to practically redesign the Kestrel but, once the Westland prototype had been ordered, the need to fit it into the airframe meant that an all-new engine would not be ready in time; accordingly the K.26 just became a natural development of

RIGHT The Westland P.9 as first proposed with twin fins and Kestrel engines (spring 1936).

MIDDLE & BELOW A model of the Westland P.9. *Joe Cherrie*

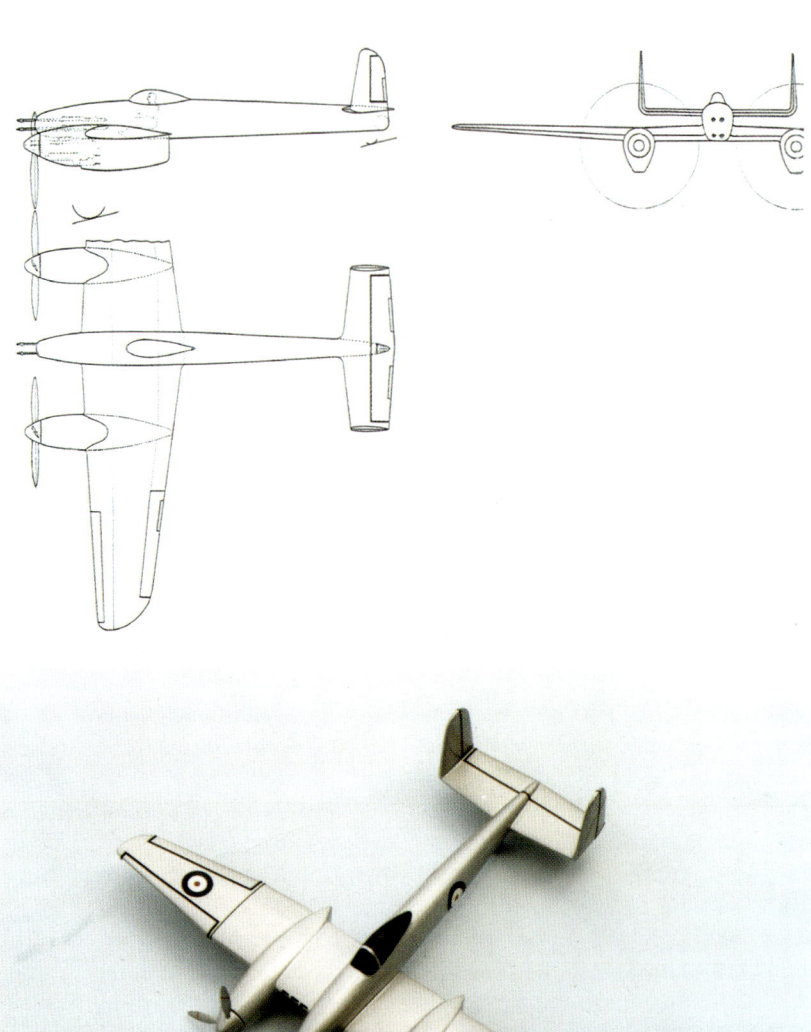

the Kestrel. A clean inline engine, the Peregrine helped the aerodynamics of the P.9 considerably and made it one of the most compact fighter designs yet proposed. The P.9's maximum rate of climb was 3,100ft/min (945m/min) and service ceiling 36,300ft (11,064m).

These designs were analysed at the Tender Design Conference held on 24 May 1936. Westland felt the chief advantage of a twin-engine layout was that the armament could be installed in the nose; if it was placed wide apart in the wings on a single-engined aircraft the recoil of the guns would be uneven and result in inaccurate fire. Opponents said that two engines would reduce manoeuvrability, but the Conference commented favourably on the twin types submitted. It initially recommended the Supermarine 313, the preference for most experts because of Reginald Mitchell's recent success with the Spitfire and his experience in designing fast aeroplanes, but the type's delivery date (twenty-seven months) was considered excessive.

Westland's P.9 thus became the more favoured. DTD considered it the most advanced project while the company was not overburdened with work and another twin-engine type would provide a competitive stimulus to Supermarine. The P.9 represented

Westland P.9 (spring 1936)	
Span:	45ft 0in (13.72m)
Length:	31ft 0in (9.45m)
Wing Area:	c250sq.ft (23.25sq.m)
All-Up-Weight:	8,400lb (3,810kg)
Powerplant:	2 x Kestrel K.26 1,710hp (1,275kW)
Max Speed / Height:	395mph (636km/h) at 15,000ft (4,572m)
Armament:	4 x 20mm cannon

LEFT These images of P7062 were part of a set taken of the aircraft on 22 October 1942.

a complete break from orthodox design and its novel features included a magnesium monocoque fuselage (a particularly innovative feature because its better strength-to-weight ratio enabled the skin to be thicker for the same weight than if aluminium was used), a radiator in the wing leading edge to cut drag, integral wing fuel tanks that were detachable for maintenance, Fowler flaps for high lift but minimum wing area, large chord lifting slots, and an internal exhaust.

The idea of modifying either the Spitfire or Hurricane to take 20mm guns was rejected because their designer's drawing offices were too busy; it seemed quicker to order a totally new design from a less occupied company (later, during the war, both types were of course fitted with cannon). Because of the experimental nature of the armament the Air Ministry was anxious to order two P.9s, two P.88s and one Type 313. However, this exceeded the financial allocation and Treasury sanction had to be obtained for these prototypes. Treasury approval was given in January 1937 but only Westland's machine was in fact built – the firm received a contract for two prototypes on 11 February and a maiden flight was expected in June 1938; a mock-up was examined on 28 May 1937.

Construction of the first prototype, L6844, began in July 1937. However, following delays caused mainly by the new design features but also from hold-ups in the delivery of undercarriages and engines, its first flight did not take place until 11 October 1938. ACAS noted, 'This fighter seemed a thoroughly practical and high-performance aeroplane and I only wish the production capacity of this firm were greater.' In fact, there were proposals to move production to either Fairey or Hawker, and because the P.9 was so experimental the Air

Westland Whirlwind Mk.I (flown)	
Span:	45ft 0in (13.72m)
Length:	31ft 6in (9.60m)
Wing Area:	250sq.ft (23.25sq.m)
All-Up-Weight:	10,377lb (4,707kg)
Powerplant:	2 x RR Peregrine I 885hp (638kW)
Max Speed / Height:	356mph (573km/h) at 15,000ft (4,572m)
Armament:	4 x 20mm cannon

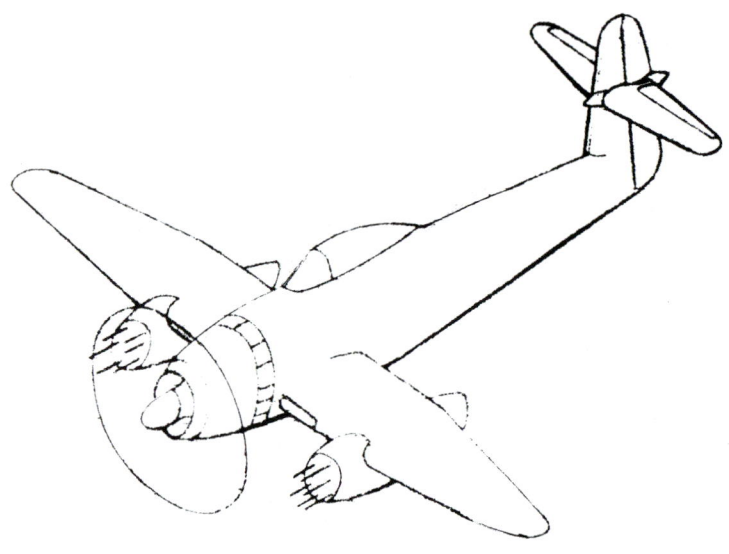

TOP Westland Whirlwind P7048 was captured in colour by legendary photographer Charles Brown on 20 April 1944. *RAF Museum*

ABOVE This manufacturer's sketch shows a development of the Whirlwind with a nose-mounted Hercules engine and guns in each of the wing nacelles. *The late Fred Ballam, Westland Archive*

Ministry would not risk ordering any production aeroplanes until flight trials were under way.

A production order for 200 aircraft, to be called Whirlwind, was placed with Westland at the start of 1939. It was intended to build 800 more at Castle Bromwich, but this plan was replaced in March 1939 by Spitfires and 200 more Yeovil-built Whirlwinds. In the end, after development work on the Peregrine had been halted, only 114 Whirlwinds were built – the second batch was dropped and the original order reduced. Early in the war Rolls-Royce decided to abandon development of the Peregrine and concentrate its efforts on the Merlin, a move that curtailed the Whirlwind's career since the engine was not required for any other production aircraft type and its teething problems, though not severe, would never be fully addressed.

It is understood that a Whirlwind Mk.II was drawn by Westland in May 1940, powered by a 'developed' Peregrine, which offered another 15% of horsepower and was suggested by Rolls-Royce before the engine was abandoned. This had a redesigned nose that was tested on a Mk.I Whirlwind, there was also 20% more fuel, and the estimated maximum speed was 422mph (679km/h) at 20,000ft (6,096m). A more radical proposed development from Westland made in November 1939 had a single 1,500hp (1,119kW) Bristol Hercules engine in the nose, and in each nacelle six of what were termed 'controllable' guns. With a span of 45ft (13.72m) and a wing area of 250sq ft (23.25sq m), this was expected to achieve a maximum of 340mph (547km/h) at 15,000ft (4,572m). Roy Fedden at Bristol also pressed strongly for an installation having two radial engines in the wing, but Westland knew that fitting larger powerplants to the basic Whirlwind structure was impossible. The original concept had been to build the smallest possible fighter compatible with two engines, so the airframe was neither roomy enough nor strong enough to take anything larger.

Thus the Whirlwind was to be denied the prolonged RAF career enjoyed by the Hurricane and Spitfire, and when it entered service in the autumn of 1940 the demand for more speed and height made it appear, at least in official eyes, to be verging on obsolescence. Nevertheless, by the

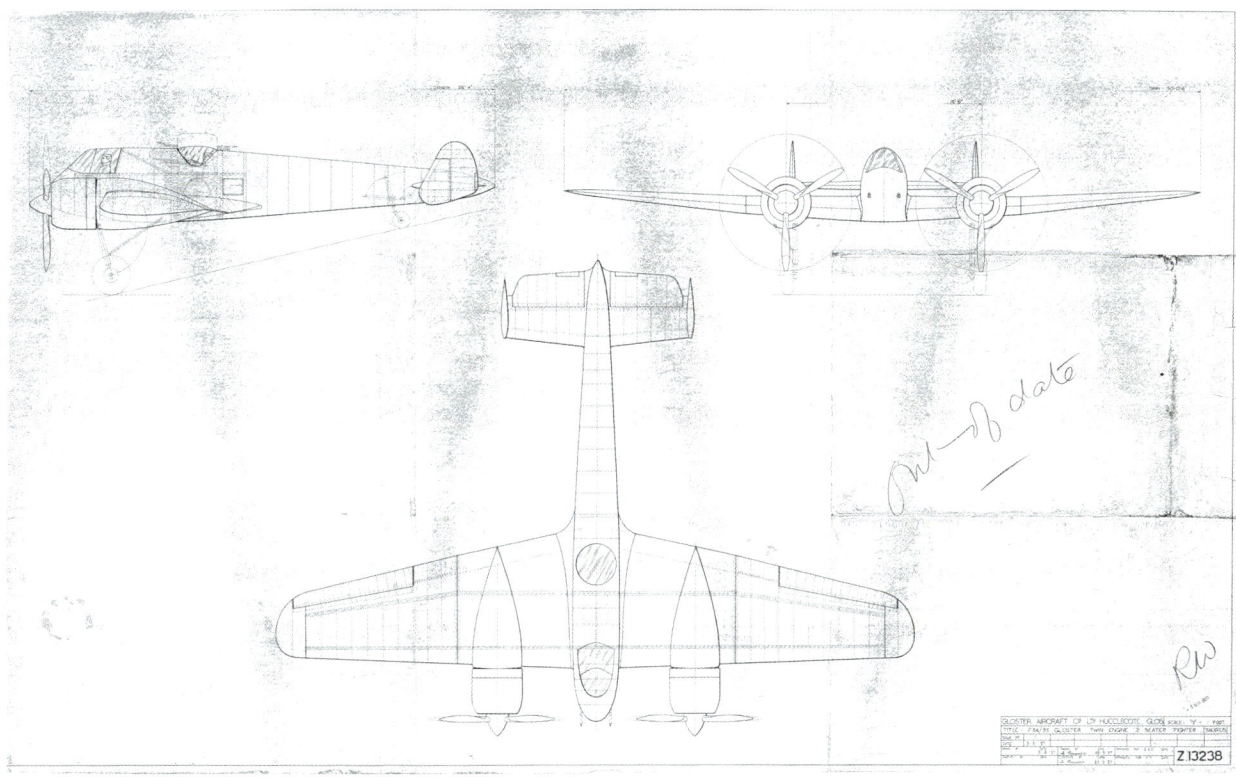

ABOVE Gloster drawing Z.13238, dated 3.5.37, shows the firm's F.34/35 design as first planned for prototype manufacture. Its span was 50ft 0.6in (15.26m) and overall length 36ft 4in (11.07m), and its Aquila power units had three-blade propellers. Note the retractable turret with four machine guns. *Jet Age Museum*

end of that year it was clear that the Whirlwind was faster than a Spitfire Mk.1 below 10,000ft (3,048m), especially close to ground level, and just about equal to it between 10,000ft and 20,000ft (3,048m and 6,096m).

BELOW A model of the Gloster F.34/35 turret fighter.

Gloster F.9/37

The first essay by Gloster for a twin-engine fighter was made to Specification F.5/33, work beginning in 1933 on a Bristol Aquila-powered turret-armed two-seater. In 1935 this scheme was brought up to date to meet F.34/35, the new design mounting a dorsal turret with two more machine guns in the nose. Gloster had also prepared a project to F.9/35 (see Chapter 5), which was satisfied by the Boulton Paul Defiant, but when the Defiant offered a performance that met both documents the Gloster F.34/35 was dropped, despite serial K8625 being allocated to a prototype ordered in 1935.

F.34/35 was replaced by another specification, F.9/37, issued on 15 September 1937 and calling for a fighter capable of at least 300mph (483km/h) at 15,000ft (4,572m). Separate cockpits housed the pilot and an observer gunner, the pilot having a pair of 20mm cannon in the nose and the observer a retractable turret, again with a battery of four 0.303 (7.7mm) machine guns. Two Rolls-Royce Kestrel or Bristol Taurus engines were

RIGHT & UPPER MIDDLE Views of the Taurus-powered Gloster F.9/37 prototype L7999.

LOWER MIDDLE L7999 pictured at Gloster's Brockworth airfield.

BOTTOM For comparison, this view shows the second F.9/37 prototype L8002, which had Peregrine engines.

to be fitted. In late autumn 1938 it was decided to delete the amidships cockpit and the Gloster project to F.9/37 was thus completed as a fixed-gun single-seat fighter. Two forward-firing 20mm Hispano cannon were placed beneath the pilot just forward of the rear spar and were inclined at a 'no-allowance' angle of 12° to the line of flight. In November 1938 a proposal was made to replace the turret with a battery of three more 20mm cannon fixed at the same angle, which were to be placed in the upper fuselage behind the pilot to fire forward over the cockpit hooding; these presented a potentially formidable armament and the fuselage would be bulged to accommodate the extra guns and allow them to fire clear of the cockpit. This idea was eventually accepted.

Two F.9/37 prototypes, serials L7999 and L8002, were ordered, but circumstances dictated that they received different powerplants. The first had two Taurus air-cooled radials while L8002 had liquid-cooled Rolls-Royce Peregrines and chin radiators. Construction of L7999 began in the Gloster Experimental Department at Hucclecote during February 1938 and the first flight was made on 3 April 1939. Early flights demonstrated performance and handling that suggested great potential, and the F.9/37 reached speeds in excess of 360mph (579km/h). The second aircraft with the less powerful Peregrines had a top speed of 330mph (531km/h), but both machines proved remarkably manoeuvrable and docile and could be rolled and looped in comfort.

There were further proposed developments to F.18/37 (see Chapter

Gloster F.9/37 (flown)	
Span:	50ft 0.5in (15.25m)
Length:	37ft 0.5in (11.29m)
Wing Area:	384sq.ft (35.71sq.m)
All-Up-Weight:	11,615lb (5,269kg)
Powerplant:	2 x Bristol Taurus TE.1 1,050hp (783kW)
Max Speed / Height:	360mph (579km/h) at 15,000ft (4,572m)
Armament:	5 x 20mm cannon

1) and F.11/37 and F.18/40 (both Chapter 5), but no design or variant in this line of development was to receive a production contract. The F.9/37 had much in common with the Westland Whirlwind in that it was built by a firm with no previous hardware experience of high-performance twin-engine fighters and made use of engines that gave problems because they were not fully developed; neither aircraft was big enough to take a larger engine. When Lord Beaverbrook, the head of the new Ministry of Aircraft Production, announced in mid-1940 an emergency production programme of only three bomber and two fighter types, the F.9/37 was not among them. Later, when the situation had improved, types such as the Mosquito had taken the state of the art beyond what had been offered by Gloster's twin.

Bristol Beaufighter

As noted already, well before the war began the Air Staff had been keen to obtain a cannon-armed fighter. The highly experimental Whirlwind's development was slow and by the autumn of 1938 the Air Staff was faced with the possibility that a suitable aircraft might not be available for some time to come. ACAS, Sholto Douglas, was anxious to find an aircraft that could be produced as a cannon fighter as soon as possible. It was too late to begin an all-new type with its inevitable prolonged period of development, so when Bristol Aircraft submitted a proposal to convert its Beaufort torpedo bomber, the Air Staff reacted favourably. Leslie Frise reported that the Beaufort's wings

TOP Merlin-powered Bristol Beaufighter Mk.IIF R2270. *Phil Butler*

MIDDLE T3032, another Mk.IIF Beaufighter, flew as a prototype with an extended dorsal fin. The picture is dated 11 February 1943. *Phil Butler*

BOTTOM This view shows another black-painted night fighter Beaufighter, this time Mk.IF T4638 with Hercules engines. Note the dipole transmitter in the nose. *Phil Butler*

had proved to be very strong, which suggested that they might be suitable for a fighter with more powerful engines and higher speeds. Bristol originally proposed mounting two 20mm Hispanos in a turret, but the firm also submitted an alternative with four fixed Hispanos and Sholto Douglas felt that this second scheme was the better of the two.

Since the Beaufort combined the functions of torpedo bomber and general reconnaissance aircraft, it did not possess an outstanding performance, but Bristol intended to improve this by substituting its Taurus engines with the new Hercules. Early estimates for the fighter conversion quoted a speed of 370mph (595km/h), but the main objective was to use as many standard Beaufort parts as possible; the fuselage body, however, would be smaller, with an all-new forward section. Bristol intended to take a partially completed Beaufort off the production line and convert it into a fighter prototype while production aircraft ordered off the drawing board would enter manufacture at the same time. In this way a competitive tender and a separate prototype stage would be avoided. The company's promise that if an immediate order was placed production would be under way in early 1940 persuaded the Air Council Committee on Supply to accept the new project and proceed immediately with 300 aeroplanes, a move agreed on 24 February 1939. The mock-up was examined on 17 April, and in July a draft specification F.17/39, which did not play its usual part in determining the design's limits, was finally approved. F.17/39 described the Beaufighter as an interim type to precede the Whirlwind with a speed at 15,000ft (4,572m) of not less than 350mph (563km/h).

In the event two converted Beauforts were ordered, together with two new-build prototypes. The aircraft was known as the Type 156 Bristol Cannon Fighter or Beau Fighter, which eventually became its official name. Construction of the converted Beauforts began immediately, but the smooth progress of both prototype and production was soon interrupted. It had been expected that the Beaufort fuselage could be converted with little trouble, but the layout of the cannon fighter was so different from a torpedo bomber that eventually the whole fuselage had to be redesigned and the

TOP Weary-looking Hercules Beaufighter X7543, a Mk.VI prototype, is pictured on 4 September 1941.

ABOVE This lovely photo of RD767 shows it banking away from the camera. This was a later TF.Mk.X Beaufighter with its nose radar protected by a 'thimble' radome. *Phil Butler*

extra drawing office time that this required thus delayed construction. Prototype R2052 finally flew on 17 July 1939. Fitted with Hercules I-SM units, in clean condition it achieved the estimated top speed of 335mph (539km/h) at 16,800ft (5,121m); however, when R2054 with Hercules

Bristol Beaufighter Mk.I (flown)

Span:	57ft 8in (17.58m)
Length:	41ft 0in (12.50m)
Wing Area:	503sq.ft (46.78sq.m)
All-Up-Weight:	21,120lb (9,580kg)
Powerplant:	2 x Hercules III 1,400hp (1,044kW)
Max Speed / Height:	330mph (531km/h) at 16,000ft (4,877m)
Armament:	4 x 20mm cannon, 6 x 0.303in (7.7mm) machine guns

Bristol Beaufighter Mk.II (flown)

Span:	57ft 8in (17.58m)
Length:	42ft 6in (12.95m)
Wing Area:	503sq.ft (46.78sq.m)
All-Up-Weight:	20,077lb (9,107kg)
Powerplant:	2 x Merlin XX 1,250hp (932kW)
Max Speed / Height:	337mph (542km/h) at 22,000ft (6,706m)
Armament:	4 x 20mm cannon, 6 x 0.303in (7.7mm) machine guns

IIIs and full operational equipment began acceptance trials at Boscombe Down in June 1940 it could only make 309mph (497km/h) at 15,000ft (4,572m).

The outbreak of war resulted in large orders for Beaufighters, but a potential shortage of Hercules engines was worrying. Consequently a Rolls-Royce Merlin variant was thought to be the most effective solution and on 17 February 1940 Sir Wilfrid Freeman arranged for three aeroplanes to be so converted. He hoped to clear the Merlin variant (which was estimated to have a similar performance to the Hercules III) in July with production following in early 1941, and the move was supported by Sholto Douglas, who felt this would be a wise insurance. This particular Merlin powerplant had been developed for the Avro Lancaster bomber's outboard positions and was adapted for the Beaufighter with an intermediate section to fit the aircraft's nacelle. The first Merlin Beaufighter, R2058, first flew on 14 June 1940.

The Beaufighter was successfully developed for a number of roles, but possibly its most significant achievement was to become Britain's first practical radar-equipped night fighter. In late 1940 the Luftwaffe's heavy night bombing Blitz brought with it a most urgent need for a night fighter. The first British aircraft to attempt to fill this role had been the Bristol Blenheim Mk.IF, but its lack of performance and poor radar ensured that this was only a stopgap. The Hercules-Beaufighter Mk.IF was the first effective RAF night fighter because it backed its radar with a powerful armament and a performance that enabled it to catch most Luftwaffe bombers. The Merlin Beaufighter served primarily as the Mk.IIF night fighter, but its main weakness was that the speeds obtained during early flight tests, which had led to strong hopes of an improved performance over the Mk.I, were not repeated. From an aerodynamic point of view the Mk.II was never satisfactory.

In early January 1939 Bristol proposed its Type 157 three-seat Hercules-powered bomber variant, and also a slim-fuselage 'sports-model' called the Type 158. The bomber conversion was known as the Beaubomber and formed part of the process that led to the Type 163 Buckingham. In August 1940 it was agreed that the Type 158 with Hercules IIIs should be the Beaufighter Mk.III, and with Merlin XXs the Mk.IV. However, producing the new slim fuselage would take many months and, if new jigs and tools were required, could stretch to a year.

The Assistant Chief of the Air Staff (Technical), ACAS(T) R. S. Sorley, hoped that the work would receive high priority because the new fuselage was expected to increase the top speed by 8 to 10mph (13 to 16km/h). Some Air Staff members felt that a 10mph increase did not justify the required jigging and tooling, but DTD pointed out that 10mph at 300mph (483km/h) was a considerable increase. The Mk.III would have six 20mm cannon and eight Browning machine guns and was expected to fly at the end of 1940, but work was eventually halted by the Battle of Britain. On 1 April 1941 the Ministry confirmed that work was unlikely to restart in the near future and the type was never completed.

The Mk.V designation went to two Merlin Beaufighters that had no wing guns but instead a dorsal turret with four 0.303in (7.7mm) machine guns. Fighter Command had an urgent need for a turret version, but the conversion took time. One example, R2274, was tested at A&AEE around the early summer of 1941 and the turret was found to operate satisfactorily even in dives up to 390mph (628km/h). The aircraft weighed 18,695lb (8,480kg) and, with the turret facing aft, gave a top speed of 302mph (486km/h) at 19,300ft (5,883m).

On 5 January 1942 Frise suggested to Air Marshal F. J. Linnell, CRD, the idea of a Torpedo Beaufighter; with the torpedo carried externally, this would keep the necessary modifications as simple as possible. Linnell examined the proposal on 11 February and noted that its 'virtues were outweighed by its vices – the approach speed was too high for torpedo dropping and the longitudinal stability was not good enough for torpedo work', so he turned the idea down. Bristol responded with a more detailed approach, which was received more favourably. After testing, Coastal Command found that it liked the type as a combined torpedo/fighter – in fact, it was really the only aircraft that could be so converted, the adaptation of the Handley Page Hampden to this role having proved a failure. A memo by Sorley dated 9 September 1942 revealed how enthusiastic he was to re-equip with the type, and the torpedo Beaufighter became the Mk.X. The Beaufighter proved to be a very successful wartime aircraft and nearly 6,000 were eventually built.

De Havilland Mosquito

The de Havilland Mosquito was first designed as a light unarmed bomber before being developed as a fighter and full multi-role aircraft, and the major part of the story really belongs to, and will be described in, the equivalent Second World War bomber volume in this series. Suffice to say here that it was developed into several night fighter and intruder versions that proved to be very successful and very valuable aeroplanes during the war. The Mosquito fighter prototype, serial W4052, made its maiden flight on 15 May 1941.

de Havilland Mosquito Mk.II (flown)	
Span:	54ft 2in (16.51m)
Length:	40ft 10in (12.45m)
Wing Area:	454sq.ft (42.22sq.m)
All-Up-Weight:	18,547lb (8,413kg)
Powerplant:	2 x Merlin 21/23 1,480hp (1,104kW)
Max Speed / Height:	370mph (595km/h) at 14,000ft (4,267m)
Armament:	4 x 20mm cannon, 4 x 0.303in (7.7mm) machine guns

TOP The de Havilland Mosquito fighter prototype was W4052, which is shown here in a photo dated 4 September 1941.

MIDDLE Another fighter intruder Mosquito Mk.II.

BOTTOM Mosquito fighter-bomber FB.Mk.VI HP854 is seen at ECFS Hullavington in around 1946. *Peter Arnold Collection*

Chapter Four
Wartime Twin Engine Fixed-Gun Fighters

ABOVE De Havilland Hornet F.Mk.1 PX244.

The development of twin-engine fighters continued after war had broken out and in the end would result in three quite separate programmes, the de Havilland Hornet, the Vickers 432 and Westland Welkin. And these three aircraft would experience quite different levels of success – the Hornet went into production and service and completed a relatively long career both with the RAF and the Royal Navy, the 432 progressed no further than one flying prototype, and the Welkin entered production but did not go into service, most of the airframes going direct to store.

Specification F.6/39 Vickers Type 432

The Type 432 was the last Vickers fighter to reach manufacture and flight test. Only two airframes were built and just one was completed which flew a mere 29 times, yet the full story stretches from spring 1939 until late 1945. Specification F.6/39 was issued in March 1939 for a two-seat fighter

BELOW The Miles M.22 variant designed to Specification F.6/39 (1939). *Miles Aircraft via Peter Amos*

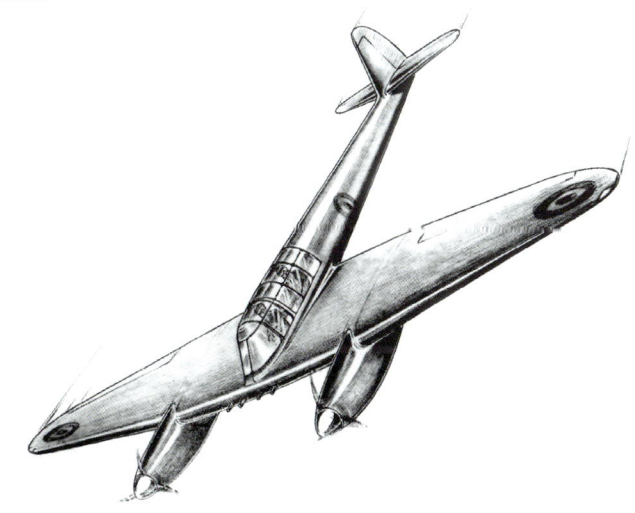

with a high speed (minimum 400mph [644km/h]) and it would carry four 20mm guns, with the possible later installation of two 40mm weapons. The following projects were proposed.

Fairey F.6/39
No details are known about this project.

Miles M.22
The Miles fighter programmes are covered separately in Chapter Nine, but one early version of its M.22 twin-engine fighter project was prepared to F.6/39.

Supermarine 334
Sadly this too is an unknown project, one of the few wartime Supermarine designs that do not appear to have survived. It is believed that a mock-up of the 334 was built.

Westland F.6/39
This covered two projects developed from the Whirlwind and powered by Rolls-Royce Griffon engines, one with conventional tractor powerplant (there was also a version with Merlins), the other with pusher engines. In fact the latter was a pusher version of the first

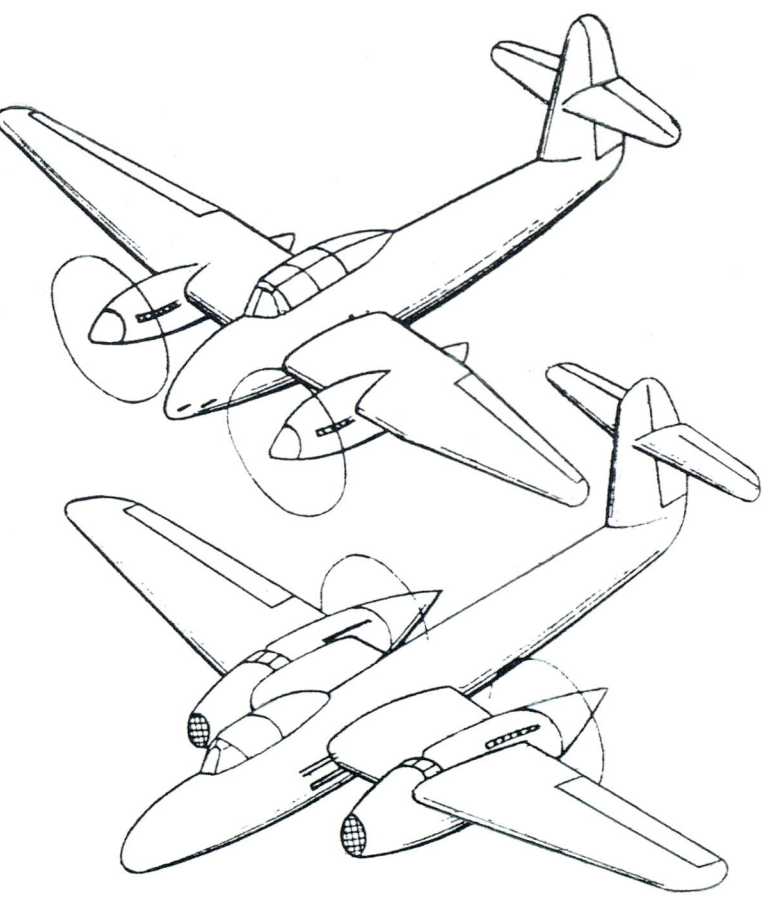

ABOVE The only known illustrations of Westland's fighter projects to F.6/39 (both 5.39). *Westland Archive via the late Fred Ballam*

Westland F.6/39 Version 1 (5.39)	
Span:	60ft 6in (18.44m)
Length:	?
Wing Area:	450sq.ft (41.85sq.m)
All-Up-Weight:	16,200lb (7,348kg)
Powerplant:	2 x Griffon 1,600hp (1,193kW)
Max Speed / Height:	396mph (637km/h) at 16,000ft (4,877m)
Armament:	4 x 20mm cannon

Westland F.6/39 Version 2 (5.39)	
Span:	52ft 0in (15.85m)
Length:	?
Wing Area:	450sq.ft (41.85sq.m)
All-Up-Weight:	16,200lb (7,348kg)
Powerplant:	2 x Griffon 1,600hp (1,193kW)
Max Speed / Height:	396mph (637km/h) at 16,000ft (4,877m)
Armament:	4 x 20mm cannon

design, it had radiators in the front of the engine nacelles and a tricycle undercarriage.

F.6/39 was soon overtaken by new requirements and these projects were all abandoned. However, further development work continued at Vickers.

Vickers 414
The Vickers design team led by Rex Pierson had been working on a proposal for a Griffon-powered fighter with a single movable 40mm gun and on 19th April 1939 Pierson and Vickers' Mr. Dunbar met Sir Wilfrid Freeman, the then Air Member for Development at the Air Ministry, to ask that their two-seat project should be continued. The powerful Vickers cannon was mounted in the extreme nose and could be elevated 45°, depressed 10° and trained 15° to either side. The range-finding sight with predictor fire control was operated by a gunner/loader seated alongside the pilot and the whole installation was based on the theory of accurate single-shot firing. If the gunner kept the sight on the target, the predictor would automatically keep the gun pointing at it. No other weapons were to be carried.

This aircraft, which became the Type 414, was to be all-metal and carried 210gal (955lit) of fuel. Top speed when fitted with forward facing intakes would be 439mph (707km/h) at 19,500ft (5,944m) and maximum rate of climb 4,560ft/min (1,390m/min) at 1,000ft (305m); top speed without forward facing intakes was 413mph (665km/h) at 15,000ft (4,572m). A draft scheme was tabled in June 1939 which, following discussions with the

CHAPTER FOUR
THE MINERVE PROGRAMME

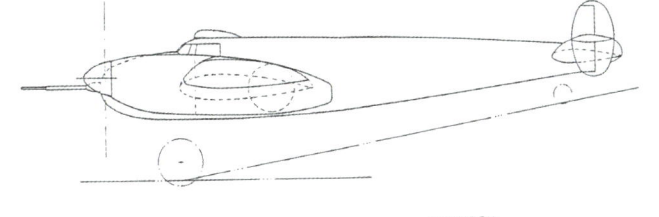

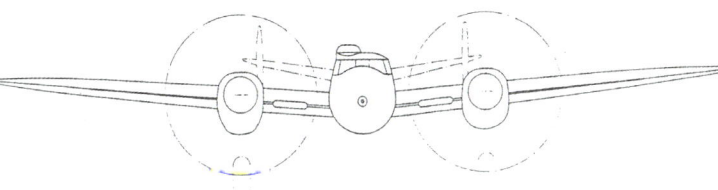

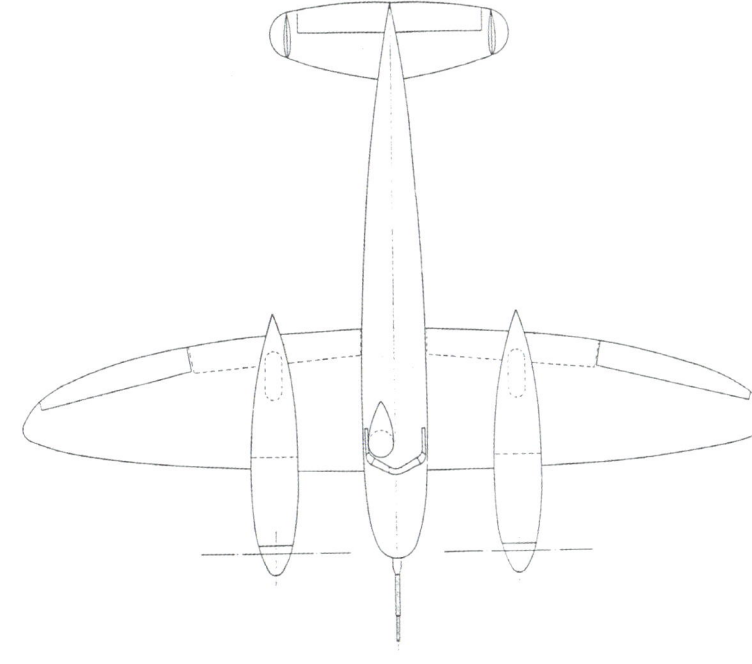

LEFT The 40mm cannon-armed Vickers Type 414 to F.6/39 (6.7.39). *The late Eric Morgan*

BELOW The Type 414's 40mm cannon installation and cockpit. *The late Eric Morgan*

Ministry, was submitted formally soon afterwards. A simultaneous effort was made to design a fixed-gun aircraft to F.6/39. Calculations were completed on the 22nd June for two versions of the fixed-gun fighter with either tractor engines or pushers and on 6th July a brochure was prepared which mainly covered the single 40mm with predictor but also included the other designs. The Ministry expressed great interest in the movable 40mm version and in autumn 1939 Specification F.22/39 was quickly prepared to cover the project. On 1st November Vickers was told that F.6/39 had been deleted from the 1939 programme.

F.22/39 requested a 40mm cannon fighter with a top speed at 20,000ft (6,096m) of not less than 400mph (644km/h). The predictor gunsight was to be operable in the height band 500ft (152m) to 25,000ft (7,620m) at ranges between 200 and 1,000 yards (183m and 914m). The primary object of F.22/39 was to obtain an aircraft that would test the principle of the heavy calibre gun and its predictor sight and a contract for two prototypes, serials R4236 and R4237, was placed on 30th

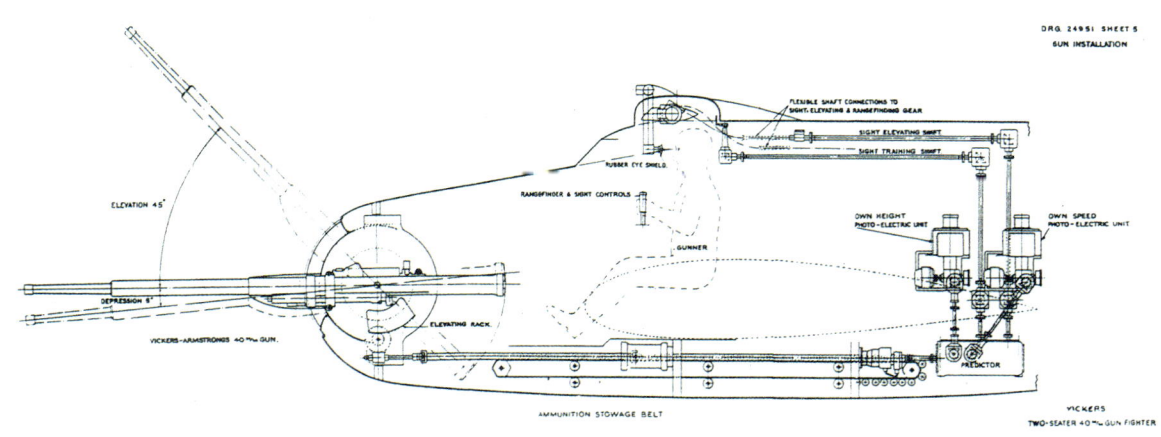

69

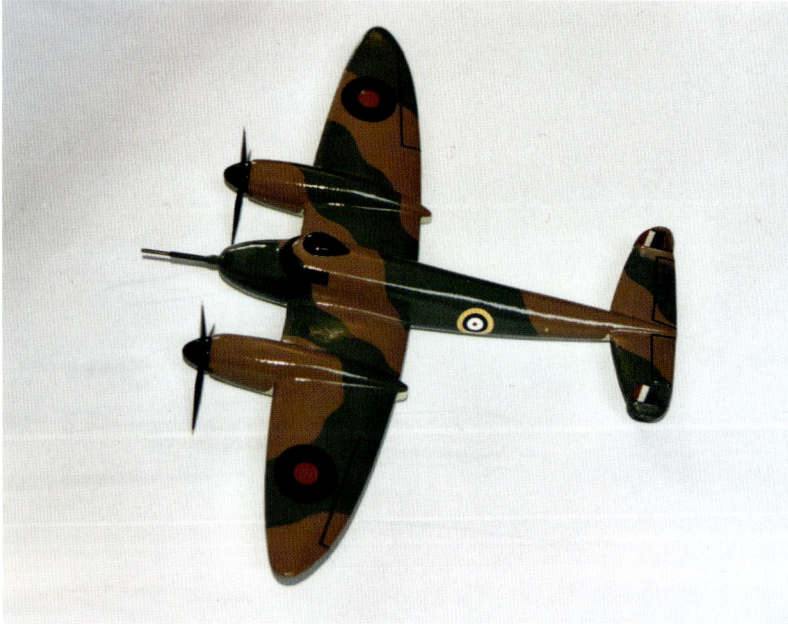

LEFT **A model of the Vickers 414.** *Joe Cherrie*

Vickers 414 to F.6/39 (6.39)	
Span:	53ft 0in (16.15m)
Length:	42ft 3in (12.88m)
Wing Area:	394sq.ft (36.64sq.m)
All-Up-Weight:	14,950lb (6,781kg)
Powerplant:	2 x Griffon RG.2.SM 1,700hp (1,268kW)
Max Speed / Height:	439mph (707km/h) at 19,500ft (5,944m)
Armament:	1 x 40mm cannon

August 1939. The 40mm gun and its sight were tested in a dorsal turret fitted on Wellington L4250. It first flew with the turret on 25th October 1940 and fired its first shots at a target (towed by a Hawker Henley) on 8th November – no hits were achieved but it was estimated that 50% of the shells came within 4ft (1.2m) of their objective.

The 414's Mock-up Conference was held on 1st February 1940 but then the Air Ministry's Wing Commander H Rowley inquired about the likelihood of fitting 20mm Hispano guns in lieu of the 40mm. In response Pierson produced a supplementary brochure to F.22/39 on 15th April showing alternate armaments of eight 20mm or two 40mm. The main external difference was a longer, slimmer cockpit because the second crewman no longer sat alongside the pilot but instead was positioned behind him facing rearwards. On the 20mm version two guns protruded from the nose while sets of three were stacked either side of the pilot, on the 40mm variant the guns were also now placed to each side of the cockpit rather than in a nose turret. The powerplant was still two Griffon RG.2SMs.

Vickers 420

Discussions regarding the proposed 20mm cannon fighter were held in June 1940 and resulted in a new specification, F.16/40, which was given very high priority. The design was called the Type 420 and Pierson reported on 19th November that 'we are to build

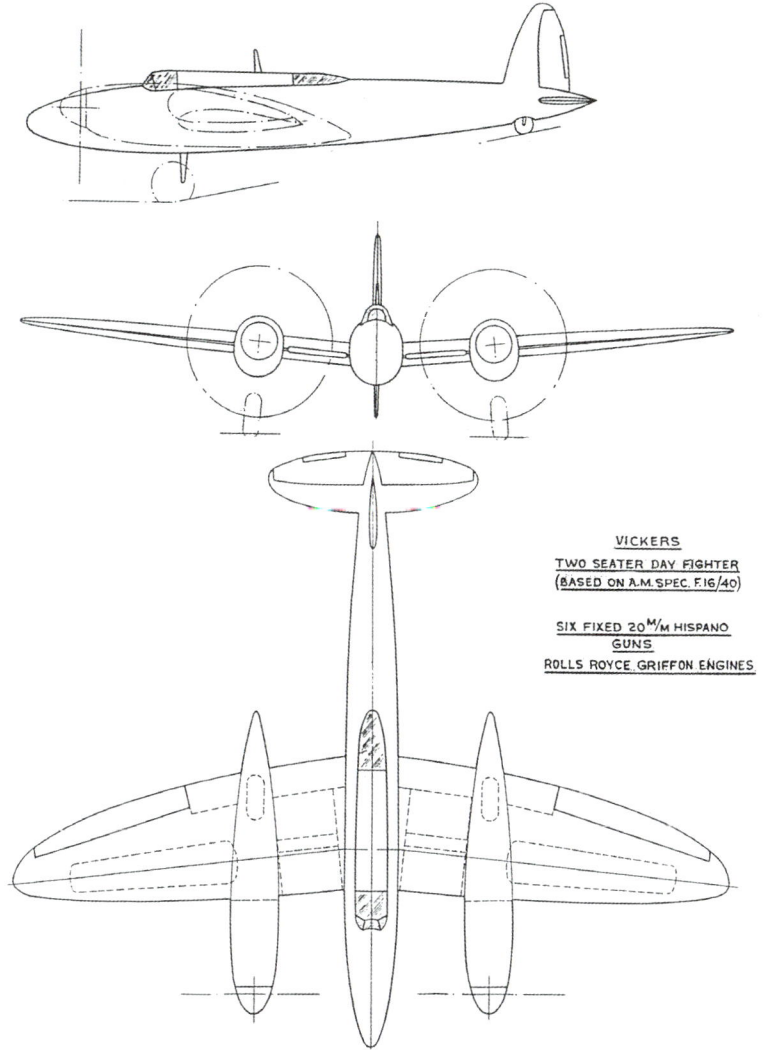

two F.22/39 Fighter Machines, also two F.16/40 Fighter Machines and the 16/40 will be urged ahead of the 22/39. In view of this the existing contract for 22/39 will presumably stand and I anticipate a further contract for the 16/40 machines'. F.16/40 stated that the design was to be basically that of the aeroplane constructed to F.22/39 and it was intended that the new requirements should be met with the minimum amount of additional work. The performance figures were identical to F.22/39 and a new brochure was prepared on 12th October to cover F.16/40 which showed for the first time a single fin and rudder. In January 1941 the armament was cut to six 20mm and the protruding nose guns were taken out. Similar projects with Merlin engines were proposed to the F.18/40 night fighter requirement (Chapter Five).

Vickers 420 to F.16/40 (1940)	
Span:	53ft 0in (16.15m)
Length:	43ft 10in (13.4m)
Wing Area:	394sq.ft (36.64sq.m)
All-Up-Weight:	16,454lb (7,463kg)
Powerplant:	2 x Griffon RG.2.SM 1,700hp (1,268kW)
Max Speed / Height:	461mph (742km/h) at 25,000ft (7,620m)
Armament:	6 x 20mm cannon

ABOVE The two-seat 20mm gun Vickers 420 to F.16/40 (1.1.41). *The late Eric Morgan*

BELOW An unnumbered project for a Vickers twin-boom three-seat night fighter with six 20mm cannon (27.8.41). This was to be powered by a single Napier Sabre NS.3SM, its span was about 60ft (18.29m) and length 50ft (15.24m), but no performance data is available. *The late Eric Morgan*

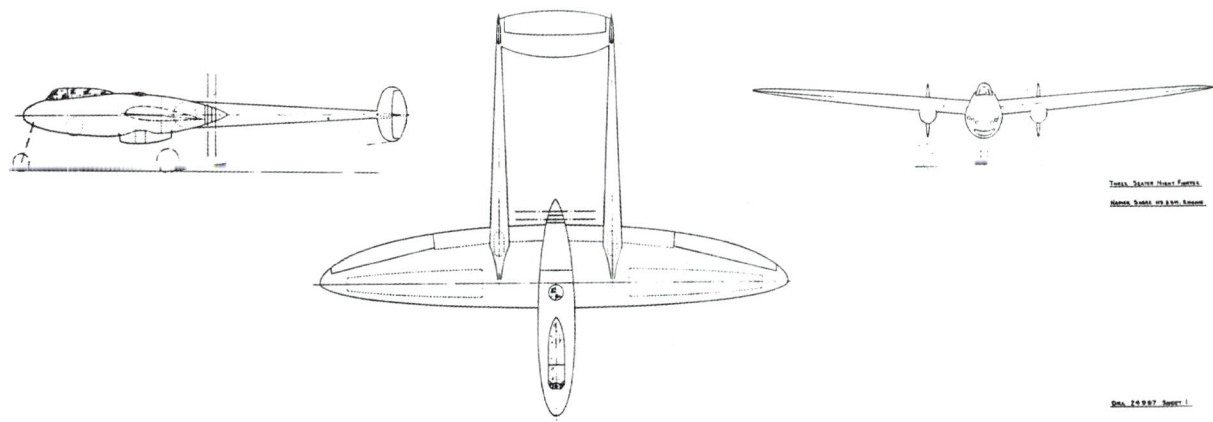

Vickers 432

On 17th January 1941 Pierson completed a brochure for a two-seat high-altitude fighter with four 20mm Hispanos and two Merlin XXII which utilised all of the components then being designed for the F.22/39. This included the fuselage which, being of circular cross-section and stressed skin construction, could easily be made into a pressure-cabin. Eventually there were two layouts – 'A' developed out of the Type 420 and 'B' (dated 7th February) with a larger span of 63ft (19.20m) to improve the ceiling.

On 5th March Pierson told Major Kilner that, following conversations with Sir Henry Tizard, Mr Farren and Mr Westbrook, 'it would appear likely that the Air Ministry will place an order with us for two experimental High Altitude Fighters based on our F.22/39 design'. Work on the Type 414 was stopped and discussions with Rolls-Royce now turned in earnest to fitting Merlins instead of Griffons. By the end of March the design had advanced with a span set at 56ft 10.5ins (17.34m) as a compromise between A and B. On 13th May the first brochure was submitted for the single-seat high-altitude fighter which was to become the Type 432. The pressure cabin was 16ft 6in (5.03m) long by 4ft 6in (1.37m) diameter and comprised the forward portion of the fuselage back to and including the rear wing frame. In order to obtain the best possible fighting view the pilot had been moved to the extreme nose and was covered by a hinged dome together with a bullet proof protecting visor. Six 20mm Hispanos were housed in an underbelly fairing.

ABOVE Vickers 432 prototype DZ217 in flight. One test flight, made on 11 November 1943, was partially devoted to photography, so this is the most likely date for one of the very few views of this aircraft in flight.

MIDDLE & BOTTOM DZ217 is seen shortly after completion. Its Merlin engines had four-blade propellers of 11ft 6in (3.51m) diameter. *Barry Guess, BAE Systems Farnborough archive*

ABOVE **The Vickers 432 takes off.** *Barry Guess, BAE Systems Farnborough*

Vickers 432 (flown)	
Span:	56ft 10.5ins (17.34m)
Length:	39ft 3in (11.96m)
Wing Area:	450sq.ft (41.85sq.m)
All-Up-Weight:	19,721lb (8,945kg)
Powerplant:	2 x Merlin 61 1,520hp (1,133kW)
Max Speed / Height:	380mph (612km/h) at 15,000ft (4,572m)
Armament:	6 x 20mm cannon

N E Rowe, DTD, discussed the single-seat fighter with Barnes Wallis and was much impressed by it. Vickers received a contract on 9th September 1941 for two prototypes, DZ217 and DZ223 to be built to a new specification F.7/41, and was told that it was important for the company to make the greatest possible use of the design data, materials and parts prepared, purchased or manufactured for the two aircraft ordered to F.22/39 and now cancelled. F.22/39 was actually stopped in May 1941 and one reason for this was that, despite being a fast aircraft, its weight was likely to prevent it from being sufficiently manoeuvrable to meet smaller enemy single and two-seat fighters. Moreover it appeared to have insufficient endurance for night fighter use and so the Air Staff had decided that there was no requirement for it.

A reference in F.7/41 to diving speed highlighted a growing problem in new high-speed aircraft, that of compressibility and its affect on the loading of the fuselage, wing and tailplane of fighters. For fighters, the capability to dive on their targets without restriction was vital and Pierson and Wallis were visited by Rowe on 17th March 1942 to discuss the maximum stressing speed of the 432. It was pointed out that the design of present-day fighters was based on the limiting diving speed of 450mph (724km/h), compressibility effects being neglected.

However the introduction of high-altitude fighters capable of entering a dive from heights far greater than had been possible in the past might lead to the attainment of diving speeds greater than the arbitrary limit hitherto assumed. Wallis stated that calculations had shown that the maximum velocity of a dive, if indefinitely continued, occurred at a height approximately 10,000ft (3,048m) above ground level, prolongation of the dive below this height resulting in a slight diminution of speed. It therefore seemed desirable that 10,000ft (3,048m) should be chosen as the height at which the design loads should be calculated and on the strength of this, and some other factors including the drag curve, Rowe decided that the limiting speed to be taken for stressing this fighter should be 500mph (805km/h) with compressibility effects now taken into account.

A few days later some independent calculations made by RAE suggested that the F.7/41 could reach 550mph (885km/h) in the dive if it was started at 43,500ft (13,259m) with a horizontal speed of 320mph (515km/h). The angle of dive, provided it was greater than 60° to the horizontal, appeared to have little effect on the ultimate speed but the question of airscrew drag at very high speeds was still being investigated by RAE. However the 500mph (805km/h) limit in F.7/41 was not changed since it was felt that to exceed this figure in the 432 would be dangerous anyway due the lack of sufficient reserve strength.

The 432's Mock-up Conference took place on 30th December 1941 and the prototypes were built during 1942. The first flight was delayed for a number of reasons but DZ217 finally climbed into the air on 24th December 1942. Five days later MAP advised that only one prototype was to be completed and all work on the second machine was cancelled, although the official confirmation of this decision did not arrive until May 1943. The maximum level speed actually achieved by DZ217, in May 1943 at an all-up-weight of 17,700lb (8,029kg), was 380mph (612km/h) at 15,000ft (4,572m) and some way off the design estimate of 435mph (700km/h) at 28,000ft (8,534m); however, 400mph (644km/h) was exceeded in a dive.

The final flights were made in November 1944 and the aircraft was never submitted for official trials; DZ217 was eventually scrapped. The Type 432 and its ancestors initially showed undoubted promise but the long period of time taken to produce hardware saw this evaporate away and no real effort was ever made to correct the aircraft's faults. Consequently, it will never be known just how good this aircraft might have been. Vickers' own war diary describes the 432 as 'an interesting experiment which resulted in a dead end'.

Specification F.4/40 Westland Welkin

By 1940 the Air Staff had a strong wish to acquire a high-altitude fighter. During the late 1930s increasing effort had been put into the development of high-altitude aeroplanes fitted with pressure cabins and, indeed, the Experimental Aircraft Programme for 1937 had included a specification, B.25/37, for a four-engined bomber with a pressure cabin (it was assumed that if a UK pressure cabin bomber became a reality then so would a German). That requirement, however, was not proceeded with but General Aircraft began working on a pressure cabin variant of its Monospar airliner and in October 1939, after the Air Staff had asked that a high-altitude fighter should be developed, the company submitted a brochure for a fighter.

General Aircraft GAL.46

General Aircraft observed that sooner or later the defences against air attack at 'low level' would become difficult to penetrate and so enemy aircraft would then have to make use of the stratosphere. Hence there was an urgent necessity to prevent the enemy enjoying immunity of operation at high altitudes while it was also desirable that Britain's own forces should enjoy the operational benefits of stratospheric aircraft. The brochure noted that 'the attainment of such heights is now well within the bounds of scientific and practical possibility' and added, after studying various patents, that 'the enemy is well advanced in its thoughts along these lines.'

General acknowledged that the development of pressure cabin aircraft in Britain was not very advanced but the fact that there was one pressurised aircraft ready to start flight testing (the Monospar) was 'due solely to the initiative of this company which, entirely at its own expense, has been engaged on this research for the last two years.' This pressure cabin research aircraft had emerged from a long series of static and blower plant tests and General now wanted to apply its knowledge and experience to a military application. The suggested twin-engined design was based on the requirements of F.6/39 and could not only perform the duties of a cannon fighter up to the highest possible level but also carry out long-range bombing and long-range high-altitude reconnaissance and photography. The company observed that once the principle of the pressure cabin had been accepted the attainable ceiling was a mainly a matter of engine design and this opened up a somewhat neglected avenue of engine supercharger development. Engines would be required with either multi-stage blowers or, better still, exhaust turbo-blowers.

However, for the time being whilst such equipment was being developed, the GAL.46 would use standard Merlins which still allowed the crew to reach high altitudes in comfort when, at present, they could only reach them by great physical endurance and by using oxygen (oxygen made crews very tired which reduced patrol times). Due to its speed and ability to fly high, the GAL.46 dispensed with any form of turret equipment (although two cannon could be reversed in their mountings to provide rear defence). It had two crew, four 20mm cannon (two on each side of the fuselage) and carried 190gal (864lit) of internal fuel. At its best operating height the GAL.46 could reach 395mph (636km/h) while estimated rates of climb were 2,940ft/min (896m/min) at sea level and 3,185ft/min 971m/min) at 9,000ft (2,743m). The aircraft would take 7.1

BELOW **The General Aircraft GAL.46 (10.39).** *Adapted from National Archives AVIA 15/65*

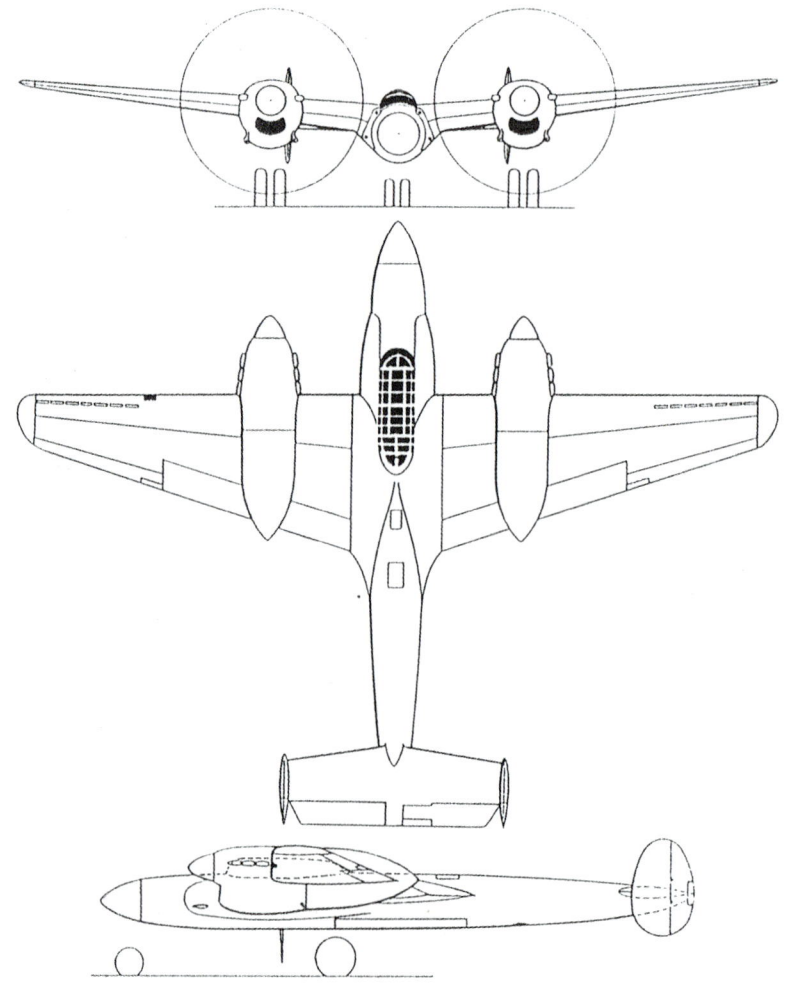

minutes to reach 20,000ft (6,096m) and 14.0 minutes to achieve 30,000ft (9,144m), service ceiling was 37,200ft (11,339m). The engines would have three-blade 12ft 6in (3.81m) diameter Hydromatic airscrews. As a bomber it could carry four 500lb (227kg) bombs under the wing roots (ceiling 29,800ft [9,083m]) while reconnaissance sorties could be made at 35,000ft (10,668m) and 2,250 miles (3,620km) range. General described its project as 'an extremely formidable weapon'.

The GAL.46 was expected to use simple construction and a tricycle undercarriage, the latter another area in which General had more experience than any other British constructor because in 1938 it had flown a Monospar with a tricycle undercarriage. Composite construction would be used where possible but a metal centre section and outer wing would be necessary because of the pressure cabin, high load factors and the need for great rigidity. Future research would embrace the need to keep the structure, windscreen and petrol systems, and so on, free of ice, plus the development of the blower system on the engines. The brochure's altitude figures, based on standard Merlins, would be much improved by such developments.

On 1st November ACAS and DGRD agreed to proceed with the GAL.46 as a 'development' to gain experience. However, the desirability of placing an order for it was discussed again on 18th April 1940 by AVM Hill (DTD), Air Commodore Saundby (the Director of Operational Requirements, DOR), Capt Liptrot, Messrs Farren, Grinstead and others. The Air Staff had for some time stated that high-altitude fighters were important and its wish to develop them was strong. It was agreed that an aircraft capable of use up to 45,000ft (13,716m) should be designed now in readiness for a suitable powerplant for that height, but General Aircraft's lack of experience in fighter design caused doubts as to whether it could produce a useful aircraft. The company's work on pressure cabins did not inspire great confidence in its ability to deal unaided with the problems of design, although help would be forthcoming from RAE. It was agreed that some other firms should therefore be asked to tender for the design and construction of a pressure cabin fighter and, provided General revised its design on satisfactory lines, it should be one of two companies to receive orders for experimental aircraft.

TOP A model of the GAL.46.

ABOVE Manufacturer's original artwork for the GAL.46. *Chris Gibson*

General Aircraft GAL.46 1st Proposal (18.10.39)	
Span:	52ft 0in (15.85m)
Length:	41ft 6in (12.65m)
Wing Area:	385sq.ft (35.81sq.m)
All-Up-Weight:	15,704lb (7,123kg) fighter, 17,845lb (8,094kg) fighter-bomber
Powerplant:	2 x Merlin RM.2.SM 1,265hp (943kW)
Max Speed / Height:	395mph (636km/h) at 20,800ft (6,340m)
Armament:	4 x 20mm cannon, 4 x 500lb (227kg) bombs

General Aircraft GAL.46 2nd Proposal (c9.40)	
Span:	59ft 0in (17.98m)
Length:	48ft 10in (14.88m)
Wing Area:	465sq.ft (43.245sq.m)
All-Up-Weight:	17,800lb (8,074kg)
Powerplant:	2 x Merlin XX 1,270hp (947kW)
Max Speed / Height:	387mph (623km/h) at 25,000ft (7,620m)
Armament:	

Hawker P.1004 (c9.40)	
Span:	52ft 0in (15.85m)
Length:	39ft 0in (11.89m)
Wing Area:	405sq.ft (37.67sq.m)
All-Up-Weight:	13,930lb (6,319kg)
Powerplant:	1 x Sabre 1S.M 1,850hp (1,380kW)
Max Speed / Height:	380mph (611km/h) at 18,500ft (5,639m)
Armament:	6 x 20mm cannon

Fairey, Hawker, Vickers-Armstrongs and Westland were invited to tender and in July Specification F.4/40 was raised to cover the new type. A top speed of at least 400mph (644km/h) was requested consistent with a high service ceiling while the pressure cabin would have to maintain conditions appropriate to 25,000ft (7,620m) when the fighter was flying above that height up to 45,000ft (13,716m). The tenders were as follows:

General Aircraft GAL.46

The original General Aircraft project was revised and refitted with 1,170hp (872kW) Merlin XX engines and six 20mm cannon. Maximum fuel capacity was 403gal (1,832lit), the aircraft had slotted flaps and, again, a tricycle undercarriage. Estimated rate of climb was 2,450ft/min (747m/min), time to 25,000ft (7,620m) 10.7 minutes and service ceiling 39,500ft (12,040m).

Hawker P.1004

This two-seat fighter with a single Napier Sabre was virtually a development of the Hawker Typhoon (Chapter One) and shared the same aerodynamic and structural features. No drawing is known to survive but its design and construction followed the Typhoon's very closely and the project was in fact a Typhoon scaled up by 25% plus the addition of the pressure cabin and the second crewman seated with his back to the pilot. For this reason the required development work was expected to be much reduced with no wind tunnel testing necessary. The two mainplanes were attached direct to the centre fuselage, which dispensed with a complicated centre plane, the aircraft used split flaps and could carry a maximum of 290gal (1,319lit) of fuel.

Rate of climb at sea level was 2,250ft/min (686m/min), time to 25,000ft (7,620m) 13.4 minutes and service ceiling 37,000ft (11,278m).

Westland P.13

Westland submitted two proposals, projects P.13 and P.14. The P.13 was a highly experimental arrangement of typical single-engined layout but in which two standard Merlin XXs in the nose were coupled in tandem to drive a pair of contra-rotating airscrews through a common gearbox. It was

BELOW Manufacturer's sketch showing the P.14 in flight. The similarity to the earlier Whirlwind fighter is at this stage quite marked. *National Aerospace Library, Farnborough*

BOTTOM Manufacturer's sketch showing the P.13 in flight. *National Aerospace Library, Farnborough*

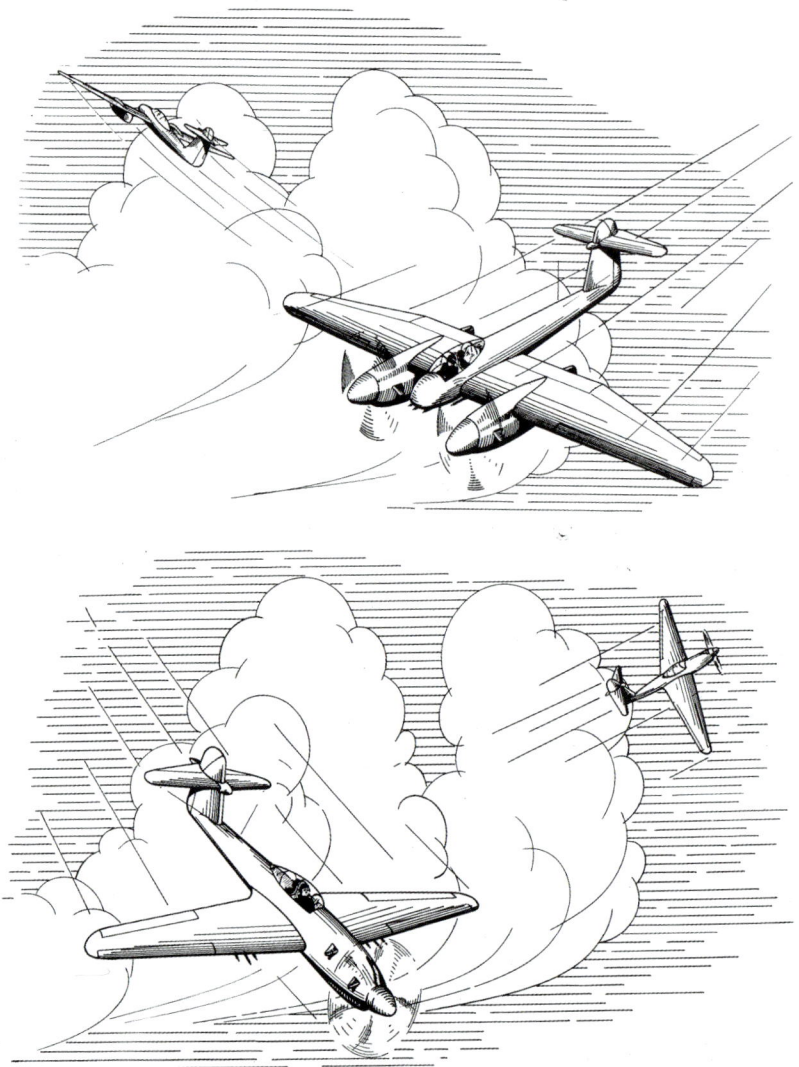

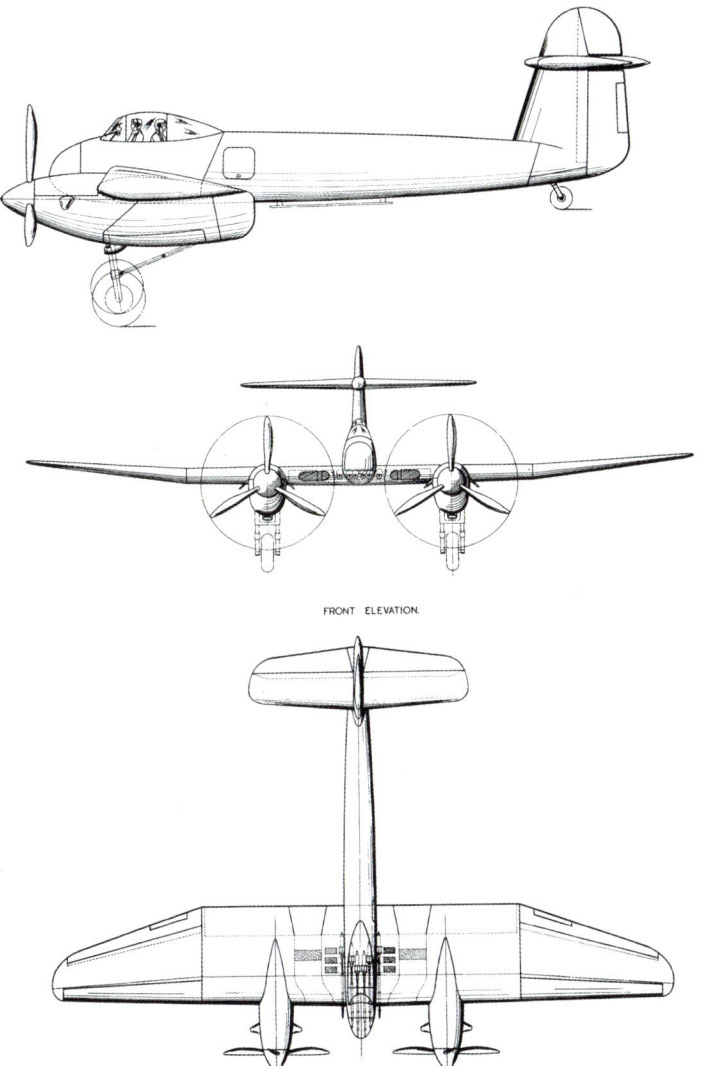

LEFT The Westland twin-engine P.14 proposal to F.4/40 (c9.40). As built, the Welkin's span had been increased by 10ft (3.05m). *National Aerospace Library, Farnborough*

Westland P.13 (c9.40)	
Span:	58ft 0in (17.68m)
Length:	46ft 6in (14.17m)
Wing Area:	450sq.ft (41.85sq.m)
All-Up-Weight:	16,420lb (7,448kg)
Powerplant:	2 x Merlin XX 1,270hp (947kW)
Max Speed / Height:	316mph (508km/h) at sea level, 398mph (640km/h) at 21,000ft (6,401m), 428mph (689km/h) at 35,000ft (10,668m)
Armament:	6 x 20mm cannon

diameter constant speed airscrews were fitted and the fuel capacity was 400gal (1,819lit). Ground level rate of climb was given as 2,320ft/min (707m/min), time to 20,000ft (6,096m) was 9.3 minutes and to 30,000ft (9,144m) 16.2 minutes, and service ceiling 37,000ft (11,278m). Both Westland designs had their second crewman sitting with his back to the pilot.

Westland P.14

Westland's two-seat P.14 design, which in due course became the Welkin, was put forward as being that which, after consideration of a number of types, best met the majority of the specification requirements. In the then present circumstances it was considered essential to contemplate only the Rolls-Royce Merlin XX engine since this was established in production and was due for high altitude development. The main reasons for choosing the twin-engine layout were:

i. It was felt that a design which was based on, and was a logical development of, the successful Whirlwind had many advantages. Thus, apart from the pressure cabin very little structural, aerodynamic or operational development would be required. Since it resembled the Whirlwind in many respects it could also take advantage of all of

disliked by the Air Staff, partly because of the very poor view for the pilot and also due to some questionable handling qualities for fighting. But Westland's own testing had shown a decidedly higher performance than did the twin-nacelle P.14 (the main proposal) and so a general arrangement and brief summary of its particulars was included in the brochure. The advantages included a gain of 30mph (48km/h) on the speed, climb about 10% better, lateral manoeuvrability should be improved due to the concentration of mass around the aircraft's cg, safety in flight on one engine at low speeds, a simpler structure, better protection for fire from ahead for crew and fuselage, and a slimmer fuselage than would be possible in any single-engine fighter having the same power. The disadvantages were that gun firing from the wings might adversely affect the steady gun platform, the fire was not concentrated except at one range, a special gear box would have to be developed and rigidly mounted, flexible engine drive couplings were necessary, the mechanism for controlling the airscrews would have to be produced, and the forward and downwards views were poor.

The construction and special features required by the twin-nacelle P.14 would in general apply to this alternative design and three 20mm cannon were to be fitted in each wing outboard of the propeller arc. Three-blade 12ft (3.66m)

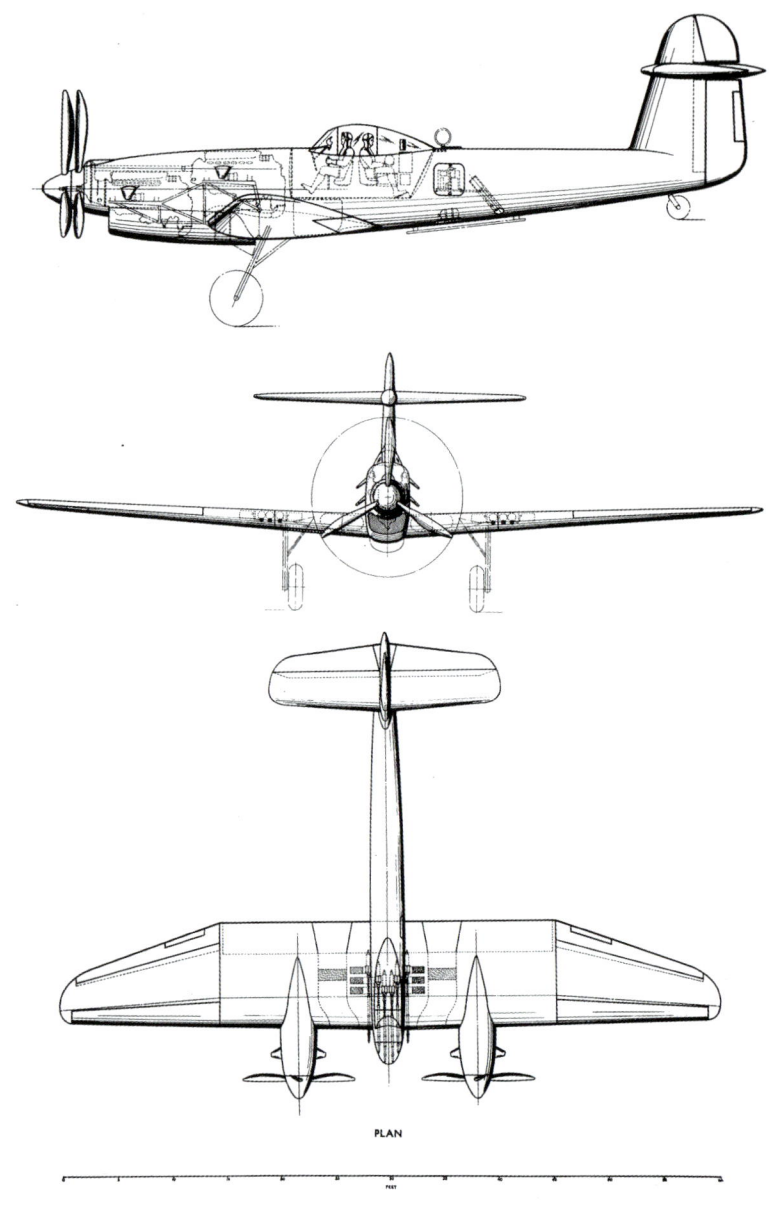

ABOVE The alternative Westland tandem twin-engine P.13 proposal to F.4/40 (c9.40) was not described in the brochure in the same depth as the P.14, but the drawing does provide good powerplant and cabin detail. Note the wing-mounted guns.
National Aerospace Library, Farnborough

while the pilot's view, and the safety of the crew in the advent of engine trouble, were greatly superior.

Other arrangements of the two engines had been envisaged including the twin-pusher and the tractor-pusher fuselage, but there was little justification for such departures. It was acknowledged that while in comparison to the Whirlwind the useful load to be carried was more than doubled, the power available at rated altitude had been increased by only 35%. And since no further aerodynamic improvement was thought possible in this type at the present time, it was to be expected that the twin-nacelle F.4/40 would be a less efficient aeroplane than the Whirlwind at least in its high speed qualities and this was in fact the case, the speeds at 15,000ft (4,572m) being 343mph and 360mph (552km/h and 579km/h) respectively. Development of the Merlin engine to maintain approximately the same power at 35,000ft (10,668m) would allow a speed of approximately 400mph (644km/h) to be attained.

The P.14 followed the same general aerodynamic and structural lines of the Whirlwind. The centre wing was built around a single spar, it occupied approximately half the span and constituted the backbone of the aircraft; the outer wing sections were of simple construction and all of the wing was covered in light alloy skin. The pressure cabin could be built and tested as a unit and was mounted well forward on the wing centre section. P.14's simple rear fuselage tubular structure would (it was preferred) be made from thick magnesium strips as in the case of the Whirlwind. Well proven aerodynamic features retained from the earlier Whirlwind were the engine cooling duct housed within the wing (just outboard of the guns) and the combination of large slots with Fowler flaps and a high tailplane position. Again three-blade 12ft (3.66m) diameter constant speed airscrews were to be used and the

the experience gained in the earlier fighter's production and service.

ii. The same considerations which led to the adoption of having the armament as near as possible to the aeroplane's centreline also applied here – in fact even more so! The number of guns (20mm cannon) had been increased to six and fitting this number into the wings could present problems from the point of view of steadiness of the aircraft as a gun platform (four were in fact housed in the lower fuselage and one in each wing root right alongside the fuselage guns).

iii. In spite of production considerations, having two Merlin engines when compared to an aircraft with one large existing single engine gave a performance that was equally good

Westland P.14 (c9.40)

Span:	60ft 0in (18.29m)
Length:	41ft 6in (12.65m)
Wing Area:	450sq.ft (41.85sq.m)
All-Up-Weight (360gal/lit fuel):	16,340lb (7,412kg)
Powerplant:	2 x Merlin XX 1,270hp (947kW)
Max Speed / Height:	290mph (467km/h) at sea level, 368mph (592km/h) at 21,000ft (6,401m)
Armament:	6 x 20mm cannon

maximum fuel was 400gal (1,819lit). Sea level rate of climb was estimated to be 1,600ft/min (488m/min), time to 25,000ft (7,620m) 13.5 minutes and service ceiling 36,500ft (11,125m).

These proposals were discussed in much detail by the Air Staff. The GAL.46 brochure was criticised for giving too little structural detail and, since the company had not yet built anything larger than a trainer, there was no background on which to guess its structure. It was considered that the tender gave insufficient information to assess its worth and the project's handling qualities as a fighter were mistrusted, while the long nose spoilt the pilot's view. The company itself had made a laudable pioneer effort in pressure cabin construction but new enquiries into its work on the pressure cabin Monospar revealed that little serious work had been done in dealing with the main problems.

An F.4/40 Tender Design Conference was held on 17th October 1940. DTD, then W S Farren, opened it by pointing out that the research and development position was such that they could not expect to immediately produce a satisfactory pressure cabin fighter for service operation – a lot of work still needed to be done. Major A A Ross (Deputy Director R & D Engines) explained that Rolls-Royce was already working actively on a development of the Merlin XX in which the M-blower was retained but the S-blower was stepped up to give a rated height of 31,000ft (9,449m) – this developed engine should be available for prototypes in one year. Napier was in the early stages of investigating high-altitude versions of its Sabre with two-stage blowers, each stage of which had two speeds and which would have rated heights of 32,000ft (9,754m) and 40,000ft (12,192m) when the second stage was in operation. Based on this information, the Air Staff's revised performance estimates for the two-stage Sabre P.1004 were a maximum 370mph (595km/h) at 32,000ft and service ceiling 38,400ft (11,704m), while the Westland twin-Merlin would achieve 381mph (613km/h) at 30,500ft (9,296m) and reach 40,700ft (12,405m). Farren pointed out the advantage of the Sabre two-stage two-speed arrangement in that it maintained the speed within +/-10mph (16km/h) at all heights between 19,000ft (5,791m) and 32,000ft (9,754m) whilst the Merlin system suffered a loss in speed from 380mph (611km/h) at 32,000ft (9,754m) to 330mph (531km/h) at 19,000ft (5,791m).

One of the advantages of the GAL.46 was that only 3,050lb (1,383kg) of light alloy would be used with almost no extrusions (the metal industry was currently very full with work) but, unlike the other pair, the design was not based on existing aircraft and the tricycle undercarriage was an additional complication. The

BELOW To illustrate how the P.14 had changed when it became the Welkin, this photo from 26 May 1943 shows prototype DG558 on test while in the hands of A&AEE Boscombe Down. *Phil Butler*

RIGHT The spindly but quite attractive appearance of the Welkin is shown in further A&AEE recognition views, this time of production Mk.I DX282 on 25 November 1943. *Phil Butler*

Westland project had the disadvantage of using a very large amount of extrusions (1,300lb [590kg]) and in all a total of 6,400lb (2,903kg) of light alloy, while the centre plane, which was equal to half of the span and contained the engine mountings, nacelles, undercarriage and cannon gear, was a large and complicated component.

Farren summarised that, in regard to their structure and general layout, all of the designs were straightforward and it was really a question of deciding which of the design staffs could best undertake what would be largely experimental work. Hawker's design was the most practicable and declared the best, Westland's (like the Whirlwind) was 'rather fancy' and considered the worst, and General's was 'half-baked structurally'. It was agreed that Hawker and Westland were the most likely to undertake the work satisfactorily and that separate discussions with these companies should proceed before recommending which would be the best choice to do it.

On 8th January 1941 Sir Henry Tizard declared that the Hawker fighter/bomber layout was not specifically intended for high-altitude work; the pressure cabin could be fitted but he did not think it would be wise to concentrate Camm's attention on that just now. He also added that if the Whittle jet engine was a success it would make the specialised Westland high-altitude fighter redundant. The following day Beaverbrook, Minister of Aircraft Production, wrote to Westland to ask the company to put its full effort into the high-altitude fighter and to collaborate with Gloster on the solution of pressure cabins (which that company would need for its jet fighter).

A meeting held on 1st May 1941 asked for design work on the Westland F.4/40 airframe fitted with Griffon engines to proceed with all speed (in

LEFT The sole Welkin NF.Mk.II PF370 displays the type's considerable wingspan at the 1946 SBAC Show at Radlett. *Jo Ware*

BELOW As an aside, and just to show that the design and development of aircraft is always continuous, in December 1943 Westland looked into the possibility of fitting a Vee tail to the Welkin. Preliminary wind tunnel tests were carried out on a set of tail units having two different dihedral angles (30° and 40°) fitted to a standard Welkin tunnel model, and the pitching and yawing moments were measured. The results showed that the pitching moment curves produced by the Vee tail were very smooth and free from erratic readings. The covering report included these drawings, but no Welkin ever flew with this feature.

fact this was never built) but it was agreed that the first batch should use Merlins. The F.4/40 was named Welkin and the first of two prototypes made its maiden flight on 1st November 1942. As proposed the twin-engine F.4/40 had looked quite like the Whirlwind, but as built it was rather different. The wing shape was much

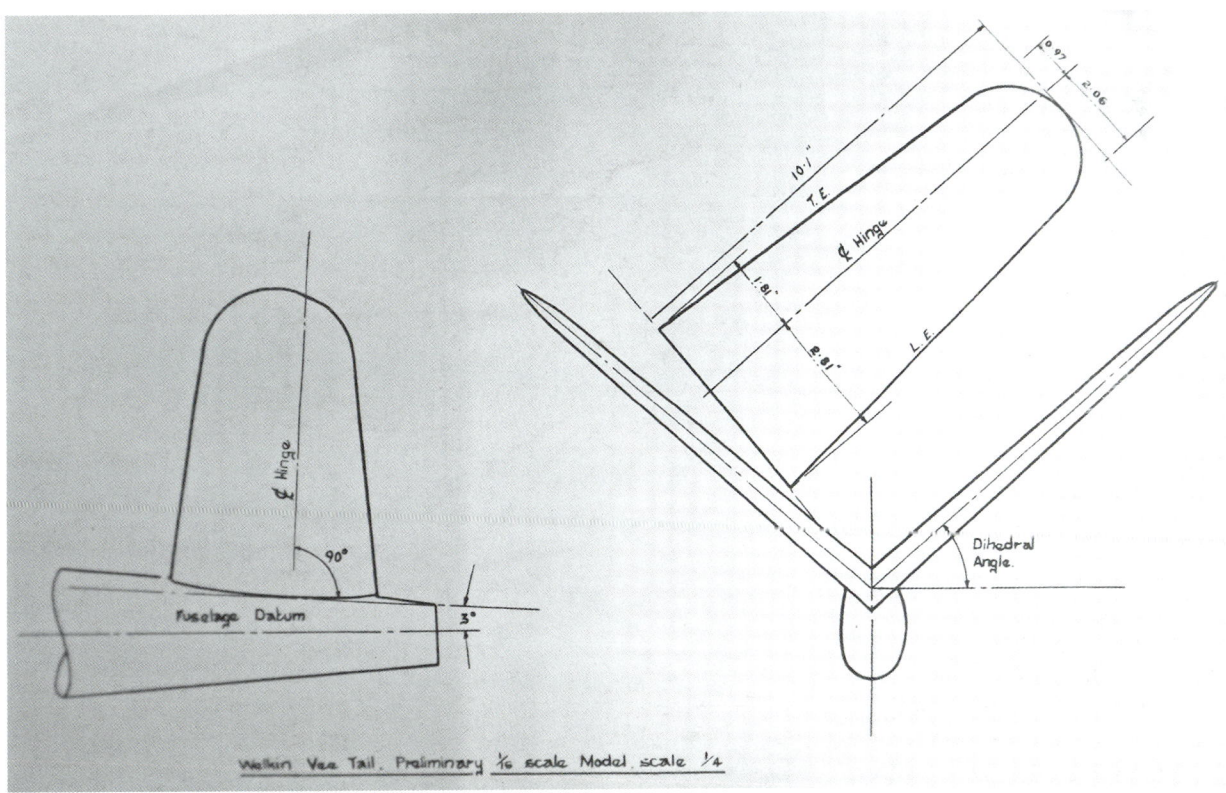

Westland Welkin Mk.I (flown)	
Span:	70ft 0in (21.34m)
Length:	41ft 6in (12.65m)
Wing Area:	460sq.ft (42.78sq.m)
All-Up-Weight:	19,775lb (8,970kg)
Powerplant:	2 x Merlin 61 1,560hp (1,163kW)
Max Speed / Height:	387mph (623km/h) at 26,000ft (7,925m)
Armament:	4 x 20mm cannon

changed, the horizontal tailplane was moved to a lower position on the fin, and the engine nacelles were altered. Altogether 75 production Welkins were eventually built (out of planned orders approaching 300) and all were Merlin-powered F.Mk.Is except for one Mk.II two-seat radar night fighter to F.9/43. Apart from the Mk.II, all of the completed Welkins were single-seaters and they all carried just the four 20mm cannon.

RAF interest in the Welkin had waned through 1944 and no example would reach a squadron. Part of the reason for this loss of interest was the performance and better manoeuvrability of the de Havilland Mosquito, which had been barely realised when F.4/40 was first laid down, but a further factor was the shortfall in the Welkin's own performance from the original estimates. Most examples were delivered straight to Maintenance Units and scrapped after the war.

De Havilland Hornet

By the middle of World War Two de Havilland was looking at what might follow its famous Mosquito multi-role aircraft (Chapter Three) and the result was two fighters, the jet-powered DH.100 Vampire (Chapter Eleven) and a scaled down development of the Mosquito called the DH.103. The initial proposals for the second project with twin Merlin engines were passed to N E Rowe on 22nd September 1942. Talks between de Havilland and MAP had concentrated on how to make use of a new and very cleaned up variant of the Merlin to meet a need for a long-range fighter to oppose Japanese single-engine fighters in the Pacific. The new engine was so free of accessories that the frontal area was virtually dictated by the crankcase and cylinder dimensions and it was not really suited to the Mosquito; a smaller aeroplane would be better. However, besides the DH.100 Vampire, the unarmed DH.102 Mosquito II bomber to B.4/42 was also being developed at this time and so the Air Staff placed the DH.103 on a low priority.

R N Liptrot assessed the DH.103 in early January 1943. The basic project covered an all-wood twin-Merlin single-seat fighter for low/medium-altitude duties to be produced generally on Mosquito lines. In low-altitude form with a span of 47ft (14.33m) and flying weight 14,700lb (6,668kg), de Havilland predicted that the DH.103 would reach 474mph (763km/h) at 27,500ft (8,382m), but Liptrot concluded that there was not a good case for the project in the form presented when compared to the new single-engined F.6/42 fighter requirement (Chapter Two), which would be smaller and lighter. A request was made to give the aircraft greater range for operation in the Pacific theatre but, because of the Air Staff's lack of interest, the firm had now stopped work on the DH.103.

Towards the end of April 1943, when the latest engine developments were assessed, it was realised that two Merlin 61 engines offered considerably greater

BELOW This splendid photograph of early Hornet Mk.I PX217 was released to the press on 20 September 1945. Note the original small fin and rudder.

BOTTOM Westland's tandem Merlin project, believed to have been prepared to F.12/43 (5.44). *Westland Archives*

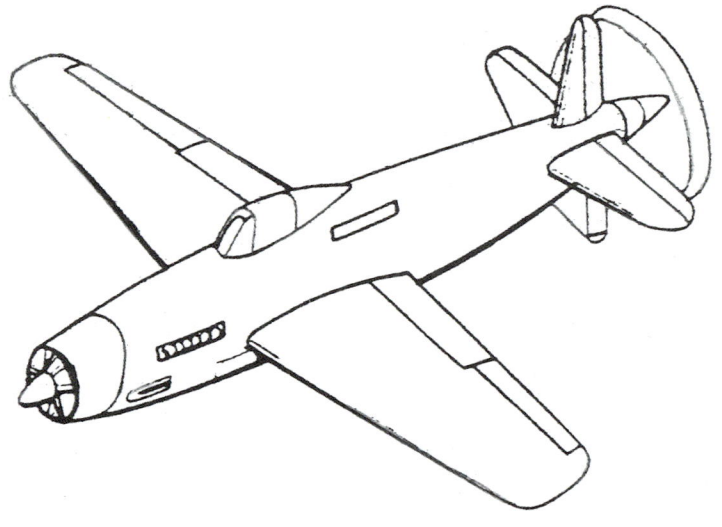

TOP PX288 was the last Mk.I Hornet to be built. Flying 'alongside' in the distance are three Avro Lancasters and Lancastrians, and one of the latter appears to be a jet engine test bed.

ABOVE PX362 was a de Havilland Hornet Mk.III with the dorsal extension to its fin.

installed power than was possible with any single unit while, at the same time, the 61 was capable of further immediate development for the highest possible power output at all altitudes. This would give the twin-engine DH.103 a superior performance in speed and climb over what could be obtained with a single-engined aircraft to the same specification. Consequently interest in the DH.103 began to grow and the manufacturer now estimated that a speed of 490mph (788km/h) at 23,400ft (7,132m) would be possible.

Up to 1943 long-range fighters had generally suffered certain drawbacks, mainly concerning their manoeuvrability. By this time the need for such a type in the RAF was becoming obvious but if a similar design technique was used to the Mosquito the production stage could be reached quickly and there would be many advantages from having a twin-engined fighter, such as greatly increased power and improved pilot's view. It was also realised that, while there was no reason why a twin-engined fighter should suffer in most manoeuvres compared with others of similar power, there would be some loss in rate of roll. However, it was felt that any more than a certain rate of roll could not be used effectively and that this limit could be reached in the DH.103, while the layout itself gave the considerable advantage of central rather than convergent fire.

Since it was a scale model of the Mosquito, the DH.103 was expected to inherit the good aerodynamic, controllability and structural features of the latter and so hopefully suffer relatively little from teething problems. Rowe felt that the performance looked so good that 'it must not be overlooked' and on 11th May 1943 wrote 'the DH.103 is a very attractive proposition and I would like to see it built. Geoffrey de Havilland would also like to build it … he has an eye for a good aeroplane … but would not be disappointed if the Air Staff decides against it. The outstanding quality is that it retains extremely high performance with the ability to fight at long range and is likely to be invaluable in the Far East War in 1945/46'.

Prototypes were agreed on 20th June and ordered on 30th July, the first (RR915) just a 'skeleton' to be completed in May 1944 while the second (RR919), two months behind, would be to the full standard. The first production aeroplane was to be ready in December 1944 and to get it into service quickly it was agreed to order 'off the board'; in early 1944 the type was named Hornet. Specification F.12/43 was written around it and called for as high a speed as possible but not less than 480mph (772km/h) at 22,000ft, plus a maximum rate of climb of not less than 4,400ft/min (1,340m/min) from ground level to 22,000ft (6,706m). Armament consisted of four 20mm cannon and, for ground attack, two 1,000lb (454kg) bombs or eight rocket projectiles under the wings. The Hornet's primary duty was to serve as a long-range medium-altitude single-seat day fighter but it would also be used as a fighter-bomber and unarmed photo-reconnaissance aircraft.

From the manufacturing point of view there was a need to combat the weathering problems suffered by the Mosquito. Consequently the Hornet employed a bonding resin called Redux which was used to cement metal to wood to make composite spars for the wings, the first time this

ABOVE Hornet F.Mk.III PX351 is seen at Hullavington at some point after its delivery to No 10 Maintenance Unit on 26 September 1946, but before the dorsal fin fillet had been added. *Peter Arnold collection*

process had been used in an aircraft structure; Redux cement had been shown to resist higher stresses than could be withstood by wood-to-wood cements, or indeed the wood fibres themselves. In September 1943 contra-rotating propellers were considered as a counter to the considerable control problem of swing on take-off, but it was eventually agreed with Rolls-Royce that handed engines with opposite-rotating propellers would be more suitable. The specially 'tailored' handed engines were known as the Merlin 130 series; the 130 was the conventional right hand rotating unit fitted in the port nacelle, the 131 in the starboard nacelle had a reverse-rotating (left hand) airscrew. These were two-speed, two-stage engines with downdraught carburettors (the first of the Merlin family to have this feature) and were mounted low so that a smooth airflow was obtained over the whole upper wing. Mosquito practice surfaced again with leading edge radiator intakes housed in an extended wing centre section; the air intakes were placed outboard of the nacelles.

A Mock-Up Conference to clear the design was held in September 1943, although the mock-up itself had been put together the previous January and for security was hidden behind a wall in Hatfield's Experimental Department. RR915 made its first flight on 28th July 1944 and by 22nd August had achieved a true airspeed at full throttle height of 491mph (790km/h) at 24,600ft (7,498m) in FS Gear (within 2mph/3.2km/h of de Havilland's latest estimate) and 460mph (740km/h) at 12,690ft (3,868m) in MS Gear – production aircraft would only reach 472mph (760km/h) at 22,000ft (6,706m). Not including special racing aircraft it is believed that the only aircraft to beat RR915 on the level with piston power was the Griffon 101-powered Supermarine Spiteful RB518 at 494mph (795km/h).

It appears possible that another Westland project used F.12/43 as a base. This design, completed in May 1944, had two 2,100hp (1,566kW) Merlins mounted in tandem with a shaft drive to contra-rotating propellers placed behind the tail. Its span was 45ft (13.72m), wing area 340sq.ft (31.62sq.m), all-up-weight 23,000lb (10,433kg) and top speed 510mph (821km/h) at 25,000ft (7,620m). Bombs would have been carried internally.

The close of the war in the Pacific ensured that the Hornet production run was curtailed and many examples were cancelled. However, 193 fighters were built for the RAF and served in the Far East until 1955 while another 182 Sea Hornets were built for the Fleet Air Arm (Chapter Seven). The Hornet was one of the most beautiful piston-engined aeroplanes ever produced, it possessed a truly remarkable performance and was a joy to fly.

Conclusion

These three most interesting twin-engine fighter types, resulting from different programmes, were in character quite different from each other. And in the same way as the single-engine types described previously they brought to a close the development of twin-piston-engined fighters in the UK, which has been discussed over the last two chapters. The next British twin-engine type would be the jet-powered Gloster Meteor.

de Havilland Hornet F.Mk.III (flown)	
Span:	45ft 0in (13.72m)
Length:	36ft 8in (11.18m)
Wing Area:	361sq.ft (33.57sq.m)
All-Up-Weight:	17,880lb (8,110kg)
Powerplant:	2 x Merlin 130/131 2,070hp (1,544kW)
Max Speed / Height:	472mph (760km/h) at 22,000ft (6,706m)
Armament:	4 x 20mm cannon, bombs or rock

Chapter Five
Turrey Fighters and Night Fighters

ABOVE Boulton Paul Defiant N1535 pictured on 17 January 1941.

When the Second World War began in 1939 the developments that had taken place in all areas of aviation since the end of the first global conflict in 1918 were immense, but there were unknowns as to just how effective some of the new military aircraft might be. The types that were designed during the build-up to war were, to some extent, produced against theory rather than fact, although the Spanish Civil War of 1936 did supply valuable experience at a vital time. Several British aircraft developed during this period, like the Spitfire and Hurricane, proved to be a great success, but others were flawed. One example was the turret fighter, which today, familiar as we are with dogfighting and close-in air-to-air combat, may seem to have been rather an odd concept. However, it was the outcome of serious thought regarding how the forthcoming conflict might be fought at a time when there was a need to cover every possible eventuality.

A theory that was generally accepted at this time was that Britain would be attacked by massed formations of enemy bombers. To counter this it was felt that the defending fighters would have to attack in formation, but there were doubts as to whether the pilots would be capable of formating with their colleagues while aiming their guns. The solution could be to concentrate the guns in a power-operated turret, and from the mid-1930s there were several attempts to acquire 'modern' turret-armed fighters. Wartime experience eventually showed that the fixed-gun Spitfire/Hurricane arrangement was superior, and after 1940 the idea of the turret-armed 'bomber destroyer' faded away.

Specification F.9/35 Boulton Paul Defiant and Hawker Hotspur

In 1934 some British companies were experimenting with power-operated gun mountings or turrets. One, Boulton & Paul Aircraft, had achieved some success with its Overstrand medium bomber, and in 1935 it acquired from the French company SAMM a four-gun power-operated turret. Boulton Paul considered this equipment to be far in advance of anything it, or the other British turret designing firm Frazer Nash, had so far achieved.

One early turret fighter specification was F.5/33, but the concept here was for a pusher fighter with a nose turret, which appears to have been abandoned when it became clear that it did not offer a sufficient

85

advance over current fighters. A prototype of one of the designs tendered, the Armstrong Whitworth AW.34, was ordered but not completed. A much more successful document was F.9/35 for a two-seat day and night fighter having a speed of not less than 290mph (467km/h) at 15,000ft (4,572m), and this brought forth the RAF's only wartime turret fighter, the Defiant. The aircraft was to have no forward-firing armament, the offensive gunnery being placed in a rear cockpit; the document added, quite delightfully, that 'the gunner shall be completely sheltered from the wind and be able to operate his guns without appreciable effort, whatever the speed of the aircraft may be.' F.9/35 was issued to Tender in June 1935 and resulted in the following proposals.

Armstrong Whitworth F.9/35

Armstrong Whitworth's design, which was unnumbered but a development of the AW.34, was the only twin-engined contender, making use of two Armstrong-Siddeley Terrier engines. The mainplane employed the then current AWA practice of a single box spar made in light alloy where the bending moment stresses and torsional loads would be accommodated by wide booms to give a light and rigid plane. The wing was covered in light alloy from the spar's leading edge through to its rear, but the areas aft of this had standard fabric covering. It was also

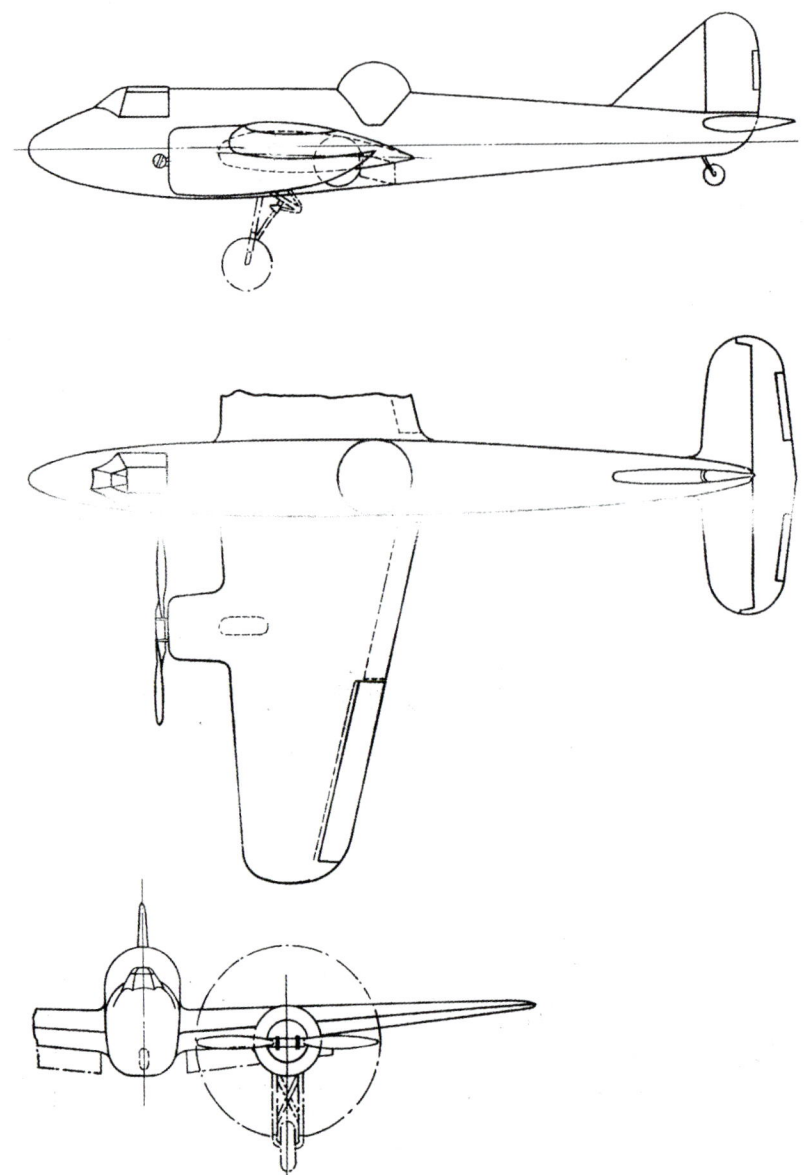

ABOVE The Armstrong Whitworth F.9/35 (c8.35). *Adapted from National Archives AVIA 14/64/18*

Armstrong Whitworth F.9/35 (8.35)	
Span:	39ft 0in (11.89m) (February 1937 drawing same)
Length:	37ft 3in (11.35m)
Wing Area:	259sq.ft (24.09sq.m) (February 1937 drawing gives 295sq.ft [27.44sq.m])
All-Up-Weight:	6,700lb (3,039kg) (February 1937 drawing gives 7,000lb [3,175kg])
Powerplant:	2 x AS Terrier 455hp (339kW)
Max Speed / Height:	328mph (528km/h)
Armament:	4 x 0.303in (7.7mm) machine guns

intended to have a fuselage and wing surface finish approaching the quality achieved at the time on motor cars, this being accomplished using flush riveting and cellulose lacquers. A contract was placed for one prototype, K8624, which may have been a conversion of the part-complete AW.34 prototype, and it seems likely that this aeroplane's assembly was well advanced when the order was cancelled. Sources suggest that cooling problems with the Terrier engines may have been partly responsible for the abandonment.

Boulton & Paul P.82

The P.82 had a completely rotating turret behind the pilot's cockpit fitted with four Browning machine guns, which covered a field of fire equal to nearly the whole of the upper hemisphere. Firing forward over the airscrew and backward and alongside the rudder was made possible by retracting local portions of fairing fore and aft of the turret. Light alloy monocoque construction was used for the fuselage, tail unit and single-spar wings, and the fuselage was novel

CHAPTER FIVE
TURRET FIGHTERS AND NIGHT FIGHTERS

Boulton Paul P.82 (8.35)

Span:	39ft 0in (11.89m)
Length:	33ft 0in (10.06m)
Wing Area:	240sq.ft (22.32sq.m)
All-Up-Weight:	5,771lb (2,618kg)
Powerplant:	1 x Merlin F.5
Max Speed / Height:	265mph (426km/h) at ground level, 323mph (520km/h) at 15,000ft (4,572m)
Armament:	4 x 0.303in (7.7mm) machine guns

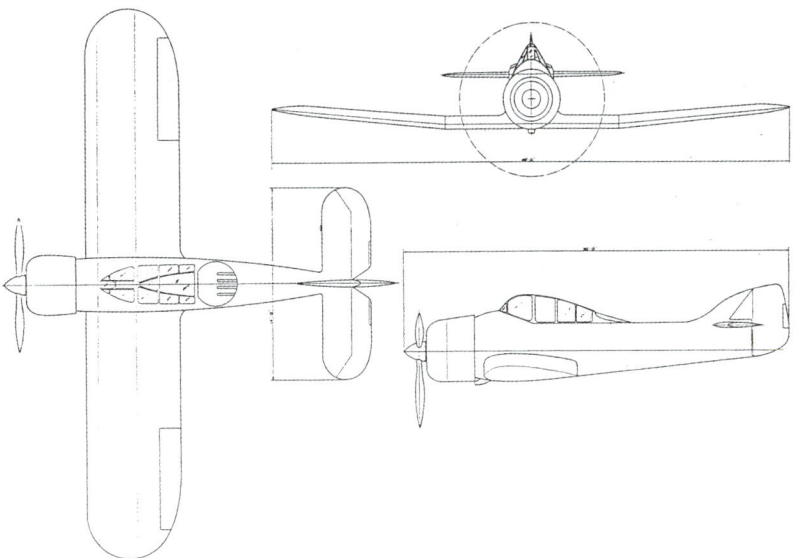

ABOVE The Bristol 147 (17.8.35).

in the sense that it was constructed in sections for bolting together, a method successfully employed on Boulton Paul's Feeder Line aircraft for Imperial Airways. This, it was considered, considerably reduced the difficulties of monocoque construction and repair brought about by the inaccessibility of many rivets. The tailplane was built integrally with the fuselage and the wing was metal throughout, except for some possible fabric covering on the ailerons. Frise ailerons and split flaps were fitted, the latter extending from the body side to the ailerons.

The Merlin was to be cooled by a honeycomb radiator mounted beneath the engine, though on the resulting Defiant this had been moved further rearwards. Recessed stowage space for racks to carry light bombs was available in the inner part of each outer wing; when no bombs were carried these recesses would be faired over by cover plates (this feature did not find its way onto the prototype Defiant). Each wing also housed a 42-gallon (191-litre) fuel tank, the rate of climb up to 15,000ft (4,572m) was 2,450ft/min (747m/min), time to 25,000ft (7,620m) 12.0 minutes, and service ceiling approximately 34,000ft (10,363m). A considerable amount of the development work carried out for Boulton Paul's tender to the B.1/35 bomber requirement was also applicable to this aircraft.

Bristol 147

This used the same wing, tail unit and pilot's cockpit as Bristol's Type 148 two-seat army co-operation aircraft designed to A.39/34, which itself used many parts standard to the Type 146 proposed to F.5/34 (see Chapter 1). The biggest change was the addition of the rear turret, faired into the rear cockpit, which housed the four Browning machine guns. The rear crewman sat inside the cockpit ahead of the guns and aimed remotely using a reflector sight and two hand wheels. A 65-gallon (296-litre) fuel tank was placed under the pilot and at least one more in the wing held another 18 gallons (82 litres). Two versions of the aircraft were tendered in August and

Bristol 147 (17.8.35)

Span:	40ft 0in (12.19m)
Length:	30ft 0in (9.14m)
Wing Area:	?
All-Up-Weight:	?
Powerplant:	1 x Perseus or Hercules
Max Speed / Height:	280mph (451km/h) or 315mph (507km/h), both at 15,000 (4,572)
Armament:	4 x 0.303in (7.7mm) machine guns

September 1935 respectively, the first using a Bristol Perseus engine while the second (the Type 147A) had a more powerful Bristol Hercules. Both were expected to achieve a service ceiling of 35,000ft (10,668m).

BELOW A rough sketch of the Fairey F.9/35.

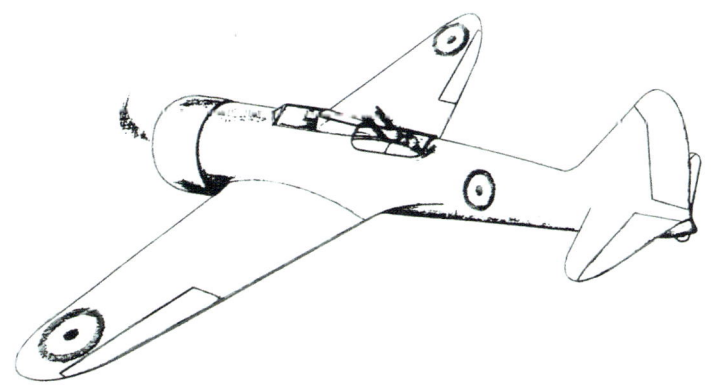

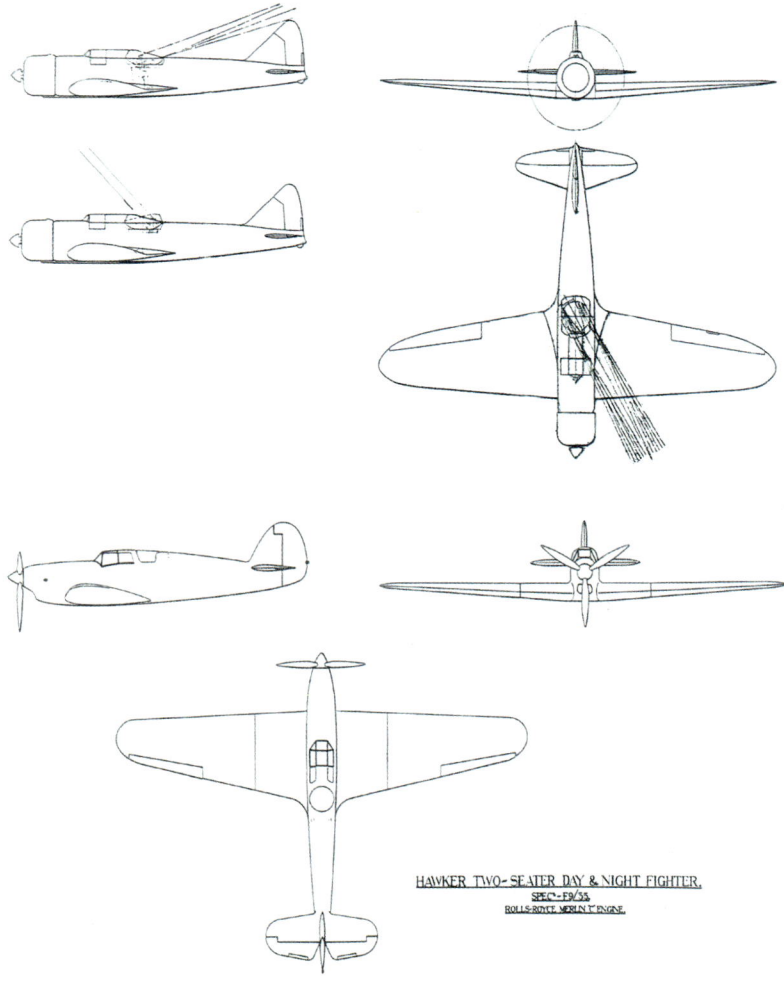

Fairey F.9/35

Fairey's submission used a single Hercules engine and its four-machine-gun turret, when facing rearwards, was blended flush with the pilot's cockpit.

Gloster F.9/35

No information has been traced for this single-engine design.

Hawker F.9/35

This project shared a close similarity in its airframe design to the Hurricane and was to fly as the Hotspur. As first proposed, however, it had a larger span and used some upper rear fuselage decking to fair the turret into the fuselage when not in use; this could be lowered when the time came to fire or rotate the turret. The four machine guns were placed in vertical pairs to each side of the turret.

Hawker F.9/35 (9.8.35)	
Span:	45ft 6in (13.87m)
Length:	33ft 2in (10.11m)
Wing Area:	260sq.ft (24.18sq.m)
All-Up-Weight:	?
Powerplant:	1 x Merlin C
Max Speed / Height:	?
Armament:	4 x 0.303in (7.7mm) machine guns

TOP The Fairey F.9/35, showing turret field of fire (4.8.35).

ABOVE The Hawker F.9/35 (9.8.35). *Hawker via Chris Farara*

BELOW The Supermarine 305 (8.35). *The late Eric Morgan*

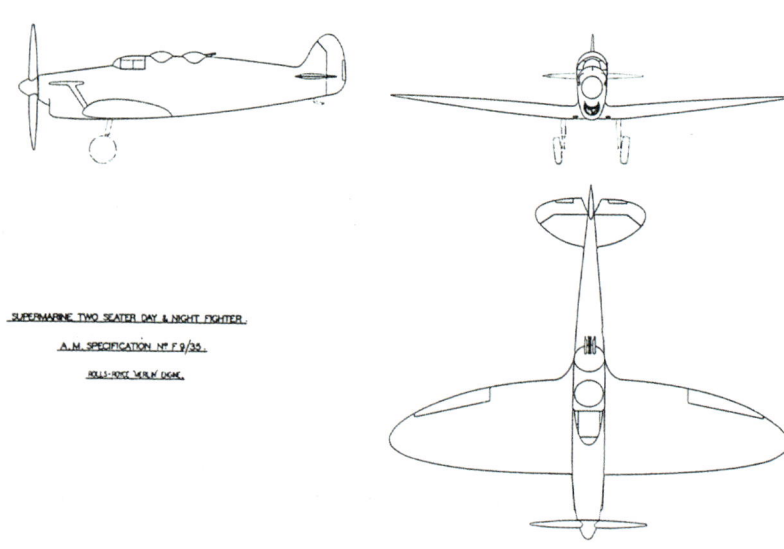

Supermarine 305

This was another development of Supermarine's F.7/30 (Type 224) and F.37/34 (Spitfire) fighters, and indeed was near identical to the latter apart from the necessary modifications to the fuselage to covert it from a single- to a two-seat aeroplane. The wings, engine installation, tail unit and chassis remained substantially unaltered, which prompted Supermarine to suggest that the aircraft could be designed and constructed in a very short time. Great attention was given to reducing 'parasite drag' with the fuselage, wing and tail covered entirely with smooth flush-riveted sheet metal, while all excrescences from the cockpits and turret were cut to a minimum. The 305's structure and chassis were

Supermarine 305 (16.8.35)	
Span:	37ft 0in (11.28m)
Length:	30ft 6in (9.30m)
Wing Area:	242sq.ft (22.51sq.m)
All-Up-Weight:	5,650lb (2,563kg)
Powerplant:	1 x Merlin 1,000hp (746kW)
Max Speed / Height:	315mph (507km/h) at 15,000ft (4,572m)
Armament:	4 x 0.303in (7.7mm) machine guns

identical to the F.37/34 (then currently building) and the Merlin installation was very similar. The cantilever wing used a single light alloy spar to which was attached the torsion-resisting leading edge box and the trailing ribs; the air brakes and landing flaps were of the split type. Flush-riveted semi-monocoque construction was used on the fuselage and only the engine mounting employed tubular construction. Originally four 0.303in (7.7mm) Browning machine guns were mounted in a turret that was separated from the gunner, but these were later replaced by four Lewis guns.

Vickers F.9/35

It appears that this Merlin-powered design was not officially tendered to the Air Ministry. It featured an unusual vertical end fin and rudder arrangement, presumably because of the presence of the turret, which was set well to the rear of the cockpit. No support data for this project has been traced.

The Tender Design Conference was held on 12 September 1935 and placed the top three designs, in order of merit, as Hawker, Boulton Paul and Armstrong Whitworth; Bristol and Gloster were eliminated because of their unsatisfactory turret design. All of the contenders quoted a speed considerably in excess of the requirements and, in particular, the French turret on the Boulton & Paul P.82 excited very favourable comment. The Air Ministry attached great importance to the operational role of this type and was therefore very anxious to order prototypes of several designs; in addition it wanted duplicate prototypes as an insurance against mishap. As a result the financial allocation was exceeded and special Treasury sanction had to be obtained to order seven prototypes, two each from Hawker, Boulton Paul and Fairey, and one from Armstrong Whitworth. Contracts for these were placed shortly afterwards (to Boulton Paul on 4 December), but in the event the Armstrong Whitworth and Fairey machines were never built and only one Hawker Hotspur was completed.

The first P.82 prototype, later named Defiant, was built during 1936 and 1937, the final Mock-Up Conference having convened on 28 February 1936; the first flight took place on 11 August 1937. To begin it appears that the Air Ministry's primary interest in the P.82 lay in its turret, and in June 1936 it was thought that, due to a production order also having been given for the Hawker F.9/35, the likelihood of the aircraft going beyond the experimental stage was remote. However, it seemed worthwhile to continue with the P.82 because of the interest that the armament division took in the turret, quite apart from the aircraft itself. However, when DTD visited Boulton Paul's factory in September to see the prototype being built, he was struck by the apparent simplicity of the methods of production used on it.

A recommendation by DTD that a small order for P.82s should be placed was rejected on the grounds that the company had not yet shown its skill as a producing unit and was in any case fully occupied with work for Blackburn. In the spring of 1937, however, this decision was reversed when an order for eighty-seven Defiants was placed following a serious setback to the Hawker Hotspur programme. Boulton Paul was enthusiastic about its design, and with turrets generally, and was also considered to have produced an excellent design for the F.11/37 fighter (below) when, on the other hand, Hawker appeared to show more interest in fixed-front-gun fighters than the turret variety, which was one reason why it took that company so long to get its prototype into the air.

Later that year CAS agreed to

BELOW **The Vickers F.9/35 (9.8.35).** *The late Eric Morgan*

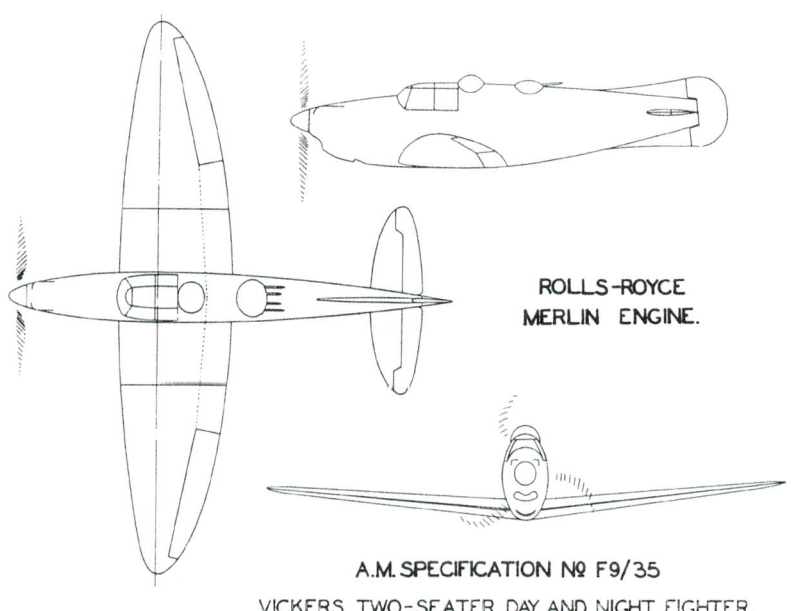

LEFT The Boulton Paul Defiant's weakness was that its sole armament was mounted in a turret to the rear of the cockpit. There were no fixed forward-firing guns to permit the fighter to make a fast head-on attack.

MIDDLE An air-to-air view of an unknown Defiant. The serial number has been removed from this photo.

BOTTOM Defiant prototype K8310 is seen in 1940 after conversion to a single-seat fighter with no turret.

drop the Hotspur altogether in favour of the Defiant, and in January 1938 the Council Committee on Supply agreed to adopt the Defiant as the sole two-seat fighter type, increasing Boulton Paul's order to 389. However, because Boulton Paul was occupied with producing the Blackburn Roc, deliveries did not begin until September 1939, and not in quantity until the summer of 1940. In April 1940 the Air Council agreed that, as an operational type, the Defiant had entered service two years too late and was thus verging on obsolescence. The manufacturer had estimated a speed of 315mph (507km/h) for the fighter, but its true speed was 304mph (489km/h). Despite achieving some success in the Battle of Britain, the Defiant had a generally unhappy career as a day fighter, and the shortcomings of the turret fighter concept were exposed. During the night bombing attacks of the winter of 1940/41 it was used extensively as a night fighter, but it could not fulfil the Air Staff's needs for speed, armament and range and was subsequently converted into a target-tug. More than 900 Defiants were eventually built.

As noted, Boulton Paul had been fully occupied building the Blackburn B.25 Roc, an adaptation of the Skua naval fighter/dive bomber into a two-seat fleet turret fighter. This project was proposed to Specification O.30/35 and the prototype first flew on 23 December 1938. Against that specification Boulton & Paul offered the P.85A (Hercules) or P.85B (Merlin) development of the P.82 (a 'Sea Defiant') with a new tail, deeper fuselage and leading edge slats to reduce the landing speed. Its span was 42ft 6in (13.0m). Despite offering an estimated top speed of 308mph (496km/h), 85mph (137km/h) more than that achieved by the Roc at 223mph (359km/h), the Roc was chosen for the Fleet Air Arm. Ironically, because Blackburn was full with work, it sub-contracted the Roc's detail design and production to Boulton Paul (which labelled the project P.93). The Roc was a failure because it was just too slow to catch enemy bombers.

Boulton Paul P.94

Prototype Defiant K8310 eventually had its turret removed and in August 1940 was flown as an unarmed flying demonstrator for a fixed-gun version called the P.94, which was intended for rapid production using many complete Defiant components. For long-range fighter duties the P.94 had its turret replaced by twelve 0.303in (7.7mm) Browning machine guns disposed in each side of the wing centre section in nests of six, while four 20mm Hispano cannon, replacing eight of the Brownings in two nests of two, made an alternative cannon fighter. The machine guns could also be depressed by 17° for ground attack work. P.94 had a 1,100hp (820kW) Merlin XX, which offered a maximum speed of 360mph (579km/h) at 21,700ft (6,614m), and a sea level rate of climb of 3,235ft/min (986m/min) would get the aircraft to 25,000ft (7,620m) in 8.1 minutes (these figures were deduced from K8310's flight trials). To allow the type to act as a long-range fighter two 30-gallon (136-litre) auxiliary fuel tanks could be carried, and in production the aircraft would use standard Defiant jigs. The long-range gun fighter had an all-up weight of 7,675lb (3,481kg) and the cannon fighter was heavier at 7,855lb (3,563kg). P.94 was never ordered, but Boulton Paul also proposed to convert the now single-seat Defiant prototype into a four-cannon fighter demonstrator. The Air Ministry's rejection of this idea was recorded at a company board meeting held on 26 September 1940.

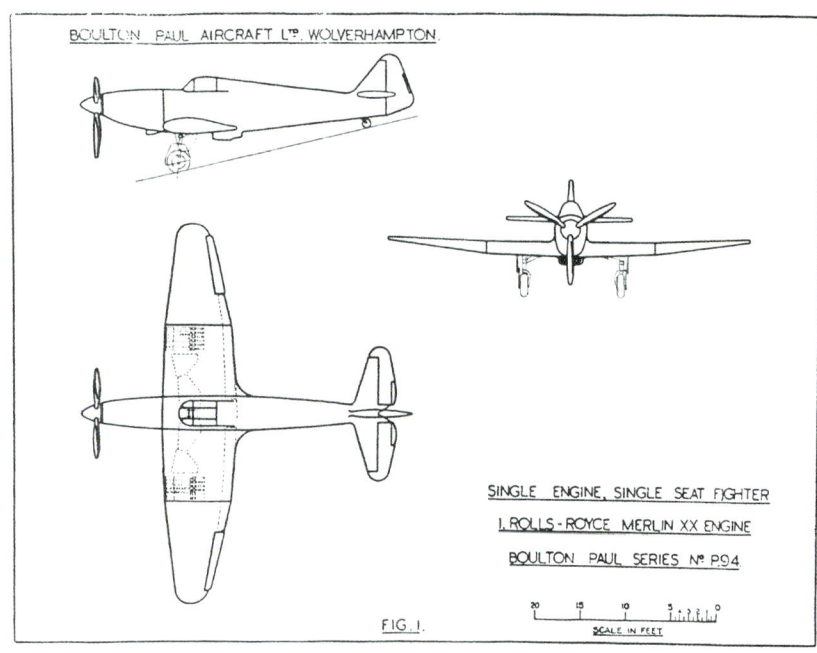

ABOVE The Boulton Paul P.94 (mid-1940). *Les Whitehouse, Boulton Paul Archive*

BELOW K8309, the only Hawker Hotspur to be completed, is seen with a wooden dummy turret and no guns. The real turret was never fitted.

Boulton Paul Defiant Mk.I (flown)

Span:	39ft 4in (11.99m)
Length:	35ft 4in (10.77m)
Wing Area:	250sq.ft (23.25sq.m)
All-Up-Weight:	8,240lb (3,738kg)
Powerplant:	1 x Merlin III 1,030hp (768kW)
Max Speed / Height:	304mph (489km/h) at 17,000ft (5,182m)
Armament:	4 x 0.303in (7.7mm) machine guns

Hawker Hotspur

Hawker's F.9/35 project was christened the Hotspur. The gunner's cockpit was built with a fully enclosed power-operated turret containing four Browning machine guns, and there was provision for one Vickers gun on the port side of the fuselage. Prototype K8309, flown on 14 June 1938, was the only Hotspur built because the planned production run was dropped when it was realised that capacity was limited for the quantity manufacture of additional new designs. Hawker was under growing pressure to accelerate quantity production of the Hurricane, while its sister Hawker Siddeley company Gloster Aircraft was fully occupied building the Henley light bomber. K8309 was used for research at RAE until February 1942.

Hawker Hotspur (flown)	
Span:	40ft 6in (12.34m)
Length:	32ft 10.5in (10.02m)
Wing Area:	265sq.ft (24.645sq.m)
All-Up-Weight:	6,850lb (3,107kg)
Powerplant:	1 x Merlin 2 1,025hp (764kW)
Max Speed / Height:	320mph (515km/h)
Armament:	4 x 0.303in (7.7mm) machine guns (not fitted)

Specification F.11/37 Boulton Paul P.92

Another turret fighter specification was F.34/35, which described a twin-engined Gloster design that was eventually abandoned and replaced by the fixed-gun F.9/37 (see Chapter 3). The next such specification, F.11/37 dated 26 May 1937, called for a twin-engined home defence day and night fighter capable of at least 370mph (595km/h) at 15,000ft (4,572m). In addition, 'in order to obtain a striking power superior to the eight gun machine gun fighter' it would have four 20mm cannon in a power-operated turret. One 250lb (113kg) bomb was also to be carried internally. The following designs are known to have been prepared to F.11/37, but available Ministry documents make reference only to Boulton Paul's project.

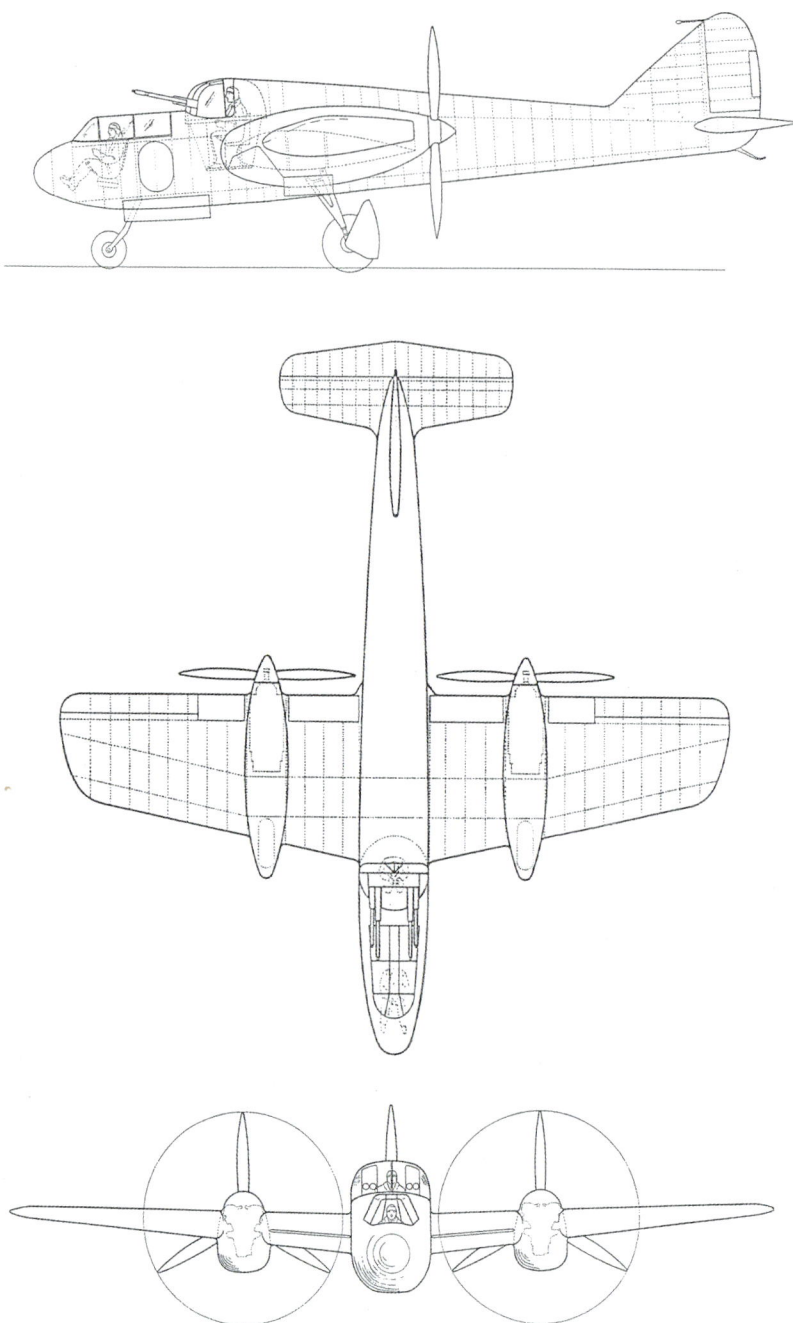

ABOVE **The Armstrong Whitworth F.11/37 (8.37).** *Ray Williams*

Armstrong Whitworth F.11/37

AWA concluded that F.11/37's primary objective was a fighter that would usually attack a target flying in front of it; consequently this unnumbered design had the pilot sitting in the nose with his gunner and turret just behind and above. Two Merlin pusher engines were fitted to allow the gunner the maximum forward field of fire, although his turret could be rotated through 360° except for a small area directly behind; in addition, the guns could not be lowered to the horizontal.

Armstrong Whitworth F.11/37 (8.37)	
Span:	43ft 0in (13.11m)
Length:	43ft 3in (13.18m)
Wing Area:	?
All-Up-Weight:	13,500lb (6,124kg)
Powerplant:	2 x Merlin
Max Speed / Height:	418mph (673km/h)
Armament:	4 x 20mm cannon

This was AWA's first project to have no fabric-covered surfaces, stressed-skin light alloy construction being used throughout, and it was also the first to have a retractable tricycle undercarriage complete with steerable nosewheel. Petrol was housed in two upper fuselage tanks directly behind the turret, and the 250lb (113kg) bomb container and rack were carried in a lower fuselage bay also behind the turret.

Boulton Paul P.92

This attractive design had a very slim fuselage and two Vulture engines and managed to accommodate a large turret 13ft (4.0m) in diameter in a combined fuselage and thickened wing centre-section mounting between the engine nacelles. To help reduce drag most of the barrels for the four 20mm Hispano cannon were housed in recessed slots, except when elevated above about 30°, and the gunner had a small offset transparent sighting hood. To prevent distortion and ensure that the turret would always rotate freely, considerable structural stiffening was required around the turret and between the wing spars. The turret itself was built in light alloy over braced ribs and the only part not housed within the wing was the carefully faired shallow dome, which ensured that the resultant drag was minimal. The fuselage was of monocoque construction throughout with light alloy sheet skinning and stiffened by longitudinal corrugated stringers built on to a series of ring formers and built-up bulkheads. Both turret and wing/fuselage centre section were mocked-up and photographed for the original submission, the wing/turret shape having already been tested in the wind tunnel.

Although ordered as a four-cannon fighter, the P.92 was in fact also tendered with a turret having four cannon and four machine guns together (two vertically opposed Browning machine guns were positioned on each side of the

Boulton Paul P.92 (30.7.37)	
Span:	62ft 6in (19.05m)
Length:	52ft 3in (15.93m)
Wing Area:	650sq.ft (60.45sq.m)
All-Up-Weight:	17,697lb (8,027kg)
Powerplant:	2 x Vulture II 1,710hp (1,275kW)
Max Speed / Height:	299mph (481km/h) at ground level, 371mph (597km/h) at 15,000ft (4,572m)
Armament:	4 x 20mm cannon

cannon, stacked one above the other). The brochure three-view drawing did not show the additional four machine guns outboard of the cannon, but a more detailed drawing did. A 250lb (113kg) bomb container could be carried as an alternative load in the underbelly. P.92's wing had split flaps and Frise ailerons and the engine radiators were placed on the front of the nacelles. A total of 270 gallons (1,228 litres) of fuel was carried in four tanks. The estimated rate of climb was 3,080ft/min (939m/min) at sea level and 3,220ft/min (981m/min) at 15,000ft (4,572m); service ceiling was 38,000ft (11,582m). This aircraft was chosen for construction and as the design evolved it acquired a fin fitted with a straight leading edge.

Bristol F.11/37

This brochure described two versions of the same design, which were distinguished as 'Small' and 'Large' but, surprisingly, not given a type number. The first had a pair of Bristol Hercules HE.6.SM units while the larger variant would take two examples of a new 2,000bhp (1,491kW) eighteen-cylinder two-row radial to be made by Bristol in the 'immediate future' (at this stage the engine was provisionally named Centaurus). To ensure a design wing loading of 30lb/sq ft (146kg/sq m), and so compensate for the differing weights and size of the powerplants, the two projects had different wing and tail areas, tail lengths and undercarriages; otherwise they were practically identical. The materials and methods

BELOW The Boulton Paul P.92 with two Vulture engines (30.7.37). *Les Whitehouse, Boulton Paul Archive*

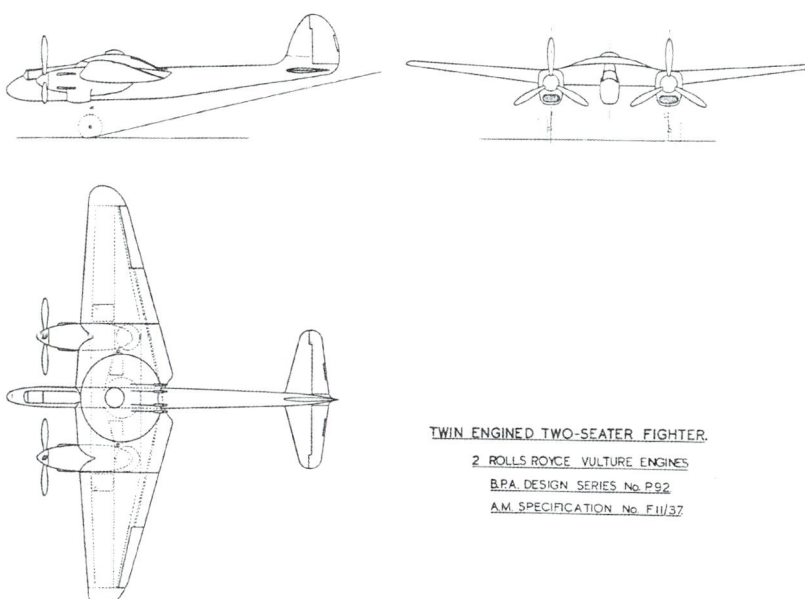

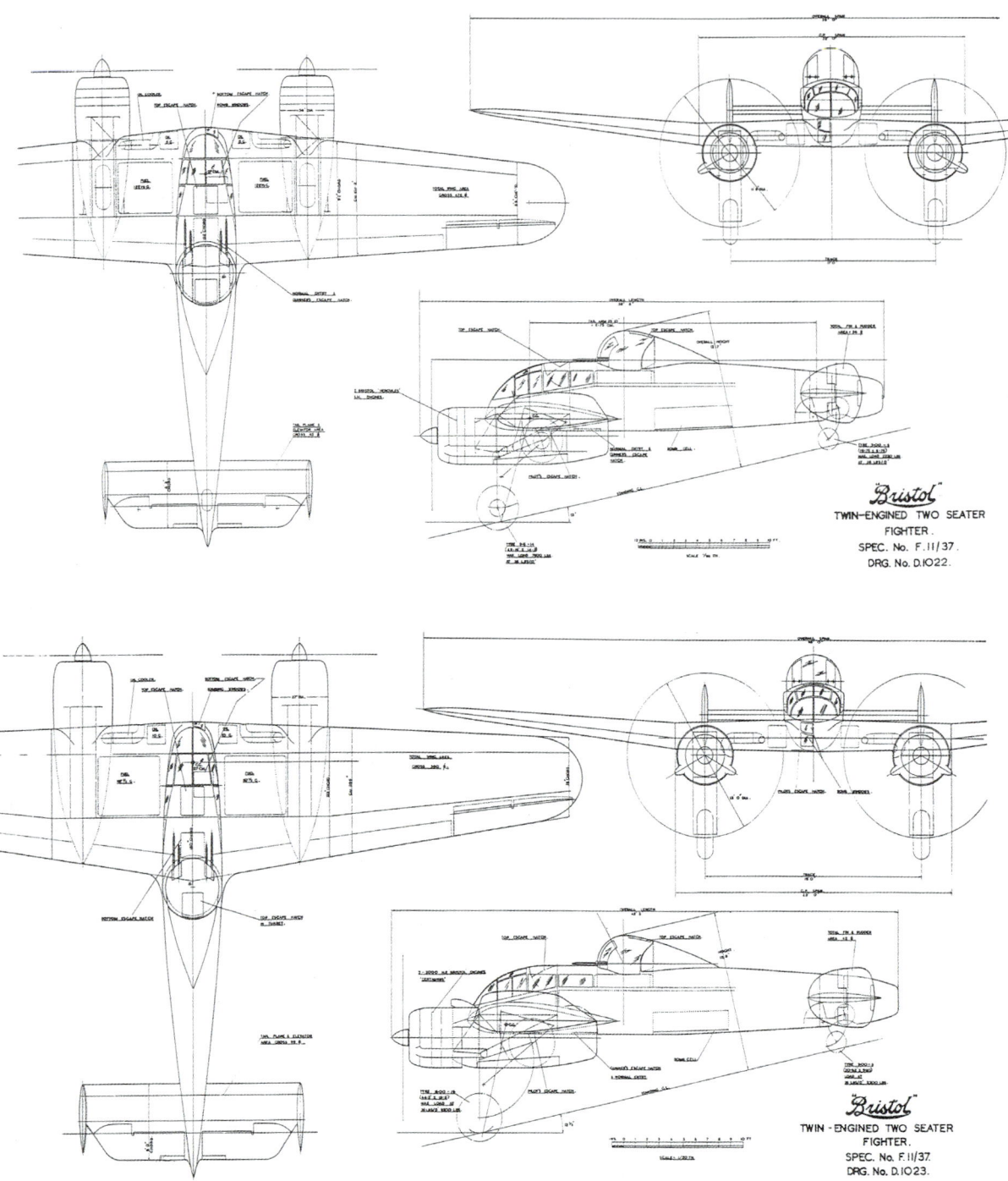

TOP *The Bristol 'Small' design to F.11/37 (8.37).* The late Jim Oughton

ABOVE *The Bristol 'Large' design to F.11/37 (8.37).* The late Jim Oughton

of construction to be employed would be generally similar to the Beaufort torpedo bomber, but incorporating any improvements thought necessary from experience.

Standard two-spar wing construction was used, with the pilot seated between the spars; to maintain the chief requirement of a clean upper hemisphere for gunfire, the engines were mounted in nacelles fitted flush with the top of the wing surface. Dependent on the type of engine fitted, engine cooling was obtained by either ducted or bottom-gilled cooling passages that exhausted below the wing surface. The low wing position enabled the guns to have a clear field of fire

ABOVE A model of the 'Small' Bristol F.11/37.

horizontally forward over the airscrews and afforded the pilot an excellent view for formation flying. The roof of the pilot's compartment was protected from gun blast by reinforced panels and just aft of the turret a cell in the floor was arranged to carry the 250lb (113kg) small bomb container on a universal rack; hydraulically operated doors opened this compartment for the bombs to be released. Both aircraft carried fuel in two wing tanks, the 'Small' design having 245 gallons (1,114 litres) in total and the 'Large' 315 gallons (1,432 litres).

The data for the 'Small' machine included a maximum rate of climb, at 5,000ft (1,524m), of 3,620ft/min (1,103m/min), which at 15,000ft (4,572m) dropped to 2,900ft/min (884m/min), time to 15,000ft was 4.6 minutes and to 30,000ft (9,144m) 12.0 minutes, service ceiling was 40,000ft (12,192m) and absolute ceiling 41,000ft (12,497m). The equivalent figures for the 'Large' version were 3,590ft/min (1,094m/min) (maximum rate of climb actually at sea level), 2,500ft/min (762m/min), 4.7 and 13.7 minutes, 41,500ft (12,649m) and 42,500ft (12,954m). The 'Small' version had a propeller 11ft 6in (3.51m) in diameter, while the 'Large' was 13ft 0in (3.96m).

Gloster F.11/37

This project followed the basic design of the Gloster F.9/37 in its original form as a two-seat fighter (see Chapter 3) but with more powerful engines. It was a cantilever mid-wing aircraft with outboard engines and retractable undercarriage, and the tail had twin rudders and fins; the pilot was seated ahead of the mainplane. A fully retractable turret, located immediately aft of the rear main spar, housed four 20mm Hispano cannon or, as an alternative, two 23mm Madson automatic guns. Apart from the gunner's head fairing, this turret was flush with the fuselage when in the

Bristol F.11/37 'Small' (8.37)

Span:	59ft 0in (17.98m)
Length:	38ft 8in (11.79m)
Wing Area:	478sq.ft (44.45sq.m)
All-Up-Weight:	14,310lb (6,491kg)
Powerplant:	2 x Hercules HE.2.SM
Max Speed / Height:	320mph (515km/h) at ground level, 370mph (595km/h) at 15,000ft (4,572m)
Armament:	4 x 20mm cannon

Bristol F.11/37 'Large' (8.37)

Span:	65ft 0in (19.81m)
Length:	42ft 3in (12.88m)
Wing Area:	590sq.ft (54.87sq.m)
All-Up-Weight:	17,680lb (8,020kg)
Powerplant:	2 x 'Centaurus' 2,000hp (1,491kW)
Max Speed / Height:	335mph (539km/h) at ground level, 390mph (628km/h) at 15,000ft (4,572m)
Armament:	4 x 20mm cannon

Gloster F.11/37 (5.39)

Span:	63ft 0in (19.20m)
Length:	45ft 6in (13.87m)
Wing Area:	565sq.ft (52.55sq.m)
All-Up-Weight:	17,100lb (7,757kg)
Powerplant:	2 x Vulture
Max Speed / Height:	378mph (608km/h) at 15,000ft (4,572m)
Armament:	4 x 20mm cannon or 2 x 23mm cannon

RIGHT A model of the Boulton Paul P.92 as proposed. It is not in good condition and has lost its cockpit canopy, but it does show the layout well. *Les Whitehouse, Boulton Paul Archive*

'down' position. A total of 280 gallons (1,273 litres) of petrol was carried and alternative powerplants were two Rolls-Royce Vultures, Armstrong Siddeley Deerhounds or Bristol Hercules; the Vulture offered an estimated 8.7 minutes to 25,000ft (7,620m).

During 1937 Gloster also proposed a sister F.11/37 bomber with Hercules HE.6.SM engines and the same centre wing, centre sections and engine installations. Nine 250lb (113kg) or six 500lb (227kg) bombs, or a single 2,000lb (907kg) torpedo, could be carried, the span was 60ft (18.29m) and for a gross weight of 20,530lb (9,312kg) the aircraft was expected to achieve 353mph (568km/h) at 15,000ft (4,572m).

Hawker F.11/37

No drawings or data are known to have survived for this twin-engined two-seat turret fighter tendered to F.11/37 in mid-1937.

The Boulton Paul P.92 was selected as the winning design and a contract for two prototypes, L9629 and L9632, was placed on 2 March 1938, one to have 1,760hp (1,312kW) Vulture IIs and the other 2,055hp (1,532kW) Napier Sabre I engines. The mock-up was examined on 31 May and their construction began in 1939. To ensure that it was a satisfactory aeroplane it was considered essential that the first should be tested without reference to the turret operation, while both prototypes would also be used to develop the engine installation. On 16 November 1938 it was recommended that an additional Vulture installation should be ordered and that both prototypes should now be completed with the Rolls engine, while a third would be ordered for the Sabre (serial V9258). At this stage Boulton Paul expected L9629 to be completed in January 1940 and L9632 about four months later, but some delays were expected due to the concentration of the company's drawing office staff on the Defiant.

On 7 January 1939 it was revealed that the first machine was now unlikely to be ready for flight test until March 1940 because the centre section turret housing involved some difficult aerodynamic problems with inevitable air leakage around the periphery of the dome and through the gun apertures. These problems were expected to be overcome, but to obtain additional aerodynamic data and help with the problem a 2/7th scale wind tunnel model was tested by RAE. This showed that, with the guns elevated to 45° and turned to 135°, drag was increased by as much as 35%. Therefore a piloted scale model prototype, labelled P.92/2 and serialled V3142, was also ordered to further examine the type's drag and aerodynamic qualities. This all-wood aircraft was built by Heston Aircraft as the J.A.8 (Boulton Paul was too busy with the Defiant to be able to build this machine as well) and it was powered by two 130hp (97kW) de Havilland Gipsy Major II engines. It had a span of 33ft 1½in (10.10m) and a length of 27ft 6in (8.38m), and the turret was represented by a wooden hump; there were no dummy guns.

LEFT The scale model Boulton Paul P.92-2 V3142 photographed on 14 August 1943.

BELOW A view of the P.92/2 on the ground.

Gross weight was 2,778lb (1,260kg) and the aircraft achieved a maximum speed of 152mph (245km/h).

A Ministry memo dated 5 March 1940 states that Boulton Paul 'was energetically pursuing the building of three prototypes', but the P.92 was then cancelled on 26 May (published sources state that at this point the prototype's structures were only about 5% complete). The reasons for the suspension were the German advance and the need to standardise on the types of aircraft being produced, but a decision was made to continue with the P.92/2. That aircraft made its first flight in the spring of 1941 and continued to fly for an extended period but was scrapped before the end of the war. When F.11/37 was suspended, its turret development was also connected to the B.1/39 heavy bomber programme.

It is thought that the Sabre-engined P.92 prototype, having an internal exhaust pipe in its cowling, was to have been armed with the four-gun turret together with another cannon or a machine gun in each wing, firing as a moteur cannon through the centreline of the Sabre and its spinner. Also, 'as built' the P.92 differed considerably from the original proposal, in particular with an increased upwards angle to the rear fuselage, the outboard wings showed more sweep, and the fin had a straight leading edge. No original three-view drawing apparently survives to show how the prototypes 'as built' would have appeared.

Specification F.18/40

Chapter 3 made brief reference to the development and use of the Bristol Beaufighter and de Havilland Mosquito for night fighter operations. By the time these impressive machines made their debuts there had been another design competition for a night fighter. On 10 July 1940 Sholto Douglas (DCAS) wrote that 'the problem of the night fighter is still far from being solved. The Blenheim is too slow and the pilot's view is bad. The [fixed-gun] Beaufighter may possibly provide the solution but at present it is a not very promising night fighter.' At the time Air Marshal Joubert and others felt that proper night fighter armament should be a fixed forward 20mm cannon for stern attack and a 0.303in (7.7mm) Browning turret for attack from below with the target silhouetted against the sky. The Douglas Havoc was also being developed for night fighting, but this aircraft was slow and looked upon as no more than a stopgap. Sholto Douglas suggested that they should put out an Air Staff requirement for an aeroplane specifically designed as a night fighter – it would have to be a two-seater and carry air-interception (AI) radar.

When the Luftwaffe's night bombing Blitz began in the autumn of 1940 the need for a new night fighter became ever more important and one result was the confirmation of Specification F.18/40, dated 31 October 1940, which called for a fixed-gun (six-cannon) two-seat night fighter, which must be produced very quickly. Single- or twin-engined types would be considered, but performance was paramount with a top speed of at least 380mph (611km/h) at 20,000ft (6,096m). On 9 December the armament was amended to include a dorsal power-operated turret.

The discussions preceding this document were considerable since night fighting was essentially a new art, particularly with the need to carry AI radar. On 2 October 1940 Squadron

Leader Leatheart of Air Tactics explained some of the problems to the Deputy Director of Operational Requirements. He maintained that unless there was a quarter moon or more the pilot of a night flying aeroplane spent his entire time concentrating on his instruments and could not do any searching. 'For all of the good he is doing he might just as well be in the Officers Mess having a nice beer.' Leatheart suggested the fitting of an automatic pilot, but clearly there was much to learn. Nevertheless, in November invitations to tender to F.18/40 were sent to Hawker, Gloster, Supermarine and Westland, and requests for permission to tender were received from Boulton Paul and Fairey.

Boulton Paul P.96

A single-engine design similar to and scaled up from the Defiant, this used many components that were identical to the Defiant and there were five versions. The first three all had a Napier Sabre engine – P.96A had no turret but six forward-firing 20mm in the wings and a long canopy to cover the AI radar operator, B had a standard Defiant turret and two wing-mounted 20mm cannon, and C had the turret and a slightly larger wing with four 20mm guns; in B and C the

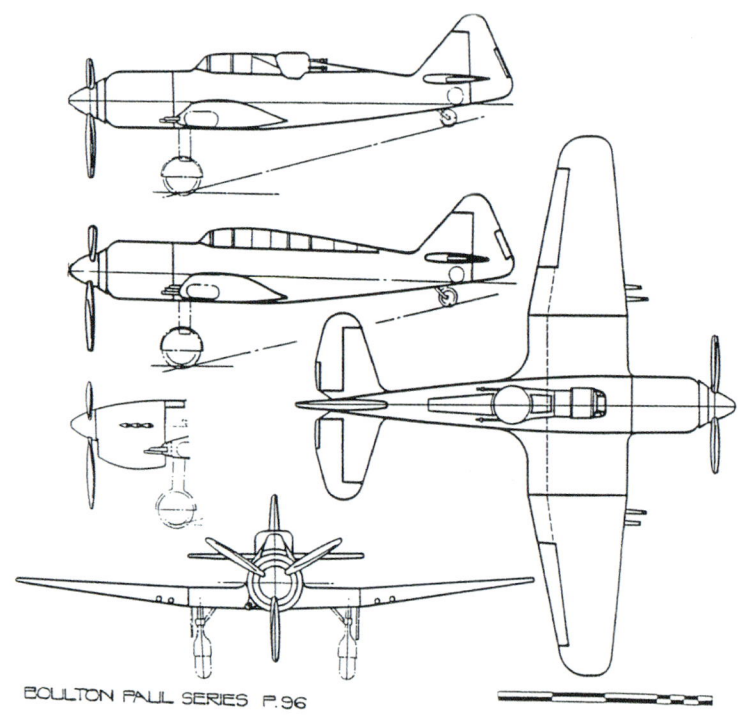

BELOW The Boulton Paul P.96 (both Sabre and Centaurus engine) with and without turret (c11.40). *Les Whitehouse, Boulton Paul Archive*

BOTTOM A model of the P.96B. *Alec Brew*

Boulton Paul P.96A (c11.40)	
Span:	44ft 0in (13.41m)
Length:	38ft 0in (11.58m)
Wing Area:	325sq.ft (30.225sq.m)
All-Up-Weight:	12,660lb (5,743kg)
Powerplant:	1 x Sabre NS.6.SM 2,300hp (1,715kW)
Max Speed / Height:	410mph (660km/h) at 34,000ft (10,363m)
Armament:	6 x 20mm cannon

Boulton Paul P.96C (c11.40)	
Span:	46ft 0in (14.02m)
Length:	38ft 0in (11.58m)
Wing Area:	340sq.ft (31.62sq.m)
All-Up-Weight:	12,680lb (5,752kg)
Powerplant:	1 x Sabre NS.6.SM 2,300hp (1,715kW)
Max Speed / Height:	400mph (644km/h) at 34,000ft (10,363m)
Armament:	4 x 20mm cannon, 4 x 0.303in (7.7mm) machine guns

Boulton Paul P.96D (c11.40)	
Span:	46ft 0in (14.02m)
Length:	38ft 0in (11.58m)
Wing Area:	340sq.ft (31.62sq.m)
All-Up-Weight:	12,306lb (5,582kg)
Powerplant:	1 x Centaurus CE.4.SM 2,300hp (1,715kW)
Max Speed / Height:	400mph (644km/h) at 22,500ft (6,858m)
Armament:	4 x 20mm cannon, 4 x 0.303in (7.7mm) machine guns

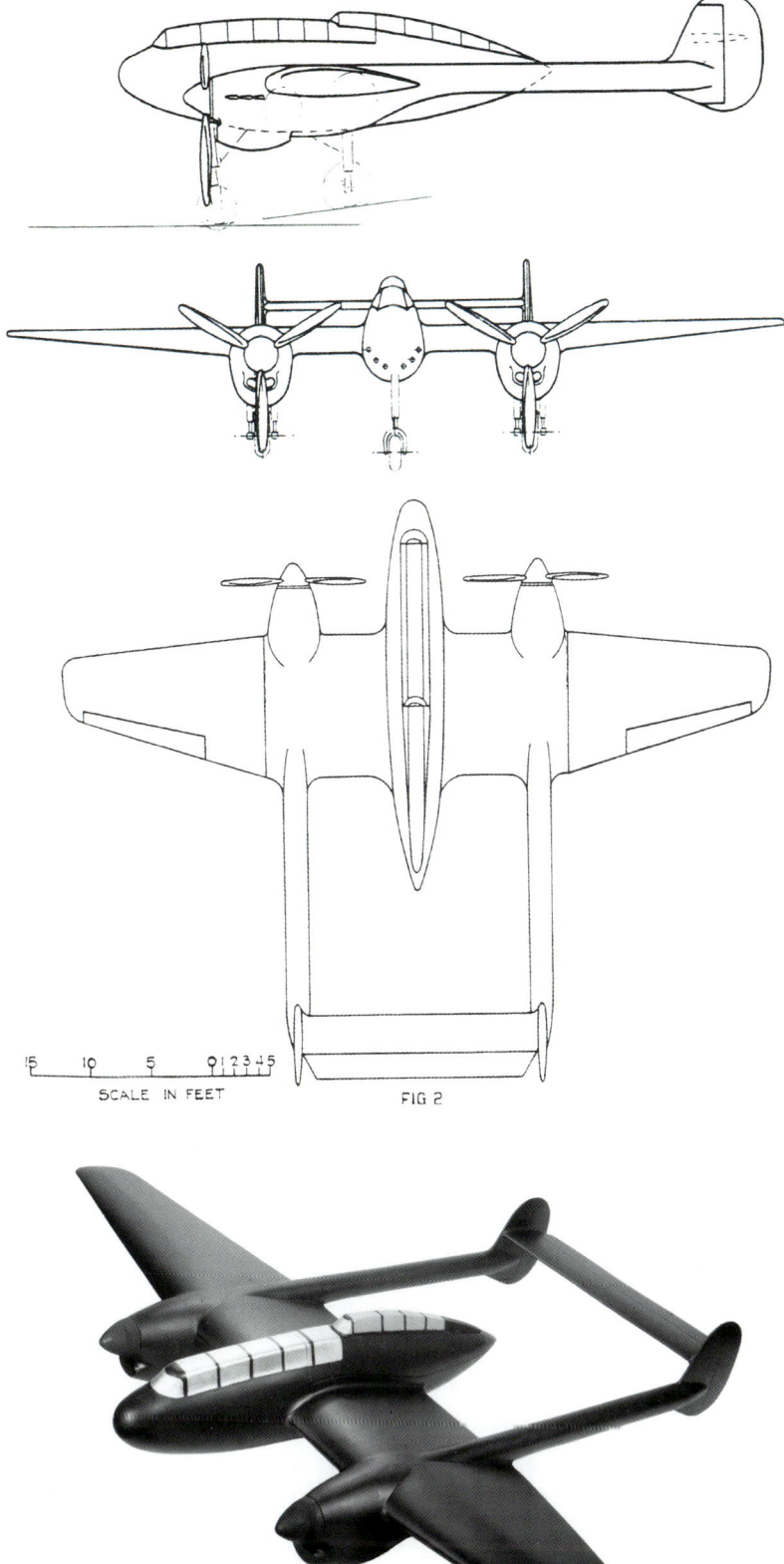

LEFT The Boulton Paul P.97A had no turret (c11.40). *Les Whitehouse, Boulton Paul Archive*

BOTTOM A model of the P.97A. *Alec Brew*

pilot operated the radar. The other pair (oddly the brochure called both types P.96D) kept the larger wing but used a Bristol Centaurus, the first with no turret and six cannon, the second with a turret and four wing cannon. All of them had two crew and, apart from P.96A, at 32,200ft (9,815m), offered a ceiling of 35,000ft (10,668m) or slightly more. The P.96 represented Boulton Paul's main tender to F.18/40.

Boulton Paul P.97

This twin-Sabre type had a short central fuselage and two tail booms, and came in two versions, with and without a turret. P.97A had six 20mm cannon mounted in a fuselage weapon bay while the P.97B had the turret and two nose cannon. The design allowed some of the fixed guns to be removed and replaced by two 550lb (249kg) bombs to provide an alternative use for the aeroplane. Engines of lower power than the NS.6.SM (which had

Boulton Paul P.97A (c11.40)

Span:	58ft 6in (17.83m)
Length:	45ft 6in (13.87m)
Wing Area:	525sq.ft (48.825sq.m)
All-Up-Weight:	19,586lb (8,884kg)
Powerplant:	2 x Sabre NS.6.SM 2,300hp (1,715kW)
Max Speed / Height:	425mph (684km/h) at 34,000ft (10,363m)
Armament:	6 x 20mm cannon

Boulton Paul P.97B (c11.40)

Span:	58ft 6in (17.83m)
Length:	45ft 6in (13.87m)
Wing Area:	525sq.ft (48.825sq.m)
All-Up-Weight:	19,232 (8,724)
Powerplant:	2 x Sabre NS.6.SM 2,300hp (1,715kW)
Max Speed / Height:	418mph (673km/h) at 34,000ft (10,363m)
Armament:	2 x 20mm cannon, 4 x 0.303in (7.7mm) machine guns in turret

RIGHT Boulton Paul's P.97B was to be fitted with a turret (c11.40). *Les Whitehouse, Boulton Paul Archive*

BOTTOM A model of the P.97B. *Alec Brew*

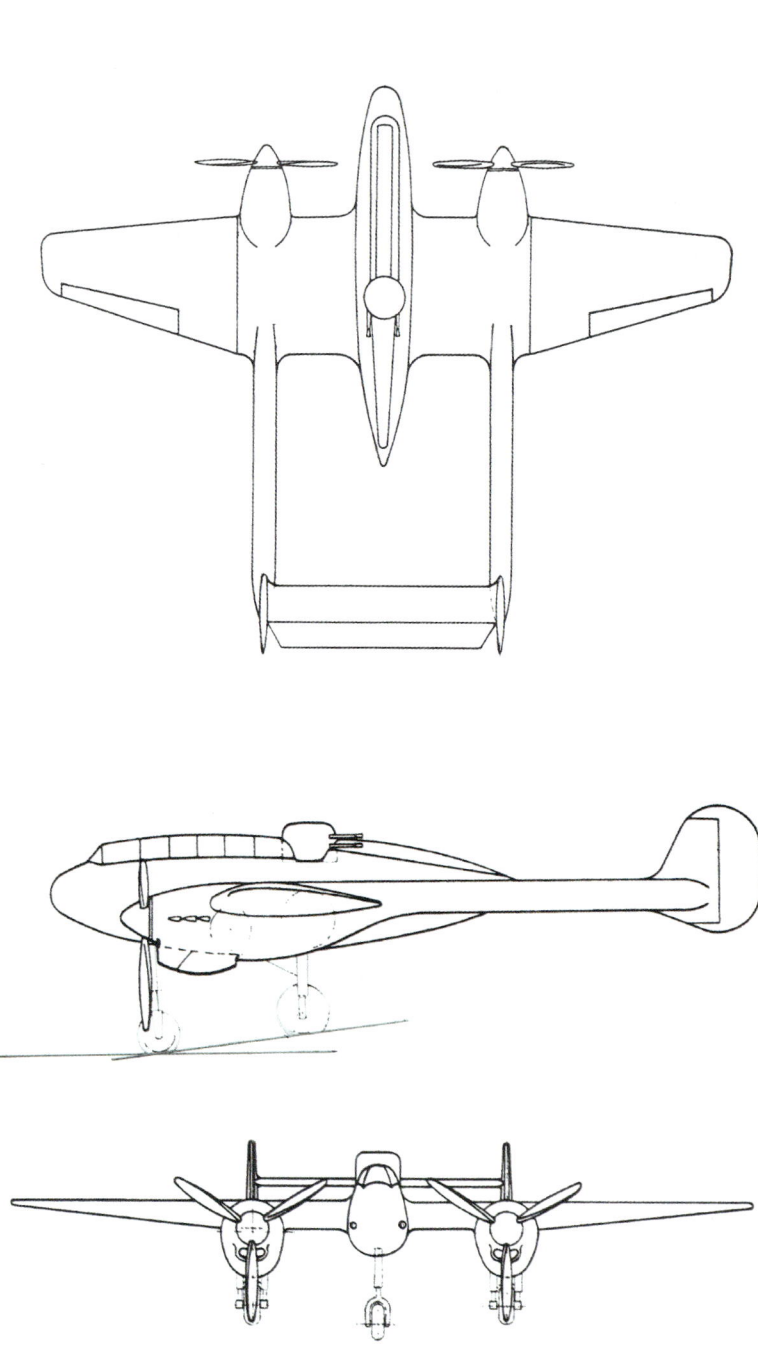

a three-speed supercharger) had not been considered because of the need to keep the performance competitive with enemy aircraft. Rate of climb at sea level was estimated to be 3,520ft/min (1,073m/min) for the P.97A and 3,560ft/min (1,085m/min) for the B, time to 20,000ft (6,096m) 6.7 and 6.6 minutes respectively, and service ceiling (for both) 39,500ft (12,040m). Internal fuel totalled 520 gallons (2,364 litres).

Fairey F.18/40

This two-seat Griffon-engined scheme was based on the Fleet Air Arm's Firefly (see Chapter 6) with very little alteration except to the equipment; there was no turret. Fairey stressed the difficulty of introducing a completely new design under the present conditions and considered that it would be impracticable to accommodate both fixed cannon and an interchangeable four-gun turret, as well as the AI operator, in a single-engined aircraft. It therefore offered a direct derivation from the N.5/40 Firefly in which that design was maintained except for the addition of two extra cannon, the necessary strengthening of the undercarriage, wing and body, and the elimination of naval features such as wing-folding, catapult and arrester gear. The estimated ceiling was 30,500ft (9,296m).

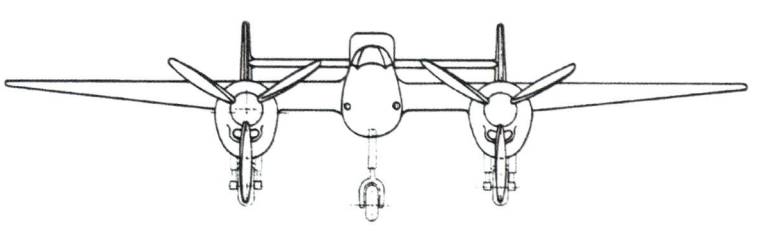

Fairey F.18/40 (late 1940)	
Span:	c44ft 6in (13.56m)
Length:	c37ft 7in (11.46m)
Wing Area:	?
All-Up-Weight:	?
Powerplant:	1 x Griffon
Max Speed / Height:	370mph (595km/h) at 23,000ft (7,010m)
Armament:	6 x 20mm cannon

CHAPTER FIVE　　　　　　　　　　　　　　　　　　　　　　　　　　TURRET FIGHTERS AND NIGHT FIGHTERS

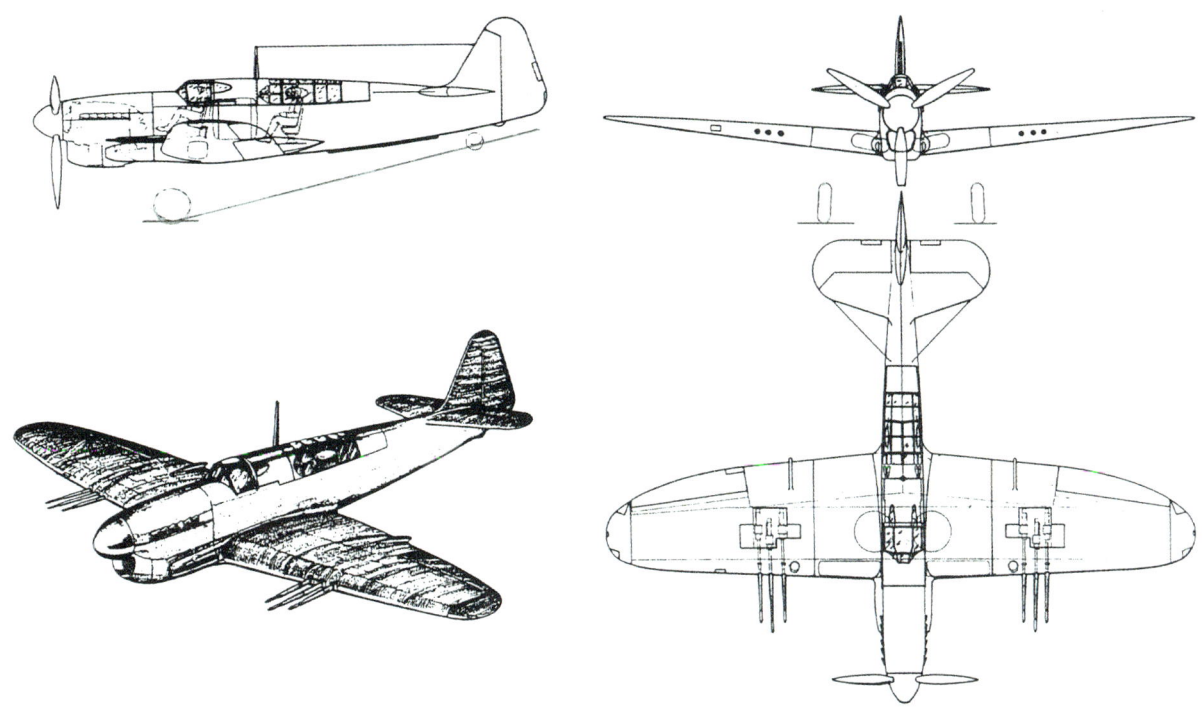

ABOVE The Fairey F.18/40 (late 1940). *Bill Harrison*

BELOW The night fighter version of the Gloster Reaper (mid-1940). *Jet Age Museum*

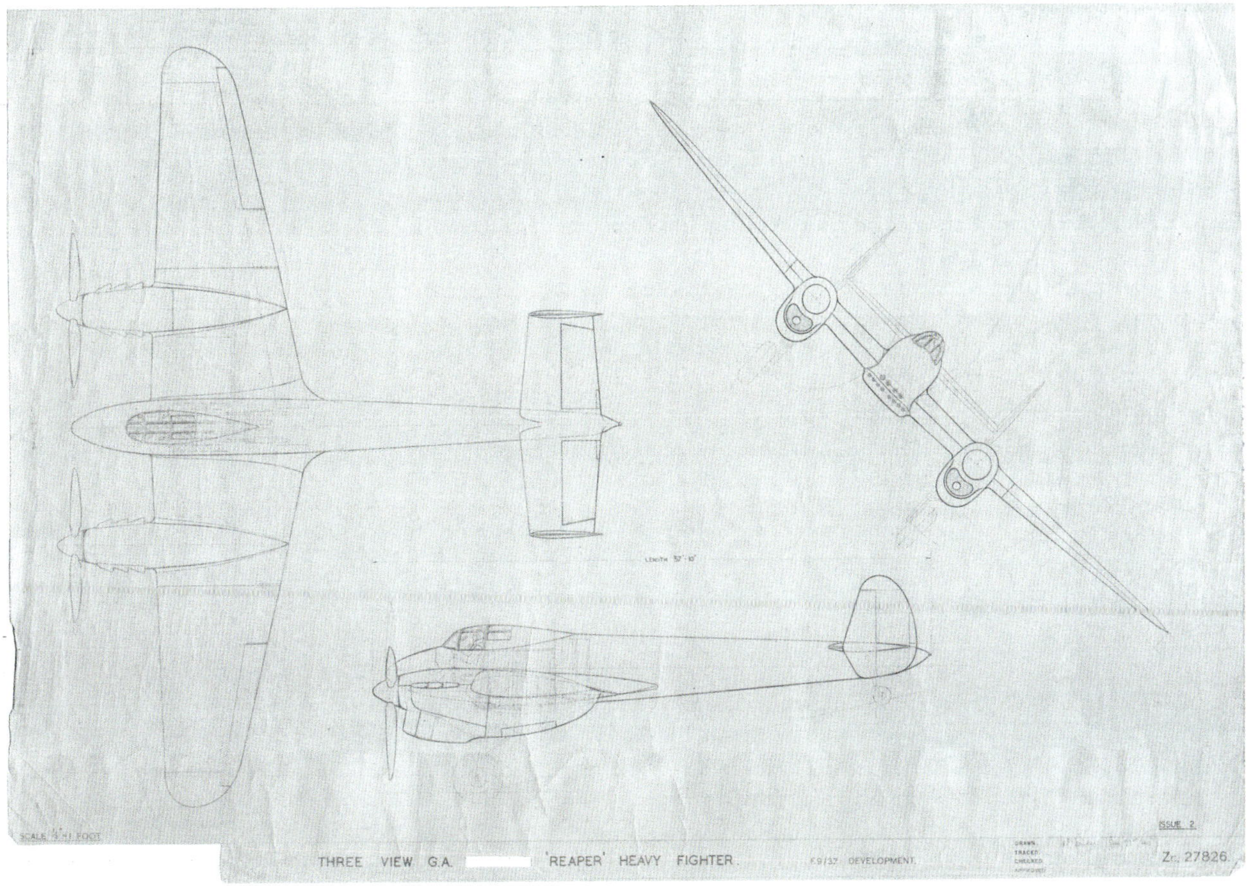

101

ABOVE The mock-up of the Gloster Reaper. *Jet Age Museum*

Gloster F.9/37 Development (Reaper)

This further development of the F.9/37 fighter (see Chapter 3) had twin Merlin XX engines replacing the Taurus, which substantially increased the type's range, endurance and military load. At an all-up weight of 14,500lb (6,577kg), the designers felt that an effective limit of development had been reached, and to meet F.18/40 in full would need a weight in excess of 15,000lb (6,804kg) with another 60sq ft (5.58sq m) of wing area; however, all of the operational requirements for a night fighter had been met here except that four cannon were carried instead of six (beneath the cockpit). Time to 10,000ft (3,048m) and 25,000ft (7,620m) was estimated to be 3.8 and 11.4 minutes respectively, and the ceiling 35,500ft (10,820m). Although drawn well before the Specification was prepared, Gloster's modified F.9/37 was accepted as the company's tender to F.18/40, but because it did not meet all of the requirements a special specification, F.29/40, was eventually drawn up to cover it.

Gloster F.18/40 Reaper (23.7.40)	
Span:	50ft 0in (15.24m)
Length:	37ft 10in (11.53m)
Wing Area:	386sq.ft (35.90sq.m)
All-Up-Weight:	14,500lb (6,577kg)
Powerplant:	2 x Merlin XX
Max Speed / Height:	390mph (628km/h) at 22,500ft (6,858m)
Armament:	4 x 20mm cannon

Hawker P.1008

This night fighter design to F.18/40 is another Hawker design for which no information has been found. In fact, Hawker did not tender officially to F.18/40 (neither did Supermarine or Westland).

Two other designs were prepared to F.18/40 but were apparently not tendered. One was the Miles M.22A, a development of that firm's M.22 project, and this has been covered in the separate section on Miles's fighter studies within Chapter 9. The second came from Vickers.

Vickers F.18/40

On 16 October 1940 a near identical version of the Vickers Type 420 to F.16/40 (see Chapter 4) was proposed to the draft F.18/40, except for a switch to Merlin XX engines. In January 1941 a new Merlin XX F.18/40 was proposed as a three-seat night fighter with two fixed 20mm Hispanos together with four 0.303 (7.7mm) Browning machine guns in a power-operated turret located in a fairing on top of the amidships fuselage. This would be controlled remotely by a gunner seated alongside the pilot and the turret guns could be elevated up to 45° and turned 60° to either side, subject to some restrictions from the airscrews; the 20mm guns were located in the bottom fuselage.

Vickers F.18/40 (1.41)	
Span:	54ft 0in (16.46m)
Length:	43ft 10in (13.36m)
Wing Area:	403sq.ft (37.48sq.m)
All-Up-Weight:	15,585lb (7,069kg)
Powerplant:	2 x Merlin XX 1,270hp (947kW)
Max Speed / Height:	409mph (658km/h) at 24,000ft (7,315m)
Armament:	2 x 20mm cannon, 4 x 0.303in (7.7mm) machine guns

F.18/40 actually raised two separate lines of research, the Gloster F.9/37 development and the alternative studies to F.18/40. Gloster's design was unofficially christened the Reaper. This project had started in around June 1940, prior to F.18/40 being

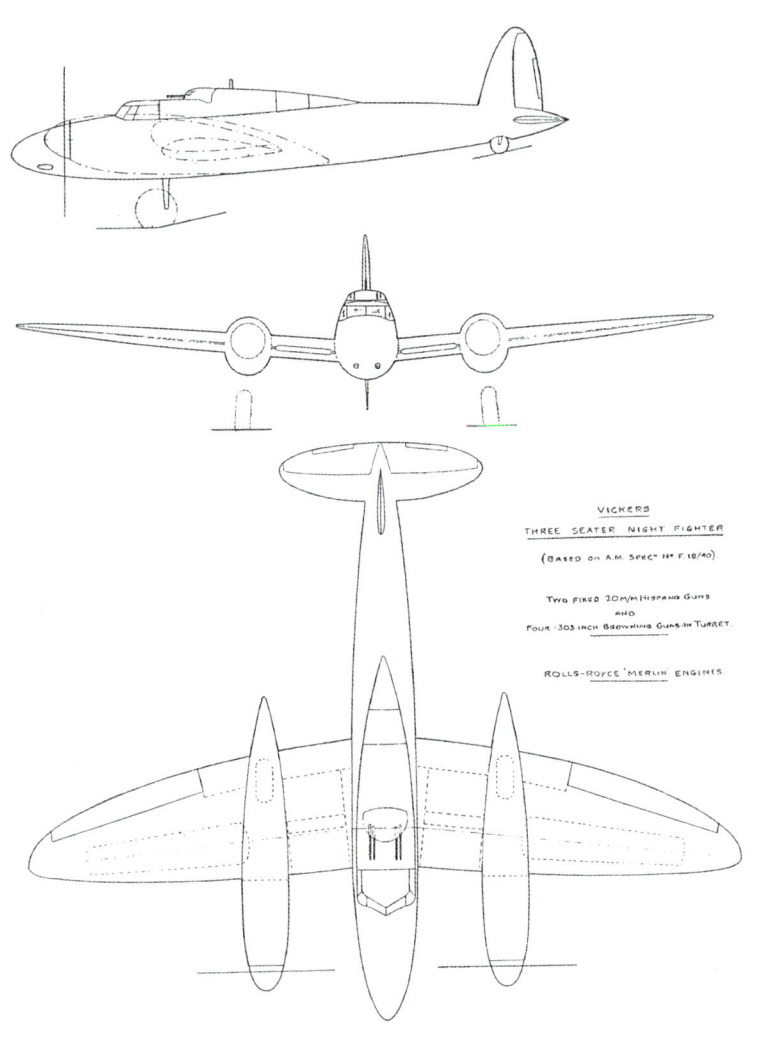

ABOVE **The Vickers F.18/40 (1.41).** *The late Eric Morgan*

formulated, and fitting Merlin XXs in the airframe was seen to be a relatively small job. The two-seat night fighter was proposed to W. S. Farren, DTD, on 8 July and, with Merlin XXs and a strengthened airframe, was looked upon as a particularly attractive idea that would nearly meet the Air Staff's requirements. On 23 September Sir Henry Tizard, AMDP, noted that the F.9/37 had shown very good handling and flying characteristics and he felt that any night fighter proposals from other manufacturers were unlikely to be appreciably superior to it. On 13 October 1940 the go-ahead was given to convert one of the F.9/37s to F.18/40 and a cockpit mock-up was examined on 26 October.

However, by December it was apparent that it would not be possible to get a reasonable number of F.9/37s, or F.18/40 Reapers, until the end of 1942; Air Marshal Joubert felt that it would be out of date by the time it came into production, while Mr Hennessy wrote that it was not sufficiently promising as a production job to be worth the effort of development. On 1 December the Secretary of State for Air requested that the Reaper should proceed because production facilities, capacity and materials would have to be allocated within the next few months.

A Ministry of Aircraft Production (MAP) meeting, including Tizard, Farren and DGRD, was held on 18 December 1940 to discuss the Reaper. The Air Staff wanted the aircraft because it was considered to be better than the Beaufighter, but MAP preferred Gloster to go easy on the Reaper and concentrate on its jet fighter (see Chapter 10). This meant that the Beaufighter would have to be developed as an insurance against the failure of the Whittle jet because de Havilland had stated that fitting the Mosquito with a turret would mean a radical redesign of that aircraft. Bristol had also declared that installing a turret in the Beaufighter would present difficulties and that its speed would be appreciably reduced. The meeting agreed to recommend to the Air Staff that the Reaper should immediately go on to a lower priority, but that it should not be suspended entirely.

Gloster's chief designer, George Carter, felt that the Reaper would not be in production within eighteen months and stated that he did not have enough design staff to undertake both it and the jet project. Twelve days later Geoffrey de Havilland was asked if a night fighter version of the Mosquito could be produced quickly to the latest requirements. Tizard felt that this would allow Gloster to stop work on the Reaper because he was anxious to see that company concentrate on its heavy commitments for Whittle-engined jet fighters, although he thought the Reaper with Merlin XXs was the best night fighting aircraft that could be expected and, had Gloster not been so involved with the jet, he would have recommended that it should continue. On 1 May 1941 both MAP and the Air Staff finally agreed that the Gloster Reaper should not proceed further and that de Havilland's Mosquito would be considered to fill the night fighter requirement.

Turning to the other F.18/40 designs, on 24 March 1941 Capt R. N. Liptrot completed an appraisal and estimated that the P.96 would be at least 1,000lb (454kg) heavier than Boulton Paul had claimed, but its performance estimates were reasonable; he also felt that the P.97 had no merits for a night fighter and introduced severe structural problems. The Fairey project did not conform to the new requirements of F.18/40 (that is, no turret) but substantially satisfied the document in its original form. However, its speed and ceiling were both low and, in spite of the ease of production, the type was unacceptable. In conclusion he felt that none of the submitted designs were considered to be really acceptable, although the P.96 was a not unreasonable interpretation of the specification as issued, and suggested that the Air Staff should reconsider the present requirements. N. E. Rowe agreed and added, 'I think it is true to say that we know very much more about night fighting requirements now than we did when F.18/40 was drafted.'

On the 28th Farren added that Fairey's project did not attempt to meet the turret requirement and, although its take-off and landing were reasonable, its speed and ceiling were indeed not up to specification (the engine power was inadequate for the load). Boulton Paul's P.96 gave a good performance with the high-altitude Sabre NS.6.SM, but the landing run was too long. The P.97 gave a higher performance, but there seemed to be little advantage in the twin-boom arrangement. Farren confirmed that none of these proposals was suitable to meet the requirements that were now emerging and maturing from operational experience.

Both Boulton Paul and Fairey were told by Farren on 11 April that no aircraft was to be ordered to F.18/40. The requirements were continuously under review and a new specification was being considered in terms of night fighter technique and the possible

ABOVE Bristol Beaufighter R2274 seen during testing at Boscombe Down in May 1941 after being fitted with a dorsal turret.

adoption of existing types. In due course the need for a night fighter was met by the Bristol Beaufighter and the de Havilland Mosquito, both of which had fixed guns, while the key to night fighting was to be the carriage of air interception (AI) radar, not turrets. Nevertheless, two Merlin Mk.II Beaufighters, R2274 and R2306, were earmarked to be fitted with a Boulton Paul dorsal turret with four 0.303in (7.7mm) guns, but the conversion took time and by 28 January 1941 only the aperture had been cut into the skin of the first example; work was expected to be completed in mid-April, with the type in production by August. The Beaufighter Mk.V R2274 was tested briefly at A&AEE around the early summer of 1941 and the turret was found to operate satisfactorily even in dives up to 390mph (628km/h). The aircraft weighed 18,695lb (8,480kg) and, with the turret facing aft, gave a top speed of 302mph (486km/h) at 19,300ft (5,883m), but the adaptation was not adopted for production.

Conclusion

Unlike other piston-engine fighters, which saw development right through to the jet age, the programmes for turret-armed fighters came to an end pretty quickly, once it was realised that the concept of such a type was in general flawed. Boulton Paul's Defiant would be the only British turret-armed fighter aircraft to enter service in the Second World War. For night fighter duties the real solution was to have fixed forward-firing guns coupled with a fully operational AI radar, and in an airframe type possessing good performance. As such versions of the Beaufighter, then the Mosquito, types already under development, eventually filled the RAF's night fighter requirements perfectly.

Chapter Six
Naval Fighters Part One

ABOVE Blackburn Firebrand prototype DD804 was caught on camera on 2 May 1942. *Phil Butler*

This and the next chapter essentially cover two categories of aircraft, pure fighters and a type that was termed 'strike fighter'. Some naval fighters were modified versions of RAF types, and the development of the Hawker Sea Fury to N.22/43, the Supermarine Seafang to N.5/45, and Supermarine's Type 391 project have been described already in earlier chapters.

Fairey Fulmar

This fighter, based on Fairey's aircraft built to the P.4/34 light day bomber specification, was ordered to Specification O.8/38 as an interim two-seat front-gun FAA fighter. The prototype, N1854, first flew on 4 January 1940 and the type entered service the following June. Although built in comparatively small numbers

BELOW An unidentified Fairey Fulmar about to touch down aboard its carrier.

Fairey Fulmar Mk.I (flown)	
Span:	46ft 4.5in (14.13m)
Length:	40ft 3in (12.27m)
Wing Area:	342sq.ft (31.81sq.m)
All-Up-Weight:	9,800lb (4,445kg)
Powerplant:	1 x Merlin VIII 1,080hp (805kW)
Max Speed / Height:	280mph (451km/h)
Armament:	8 x 0.303in (7.7mm) machine guns

Blackburn B.33 (9.39)	
Span:	49ft 0in (14.94m)
Length:	39ft 8in (12.09m)
Wing Area:	356sq.ft (33.11sq.m)
All-Up-Weight:	10,080lb (4,572kg)
Powerplant:	1 x Hercules HE.6.SM
Max Speed / Height:	313mph (504km/h) at 15,000ft (4,572m)
Armament:	8 x 0.303in (7.7mm) machine guns or 4 x 20mm cannon

and suffering from a relatively low speed, it carried a heavy forward armament of eight machine guns and proved quite successful, serving through much of the war.

Specification N.8/39 and N.9/39 Blackburn Firebrand and Fairey Firefly

In 1938 work began on two new specifications for the Fleet Air Arm (FAA) – N.5/38 for a two-seat fighter and N.6/38 for a turret fighter. These were quickly updated to N.8/39 and N.9/39, both dated 21 June 1939. N.8/39 called for a top speed at 15,000ft (4,572m) of at least 275 knots (317mph/510km/h) and an interchangeable armament of eight forward-firing 0.303in (7.7mm) Browning machine guns or four 20mm cannon; N.9/39's requirements were identical apart from having four Brownings in a turret. On 10 August the two documents were issued to tender to seven companies, and five had replied by 19 September.

Blackburn B.33

Powered by a single Bristol Hercules, the Blackburn project's mainplanes and tailplane were formed from light alloy tube and plate construction with fabric-covered control surfaces, while the fuselage used Alclad monocoque. The layout had a symmetrical inboard wing section that was then cambered towards the tips and employed 35% slotted flaps and a fixed undercarriage (which could be jettisoned when alighting on the sea). Fuel capacity was 190 gallons (864 litres) and service ceiling 33,800ft (10,302m). Blackburn quoted eighteen months to complete three aeroplanes, with the first prototype to be supplied in twelve months.

Fairey N.8/39

Fairey's design was offered with four alternative engines – the Rolls-Royce Boreas (=Exe) or Griffon, the Bristol Taurus, or Fairey's own 'Queen' power unit – the respective fuel capacities being 145 gallons (659 litres), 192 (873), 143 (650) and 159 (723). The wing and tail were to be built of conventional light

BELOW The Fairey N.8/39 with four fixed forward-firing cannon and alternative engine choices (8.39).

BOTTOM For comparison, the Fairey N.9/39 with turret armament.

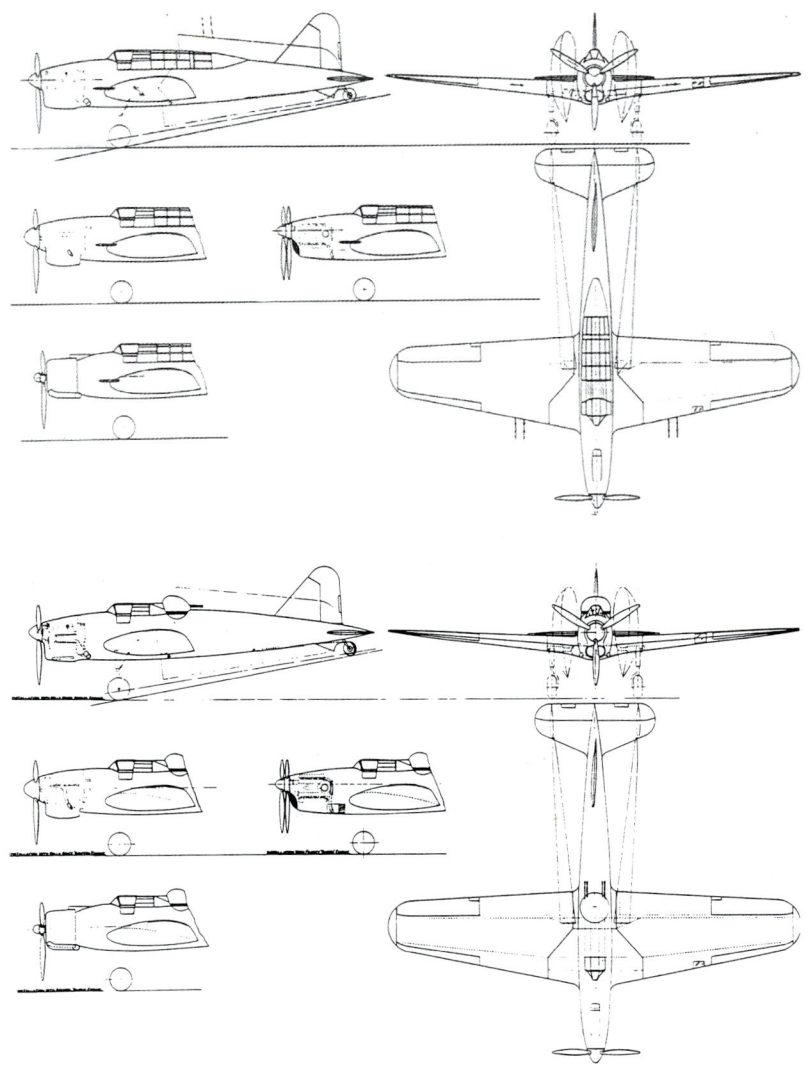

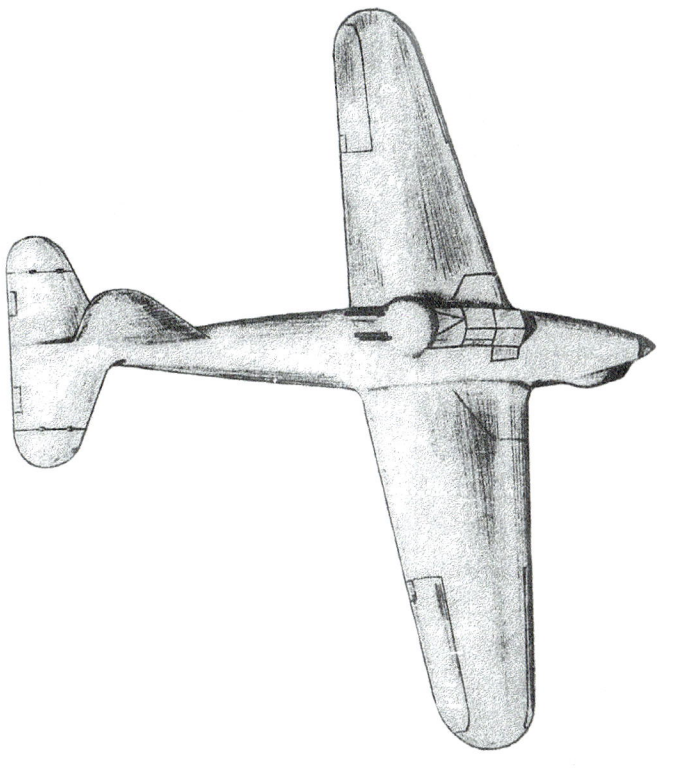

ABOVE An artist's impression of the Fairey N.9/39. *RAF Museum*

alloy, except for the wing centre section rear spar, which used tubular steel, and they had fabric-covered control surfaces. Wingtip slots were fitted, the flaps were hydraulically operated, and the guns were mounted in the wings. Fairey noted that an extremely limited folded width had been achieved by reducing the width of the centre section to an absolute minimum. As a result the length of the folding wing portion was considerable and it had been necessary to place the tailplane at the extreme aftermost limit possible within the required overall dimensions. In addition, the fin and rudder had been arranged forward of the tailplane and the resulting arrangement was excellent from an anti-spinning point of view. The rear fuselage was monocoque and both front and rear ends used tubular construction. The Griffon gave a service ceiling of 31,600ft (9,632m) and the first aircraft would need eighteen months for delivery, with the second and third following at two-month intervals.

Gloster N.8/39

Gloster's engine choice was the Hercules HE.6.SM or Napier E.112 with respective fuel capacities of 210 gallons (955 litres) and 200 gallons (909 litres). Again a conventional light alloy stressed-skin wing and tail structure was employed with fabric covering on the control surfaces, but the fuselage was fabric-covered tubular steel and duralumin. Wingtip slots, Handley Page slotted flaps and a retractable undercarriage were fitted, although the main wheels did not retract completely. Service ceiling with the Hercules was 33,000ft (10,058m). The first two machines would take eighteen months and the third another three.

Hawker N.8/39

Sydney Camm offered just the one engine choice, a Napier E.112, but no performance figures were given, although 200 gallons (909 litres) of fuel would be carried. The front fuselage used tubular construction, the centre and rear monocoque, and the wing had a D spar as far as the outer guns, then became a two-spar type. Extrusions and Alclad were used

Fairey N.8/39 (8.39)

Span:	48ft 0in (14.63m)
Length:	39ft 3in (11.96m)
Wing Area:	340sq.ft (31.62sq.m)
All-Up-Weight:	9,422lb (4,274kg), 10,627lb (4,820kg), 9,827lb (4,450kg) or 9,207lb (4,176kg)
Powerplant:	1 x RR Boreas, RR Griffon, Fairey Queen or Bristol Taurus
Max Speed / Height:	Griffon 319mph (513km/h) at 15,000ft (4,572m)
Armament:	8 x 0.303in (7.7mm) machine guns or 4 x 20mm cannon

Gloster N.8/39 1st version (8.39)

Span:	50ft 0in (15.24m)
Length:	39ft 4in (11.99m)
Wing Area:	396sq.ft (36.83sq.m)
All-Up-Weight:	9,929lb (4,504kg)
Powerplant:	1 x Hercules HE.6.SM
Max Speed / Height:	330mph (531km/h) at 17,000ft (5,182m)
Armament:	8 x 0.303in (7.7mm) machine guns or 4 x 20mm cannon

Gloster N.8/39 2nd version (8.39)

Span:	47ft 6in (14.48m)
Length:	39ft 0in (11.89m)
Wing Area:	374sq.ft (34.78sq.m)
All-Up-Weight:	9,462lb (4,292kg)
Powerplant:	1 x Napier E.112
Max Speed / Height:	?
Armament:	8 x 0.303in (7.7mm) machine guns or 4 x 20mm cannon

Hawker N.8/39 (8.39)

Span:	50ft 0in (15.24m)
Length:	39ft 6in (12.04m)
Wing Area:	365sq.ft (33.95sq.m)
All-Up-Weight:	9,720lb (4,409kg)
Powerplant:	1 x E.112
Max Speed / Height:	?
Armament:	8 x 0.303in (7.7mm) machine guns or 4 x 20mm cannon

on the wing, the tail unit was made in stressed light alloy skin, and the ailerons, rudder and elevators were fabric-covered. The construction was described as orthodox and followed Hawker practice on the Hurricane and Tornado; the aircraft had wingtip slots, 25% slotted flaps and drooping ailerons. Hawker estimated that about twenty months would be needed to supply the first aeroplane.

Supermarine 333

Supermarine's Type 333 designation covered two alternative designs, both developed from the Spitfire and very similar but of different sizes. Each of them had liquid-cooled engines, the smaller a Merlin, the larger a Griffon, with twin radiators mounted in the centre section. The important differences came with their performance and their folded width (the larger was 13ft 6in [4.11m] when every other N.8/39 project was 11ft [3.35m]). The monocoque fuselage (a shell structure in light alloy Alclad sheet) and single-spar metal-covered wing followed the practice developed by Supermarine over a number of years, while the fuel tanks in the wing nose contributed to the structural strength and stiffness and saved a lot of weight.

The main difference between the Spitfire wing and the N.8/39 was that the elliptical planform had been discarded in favour of a form incorporating two straight tapers, which approximated very closely to the elliptical form and possessed almost identical aerodynamic properties. The big advantage of the straight taper was that double curvature was avoided and the covering would require no working. No fabric was used except on the control surfaces, and slotted flaps were provided over a large percentage of the span; the undercarriage followed Spitfire experience. The four cannon were mounted two per wing just outside the wing fold joint, the eight Brownings (four per wing) were placed outboard of the cannon

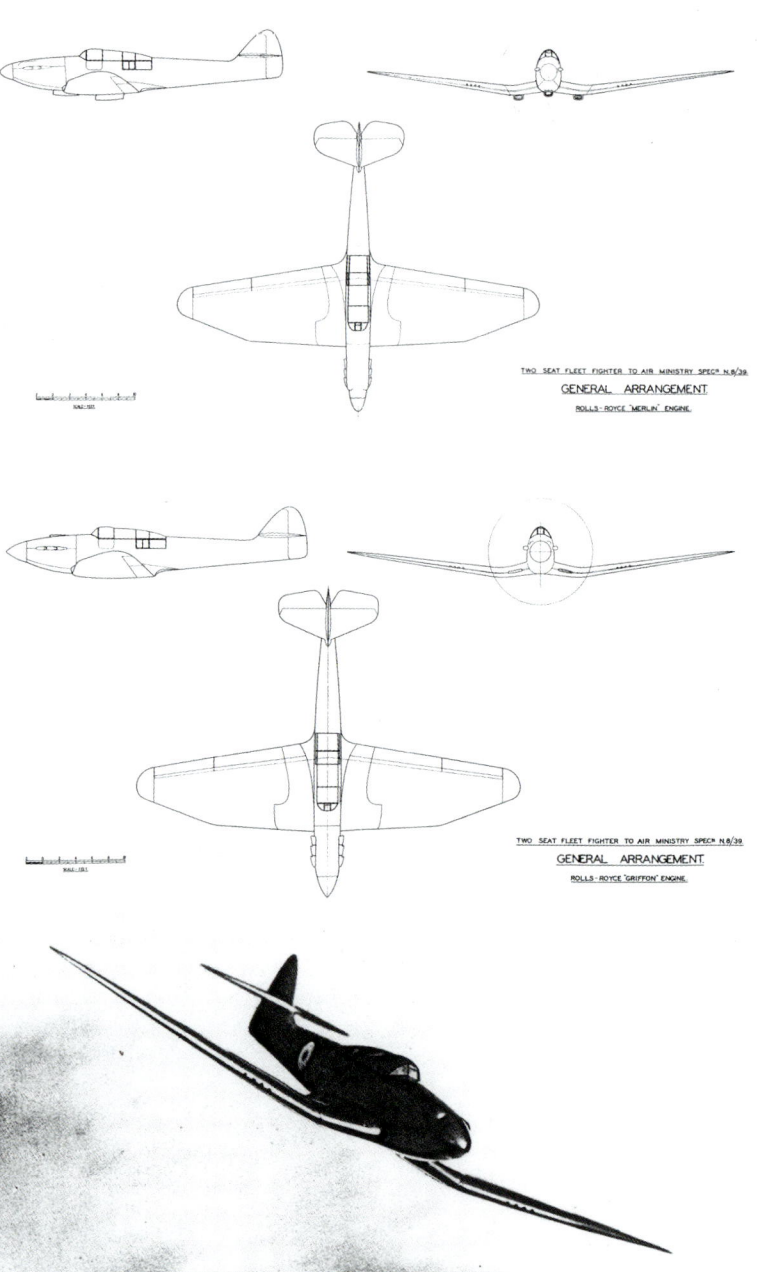

TOP The Supermarine Type 333 to N.8/39 with Merlin powerplant (6.9.39). *The late Eric Morgan*

MIDDLE The Supermarine Type 333 with Griffon powerplant (6.9.39). *The late Eric Morgan*

BOTTOM An artist's impression of the Supermarine 333. *The late Eric Morgan*

position. Service ceilings for the two types were 34,700ft (10,577m) (Merlin) and 36,900ft (11,247m) (Griffon), sea level rates of climb 2,650ft/min (808m/min) and 3,150ft/min (960m/min), times to 15,000ft (4,572m) 5.75 and 5.0 minutes, and internal fuel 320 gallons (1,455 litres) and 360 gallons (1,637 litres). The first aircraft would take eighteen months, the second and third following at six-week intervals.

Supermarine 333 'small' (6.9.39)	
Span:	44ft 0in (13.41m)
Length:	34ft 0in (10.36m)
Wing Area:	320sq.ft (29.76sq.m)
All-Up-Weight:	8,745lb (3,967kg)
Powerplant:	1 x Merlin RM.2.SM 1,205hp (899kW)
Max Speed / Height:	342mph (550km/h) at 18,750ft (5,715m)
Armament:	8 x 0.303in (7.7mm) machine guns or 4 x 20mm cannon

Supermarine 333 'large' (6.9.39)	
Span:	46ft 0in (14.02m)
Length:	36ft 0in (10.97m)
Wing Area:	360sq.ft (33.48sq.m)
All-Up-Weight:	9,630lb (4,368kg)
Powerplant:	1 x Griffon RG.1.SM 1,560hp (1,163kW)
Max Speed / Height:	375mph (603km/h) at 17,500ft (5,334m)
Armament:	8 x 0.303in (7.7mm) machine guns or 4 x 20mm cannon

In each case the sister N.9/39 projects were, from the aerodynamic and structural points of view, practically identical to their N.8/39 companions, but the wing guns had been taken out and a rear four-gun turret added; Supermarine did not tender.

Blackburn B.31

The main difference from the B.33 came in the centre and rear fuselage. The all-up weight was 9,973lb (4,524kg).

Fairey N.9/39

The only basic difference from the N.8/39 project came at the top of the fuselage in the area of the turret, and Fairey stated that a design that, up to a certain stage in manufacture, was common to both types was highly desirable; however, it was stressed that when completed it would not be possible to convert one type to the other. The Boreas gave an all-up weight of 9,500lb (4,309kg), a top speed of 259mph (417km/h) at 15,000ft (4,572m), time to 10,000ft (3,048m) 6.8 minutes, and service ceiling 27,000ft (8,230m). For the Griffon the figures were 10,650lb (4,831kg), 303mph (488km/h) at 15,000ft, 4.5 minutes, and 31,000ft (9,449m); for the Taurus 9,260lb (4,200kg), 281mph (452km/h) at 15,500ft (4,724m), 5.83 minutes, and 29,000ft (8,839m); and for the Queen 9,875lb (4,479kg), 276mph (444km/h) at 15,000ft, 7.5 minutes, and 27,500ft (8,382m).

Gloster N.9/39

Here the centre fuselage was altered to accommodate the turret, which reduced the length of the Hercules version to 39ft 1in (11.91m). All-up weights were 9,986lb (4,530kg) (Hercules) and 9,486lb (4,303kg) (E.112). The top speed was 321mph (516km/h) at 17,000ft (5,182).

Hawker N.9/39

Again only the centre fuselage was affected by fitting a turret; no weights were given.

Westland N.8/39 and N.9.39

In July 1939 Westland began preparing a joint project to N.8/39 and N.9/39, which also included proposals to A.7/39 for an army co-operation aircraft. A 'common' layout for the three specifications used a 1,260bhp (940kW) Bristol Taurus and had a span of 50ft (15.24m), a wing area of 375sq ft (34.875sq m), an all-up weight (N.9/39) of 11,600lb (5,262kg), and a top speed (for N.8/39) of 255mph (410km/h) at 15,000ft (4,572m). On 9 August Westland reported that its investigations were not sufficiently advanced for the specification and asked for an extension of time to complete the work, but this was refused.

Aerodynamically all of the N.8/39 designs were straightforward low-wing monoplanes and, except for Blackburn's fixed arrangement, had retractable or part-retractable undercarriages. Supermarine's was the cleanest design, but a small tail suggested that its longitudinal stability might be inadequate, as well as possibly also the directional stability and spinning characteristics. The most important structural feature was the wing fold mechanism, which produced exceptionally difficult problems. Blackburn had put forward a sound engineering proposition based on its Skua, but some of the other companies did not seem to have appreciated

BELOW A 'combined' sketch showing the Westland N.8/39 (wing cannon) and N.9/39 (turret) projects (7.39). *Westland Archive via the late Fred Ballam*

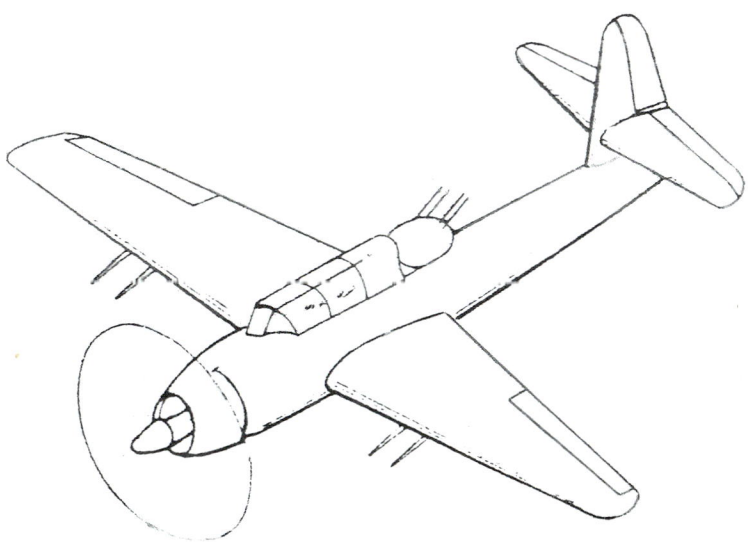

the difficulties. Hawker and Fairey were working on reasonable lines but more advanced detailed design was needed, Gloster proposed to adopt Blackburn wing fold practice but its adoption to Gloster's own methods of construction might give problems, while the Supermarine's method gave some concern.

Nevertheless the various Ministry departments placed the Supermarine 333 first, Gloster second (a thoroughly sound design with a good layout), Fairey third (a sound but unimpressive design), Blackburn fourth, and Hawker fifth. The order for the N.9/39s was Gloster first (with a rear turret that was aerodynamically very good), Fairey, Blackburn and Hawker. However, by 9 December the Admiralty, having postponed the Tender Design Conference twice because it was not ready to discuss the matter, was expected to abandon N.9/39 in favour of a single-seat fixed-gun fighter.

On 23 December the Admiralty reported that the N.8/39 tenders were unsatisfactory and revealed fresh requirements for single- and two-seat fighters, while the turret fighter was now abandoned. The specifications were modified under a document called NAD.925/39 and proposals for alternative single- and two-seat types were requested. The former required a maximum speed of 330 knots (380mph/611km/h) at 15,000ft (4,572m), the two-seaters 300 knots (345mph/556km/h). The designs produced to this unofficial document were relatively quick investigations with folding wings and other naval fittings.

Blackburn (B.37?)

The structure of Blackburn's single-seater was based on the N.8/39 and the aircraft had 40% chord full-span flaps, spoiler ailerons and 120 gallons (546

Blackburn 'single seat' design (late 12.39)	
Span:	40ft 0m (12.19m)
Length:	31ft 9in (9.68m)
Wing Area:	236sq.ft (21.95sq.m)
All-Up-Weight:	8,881lb (4,028kg)
Powerplant:	1 x Griffon
Max Speed / Height:	381mph (613km/h) at 15,000ft (4,572m)
Armament:	8 x 0.303in (7.7mm) machine guns or 4 x 20mm cannon

litres) of internal fuel. The dimensions of the two-seater were unchanged from the N.8/39. This design was described by RAE Farnborough as the best aerodynamically.

Fairey

The new single-seat requirement was of great interest to Fairey, indicating as it did a performance considerably in excess of that hitherto called for in FAA fighters. The greatest attention to clean design had been given to this project and the estimated speed was higher than that obtained in any single-engined fighter presently in service and operating from land aerodromes. This was achieved after taking into account wing-folding, deck catapulting and arresting, a stronger structure than would be needed on land, and freedom from corrosion in a salt-laden atmosphere. Two projects were in fact submitted, one with a Griffon (the 'primary design') and an alternative with a Sabre, the real difference between the two being one of scale only; their layouts were similar but the Sabre was somewhat larger and offered a higher top speed.

The aircraft had been designed primarily as a single-seat front-gun fighter but was adaptable, without changes to the airframe or too much weight penalty, to accommodate an

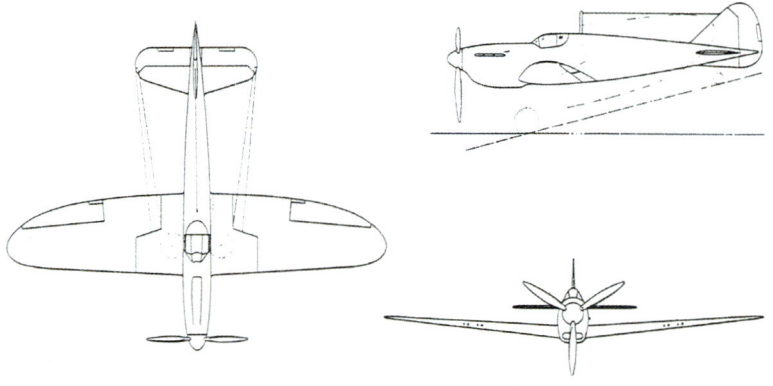

ABOVE The Fairey single-seat fighter to NAD.925/39 was powered by a Griffon engine and armed with eight machine guns (21.12.39).

LEFT An impression of the Fairey single-seat fighter.

CHAPTER SIX   NAVAL FIGHTERS PART ONE

Fairey NAD.925/39 1st design (late 12.39)	
Span:	42ft 0in (12.80m)
Length:	34ft 3in (10.44m) tail down
Wing Area:	292sq.ft (27.16sq.m)
All-Up-Weight:	9,232lb (4,188kg) machine guns only, 9,380lb (4,255kg) cannon, 9,850lb (4,468kg) 2 seat + cannon
Powerplant:	1 x Griffon RG.1.SM 1,600hp (1,193kW)
Max Speed / Height:	382mph (615km/h) at 15,000ft (4,572m)
Armament:	8 x 0.303in (7.7mm) machine guns or 4 x 20mm cannon

Fairey NAD.925/39 2nd design (late 12.39)	
Span:	44ft 0in (13.41m)
Length:	35ft 10in (10.92m)
Wing Area:	335sq.ft (31.16sq.m)
All-Up-Weight:	10,732lb (4,868kg) machine guns only, 10,880lb (4,935kg) cannon, 11,350lb (5,148kg) 2 seat + cannon
Powerplant:	1 x Sabre 2,500hp (1,864kW)
Max Speed / Height:	411mph (661km/h) at 15,000ft (4,572m)
Armament:	8 x 0.303in (7.7mm) machine guns or 4 x 20mm cannon

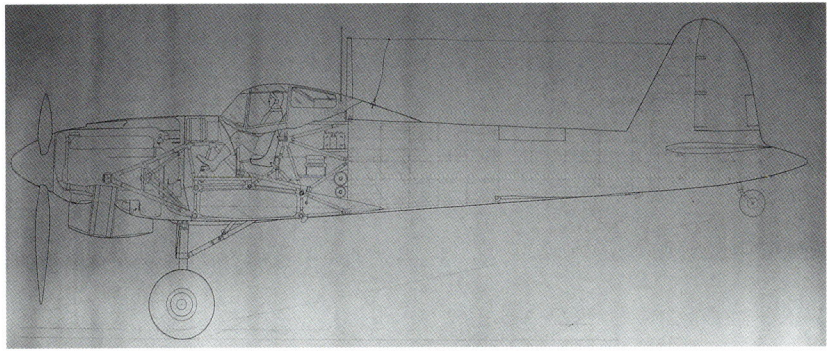

ABOVE This side view is the only known surviving drawing of Gloster's single-seat fighter project to NAD.925/39 (22.11.39). *Jet Age Museum*

observer and his equipment and canopy; however, he would not have the level of comfort and space provided in the firm's Barracuda torpedo bomber. In view of the high performance required, metal construction was employed throughout for stressed parts and every effort was made to achieve the maximum possible speed and rate of climb while fulfilling the specification. The single-seat Griffon offered a time to 10,000ft (3,048m) of 3.0 minutes, a service ceiling of 34,000ft (10,363m) and an absolute ceiling of 35,250ft (10,744m), the Sabre 2.67 minutes, 40,000ft (12,192m) and 41,000ft (12,497m); their respective fuel loads were 123 gallons (559 litres) and 128 gallons (582 litres). The brochure noted that if the Griffon had a 20,000ft (6,096m) supercharger, the speed at that height would be 408mph (656km/h). RAE considered that this was the best design from a structural point of view.

Gloster

Again the Gloster design's structure was based on the company's earlier N.8/39. It had slotted flaps and drooping ailerons and could carry 130 gallons (591 litres) of fuel. The two-seater had the same span but its length was 34ft 4in (10.46m) and weight 9,700lb (4,400kg).

Gloster NAD.925/39 (drawing dated 22.11.39)	
Span:	40ft 0in (12.19m)
Length:	33ft 7in (10.24m)
Wing Area:	283sq.ft (26.32sq.m)
All-Up-Weight:	9,102lb (4,129kg)
Powerplant:	1 x Griffon
Max Speed / Height:	368mph (592km/h) at 15,000ft (4,572m)
Armament:	8 x 0.303in (7.7mm) machine guns or 4 x 20mm cannon

Hawker

The Hawker project employed a Griffon and used slots and slotted flaps. The structure was based on the Hurricane and Hawker's N.8/39 work, and 111

Hawker NAD.925/39 (late 12.39)	
Span:	42ft 0in (12.80m)
Length:	32ft 1in (9.70m)
Wing Area:	277sq.ft (25.76sq.m)
All-Up-Weight:	8,750lb (3,969kg)
Powerplant:	1 x Griffon
Max Speed / Height:	363mph (584km/h) at 15,000ft (4,572m)
Armament:	8 x 0.303in (7.7mm) machine guns or 4 x 20mm cannon

gallons (505 litres) of fuel were carried. Service ceiling was 35,000ft (10,668m). Hawker's two-seat suggestion showed no change from its N.8/39 project.

Supermarine

The designers described the first of two projects as a 'Spitfire with Griffon engine'. It had folding wings and was offered as the most suitable aeroplane that could be put into production in a reasonable time. It was pointed out that the Spitfire had already flown with a 2,000bhp (1,491kW) engine and had

Supermarine NAD.925/39 'small' design (16.12.39)	
Span:	36ft 10in (11.23m)
Length:	30ft 7in (9.32m)
Wing Area:	242sq.ft (22.51sq.m)
All-Up-Weight:	8,100lb (3,674kg)
Powerplant:	1 x Griffon
Max Speed / Height:	396mph (637km/h) at 15,000ft (4,572m)
Armament:	8 x 0.303in (7.7mm) machine guns or 4 x 20mm cannon

Supermarine NAD.925/39 'large' design (16.12.39)	
Span:	39ft 0in (11.89m)
Length:	31ft 3in (9.53m)
Wing Area:	282sq.ft (26.23sq.m)
All-Up-Weight:	9,205lb (4,175kg)
Powerplant:	1 x Sabre
Max Speed / Height:	428mph (689km/h) at 15,000ft (4,572m)
Armament:	8 x 0.303in (7.7mm) machine guns or 4 x 20mm cannon

handled quite normally. The second project was a Spitfire development with a Sabre, which used the original wings, rear fuselage and tail but introduced a new centre section. The respective internal fuel capacities were 134 gallons (609 litres) and 186 gallons (846 litres) and RAE described these designs as 'an extremely neat job'. The original N.8/39 work was retained for the two-seater.

Westland

Westland finally got to tender a design officially and the result was powered by a Griffon and carried 220 gallons (1,000 litres) of fuel. The service ceiling was 34,000ft (10,363m).

The Research & Development (Technical) Department (RDT) re-estimated the weights and performance figures for this latest series of designs and in most cases the former went up and the maximum speeds came down (the Supermarine designs by 22mph to 37mph [35km/h to 60km/h]). However, both Blackburn and Westland were expected to be lighter than estimated, with the latter 8mph (13km/h) faster.

The Tender Design Conference for the original N.8/39 designs was finally held on 5 January 1940. Capt M. S. Slattery, Admiralty Director of Air Material (DAM), outlined the reasons for the recent changes to its requirements, which had originally been laid down before the war. The original tenders had been submitted after two months of war and it had now become evident that performance was paramount and that a fighter of low speed could not be countenanced. To obtain the desired performance, the navigation and radio facilities would have to be drastically reduced. It had also become evident that the linking of designs for front gun and turret fighters would have a serious effect on the design, and the new series of single-seat projects (to NAD.925/39) had been invited primarily to give a datum for comparative purposes. If the tenders showed that little would be lost by imposing such minimum requirements for navigation, and if two designs could be selected as suitable for development, Slattery felt the purpose of the investigation would have been achieved. Production was desired in eighteen months time.

Gloster's original design was reasonable and of relatively simple construction, that of Vickers was the 'cleanest' but, as noted, its stability was doubtful because of the small tail. There had not been sufficient time to examine the latest single-seat proposals thoroughly, but the 'Griffon Spitfire' was regarded as 'closely approaching the Fairey design in technical merit'. However, the Spitfire's view was considered poor for deck landing while Fairey's tender to the modified two-seat requirements showed a 500lb (227kg) increase in weight and a loss of about 7mph (11km/h) in speed from the single-seater. The claimed 380mph (611km/h) top speed was regarded as optimistic, but it was thought that this design showed better appreciation of the Admiralty's requirements than the others. Discussion established that the Fairey design was the most acceptable and least speculative of those submitted. However, concern was expressed that the placing of further FAA development work with Fairey could lead to the company undertaking an undue preponderance of such work, a position that might ultimately result in a lack of interest from other design staffs.

Therefore it was felt necessary to make some provision for extending FAA aircraft design problems to as many companies as possible. The Blackburn design indicated a method of improved stalling speed that ought not to be neglected, and it was considered that this scheme was worthy of a trial, even in wartime. War conditions had shown that

BELOW A rough sketch of Westland's 'N.8/39' single-seat fighter (12.39). *Westland Archive via the late Fred Ballamum*

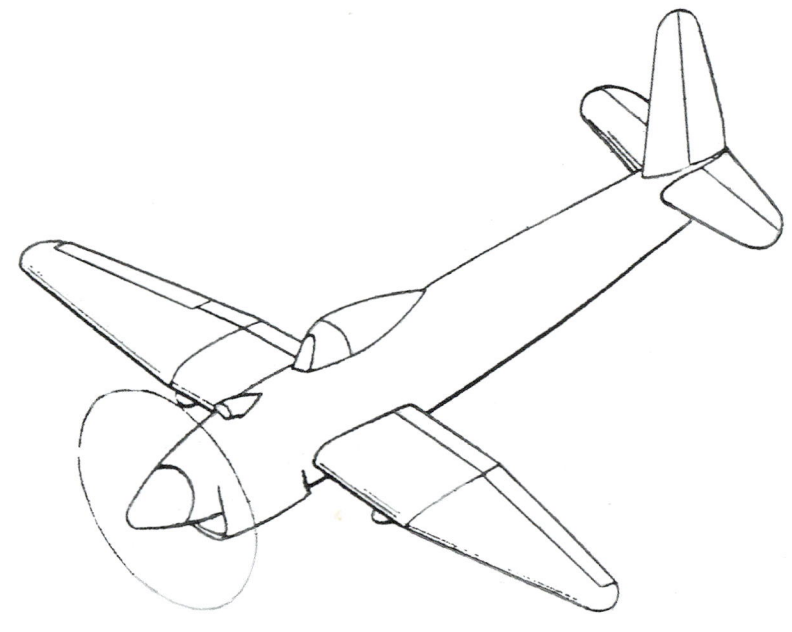

Westland NAD.925/39 (12.39)	
Span:	45ft 0in (13.72m)
Length:	?
Wing Area:	254sq.ft (23.62sq.m)
All-Up-Weight:	9,600lb (4,355kg)
Powerplant:	1 x Griffon 1,600hp (1,193kW)
Max Speed / Height:	359mph (578km/h) at 15,000ft (4,572m)
Armament:	8 x 0.303in (7.7mm) machine guns or 4 x 20mm cannon

less wind speed than expected was often available for operating aircraft, and exhaustive discussions had indicted that the overriding factor controlling the designs was the stalling speed. Therefore it was decided to recommend that a small order for twenty-five aircraft should be placed with Blackburn as an experiment. The modified Fairey N.8/39 with Griffon engine was considered to be the most suitable project for service and it was thought that a production order could be placed 'off the drawing board'.

Fairey Firefly

To avoid any confusion, on 24 February 1940 it was requested that N8/39 should be replaced by a new specification, N.5/40. Five days later the Admiralty requested approval for an order covering 200 examples of Fairey's fighter to follow the Fulmar. War experience had shown that they should concentrate on performance and speed, but in March the Air Ministry advised that the two-seater policy was still in force because the speed discrepancy between single- and two-seat types was quite small. Under normal circumstances the FAA's needs for a fighter differed from that of the RAF – the Navy would know that enemy bombers had one objective, the fleet, while the RAF had to deal with bombers that might have several targets, each of them unknown to the defenders. Hence a large speed differential was less critical for the FAA and this would tend to disappear at high altitudes anyway. In addition, a large range was required to find enemy reconnaissance aircraft before they found the fleet, which would also give warning for extra fighters to get airborne before the bombers arrived. At this early stage of the war it was not expected that the new aircraft would have to meet enemy single-seat escort fighters because of the latter's restrictions in range.

Thus, after a great deal of discussion it was confirmed that, for the normal and general functions of

TOP This Fairey Firefly Mk.I with the original chin radiator was photographed in 1945.

ABOVE An early Firefly displays the type's extraordinary wing fold system in a view dated October 1944.

ABOVE FR.Mk.4 VG979 was one of the later versions of the Firefly that had the radiators moved to the wing.

FAA fighters, the two-seater should be retained in preference to the single-seat alternative. Consequently, at the Advisory Design Conference held on 11 March it was decided that Fairey's project should be a two-seater. The Mock-up Conference was held on 6 and 7 May and the contract was placed for the first order (for 200 aeroplanes) on 12 June. The first three machines, Z1826 to Z1828, were to serve as prototypes, and the first made its maiden flight on 22 December 1941. Named Firefly, a total of 1,702 production aircraft were built and the type served the FAA in several versions until the mid-1950s. The later Mk.4 lost its elliptical wing for a clipped version and had the radiators moved from the chin position into the wing leading edge.

Blackburn Firebrand

Experience, however, had shown that there were occasions when a single-seat fighter, with its generally superior performance, could be employed with advantage. This included the defence of naval bases or ships in harbour against shore-based enemy aircraft by an interceptor type. Constitutionally the defence of fleet bases was an RAF commitment for which no provision had been made in the FAA programme, but the Admiralty now stated that in practice the FAA would have to perform much of this task itself. In addition, the advantage of having a force of high-performance fighters that could readily be transported by and operated from a carrier had been made clear by experiences in Norway during the spring of 1940. For this reason it was now proposed to introduce a limited number of high-performance single-seat fighters to Blackburn's B.37 design, which had an estimated top speed of 390mph (628km/h).

By 21 June 1940 the design had been approved by the Air Ministry's technical experts and, to speed delivery, it was proposed to order it 'off the board' without prototypes. Specification N.11/40 of 24 August was raised to cover the aircraft, stating that the minimum top speed had to be 350 knots (403mph/648km/h). The mock-up was examined in the autumn and three prototypes, DD804, DD810 and DD815, were ordered in January 1941. On 11 July the new aircraft was named Firebrand, and DD804 was first flown on 27 February 1942 with a Napier Sabre II. On trials it was found to be 32mph (51km/h) below Blackburn's maximum speed estimate, but fitting a Sabre III brought the figure up

BELOW A view of Blackburn Firebrand DD804 taken on 2 April 1942. *BAe Brough Heritage*

Fairey Firefly F.Mk.I (flown)	
Span:	44ft 6in (13.56m)
Length:	37ft 7in (11.46m)
Wing Area:	328sq.ft (30.50sq.m)
All-Up-Weight: 1	4,020lb (6,359kg)
Powerplant:	1 x Griffon IIB 1,720hp (1,283kW)
Max Speed / Height:	316mph (508km/h) at 14,000ft (4,267m)
Armament:	2 x 1,000lb (454kg) bombs or 8 RP, 4 x 20mm cannon

CHAPTER SIX   NAVAL FIGHTERS PART ONE

Blackburn B.37 Firebrand Mk.I (flown)

Span:	50ft 0in (15.24m)
Length:	38ft 2in (11.63m)
Wing Area: 3	81.5sq.ft (35.48sq.m)
All-Up-Weight:	13,643lb (6,188kg), 15,557lb (7,057kg) with bombs
Powerplant:	1 x Sabre III 2,305hp (1,719kW)
Max Speed / Height:	358mph (576km/h) at 17,000ft (5,182m)
Armament:	2 x 500lb (227kg) bombs, 4 x 20mm cannon

Blackburn B.45 Firebrand Mk.IV (flown)

Span:	51ft 3.5in (15.63m)
Length:	38ft 9in (11.81m)
Wing Area:	381.5sq.ft (35.48sq.m)
All-Up-Weight:	15,671lb (7,108kg)
Powerplant:	1 x Centaurus IX 2,520hp (1,879kW)
Max Speed / Height:	350mph (563km/h) at 13,000ft (3,962m) clean
Armament:	1 x 1,790lb (812kg) torpedo, 2 x 1,000lb (454kg) bombs or RPs, 4 x 20mm cannon

TOP This photo, dated 29 March 1943, shows an unidentified early mark of Firebrand and provides a good view of the wing radiators and cannon.

ABOVE The prototype Firebrand TF.Mk.III with the Bristol Centaurus, DK372, is seen in this recognition photo taken on 31 March 1944.

to 358mph (576km/h) at 17,000ft (5,182m). However, problems, delays and doubts regarding the Sabre's development would lead to a switch to the Bristol Centaurus.

The Firebrand was a large and heavy machine, which, although possessing considerable endurance, suffered in manoeuvrability compared with lighter shipboard fighters. It was also to suffer many development problems and consequent changes to its role, before being turned into a torpedo bomber fighter (that is, a strike fighter) for which the centre section was widened to make room for a torpedo. The first order for fifty machines eventually comprised nine TF.Mk.Is and twelve TF.Mk.IIs, all with Sabres, two B.45 Firebrand TF.Mk. III prototypes to Specification S.8/43 with Centaurus VII engines (DK372, first flown on 21 December 1943, and DK373), and the rest production Mk.IIIs with the Centaurus. All of these were used for development and trials but they were followed by another 170 built to Mk.IV or Mk.V (Blackburn B.46) standard, which had many modifications including a larger fin and more powerful 2,520bhp (1,879kW) Centaurus IXs or 57s. After a long wait the Firebrand at last began to reach operational units in 1945; it served until 1953 before being replaced by the Westland Wyvern (see Chapter 7).

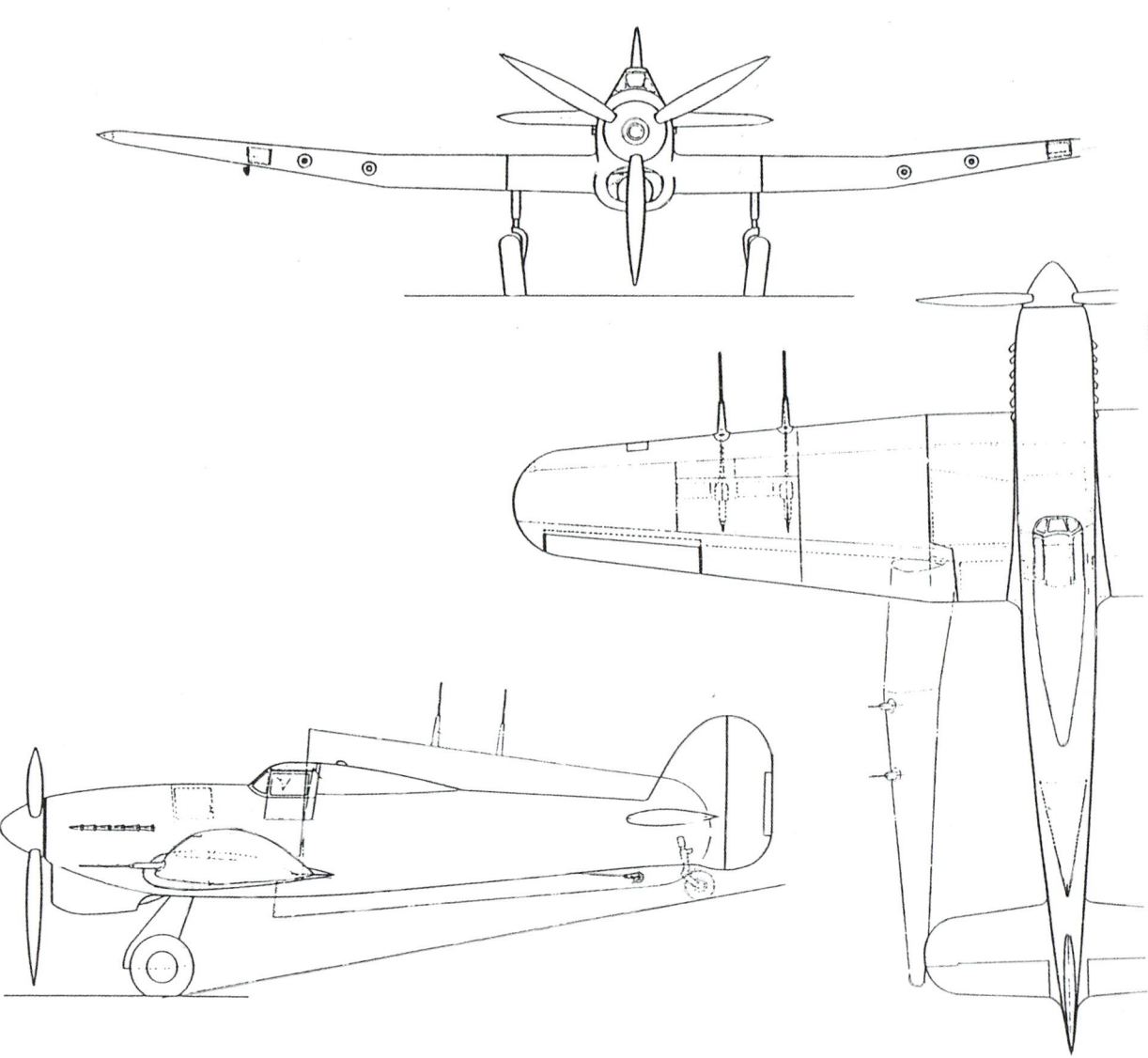

ABOVE **The Hawker P.1009 (c2.41).** *Hawker via Chris Farara*

Hawker P.1009 'Sea Typhoon'

On 20 February 1941 delays with the N.11/40 Firebrand prompted the Admiralty to agree to examine a navalised version of the Hawker Typhoon, a 'Sea Typhoon', as an alternative. The result was the P.1009 variant, converted to N.11/40 with larger folding wings and a fuel capacity of 264 gallons (1,200 litres). However, A. V. Alexander, the First Lord of the Admiralty, told Lord Beaverbrook that he saw no hope of the Sea Typhoon being produced by the end of the year, even if the design work was done by Hawker. In addition, a separate company would not have a prototype ready until the late spring or early summer of 1942, when the Blackburn was expected to fly in August/September 1941, so any Sea Typhoon prototypes would be some months behind, regardless of who built them. On 21 March 1941 it was decided that modifying the Typhoon would mean a major redesign of the aircraft. Some 25% of Typhoon parts might be used in the sea version, but the result would be inferior in performance to the N.11/40 and less suitable for naval purposes, so it was unanimously recommended that production of the Blackburn N.11/40 should proceed in preference to the Sea Typhoon. Moreover, the RAF reported that the Typhoon was a good 'bomber destroyer' but lacked the manoeuvrability needed for combat.

A 'hooked' Typhoon or Tempest for carrier operation was considered

Hawker P.1009 (c2.41)	
Span:	50ft 0in (15.24m)
Length:	35ft 8.5in (10.88m)
Wing Area:	354sq.ft (32.92sq.m)
All-Up-Weight:	?
Powerplant:	1 x Sabre
Max Speed / Height:	?
Armament:	4 x 20mm cannon

CHAPTER SIX

NAVAL FIGHTERS PART ONE

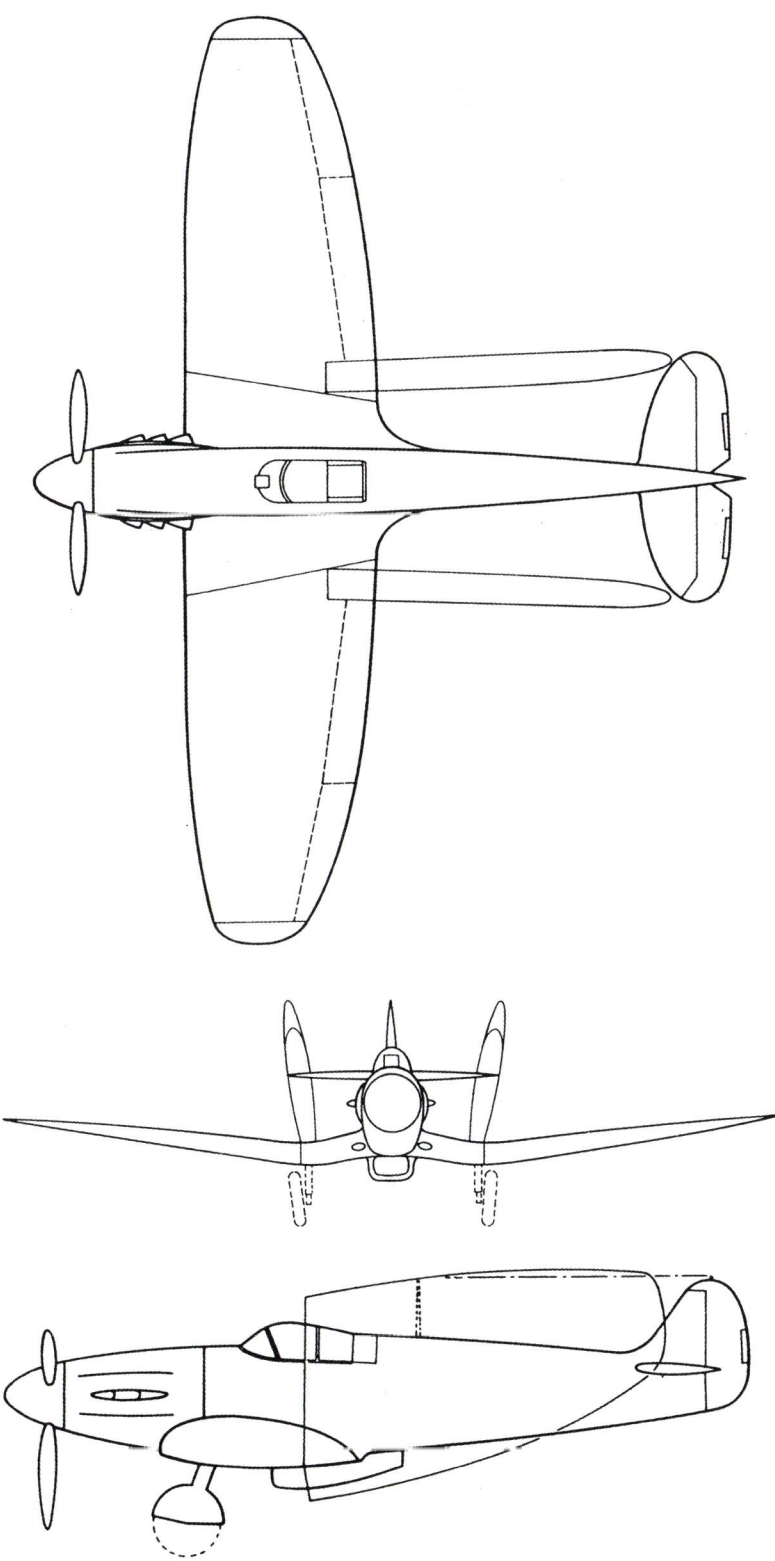

ABOVE This is the provisional general arrangement drawing of the first single-seat Griffon-engined Supermarine 'Spitfire for the Fleet Air Arm' (1939). The design was based on the Griffon Spitfire Mk.IV and differences from the Spitfire included a gull wing that folded rearwards and a ventral radiator on the centreline. *The late Eric Morgan*

again in November 1942. By then the Seafire (see below) was in service, which, although in many respects not meeting the Naval Staff requirements for a single-seat fighter, had proved valuable and was appreciated as the best fighter with which the Navy had been equipped so far. However, it showed certain disadvantages including a restricted view for landing and a lack of robustness, particularly with the undercarriage. The CinC Home Fleet wrote on 28 November that the new Hawker aircraft were less handicapped in these respects: 'The view over the Sabre engine is better [and] these aircraft are also built with all of the traditional strength of Hawkers; the undercarriage seems especially strong.' He suggested that a Typhoon or Tempest should be obtained for Admiralty use as soon as possible and hooked for trials.

He added that 'it must be remembered that these aircraft are cart-horses, being pulled along by immense engines, while Vickers (Supermarine) products are more of the racehorse class,' but acknowledged that the size of these aircraft would control the numbers that could be put onto a carrier. Discussions continued and a Typhoon Mk.IB, DW419, was allocated, but it crashed on 8 February 1943. Finally, on 23 December 1943 Capt Casper John declared that the Typhoon was difficult to use as a carrier fighter, largely because of its long take-off run and high stalling speed. The control of its stalling speed was nothing like as good as that of the Seafire, and the Typhoon test pilot, Lt Cdr Campbell, felt that the Firebrand (which was shortly to begin its initial deck trials) would be a better aeroplane to and from the deck.

Supermarine Seafire

As an intermediate step between the Fulmar and its N.5/40 replacement, the Admiralty also decided to pursue the possibility of obtaining a number of 'Spitfires' with folding wings and arrester hooks. The Sea Lords were

117

ABOVE LEFT A beautiful photo of Seafire Mk.46 LA544. During 1946, when this picture was taken, this aircraft was another resident of ECFS Hullavington. *Peter Arnold collection*

ABOVE RIGHT NS493 served as a prototype Seafire Mk.XV with a Rolls-Royce Griffon powerplant.

LEFT This well-known photo of Supermarine Seafire Mk.IIc MB156 of 885 Squadron was taken aboard the carrier *Formidable* in December 1942. *Crown Copyright*

BELOW In 1942 Supermarine proposed to the Navy two rather more radical developments of the standard Spitfire/Seafire family. This is the first, a Griffon-powered project dated 23 March 1942, which had an elliptical-shaped gull wing and, most dramatic of all, a 'butterfly' V-tailplane and rudder with the same configuration as the wings. It also had a four-blade propeller, a ventral radiator with the oil coolers in the wing leading edge, an inward-retracting undercarriage, and a wing that folded and then swivelled to sit alongside the fuselage. Four Hispano cannon were installed just outside the wing fold. *The late Eric Morgan*

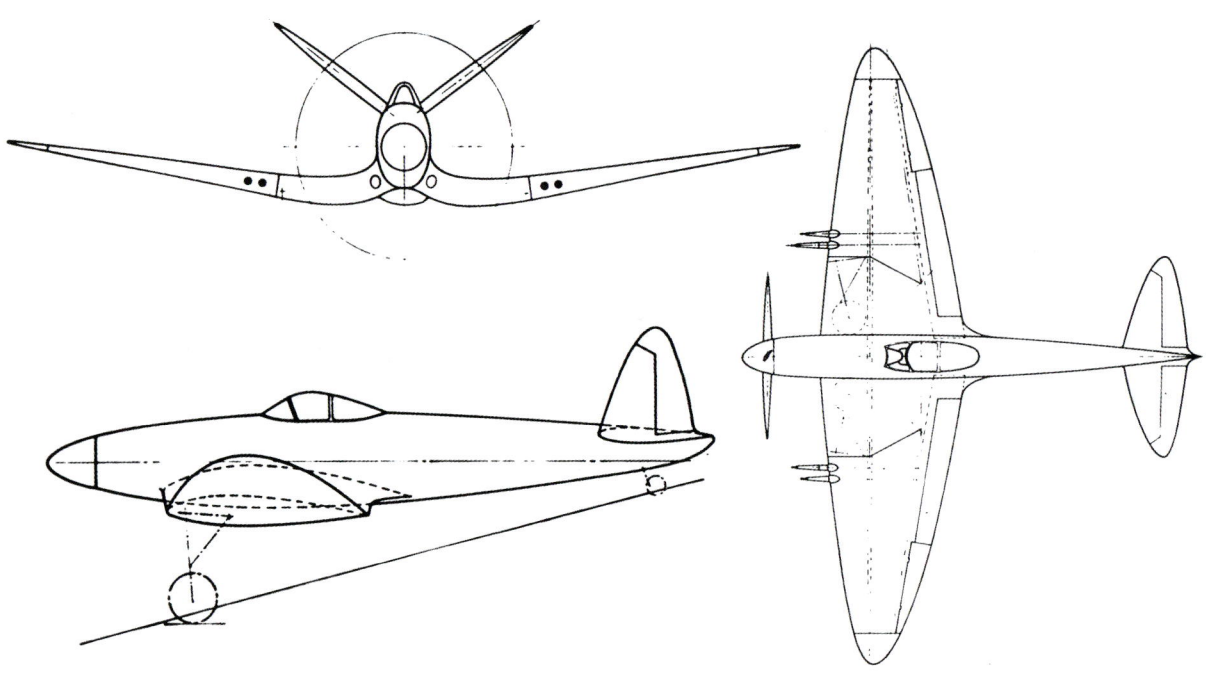

LEFT Seafire F.Mk.47 PS946. *Crown Copyright*

BELOW In October 1942 Supermarine made a proposal for a Navy fighter that was smaller and lighter compared to the design submitted in March (the drawing is dated 3.9.42). This new effort retained the outer folding wing panels but these now folded upwards. There was a conventional empennage and the fuselage was changed to accommodate a Napier Sabre engine driving a six-bladed contra-rotating propeller with its cooling radiator placed below the engine cowling. The exhaust came out via ducts at the rear of the engine and once more the armament comprised four cannon. The wing area was 200sq ft (18.60sq m), but no other dimensional data is available for either of these designs. *The late Eric Morgan*

anxious that a fighter of higher performance should be brought into service as early as possible, and the feasibility of fifty Spitfires so modified had already been discussed informally. The idea was officially put to the Air Ministry on 29 February 1940, but the project was dropped on 29 March, a key reason being that the construction of a certain quantity of 'Sea Spitfires' would reduce the number of land Spitfires coming off the lines by a much greater figure, aircraft that would be desperately needed by the RAF. The gap was to be partially filled by the acquisition of the American Grumman Wildcat fighter, which entered FAA service in late 1940 as the Martlet. However, the idea of a 'Sea Spitfire' did not go away and in the second half of 1941 some were ordered. Initial deck landing trials were made towards the end of that year and the first squadrons received their aircraft in 1942. In due course there were to be both Merlin- and Griffon-powered Seafires, and the type stayed in service with the FAA until 1954.

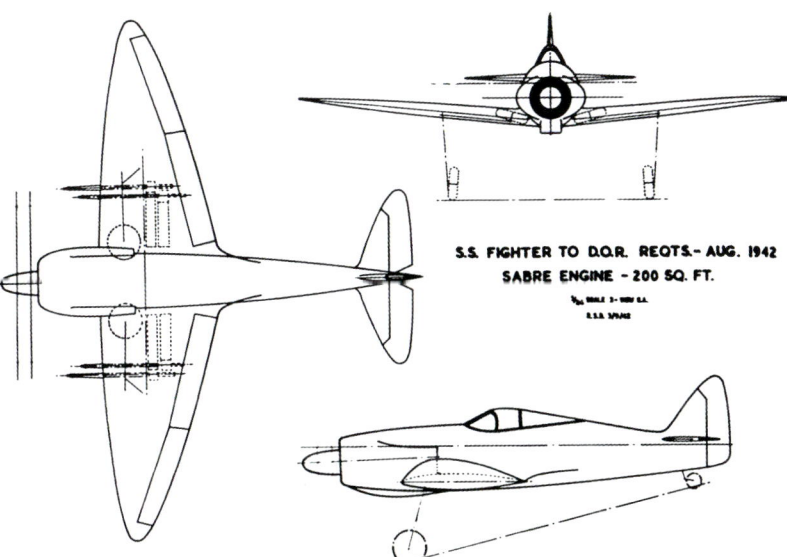

Chapter Seven
Naval Fighters Part Two including Strike Fighters

ABOVE A Westland Wyvern TF.Mk.4 on display at the Farnborough Air Show in September 1951. *Terry Panopalis*

This chapter concludes the coverage of wartime naval piston fighter development and takes in several projects that came under the strike fighter category.

Specification N.7/43

The Navy continued its search for a top-class single-seat fighter and during the early spring of 1943 some unofficial design studies for a fleet fighter were submitted by a number of companies, and they brought a review

RIGHT The Boulton Paul P.103A (4.43). *Les Whitehouse*

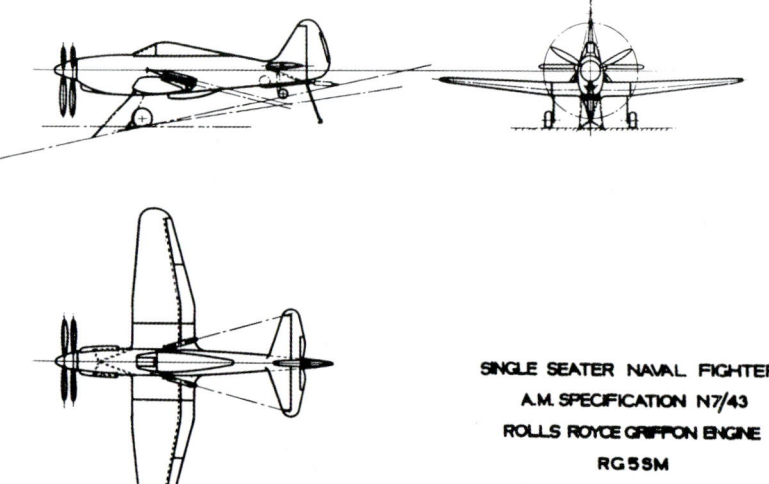

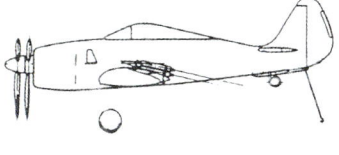
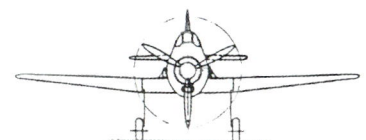
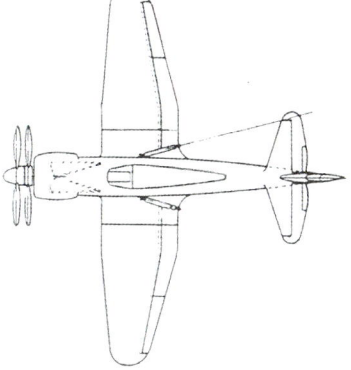

SINGLE SEATER NAVAL FIGHTER
A.M. SPECIFICATION N7/43
BRISTOL CENTAURUS ENGINE
C.E.12SM
BOULTON PAUL SERIES P.103.B.

TOP The Boulton Paul P.103B (4.43). Both P.103 drawings show take-off rocket gear on the upper wing. *Les Whitehouse*

MIDDLE An artist's impression of the P.103A. *Les Whitehouse*

BOTTOM An artist's impression of the P.103B. *Les Whitehouse*

of some new draft requirements that had recently been drawn up. The Navy's Design Committee realised that if the fleet interceptor fighter was to have the necessary very high performance to enable it to compete with shore-based fighters, it would be necessary to keep the endurance, ammunition and so on as low as possible. The normal permanent fuel load was cut to give just 1¾ hours at maximum cruising speed rather than the 2¼ hours previously desired. The resulting specification, N.7/43, brought several formal submissions.

Boulton Paul P.103

There were two versions of Boulton Paul's offering, the P.103A with a Griffon and the Centaurus-powered P.103B, both with contra-rotating 'dive brake' propellers. P.103 featured a low-drag wing and a rocket-assisted take-off facility on the upper wing centre section, together with a number of innovative features such as an undercarriage that was long enough to ensure that the airscrew had sufficient ground clearance but became shorter when it retracted. Boulton Paul stressed that the general lines of both machines were so clean that there was no doubt that the avoidance of shock stall was practicable (some wartime and late-1940s aircraft experienced shock stall, a marked increase in drag coupled with a loss of lift and control, as they approached supersonic speed in a dive). The wing thickness/chord ratio varied from 20% to 12%, the elevator had automatic trim tabs, and an American-style sting arrester hook was fitted. Internal fuel totalled 160 gallons (728 litres) and the folded span was 13ft 10in (4.23m). Certain 'special

Boulton Paul P.103A (4.43)

Span:	38ft 8in (11.79m)
Length:	36ft 4in (11.07m)
Wing Area:	250sq.ft (23.25sq.m)
All-Up-Weight:	10,221lb (4,636kg)
Powerplant:	1 x Griffon RG.5.SM
Max Speed / Height:	366mph (589km/h) at sea level, 462mph (743km/h) at 28,000ft (8,534m)
Armament:	4 x 20mm cannon

Boulton Paul P.103B (4.43)

Span:	38ft 8in (11.79m)
Length:	37ft 0in (11.28m)
Wing Area:	260sq.ft (24.18sq.m)
All-Up-Weight:	11,180lb (5,071kg)
Powerplant:	1 x Centaurus CE.12.SM
Max Speed / Height:	365mph (587km/h) at sea level, 435mph (700km/h) at 23,000ft (7,010m)
Armament:	4 x 20mm cannon

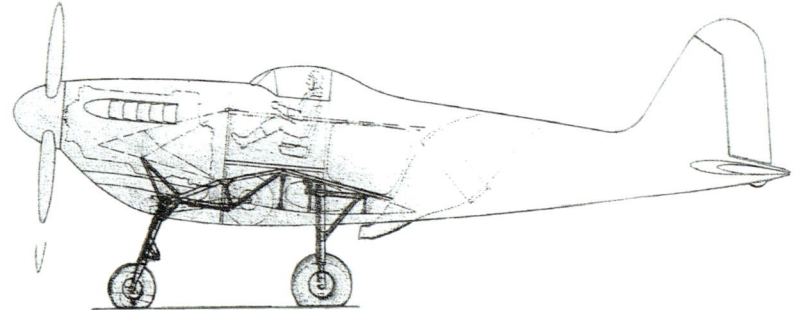

features' on the P.103 generated much interest, and Defiant DR895 was later adapted to try out some of them. Proposals were also made for Boulton Paul to work in cooperation with Hawker on its fighter proposals, in particular the suggested 'Fury with Griffon' airframe. However, Hawker turned this idea down, and almost immediately (on 22 May 1943) Boulton Paul submitted a revised P.103 brochure in response.

Boulton Paul P.104

The P.104 was a further attempt to produce a lightweight canard fighter similar to the company's earlier P.98 project (see Chapter 2), but this time designed for carrier operations. A tail-first single-seater, it was fitted with a pusher RG.5.SM Griffon engine but seems to have been abandoned pretty quickly. No further details survive.

Fairey N.7/43

Fairey considered that the pilot's view out on the approach was a key element of the new naval fighter project, and Part I of the firm's studies (dated 24 April 1943) centred on a conventional design called the A.1 with a single 2,100bhp (1,566kW) Griffon 61, a

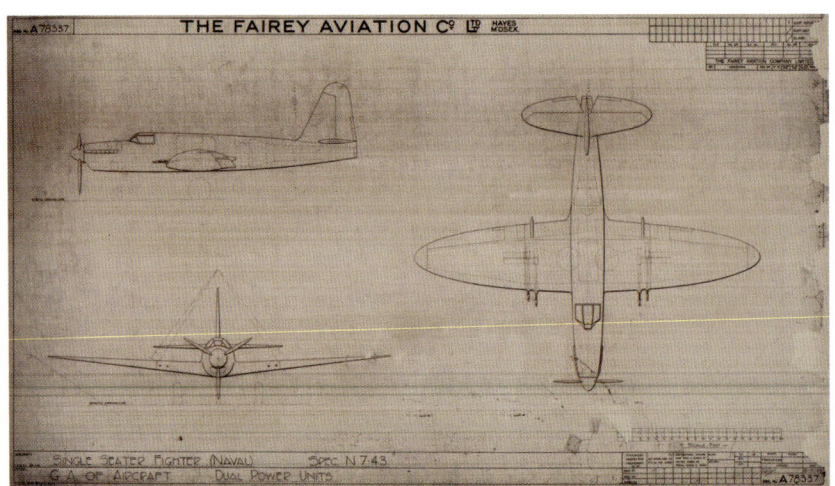

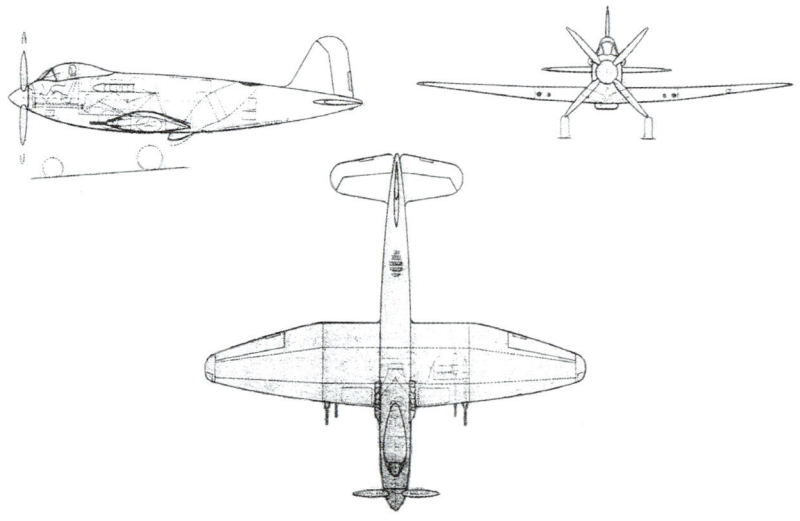

TOP A side view of Fairey's initial N.7/43 Design 'A.1' (24.4.43).

MIDDLE This drawing, dated 8 May 1943, shows the first Fairey dual-powerplant piston/jet design to N.7/43. *Chris Stainer*

BOTTOM The Fairey N.7/43 Design 'C' (26.5.43). *RAF Museum*

tricycle undercarriage and, possibly, a variable-incidence wing; Fairey acknowledged, however, that the latter could become quite complicated. The all-up weight was 12,000lb (5,443kg), maximum speed 337mph (542km/h)

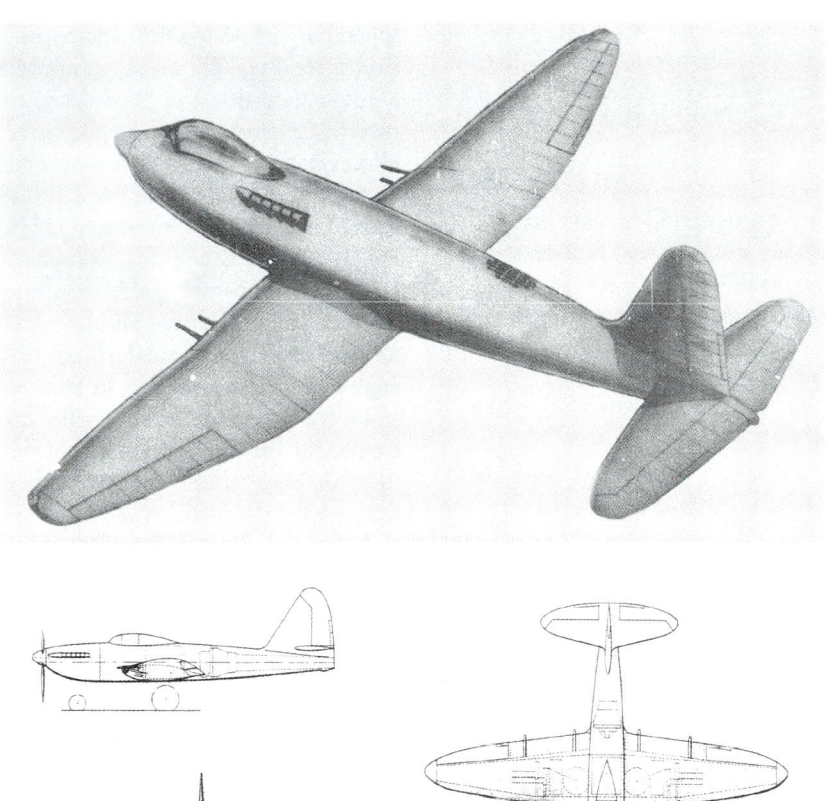

TOP An artist's impression of the Fairey N.7/43 Design 'C'. *RAF Museum*

ABOVE The final Fairey N.7/43 dual-power design (7.6.43). *RAF Museum*

at 1,000ft (305m), and time to 5,000ft (1,524m) 2.17 minutes.

Part II (dated 10 May) introduced a dual power unit comprising one Rolls-Royce Peregrine piston engine and one Whittle jet, which offered a much higher top speed. Both engines would be used for take-off, climb and combat, but the piston only would be run during cruising flight. Described as a simple design with stressed-skin construction (with thicker skins for a superior surface finish), it was hoped that the speed could be achieved without resorting to any aerodynamic or structural developments. The Peregrine had a relatively small radiator and the cooling air for this, together with all of the air for the jet, would be ducted in from the nose. Time to 10,000ft (3,048m) was given as 2.67 minutes, range 745 miles (1,199km) and service ceiling 41,000ft (12,497m). For comparison, an alternative design with a single jet of 4,000lb (17.8kN) thrust had also been assessed and this offered the same top speed but a much shorter range.

On the advice of DTD a revised Design A.1 was completed on 26 May, with the Griffon moved to the centre fuselage so that the pilot could be seated ahead of the engine behind a tractor airscrew (which was driven by a high-speed shaft from the engine). This gave the pilot a near optimum view over the airscrew spinner. On this variant, called Design C, the fuselage forward of the wing had been extended some 30in (76.2cm) compared to the A.1, but in most other respects it was similar, including the cannon position in the centre plane and its tricycle undercarriage. The radiators were positioned behind the engine and main fuel tank, and the folded span was 16ft (4.88m). Finally, on 7 June 1943 Fairey completed Part III, which was essentially a blending of design A.1 together with a dual powerplant of one Merlin and a Whittle jet. The estimated time to 10,000ft (3,048m) was 2.75 minutes and the ceiling was 42,000ft (12,802m). A version was also suggested for the RAF, but on 20 June Fairey received a letter from DTD requesting that the company's work on single-seat naval fighters should now cease.

Fairey N.7/43 (dual powerplant 10.5.43)

Span:	44ft 0in (13.41m)
Length:	37ft 0in (11.28m)
Wing Area:	301sq.ft (27.99sq.m)
All-Up-Weight:	12,670lb (5,747kg)
Powerplant:	1 x Peregrine 850hp (634kW) plus 1 x jet 3,000lb (13.3kN)
Max Speed / Height:	418mph (673km/h) at sea level, 492mph (792km/h) at 30,000ft (9,144m)
Armament:	4 x 20mm cannon

Fairey N.7/43 (design C) (26.5.43)

Span:	40ft 0in (12.19m)
Length:	35ft 9in (10.90m)
Wing Area:	?
All-Up-Weight:	?
Powerplant:	1 x Griffon 61 2,100hp (1,566kW)
Max Speed / Height:	?
Armament:	4 x 20mm cannon

Fairey N.7/43 (dual powerplant 7.6.43)

Span:	45ft 3in (13.79m)
Length:	36ft 4in (11.07m)
Wing Area:	313sq.ft (29.11sq.m)
All-Up-Weight:	14,000lb (6,750kg)
Powerplant:	1 x Merlin 1,620hp (1,208kW) plus 1 x jet 3,000lb (13.3kN)
Max Speed / Height:	447mph (719km/h) at sea level, 490mph (788km/h) at 30,000ft (9,144m)
Armament:	4 x 20mm cannon

Hawker Sea Fury F.Mk.X (flown)	
Span:	38ft 4in (11.68m)
Length:	34ft 7in (10.54m)
Wing Area:	280sq.ft (26.04sq.m)
All-Up-Weight:	9,070lb (4,114kg)
Powerplant:	1 x Centaurus XVIII 2,480hp (1,849kW)
Max Speed / Height:	465mph (748km/h) at 18,000ft (5,486m)
Armament:	4 x 20mm cannon

BELOW Hawker Sea Fury FB.Mk.11 WF619. Note the later naval colour scheme.

BOTTOM & OPPOSITE TOP These gorgeous views show Sea Hornet F.Mk.20 TT202 flying over the Solent in about June or July 1947. Barry Guess, BAE Systems, Farnborough

appeared, by a small margin, to offer the greater potential, but this manufacturer lacked the resources to put such an advanced type into full production on a large scale. It was also felt that there would be many advantages in the new naval interceptor being a modification of the best RAF type, and this policy was accepted by the Ministry.

Consequently, the P.1022 was selected and a new Specification, N.22/43, together with Operational Requirement OR.155, was written to cover the aircraft, which became the Sea Fury. Actually this document related to production aeroplanes, and when it was issued in April 1944 it had officially been retitled 22/43/H (although Hawker files still referred to N.22/43). Folland was told of the Fo.118's rejection on 20 May 1943, N. E. Rowe's letter stating that the decision had been taken not to proceed with an entirely new design at present, but to endeavour to meet the need by the development of established types (which the P.1022 was). The full background to the Sea Fury's development is explained in Chapter 2.

De Havilland Sea Hornet

With the supreme level of power available to the RAF's Hornet (see Chapter 4), it seemed a logical step to exploit its potential in a naval version. The Fleet Air Arm needed to re-equip with a modern aircraft, while the Hornet's handed propellers would be most helpful for carrier operations. After the Admiralty had revealed its interest in the type, Specification N.5/44 of 15 July 1944 was raised to cover a naval long-range fighter variant, with the Merlin 130/131 powerplants, warload, top speed and climb rate unchanged from the RAF version. The principal changes for the Sea Hornet included hydraulic folding wings, an arrester hook, rocket-assisted take-off accelerator gear, and the replacement of the Hornet's rubber-in-compression main legs with Airdraulic shock-absorber legs. The Airdraulic chassis brought a weight penalty but was necessary to eliminate bounce on carrier landings; the RAF Hornet's rubber leg could not quite absorb the energy at the high rate of descent allowed on carriers. Navalising the Hornet added 550lb (249kg) of weight and Heston Aircraft was entrusted with the detail design of the naval modifications. Eventually

MIDDLE An official recognition view of Sea Hornet FR.Mk.22 prototype TT187. *Phil Butler*

BOTTOM Serial PX239 served as a Sea Hornet NF.Mk.21 prototype with a second crewman in a new mid-fuselage position. *Phil Butler*

seven RAF Hornets were modified as prototype F.Mk.20s and the first, PX212, flew on 19 April 1945.

The next Sea Hornet fighter variant, the NF.Mk.21, brought some changes to the type's external appearance. So urgent was the Navy's need for up-to-date high-performance aircraft that Specification N.21/45 was written around a Sea Hornet night fighter to replace the Fairey Firefly. To perform this role the aircraft would need an observer and employ drop tanks to increase its range to more than 1,300 miles (2,092km). A night fighter mock-up was examined on 22 May 1945 and the mark would have the same weapon load and engines (although many aircraft actually had Merlin 134/135s); the engine's exhausts would be screened for night flying.

There was concern that the full equipment needed for night fighting might not fit inside the Hornet airframe, but the only alternative would be a version of the Short S.11/43 Sturgeon torpedo bomber developed for the role. However, while it was possible that the Sturgeon would be more lavishly equipped, there was no doubt that its performance would fall far short of the Sea Hornet, and far short of the minimum required. Nevertheless, in June Short was asked to consider the design of a night fighter based on the Sturgeon, and on 4 July the Assistant Chief of the Naval Staff (Air) (ACNS[A]) stated that the result 'would be very different from the Sturgeon in having more powerful engines which would be so installed that the arcs covered by the AI scanner (an essential feature of the night fighter) would be very much increased over what would be possible in the existing S.11/43'. At this

127

de Havilland Sea Hornet F.Mk.20 (flown)

Span:	45ft 0in (13.72m)
Length:	36ft 8in (11.18m)
Wing Area:	361sq.ft (33.57sq.m)
All-Up-Weight:	c20,000lb (9,117kg)
Powerplant:	2 x Merlin 130 series 2,070hp (1,544kW)
Max Speed / Height:	c465mph (748km/h) at height
Armament:	2 x 1,000lb (454kg) bombs or 8 x RPs, 4 x 20mm cannon

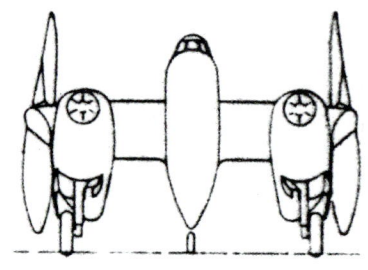

stage the Sturgeon was still to fly, but ACNS(A) concluded that he proposed to approve:

i. that the future of the S.11/43 should be considered after the prototype had flown.

ii. the investigation of a night fighter based on the S.11/43 as an insurance in case the night fighter Sea Hornet proved more difficult to land on a deck at night than was expected.

iii. the development of the Sea Hornet night fighter to the prototype stage.

Short 'Jet Sturgeon'

An undated drawing is available for a Short Brothers Fleet Air Arm Night Fighter. There is no documentation linking it to the Sturgeon or the Sea Hornet, but it seems most likely to be the result of the June 1945 request for such a design. Clearly based on the Sturgeon, with the same wings and a similar body and empennage, the Merlins had been replaced by two Rolls-Royce AJ.40 jets and the tail moved higher up on the fin to keep it clear of the jet exhaust. Four 20mm cannon were mounted in the lower nose and there were nine fuel tanks, six in the wings taking up the space vacated by the leading edge radiators, and three in the fuselage behind the cockpit; the total capacity was 910 gallons (4,138 litres). (Author's note: Published sources state that the Short S.41/S.A.3 project was prepared to Specification N.7/46, which covered the Hawker Sea Hawk. This drawing may be the S.41 but it gives no project number.)

The Short Night Fighter was never ordered and the prototype Sea Hornet Mk.21, PX230, first flew on 9 July 1946; it featured a new dorsal cockpit behind the pilot where the observer could work the radar. The eventual 'thimble'-shaped radome on a longer nose was selected after several other styles had been tried and test flights showed that the alterations to the external shape had cost just 5mph (8km/h) of speed over the Mk.20 with handling near identical. The last Sea Hornets were withdrawn in 1955.

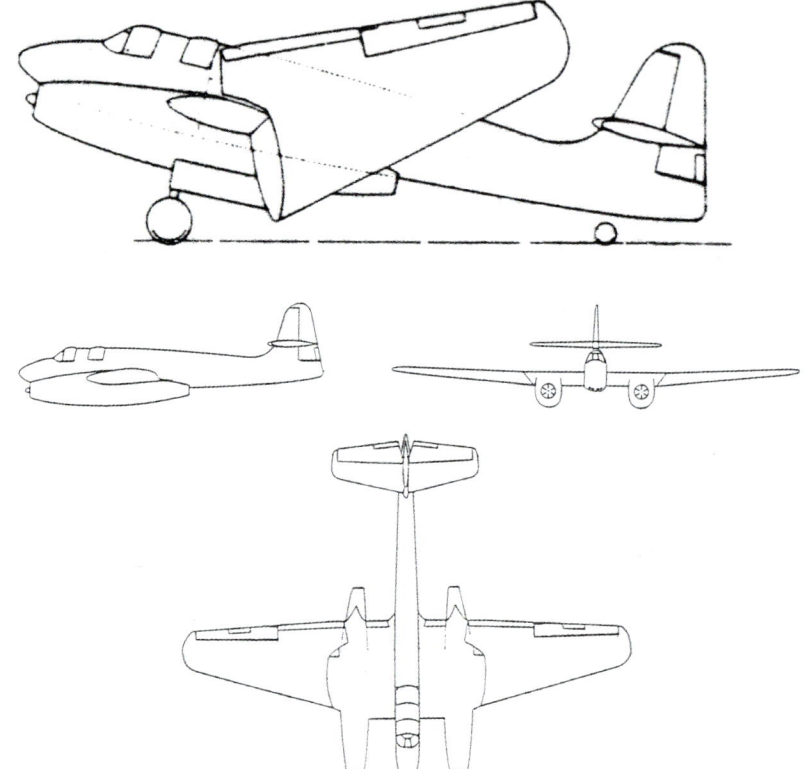

ABOVE The Short 'Jet Sturgeon' (c1945). The wings folded rearwards. *RAF Museum*

Short 'Jet Sturgeon' (c1945)

Span:	61ft 11in (18.87m)
Length:	46ft 6in (14.17m)
Wing Area:	590sq.ft (54.87sq.m)
All-Up-Weight:	23,500lb (10,660kg)
Powerplant:	2 x RR AJ.40
Max Speed / Height:	?
Armament:	4 x 20mm cannon

CHAPTER SEVEN — NAVAL FIGHTERS PART TWO INCLUDING STRIKE FIGHTERS

Strike fighters

Towards the end of the war the Fleet Air Arm began a search for a strike fighter. A tendency to combine the duties of the bomber and fighter led to the development of a number of such designs, which were capable of carrying heavy offensive loads over long distances then, after reaching and attacking their objectives, possessing a performance equal to that of contemporary fighters. The projects described in the remainder of this chapter were not totally related but they group together into one section very neatly.

Boulton Paul P.105

J. D. North, Boulton Paul's designer, continued his naval studies with the P.105 project for a multi-role design. The intention was to provide the smallest possible high-performance naval carrier-borne aircraft that could undertake, by quick conversion (if necessary on the carrier itself), either torpedo bombing (P.105A), bomber, reconnaissance (P.105B) or escort fighter (P.105C) duties. The idea was to have one basic airframe together with several modules, made up of new underbelly or cockpit sections, for role conversion. Thus a greater number of this small aeroplane and its compact conversion units could be housed in a carrier than contemporary types, thereby increasing the number

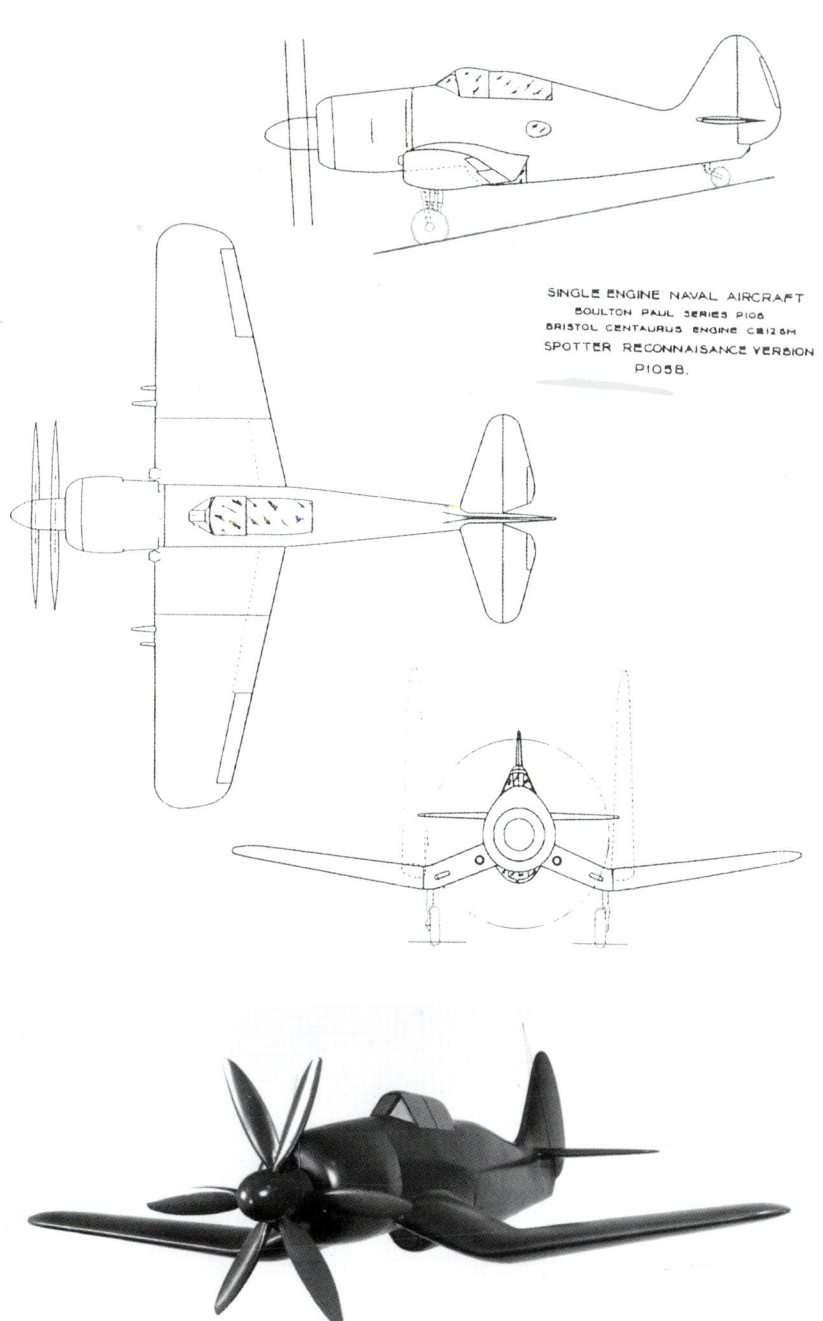

TOP The spotter reconnaissance version of the Boulton Paul P.105B (1.44). *Les Whitehouse*

ABOVE A model of the P.105. *Alec Brew*

Boulton Paul P.105 (1.44)	
Span:	38ft 0in (11.58m)
Length:	34ft 5in (10.49m) tail down
Wing Area:	250sq.ft (23.25sq.m)
All Up-Weight:	12,285lb (5,572kg) torpedo, 12,509lb (5,674kg) bomber
Powerplant:	1 x Centaurus CE.12.SM
Max Speed / Height:	as a fighter 407mph (655km/h) at sea level, 469mph (755km/h) at 20,000ft (6,096m) at 12,500lb (5,670kg)
Armament:	1 x torpedo or 2 x 1,000lb (454kg) bombs, 2 or 4 x 0.5in (12.7mm) machine guns or 4 x 20mm cannon (fighter)

of aircraft available for the diverse operations to be performed. Boulton Paul declared that this aircraft's very high performance would ensure an effective penetration of enemy defences. However, before any detailed performance estimates were completed it was decided to change from the original Griffon 61 engine to the Centaurus (fitted with a contra-rotating reversible-pitch propeller). The folded width was 15ft 4in (4.67m),

129

internal fuel 260 gallons (1,182 litres), and initial rate of climb (at 14,000lb [6,350kg] overload) 3,660ft/min (1,116m/min). The full brochure was submitted to DTD but not taken up.

Boulton Paul P.107

The P.107 was essentially a landplane two-seat long-range escort fighter derivative of the P.105 that introduced twin fins and rudders and a rear gun station, and had the torpedo blister removed. It could also be converted for photo-reconnaissance and fighter bomber duties and, although not belonging to the naval fighter category, followed the P.105 very closely. Sufficient fuel (495 gallons [2,251 litres] internal plus 140 gallons [637 litres] in two drop tanks) was carried to give a range of 3,000 miles (4,827km) plus 30 minutes of combat; without drop tanks the range was 2,200 miles (3,540km). There was a fixed forward armament (four 20mm cannon) together with two rear defence 0.5in (12.7mm) remotely controlled 'free' guns (housed completely within the fuselage except for the ends of the barrels); the latter's field of fire was considered adequate to deal with a rear attack. Some of the fuel could be substituted by 2,000lb (907kg) of bombs to give a fighter bomber with a range of 700 miles (1,126km). A six-blade contra-rotating propeller was fitted.

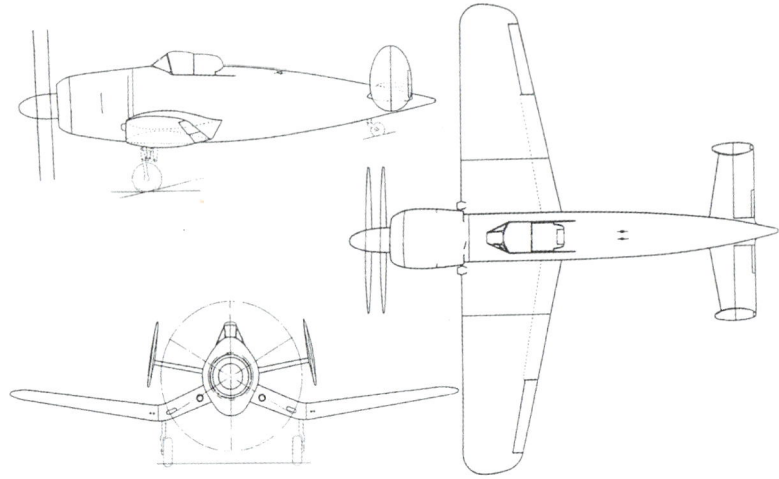

ABOVE The Boulton Paul P.107 (4.44). *Les Whitehouse*

Blackburn B.48 'Firecrest'

Blackburn spent much of the war working hard to develop and perfect its troublesome Firebrand (see Chapter 6). Air Marshal Linnell, CRD, wrote as early as August 1942 that future plans for the Firebrand were to try and 'develop it into something useful', and one line of development by George Petty's design team brought a new aircraft. The Blackburn B.48, unofficially known at Brough as the

BELOW Prototype Blackburn S.28/43 'Firecrest' RT651 is seen at the SBAC Show at Radlett in September 1947.

Boulton Paul P.107 (4.44)	
Span:	38ft 0in (11.58m)
Length:	34ft 8in (10.57m) tail down
Wing Area:	250sq.ft (23.25sq.m)
All-Up-Weight:	15,900lb (7,212kg)
Powerplant:	1 x Centaurus CE.12.SM
Max Speed / Height:	470mph (756km/h) at 22,000ft (6,706m)
Armament:	4 x 20mm cannon plus 2 x 0.5in (12.7mm) machine guns

TOP Firecrest prototype VF172 on display at the Farnborough Show on 8 September 1948.

MIDDLE This picture of VF172 was taken on 3 February 1949. *BAe Brough Heritage*

BOTTOM The sister volume in the 'British Secret Projects' series covering jet fighters since 1950 referred to versions of the Blackburn B.50 jet fighter-striker proposed in a brochure dated 17 February 1945. Since that book was published this artwork has been discovered showing another B.50 design, this time a turboprop-powered FAA strike aircraft. No other details are known (c1945). *BAe Brough Heritage*

Firecrest but always called in official circles by its specification number S.28/43, was a full redesign of the Firebrand, but it would not progress beyond the prototype stage.

The first ideas to incorporate new laminar flow wings were discussed in September 1943 and it was estimated that these would increase speed by about 13mph (21km/h) and cut wing weight by 700lb (318kg). Later it was decided to extend the scope of development and S.28/43 evolved from collaborations between Ministry and manufacturer. A redesigned fuselage with the pilot raised and moved forward relative to the engine resulted in a much improved view, while a contra-rotating propeller was included, used by Blackburn to reduce the rudder power (the Firebrand's rudder size had been determined by the need to control swing on take-off). The opportunity was also taken to eliminate other undesirable features and, with a simplified structure, a saving in structure weight of some 1,400lb (635kg) was achieved, which allowed another 70 gallons (318 litres) of fuel to be carried while still operating at a gross weight of around 900lb (408kg) less than the Firebrand. The Hawker Tempest's windscreen and blister hood were also adapted for the new aircraft.

A decision to proceed with two Centaurus-powered prototypes was made on 11 November 1943, and the aircraft was designated Blackburn Y.A.1. It was seen as a valuable type because it would be able to do a certain amount of steep dive-bombing work beyond its fighter role, but estimates for a spring 1944 first flight were to prove optimistic. As work proceeded proposals were made for alternative engines, while competition was also forthcoming from other types like the Wyvern (below). In January 1945 Blackburn supplied a brochure for installing a Napier E.122 NS.79.SM, a development of the Sabre, which looked attractive, and on 14 March a go-ahead was given for three E.122 prototypes together with a third Centaurus machine. The Ministry felt that this work would enable Blackburn to learn up-to-date techniques of design in aerodynamics and structures, while the E.122 project would support a reasonable programme of development at Napier.

In March 1945 the Sabre project was expected to have an all-up weight of 16,641lb (7,548kg), maximum rate of climb 2,740ft/min (835m/min) at 7,500ft (2,286m), take 3.8 minutes to get to 10,000ft (3,048m), and have a ceiling of 34,500ft (10,516m); in June the estimated top speed in the fighter role was 403mph (648km/h) at 19,000ft (5,791m). Specification S.10/45 was raised to cover the Sabre Firecrest, and N. E. Rowe considered that this aircraft and the piston-engined Westland N.11/44 Wyvern were vital to the Navy. To date the S.10/45 was the only aircraft envisaged to take the E.122, and this was an added incentive for production. On 12 June it was agreed that construction of the S.10/45 prototypes should be 'energetically pursued', but a final decision on the version's production would come later.

However, it was eventually discovered that the overall balance of the Sabre Firecrest was too far forward and the design could only proceed if the engine was placed behind the pilot with a shaft drive to the propeller in the nose. This entailed some major redesign and, coupled with an increase in weight of 1,000lb (454kg), helped to bring the cancellation of the Sabre project on 8 October 1945. In addition, on 10 August, during Admiralty staff discussions, the S.10/45 had been described as a post-war project that would be in competition with other projects for limited funds. On 16 September it was agreed that the S.10/45 fell short of staff requirements, so was neither justified nor sound policy. It was proposed that the project be dropped and that Blackburn should be asked to produce a single-seat strike aircraft that would meet all of the Navy's new requirements.

In mid-1946 brochures were offered for Firecrests fitted with Proteus, Clyde or Python propeller gas turbines. These were collectively designated Y.A.6 and B.62 and generated much interest within the naval staff, who were keen to encourage them because this aircraft was seen as a useful hedge against failure of Westland's N.12/45 Clyde-powered Wyvern. With its lower all-up weight and smaller dimensions, the Blackburn could also operate from the Navy's older carriers without modifications being made to their lifts and arrester gear. Blackburn's preliminary estimates suggested that the Proteus would have an all-up weight of 16,174lb (7,337kg), a sea level rate of climb of 4,440ft/min (1,353m/min), a service ceiling of 41,000ft (12,497m) and a top speed of 423mph (681km/h); the Python's figures were 16,530lb (7,498kg), 4,260ft/min (1,298m/min), 40,000ft (12,192m), and 442mph (711km/h), while the Clyde's were 16,406lb (7,442kg), 4,255ft/min (1,297m/min), 39,000ft (11,887m), and 410mph (660km/h). However, to some extent these projects were viewed as test beds and also new aircraft, with the extra design work that would be entailed, so they were not adopted.

The Centaurus Firecrest continued, but in January 1946, during final design work, development on

Blackburn B.48 Firecrest (flown)	
Span:	44ft 11.5in (13.70m)
Length:	39ft 3.5in (11.98m)
Wing Area:	361.5sq.ft (33.62sq.m)
All-Up-Weight:	16,800lb (7,620kg)
Powerplant:	1 x Centaurus 59 2,825hp (2,107kW)
Max Speed / Height:	380mph (612km/h) at 19,000ft (5,791m)
Armament:	1 x 2,097lb (951kg) torpedo, 2 x 500lb (227kg) bombs or 8 x RP, 2 x 0.5in (12.7mm) machine guns (none carried)

the Centaurus 77 with its contra-propellers was stopped, which forced the substitution of a Centaurus 57 type to give the required power. This also meant a redesign of the fin and rudder to increase their combined area from 33sq ft to 41sq ft (3.1sq m to 3.8sq m), and the new engine itself needed special flexible mountings; in this form it was redesignated the Centaurus 59.

The Firecrest suffered long delays before its first flight, then the end of the war removed much of the urgency behind the programme. On 18 February 1947, in the snow of that year's dreadful winter, the first prototype RT651 was finally rolled out for engine testing, and on 1 April it made its maiden flight. The second machine was RT656 and the third, ordered together with the Sabre aircraft, VF172. However, in September 1946 S. Scott-Hall at the Ministry of Supply revealed that the type would need strengthening to make it acceptable as a strike fighter. Considerable redesign was necessary to produce a weight and performance similar to the Wyvern, and the aeroplane would thus be a second string to the Westland machine at a considerable expenditure in design effort. Therefore, by the time the Firecrest became airborne its chances of production were gone, although no decision had been reached officially.

On 10 November 1947 the MoS requested that flying should cease, but a week later VF172 was reinstated to examine power-operated ailerons. In

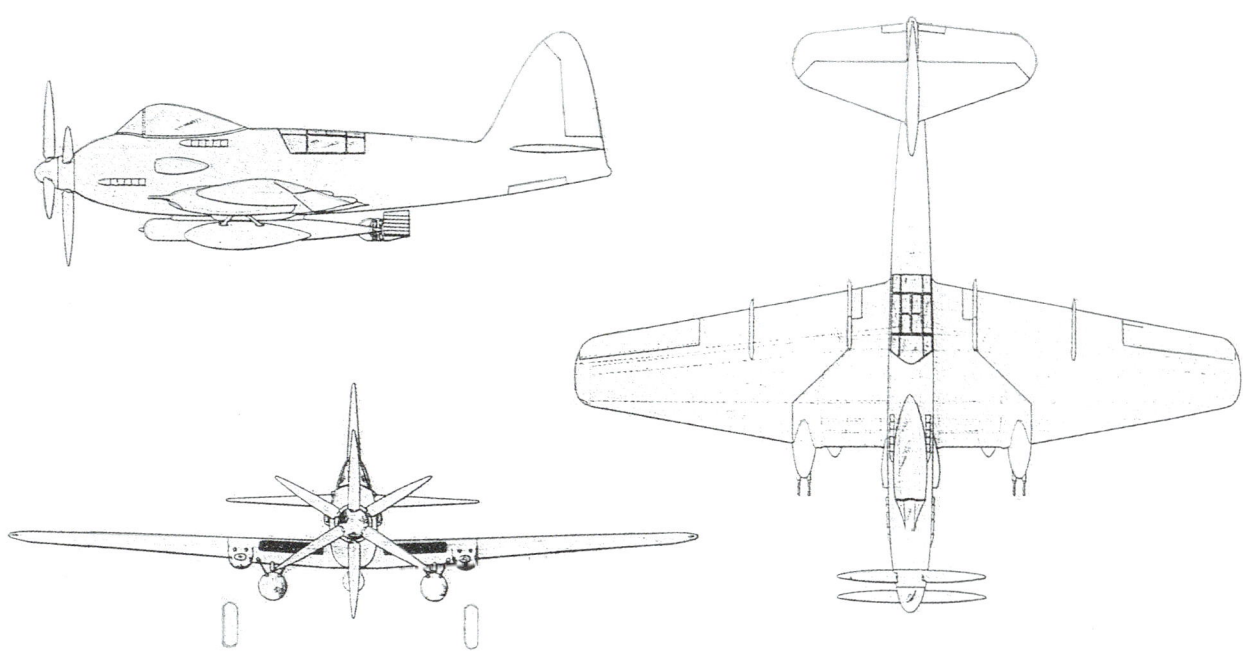

ABOVE The Fairey Strike Fighter 'Project A' with a tandem Merlin powerplant (27.9.44).

mid-1947, following discussions with RAE, Blackburn had concluded that the comparatively thick laminar flow section gave rise to speed variations and non-linear hinge moments that were very difficult to surmount by aerodynamic balance. To improve lateral control Blackburn felt that satisfactory forces throughout the speed range could be achieved by power control with artificial feel, so in October VF172 had power operation components fitted to the elevator and rudder. Flight testing had also shown that it would be beneficial to reduce the dihedral, and VF172 was completed with just 3° of outer-wing dihedral. This aircraft began prototype flight tests on 6 February 1948 and the power control trials that followed produced some valuable general information. On 14 April 1950 RT651 and VF172 were sold to Blackburn to be broken up; RT656, which never flew, lasted into 1952.

Fairey Strike Fighter

In August 1944 Fairey was asked to assess the possibilities of some tandem twin-engine studies it had been pursuing being applied to a naval strike aircraft. A brief verbal statement of the requirements was given and in October a full tender with a twin-tandem two-stage Merlin powerplant (called 'Project A'), together with a slightly larger alternative twin two-stage Griffon arrangement ('Project B'), was submitted. The design was intended primarily to be a single-seater, although there was the possibility of fitting a rear compartment for an observer. The engine arrangement was precisely similar to Fairey's concurrent O.21/44 torpedo bomber and had contra-rotating propellers. Two cannon were housed in each of two wing 'nacelles' (which also contained the main undercarriage), one torpedo or a 2,000lb (907kg) or 1,600lb (726kg) bomb could be carried on the fuselage centreline between the spars, and another 1,000lb (454kg) bomb (or a drop tank) could go under each of the inner wings. Internal fuel totalled 300 gallons (1,364 litres), but the drop tanks increased the capacity to 520 gallons (2,364 litres) and allowed the aeroplane to act as a long-range fighter.

The torpedo cut the top speed at 20,000ft (6,096m) from 460mph (740km/h) to 388mph (624km/h) and increased time to 10,000ft (3,048m) from 4.1 minutes to 6.85 minutes; service ceiling for the short-range fighter condition was 36,000ft (10,973m), which fell to 29,600ft (9,022m) with the torpedo. The long-range fighter had a range of 820 miles (1,319km). Equivalent figures for the Griffon were 397mph (639km/h) at 20,000ft, down from 473mph (761km/h), 4.25 and 7.0 minutes, 38,000ft (11,582m) and 31,750ft (9,677m), and 860 miles (1,383km). The twin-Merlin 'Project A', the main proposal, did not compare at all well with the concurrent Westland N.11/44 (later the Wyvern). Although Fairey's design was expected to have a better take-off and climb performance, in other respects it fell short of the N.11/44 and the naval staff's requirements.

In March 1945 Fairey revised and improved the design, which, although still schemed around two Merlin RM.17.SMs and carrying additional internal fuel, was made more compact. Some Ministry staff thought the project in its revised

TOP ROW & ABOVE RIGHT These poor-quality but unique illustrations show a model of the Fairey Strike Fighter of October 1944. *RAF Museum*

ABOVE LEFT An impression of the October 1944 Fairey Strike Fighter. *RAF Museum*

form was quite promising and at last compared reasonably well with the Westland. Up to 20,000ft (6,096m) it was better in the climb and as good in speed as the N.11/44, but above this height the Westland pulled away and had a considerable advantage in speed. However, the Merlin had practically reached its design peak and it was becoming increasingly obvious that the piston engine as a whole would inevitably be superseded by the gas turbine. N. E. Rowe observed that this aircraft was more suited to a turbine propeller, so, after a request from the Ministry, Fairey also investigated using a Rolls-Royce Clyde or other jet-cum-propeller gas turbine engines (i.e. turboprops) as an alternative. However, it was found that these did not offer such a good performance as two Merlins.

Next Rolls-Royce provided advance data for three different sizes of turboprop, referred to as the RB.52 (an improved Clyde), RB.52 + 30%, and RB.52 + 50%. These were also investigated as alternatives for the strike fighter, but the twin Merlins still gave better results and Fairey concluded that the high cruising consumption of the single turbine engine running in a throttled condition was mainly responsible for the poor comparison. The company suggested that the use of small twin turbines driving contra-rotating propellers, in a manner similar to the tandem piston scheme, would show much better results than a single turbine of the same aggregate power; one of the small turbines alone would be used for cruising. Fairey now prepared two new naval strike fighter studies, one having a single RB.52 + 50% turboprop with contra-rotating propellers, the other two 75% RB.52s arranged in tandem with a separate contra-propeller gearbox, each propeller being driven by its own turbine.

A summary of these projects, together with a twin piston scheme for comparison, was submitted to MAP on 30 June 1945, each of them having a span of 52ft (15.85m), four 20mm cannon and a torpedo. The pistons offered a total of 3,920bhp (2,923kW), gave an all-up weight of 23,900lb (10,841kg), a maximum speed of 410mph (660km/h) at 10,000ft (3,048m), and 6.8 minutes to 10,000ft; the RB.52 + 50% provided 3,525bhp (2,629kW) and 1,090lb (4.8kN) thrust and gave figures of 24,400lb (11,068kg) weight, 395mph (636km/h) at 10,000ft, and 2.67 minutes to that height; the two 75% RB.52s gave the same power, 23,300lb (10,569kg), 413mph (665km/h), and 2.50 minutes. The twin turbine saved 1,100lb (499kg) in weight, cut down the frontal area and increased the speed over the single-turbine alternative, and it also offered a performance that was better in some respects that the twin Merlins.

A Ministry report suggested that a single Clyde was, generally speaking, inferior to the twin Merlins on all counts of performance, but the higher-power engines gave an aircraft that was much more attractive and became a strong competitor to the N.11/44. In mid-June the Admiralty approved in principle the Fairey strike fighter as a type that it would like to encourage, and during September the company made considerable progress with the turbine versions of the aircraft. In due course Staff requirements were raised for an O.5/43 (Spearfish torpedo bomber) replacement based around Fairey's project; this became Specification N.16/45, but no prototypes were ordered until 20 June 1946.

At the end of the war it became necessary for the Ministry to review a large number of engine projects, and Rolls-Royce was requested to state its views as to whether the twin-tandem piston engine designs should be continued or abandoned in favour of the turboprop. At a meeting held at MAP, Rolls-Royce stated that it was entirely in favour of using Fairey's twin-turboprop arrangement for the naval strike project and undertook to produce the special engine and gears. The decision was also taken here to abandon four Fairey torpedo bomber prototypes to O.21/44 while the naval strike project was now reconsidered around the twin-turboprop arrangement. Strike had become the primary role for Fairey's aircraft – whereas Westland's Wyvern was essentially designed as a fighter but with provision to carry offensive weapons, the Fairey had become a strike aircraft that, after releasing its load, was expected to be capable of offensive combat against all of the enemy aircraft it was likely to meet. Rolls-Royce also stated that, for this particular purpose, its policy now was to develop axial flow jet engines, so Fairey abandoned its tandem arrangement in favour of putting the two engines side by side behind the main gearbox and beneath the floor of the pilot's cockpit.

A draft of the layout was shown to Rolls-Royce, which was entirely in favour, and it was adopted as the latest scheme for the naval strike aircraft; the engine itself was now called the AP.25. A full brochure was submitted to Rowe, now DGTD, on 13 November 1945 and noted that, although the AP.25 was still only a paper engine, Rolls-Royce had undertaken to provide a powerplant ready for installation by December 1946. Fairey had become quite frustrated by so many changes to its naval aircraft programmes, and Hollis-Williams stated in his covering letter that

'…this investigation has hung about now for 18 months, and probably constitutes a record in time wastage for the start of a new design, but it has been influenced very largely by the changeover from reciprocating engines to turbines and we have to admit that the design has steadily improved with each successive effort.'

The turbine engine favoured naval aeroplanes very much because so much power was available for take-off, which made the 'take-off problem' no longer a criterion of the design. This meant that Fairey had to revise its ideas on flap systems and the new study abandoned the Youngman type flap (whose chief virtue was a very efficient take-off setting) and adopted a new design based on Fowler principles. As a result it also had a completely clean trailing edge without hinge brackets, which had been a feature of Fairey's recent designs. The all-metal structure was built on normal lines, but improvements had been introduced to the wing structure to simplify the production problem of producing the high finish necessary to maintain laminar flow. The torpedo was still carried on the fuselage centreline, but bombs, depth charges or rockets would be carried under the wing outboard of the undercarriage between and below the cannon.

Each of the two side-by-side power units drove its own propeller through an independent gear train carried by a common centrally disposed gearbox. The two jet pipes ejected through the bottom of the fuselage just behind the wings and were disposed in such a manner that, in the event of one engine and propeller being stopped, any loss of aircraft stability resulting from the consequent introduction of torque reaction and single-propeller slipstream effects would be wholly or partly balanced by an equal and opposite loss of thrust from the relevant outlet pipe. Internal fuel for the torpedo role was 545 gallons (2,478 litres), but 595 gallons (2,705 litres) could be carried for fighter escort work; these versions' respective times to 10,000ft (3,048m) were 2.1 and 1.9 minutes, with service ceilings at 44,000ft (13,411m) and 49,000ft (14,935m). The type could also be adapted as a two-seat night fighter and for photo-reconnaissance work.

On 21 November 1945 R. S. Sorley noted that the subtle proposal to balance torque reaction when only one propeller was in action was a selling point on which it would be difficult to produce data. Rowe then advised Fairey that there was ample reserve on the take-off specification and cruising range to allow the wing area and overall size to be reduced, and on 10 December Fairey completed an amended design to the draft N.16/45, whose functions had now also been altered (all reference to the fighter and reconnaissance roles was gone and dive bombing had been introduced). The folded span was 20ft (6.10m), as previously, and a generous tail volume was provided to give a desirable standard of stability. Time to 10,000ft (3,048m) was now 2.25 minutes, the service ceiling was 38,500ft (11,735m), and range 700 miles (1,126km).

On 2 January 1946 the Admiralty announced that it wished to go ahead with the project as rapidly as possible, with a target date for first flight eighteen months from the date of the Advisory Design Conference; however, it became apparent that the coupled powerplant was not expected to be available until early 1949. On 14 August the idea of leaving out the gun

Fairey Strike Fighter (Project A) (3.10.44)

Span:	49ft 0in (14.94m)
Length:	40ft 4in (12.29m)
Wing Area:	415sq.ft (38.595sq.m)
All-Up-Weight:	17,900lb (8,119kg) naval fighter, 21,935lb (9,950kg) torpedo strike
Powerplant:	2 x Merlin RM.14.SM 2,200hp (1,641kW)
Max Speed / Height:	474mph (763km/h) at 23,000ft (7,010m)
Armament:	1 x torpedo or 1 x 2,000lb (907kg) or 1,600lb (726kg) bomb, 2 x 1,000lb (454kg) bombs, 4 x 20mm cannon

Fairey Strike Fighter (Project B) (3.10.44)

Span:	52ft 4in (15.95m)
Length:	42ft 9in (13.03m)
Wing Area:	475sq.ft (44.175sq.m)
All-Up-Weight:	21,100lb (9,571kg) naval fighter, 25,555lb (11,592kg) torpedo strike
Powerplant:	2 x Griffon RG.25.SM 2,625hp (1,957kW)
Max Speed / Height:	480mph (772km/h) at 23,000ft (7,010m)
Armament:	1 x torpedo or 1 x 2,000lb (907kg) or 1,600lb (726kg) bomb, 2 x 1,000lb (454kg) bombs, 4 x 20mm cannon

Fairey Strike Fighter (13.11.45)

Span:	51ft 0in (15.54m)
Length:	44ft 7in (13.59m)
Wing Area:	390sq.ft (36.27sq.m)
All-Up-Weight:	23,100lb (10,478kg) torpedo fighter, 23,100lb (10,478kg) escort fighter
Powerplant:	2 x RR AP.25 2,517hp (1,877kW) plus 1,015lb (4.5kN) each
Max Speed / Height:	435mph (700km/h) at 6,000ft (1,829m) torpedo, 494mph (795km/h) at 9,500ft (2,896m) escort
Armament:	1 x torpedo, 2 x 1,000lb (454kg) or 500lb (227kg) bombs, depth charges or 6 x RP, 4 x 20mm cannon

Fairey Strike Aircraft (10.12.45)

Span:	46ft 0in (14.02m)
Length:	44ft 7in (13.59m)
Wing Area:	370sq.ft (34.41sq.m)
All-Up-Weight:	23,000lb (10,433kg), 21,100lb (9,571kg) no bombs
Powerplant:	2 x AP.25 2,517hp (1,877kW) plus 1,015lb (4.5kN) each
Max Speed / Height:	443mph (713km/h), 497mph (800km/h) clean at 10,000ft (3,048m)
Armament:	Bombs, plus torpedoes

to save weight was considered, which gave a maximum speed in the clean condition of 476mph (765km/h), and on 18 September Fairey was asked to study a tricycle undercarriage. On 7 October the project was described as becoming too heavy for naval requirements, and two days later, at the Design Conference, Fairey was asked to take out 1,000lb (454kg) of weight. On that day a target date was also discussed for the Fairey GR.17/45 project (later to become the Gannet), and it was agreed to give this aircraft definite priority over the N.16/45.

By 20 January 1947 the powerplant had been named the 'Coupled Tweed' and each unit gave 3,020shp (2,252kW) and 380lb (1.7kN) of thrust. On 12 March the Admiralty no longer considered that the aircraft was promising enough to warrant the

RIGHT Impressions of the Fairey Strike Aircraft at 11.45. *RAF Museum*

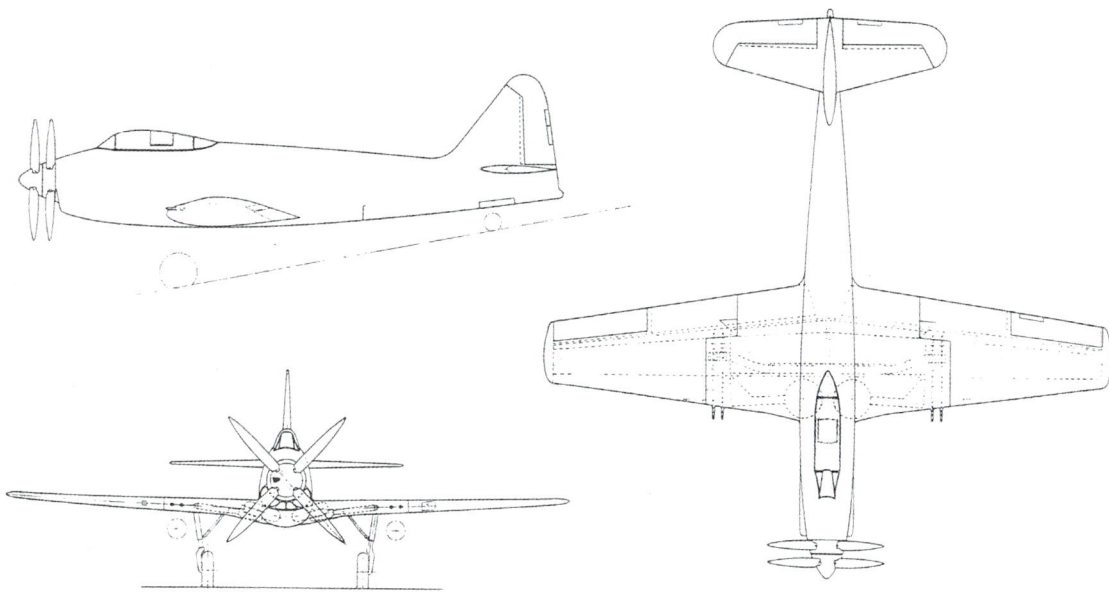

ABOVE **The Fairey Strike Aircraft (7.12.45).** *RAF Museum*

expenditure and effort that would be involved, and made it clear that it desired not to continue with the project. Cancellation of the N.16/45 would, from the Admiralty's point of view, also make it agreeable to abandon work on the AP.25. Fairey had put a considerable amount of work into this aircraft, while also being in competition with Westland with its Wyvern studies, but Rolls-Royce eventually fell into programme difficulties and was forced to cut out a vast amount of development work. The twin-coupled AP.25 was one of the developments to be cancelled and, since there was no other powerplant that could be conveniently installed in Fairey's design, it was agreed that further work on the N.16/45 should also be discontinued. The Wyvern, however, was continued.

Fairey itself carried on with the Gannet and that story is taken up in *British Secret Projects Volume 2: Jet Bombers since 1949*. The early 'Gannet' layouts were quite similar to the N.16/45 because Fairey's Design Office made use of the experience it had gained with the older project to save time.

Westland Wyvern

In the early months of 1944 W. E. W. Petter, Westland's technical director, proposed a single-seat fleet fighter powered by Rolls-Royce's new and large 'H' reciprocating engine (later to be called the Eagle). In April the initial work was expanded to embrace three versions of the design, one with a shaft drive 'H', one with a nose-mounted 'H', and one with a nose 'turbine airscrew' (turboprop), and each of them was offered as a naval or RAF fighter. A MAP meeting held on 19 April agreed that a long-range fighter striker for RAF and naval use should be of outstanding value, and it was also agreed that Westland should proceed with its design (presumably with the nose-mounted 'H' engine, as built).

On 23 June 1944 Petter tendered the basic aircraft under the designation W.34, powered by the 'H' engine with an initial output of 3,230hp (2,409kW) at 23,000ft (7,010m) – the target output was 4,500hp (3,356kW). The span was 44ft (13.41m) and the wing area 350sq ft (32.55sq m). For short-range operations 230 gallons (1,046 litres) of fuel would be carried, and for torpedo work 430 gallons (1,955 litres). Gun armament was four 20mm cannon (reduced to two when carrying a torpedo), and the following data was given for short-range fleet fighter, torpedo bomber and RAF short-range fighter forms: take-off weight 17,355lb (7,872kg), 20,420lb (9,263kg) and 16,735lb (7,591kg); maximum speed at 25,000ft (7,620m) 472mph (759km/h), 432mph (695km/h) and 480mph (772km/h); and rate of climb at 5,000ft (1,524m) 3,970ft/min (1,210m/min), 2,860ft/min (872m/min) and 4,150ft/min (1,265m/min). As a fighter the service ceiling was given as 39,000ft (11,887m).

By early July 1944 the Admiralty was showing a keen interest in the aircraft. However, AVM J. D. Breakey, ACAS(TR), told CRD that he felt that the estimated performance was disappointing. The top speed, given as 480mph (772km/h) by Westland and re-estimated at 463mph (745km/h) by Liptrot, was less than that expected from the F.2/43 and Hornet, both of which would be in service some two to three years earlier. Its ceiling and rate of climb were inferior, and its range no greater except in the one condition when carrying 2,000lb (907kg) of bombs. Breakey declared that this last feature

'...is virtually the aircraft's only merit and seems a very small return for the large step up in power given

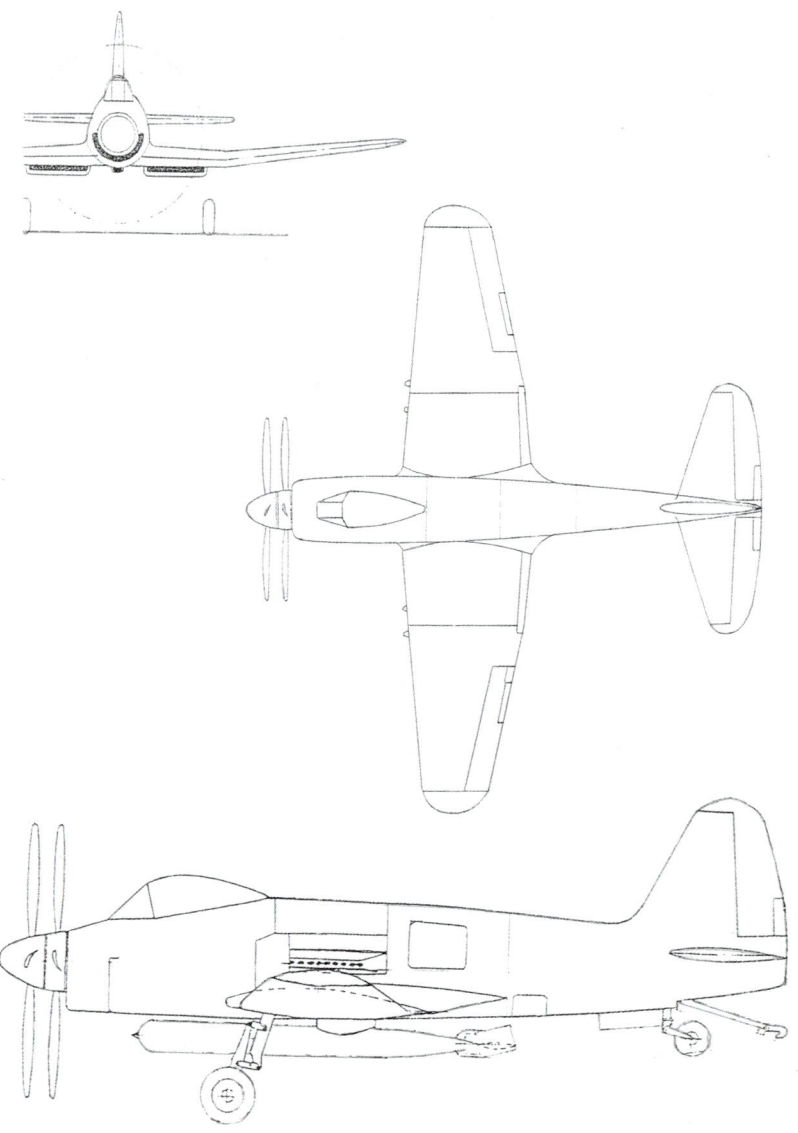

ABOVE Early layout for Westland's single-seat naval fighter and strike aircraft, with a fuselage-mounted 3,000bhp (2,237kW) 'H' engine (mid-1944). The span was 40ft (12.19m), wing area 320sq ft (29.76sq m), all-up weight 17,300lb (7,847m), and maximum speed 420mph (676km/h). *The late Fred Ballam, Westland Archive*

by the "H" engine, and an increase in weight of some 6,000lb (2,722kg) over the F.2/43. While we are, of course, decidedly interested in any new fighter project built around the "H" engine, and particularly in one designed for further development using a turbine driven propeller, I feel it would be wrong to encourage Westland in believing that there is likely to be any considerable RAF use for this aeroplane. I should have much preferred to see this firm tackling a straightforward fighter of the F.2/43 type but built around the "H" and capable of development with the turbine-cum-propeller. I realise that such an aircraft must be heavier than the F.2/43 but I am quite sure that it need not go up to 16,000lb (7,258kg).'

Nevertheless the Admiralty went ahead. Specification N.11/44 was written around the type and in August 1944 six prototypes were ordered; F.13/44 was also written to cover an RAF version, but this was soon dropped. In fact, the W.34 was designed from the start (but at a later stage as suggested by the first brochure) with the installation of the Rolls-Royce RB.39 Clyde turboprop in mind. The Clyde version (called the W.35) had wings, tail, fin and empennage that were common to the W.34, but an all-new fuselage. In 1945 a new specification, N.12/45, was produced for this version, and three prototypes were eventually ordered in February 1946.

Rolls-Royce intimated that it had insufficient facilities to permit the Eagle (as the 'H' had become) and Clyde to be developed concurrently, and it was essential to concentrate its effort on just one of these engines. Rolls-Royce's E. W. Hives explained that the Eagle in its present form could only be regarded as an interim version. and two years of work would be required to develop the engine fully (to 4,000hp [2,983kW]). In the case of Westland's aircraft it appeared that progressive improvements in performance were much more likely to accrue from development of the Clyde than from the Eagle. Rolls-Royce felt that energy should now be concentrated more on turbine engines and, as a result, the turboprop became the more important power unit for Westland's strike fighter.

In June 1945 RAE reported that the original piston W.34 had been handicapped by the choice of an undeveloped engine of high specific weight and, for a high-speed aircraft designed to carry a large load in fuel and weapons, this had led to a high all-up weight (in fact, an extremely heavy aircraft) and (to keep down drag) a high wing loading. The chief effect of substituting the light Clyde for the heavy Eagle was a lower all-up weight and wing loading. The take-off and landing performance of the Eagle version was poor, but RAE stated that the Clyde would improve this and also provide a 50mph (80km/h) gain in speed and 1,000ft (305m) gain in climb at sea level, although

LEFT A model of Westland's early design for a single-seat naval fighter and strike aircraft. *Joe Cherrie*

the top speed at 20,000ft (6,096m) was unchanged. The performance at 20,000ft – 445mph (716km/h) and 2,500ft/min (762m/min) – was not thought to be particularly good for a fighter that would not be in service for two years, but its combat range (550nm [1,019km] radius) was excellent for such a type. At this stage the Clyde was expected to give 2,300bhp (1,715kW) and 1,040lb (4.6kN) thrust at sea level.

By now Petter had left Westland for English Electric and had been succeeded as chief designer by John Digby and as technical director by Arthur Davenport. On 27 June 1945 Davenport was able to supply some extra data. The Eagle fighter would now have an all-up weight of 19,194lb (8,706kg) and the torpedo striker 21,879lb (9,924kg), while the W.35 Clyde would give respective weights of 16,300lb (7,394kg) and 19,045lb (8,639kg). By early June 1945 four Eagles had been running for around six months, during which a redesign of the crankcase had already been completed.

During the first half of 1946 the Armstrong Siddeley Python turboprop entered the picture. On 7 February it was agreed that this engine was a very satisfactory alternative and there were good reasons for installing it in the fifth and sixth N.11/44s. However, by May the prototype and pre-production programme comprised six Eagle N.11/44s to fly between September 1946 and February 1947, twenty pre-production N.11/44s to follow them, two Python-powered N.12/45s to fly in August and September 1947, and three Clyde N.12/45s to fly between December 1947 and February 1948. Soon afterwards, however, in the interests of economy, it was agreed to call for one Python instead of the Clyde in one of the three Clyde machines and to order only one further Python prototype.

TOP TS380 was the fourth prototype Rolls-Royce Eagle-powered Westland Wyvern.

MIDDLE The Clyde-powered Wyvern prototype was serial number VP120, seen here on 2 September 1949..

BOTTOM An excellent air-to-air photo of Westland Wyvern S.Mk.4 VW885.

In June 1946 Westland began to examine a variant fitted with an Armstrong Siddeley Cobra powerplant (a new low-power jet), which would need a smaller jet pipe. Although three and a half years away, the Cobra was seen as another suitable alternative to the Clyde and little difficulty was expected in fitting it. However, a report dated 14 January 1947 confirmed that, although the study

Westland Wyvern TF.Mk.1 (flown)	
Span:	44ft 0in (13.41m)
Length:	39ft 3in (11.96m)
Wing Area:	355sq.ft (33.015sq.m)
All-Up-Weight:	21,879lb (9,924kg) torpedo, 19,194lb (8,706kg) clean
Powerplant:	1 x Eagle 22 3,560hp (2,655kW)
Max Speed / Height:	456mph (734km/h) at 23,000ft (7,010m)
Armament:	1 x 20in (510mm) torpedo or 1,000lb (454kg) bomb under fuselage, 2 x 1,000lb (454kg) bombs or 8 x RP under wings, 4 x 20mm cannon

Westland Wyvern S.Mk.4 (flown)	
Span:	44ft 0in (13.41m)
Length:	42ft 3in (12.88m)
Wing Area:	355sq.ft (33.015sq.m)
All-Up-Weight:	21,200lb (9,616kg) normal
Powerplant:	1 x Python 3 3,670hp (2,737kW) plus 1,180lb (5.2kN)
Max Speed / Height:	388mph (624km/h) at sea level
Armament:	1 x 2,500lb (1,134kg) torpedo or 1,000lb (454kg) bomb under fuselage, 2 x 1,000lb (454kg) bombs or 16 x RP under wings, 4 x 20mm cannon

had been completed, the design would not proceed (it was also subsequently agreed that the Cobra engine should not be produced). In the event all six Eagle-powered W.34 prototypes were built and flown, the first TS371 becoming airborne on 12 December 1946, but only three turboprop W.35 prototypes were completed. VP109 (flown on 22 March 1949) and VP113 had the Python, while VP120 (flown on 18 January 1949) was to be the only aircraft anywhere to be powered by a Clyde (the development of this engine was also abandoned). The fourth W.35 prototype was cancelled, and the name Wyvern was not applied until early 1947.

There were long delays getting the Wyvern into service and many development problems. Out of the twenty pre-production Eagle W.34s just the first four were delivered and only ten were built, but ninety-six production examples of the turboprop W.35 were completed. The first Wyvern squadron received its aircraft in 1954, but the type stayed in front-line service for just four years. The ultimate version was the S.Mk.4, the torpedo fighter TF designation having been dropped for strike after the Hawker Sea Fury had taken on the Wyvern's fighter duties.

Westland Wyvern S.Mk.5

Although essentially falling outside the date parameters of this book, and again a strike aircraft rather than a fighter, for completeness coverage is presented here of an S.Mk.5E Wyvern proposed in March 1954 and fitted with a Napier E.141 Double Eland turboprop in a new cowling and with wingtip tanks. It was not built.

In early 1954 the Admiralty was considering a Wyvern strike aircraft replacement. Westland had studied the newly proposed Specification NA.39 requirement and from January 1952 had carried out preliminary design study work on a Wyvern S.Mk.5. Estimates had shown that perhaps eight years would be required

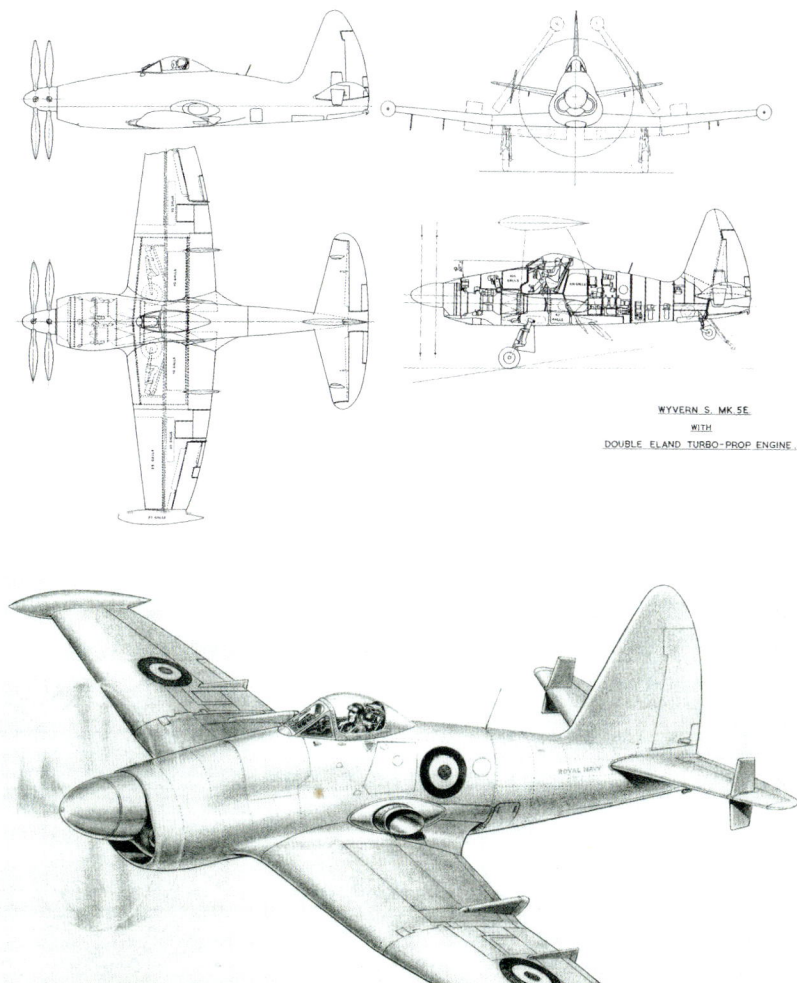

TOP The Westland Wyvern S.Mk.5E proposal with a Napier E.141 Double Eland turboprop (3.54). *The late Fred Ballam, Westland Archive*

ABOVE An artist's impression of the Wyvern S.Mk.5E. *The late Fred Ballam, Westland Archive*

to have an all-new type in service, but in the meantime the air striking power of the Royal Navy would depend on the current Wyvern. Hence Westland, foreseeing a long service life for its aeroplane, had sought ways and means of improving its performance and operational suitability. This improved Wyvern could be in service within three years and so help bridge the gap.

For a powerplant Westland had explored the possibilities of British turboprop engines of suitable size. Interest had at first centred on the Bristol Proteus Mk.3, which was geometrically suitable for the Wyvern, but which would have to be converted to a contra-rotating propeller arrangement to make it operationally suitable. Consequently the engine most favoured by Westland was a development of the Napier Eland, then under prototype development. If this could be converted to a double engine (on the lines of the Armstrong Siddeley

141

Westland Wyvern S.Mk.5E (3.54)	
Span:	46ft 0in (14.02m)
Length:	40ft 3.5in (12.28m)
Wing Area:	377sq.ft (35.06sq.m)
All-Up-Weight:	26,060lb (11,821kg)
Powerplant:	1 x Napier E.141 Double Eland 6,000hp (4,474kW)
Max Speed / Height:	450mph (724km/h) clean, 426mph (686km/h) with torpedo at sea level, 488mph (785km/h) and 461mph (742km/h) at 22,000ft (6,706m)
Armament:	1 x torpedo or various ground attack stores

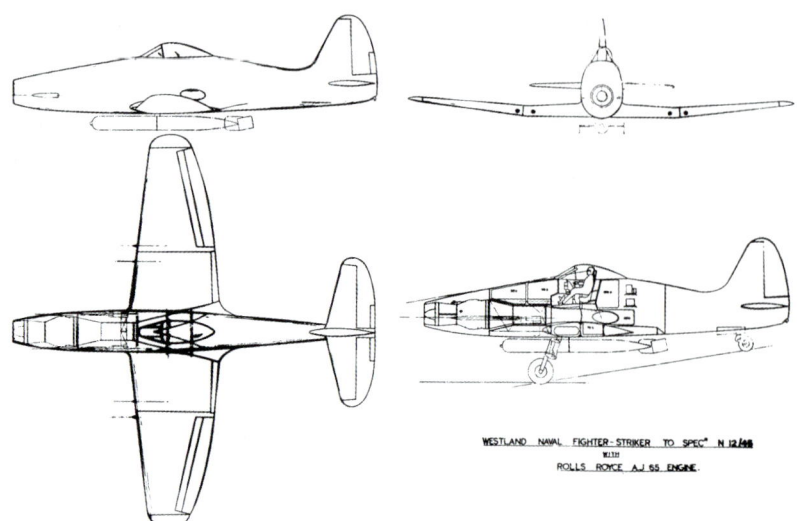

ABOVE The Westland W.36 Wyvern development with a single Rolls AJ.65 jet engine (1946). *The late Fred Ballam, Westland Archive*

Double Mamba) then it would make an ideal powerplant for the Wyvern, with 6,000hp (4,474kW) available initially and with development potential for more than 8,000hp (5,966kW).

This new brochure also introduced a number of other improvements, such as an increased-span centre section to give greater store-carrying space, a high-energy-absorption undercarriage, and wingtip tanks. The resulting design would go a long way towards meeting the requirements, yet would not constitute a great departure from the existing Wyvern. It would have a maximum striking radius of 810nm (1,501km) at high altitude and 580nm (1,074km) for low-level attack. The new type was in fact offered in two forms, as a single-seat strike aircraft and as a two-seater combined strike and radar guide, and was fitted with an eight-blade 13ft 6in (4.11m) contra-rotating propeller. Wing thickness/chord ratio was 14.3% at the fuselage and 12% at the tip, the maximum rate of climb and operational ceiling in clean condition were given as 5,250ft/min (1,600m/min) and 34,000ft (10,363m) respectively, and with a torpedo 4,500ft/min (1,372m/min) and 30,000ft (9,144m).

Westland W.36 Jet Wyvern

In 1947 a version of the Wyvern called the W.36 was drawn, powered by a Rolls-Royce AJ.65 or MetroVick F.9 axial jet engine. Westland described this as an attractive proposition that would exploit to the full the speed and climb potential of an existing design without any major structural alteration. The fuselage and tail were basically as the W.34, there was a new wide-chord inner wing, the jet pipe would be similar in size and dimensions to the current Wyvern Python arrangement, and the W.36 would have a new tricycle undercarriage and carry 600 gallons (2,728 litres) of internal fuel. The absence of the propeller would give an increase in longitudinal stability. With the F.9 engine a short-range fighter version had a sea level rate of climb in dry thrust of 7,600ft/min (2,316m/min) and 13,100ft/min (3,993m/min) in reheat, and a service ceiling of 47,700ft (14,539m); the equivalent figures for the torpedo striker version were 5,300ft/min (1,615m/min), 7,160ft/min (2,182m/min) and 40,600ft (12,375m). Fitted with the AJ.65 these sets of figures were fighter 6,620ft/min (2,018m/min) dry and 11,040ft/min (3,365m/min) in reheat, and 47,000ft (14,326m), and for the striker 5,100ft/min (1,554m/min) dry, 7,820ft/min (2,386m/min) reheat, and 40,200ft (12,253m).

Westland W.36 (2.4.47)	
Span:	44ft 0in (13.41m)
Length:	42ft 3in (12.88m)
Wing Area:	360sq.ft (33.48sq.m)
All-Up-Weight:	Avon engine short range fighter 16,140lb (7,321kg) and torpedo striker 18,774lb (8,516kg); F.9 16,150lb (7,326kg) and 19,075lb (8,652kg)
Powerplant:	1 x Rolls-Royce AJ.65 6,500lb (28.9kN) or MetroVick F.9 7,000lb (31.1kN)
Max Speed / Height:	AJ.65 short range fighter 560mph (901km/h) at sea level, 515mph (829km/h) at 30,000ft (9,144m), torpedo striker 517mph (832km/h) and 498mph (801km/h); F.9 short range fighter 576mph (927km/h) at sea level and 522mph (840km/h) at 30,000ft (9,144m), torpedo striker 576mph (927km/h) and 518mph (833km/h)
Armament:	4 x 30mm Aden cannon, 1 x torpedo, 1 x 'Bootleg' high-speed airborne tossed torpedo, 2,000lb (907kg) bombs, 2 x Red Angel missiles, or rocket projectiles

Chapter Eight
Advances in Technology

ABOVE The Centaurus and four-blade propeller installation on Hawker Fury prototype NX798.

The time period covered by this book just about overlaps with the start of the development and introduction of the first generation of guided weapons for air-to-air and air-to-ground operations, a subject that was described briefly in the post-1950 volumes of this series. However, the advances in technology made during the Second World War to make the aircraft described in this volume work, and for the equivalent types covered in the follow-on bombers and attack aircraft book, were still considerable. Major development programmes included the final generation of high-performance piston engines, the first jet engines, airborne radars, guns and rocket projectiles as the most obvious fields of research, but 'behind the scenes' major advances were also made, for example in the fields of engine fuels, aerodynamics and materials. So let us pause for a moment from the projects themselves to take a quick look at some of the progress that was made during this period.

To begin however, the major re-equipping of the RAF and FAA would not have been possible without a huge expansion in the facilities and production capacity of the industry itself. Many new factories were built (mostly under the 'shadow' scheme, where they came under the control of the individual aircraft companies), but these were supplemented by the production of aircraft and engines in quite a number of car factories. In addition, aircraft were built in Canada and Australia, while the armed forces also received a great number of American types. By the end of the war the aircraft and weapon supply facilities formed an immense, and immensely impressive, organisation.

Looking at aero engines, piston-engine power at altitude had been much improved by the process of supercharging. As an aircraft ascends to higher altitudes the diminishing density of the aspirated air, combined with a reduction of the atmospheric pressure upon which aspiration depends, results in a smaller mass of air entering the cylinder; consequently the mass of fuel to be burned has to be reduced and with it the power of the engine. Supercharging employs a compressor (also called a 'blower') to increase the density of the air taken into the cylinders and it takes the form of an impeller (a wheel with a number of radial vanes formed on one face) turning inside a casing. When the impeller revolves at high speed, the air that enters is carried around between the vanes then thrown outwards by centrifugal force, before escaping through peripheral outlets into a collecting chamber from which it passes to the engine. To keep the engine running at a constant speed at all heights, the supercharger required some form of variable speed drive and, as a result, two-speed superchargers were commonly fitted in which different gear ratios were used according to the altitude. Work on supercharging actually began as early as 1915 and its success was dependent on the ever-increasing quality of fuels to prevent detonation (the spontaneous combustion of the remaining fuel/air mixture or 'end-gas', which can occur following normal combustion with the spark plug).

The power generated by the piston engine is used by the propeller or airscrew. The engine turns a shaft and the propeller is placed on the end or hub where, to pull the aeroplane forward, its blades are set at an angle (or pitch) to

ABOVE The contra-rotating propeller fitting on Supermarine Seafang VB895.

the plane of rotation; however, it is not possible to fix the blades at just one angle and get good results at all speeds. On early aircraft the blades did have a fixed pitch (a set angle), which was intended to form a compromise between good performance at high speed and good performance at low speed. However, the ever-increasing power, speed and performance of military engines and aircraft, particularly fighters like the Spitfire, needed something better. Fine pitch is best for take-off (that is, a small angle to the plane of rotation) and course pitch is best for high speeds (because the large angle will exert the maximum force to drive the aircraft forward).

The answer was the variable-pitch propeller, which altered the blade angle during flight, and also imposed much less strain on the engine while considerably improving the fuel economy. The simplest form was the two-pitch bracket propeller, which had a fine pitch setting for take-off and climb and a course setting for level flight (both were pilot-operated), but the best solution was the constant-speed unit. This had a small pump that,

CHAPTER EIGHT

ADVANCES IN TECHNOLOGY

TOP A wonderful view of the Heat Treatment Bay (formerly the 'Old Prop Shop') at High Duty Alloys, Slough, in 1937. Aluminium propeller blades and piston forgings wait to be heat-treated, an operation that will give them their optimum strength properties. *HDA Forgings*

MIDDLE The Napier Sabre II piston engine. *Rolls-Royce Heritage Trust*

BOTTOM A Sabre installation in a Hawker Typhoon, photographed at RAE Farnborough on 9 July 1941.

without any intervention by the pilot, adjusted the pitch of the propeller as the aircraft climbed or dived, so that the blades were always set at the correct angle whatever the speed selected by the pilot. Early in the war propellers were usually fitted with two or three blades but, with the increasing size of aero engines, it became necessary to fit four or even five blades to absorb all of the extra power. The biggest engines needed six blades, which brought the introduction of the counter-rotating airscrew or contraprop, where two three-bladed propellers were mounted one behind the other and turned in opposite directions. The contraprop had the added benefit that the torque produced by the two propellers was cancelled out, removing an aircraft's tendency to swing to the side, in particular when it was taking-off.

The materials used for blade manufacture were either metal or wood, and Duralumin (aluminium alloy) blades were machined from forgings, as were the aluminium pistons used in the engines themselves. Extra factory space had to be built for all of these components, an example being High Duty Alloys, whose factory at Slough was clearly going to be too small for wartime production. On 16 August 1939 HDA's 'shadow' factory at Redditch was opened and, following bomb damage to the forge at Slough, this new site became responsible for nearly all of the forged aero engine pistons produced in Britain during 1939-45, the final total exceeding 10 million.

ABOVE On the Hawker Tempest V production line is an example showing the fighter's Napier Sabre installation.

There were numerous other developments in engine technology, such as water injection and sleeve valves. Engine development also demanded better materials, and great progress was made in aluminium alloys, while the introduction of the jet brought with it the development of the nickel-chromium alloy 'Nimonic', which offered outstanding strength properties at very high temperatures. This alloy was to prove crucial in the successful operation of jet engines because it allowed them to run for long periods without having to replace any parts – a luxury denied to Germany, whose jet engines consequently had a service life of just a few hours.

During the war the three principal companies to produce piston engines for fighters and bombers were Bristol, Napier and Rolls-Royce. Armstrong Siddeley's last big engine project was the Deerhound (abandoned in 1941) and its only major wartime contribution was the Cheetah, which was virtually confined to trainers. In 1941 Armstrong Siddeley was asked to give up development work on reciprocating engines and instead to undertake work on jet projects. Napier's most important engine was the liquid-cooled Sabre, initially intended to give 2,000bhp (1,491kW) and primarily flown on the Hawker Typhoon and Tempest at rather higher figures, but it was to suffer many development problems and setbacks before making a valuable contribution from 1944 onwards.

Bristol and Rolls-Royce were the most successful engine companies, the first specialising in air-cooled radials, the second in liquid-cooled inline engines. During the 1930s Bristol developed versions of the Aquila, Mercury, Pegasus and Perseus engines before moving on to the Taurus and Hercules. The design of the 1,130bhp (843kW) Taurus was completed in the early 1930s specifically for FAA and Coastal Command purposes, and was installed in the Bristol Beaufort and Fairey Albacore; however, neither of these types was a great success and the engine saw little alternative use. In the early days of the war by far the most important of Bristol's products was the Hercules, and several 'families' of this type were produced, each an improvement over the previous generation. The engine powered many RAF bombers and some fighters, and started life at around 1,400bhp (1,044kW), but the final versions offered as much as 1,700bhp (1,268kW). Bristol's last piston engine to reach wartime production (in 1943) was the 2,300bhp (1,715kW) Centaurus, which served primarily as a fighter powerplant.

The jewel in the Rolls-Royce crown was the Merlin, a design begun in 1932 as a high-performance fighter engine. Its reputation was made by the achievements of the Spitfire and Hurricane, and there were many versions with power ratings from the initial 1,000bhp (746kW) up to the 1,700bhp (1,268kW) of the 100-series used by the Hornet fighter and Short Sturgeon torpedo bomber. The Merlin also famously powered the Lancaster and Mosquito, and its success overshadowed other Rolls engines. At the start of the war these included the Kestrel (used mostly by training aircraft), the Peregrine, Exe and Vulture. Two 860bhp (641kW) Peregrines were used to power the Whirlwind, but the unit was much smaller than the Merlin and thus offered less power. The 2,000bhp (1,491kW) Vulture, intended to rival the Napier Sabre, suffered severe development problems that eventually led to its abandonment and the withdrawal of the Manchester bomber that used it. The progress of the Merlin, with ever more versions, ensured that the staff and time devoted to the development and clearance of both the Peregrine and Vulture proved insufficient and they died a natural death. The Exe was an air-cooled inline type that reached an advanced state of development, but to relieve some of the strain on the organisation Rolls asked for it to be cut out of its plans. The Air Ministry agreed on 12 December 1939 and Rolls did not renew its interest in the engine until the middle of 1943.

The next Rolls piston engine was the Griffon. This had in fact been first proposed for installation in Spitfires in late 1939 but it did not, at the time, offer a sufficient advance

TOP A Bristol Hercules installation in a Beaufighter.

MIDDLE The Rolls-Royce Merlin XX piston engine powered the Bristol Beaufighter Mk.II and Avro Lancaster bombers. *Rolls-Royce Heritage Trust*

BOTTOM A Merlin 130-series engine fitted in a de Havilland Hornet. The picture is dated 22 March 1945.

over the latest Merlin to compensate for the extra weight. The Griffon returned to the agenda in 1941 but was dropped again for the Merlin 61, and it was not until April 1942 that the 1,720bhp (1,283kW) Griffon Mk.II entered production. Later versions reached 2,000bhp (1,491kW), but the type appeared too late to exert any strong influence on air battles against Germany. The last Rolls-Royce piston engine was to be the 3,500bhp (2,610kW) Eagle, flown in a prototype Westland Wyvern naval strike fighter, but this complicated machinery was overtaken by the jet engine and eventually dropped.

The creation of the jet engine is one of the best-known of aviation stories. All that needs to be told here is that the development of Frank Whittle's early engines, with centrifugal compressors and a large aluminium impeller, was taken under the Rolls-Royce umbrella during 1943. The first result was the 1,600lb (7.1kN) Welland, which entered service in the earliest marks of Gloster Meteor fighter in 1944, and this was followed by the Derwent, then the all-new Nene with 5,000lb (22.2kN) thrust. From the spring of 1941 de Havilland began to work on its own jet engines and ran the first 2,300lb (10.2kN) H.1 (later called Goblin) in April 1942. This went on to power the first Meteor prototype and de Havilland's own Vampire fighter, and was followed by the H.2 Ghost, which reached 4,850lb (21.6kN) and was used by the Venom fighter. Mention must also be made of Metropolitan-Vickers (MetroVick), which worked on the first axial jet. This was called the F.2 and, having been initially

ABOVE LEFT The Rolls-Royce Peregrine engine. *Rolls-Royce Heritage Trust.*

ABOVE RIGHT The Rolls-Royce Griffon. *Rolls-Royce Heritage Trust*

RIGHT The Rolls-Royce Welland jet engine. *Rolls-Royce Heritage Trust*

BOTTOM The Power Jets W.1 was the first British jet engine to fly, in the small Gloster E.28/39 research aircraft. *Rolls-Royce Heritage Trust*

rated at 1,800lb (8.0kN), was flown in Meteor prototype DG204; later the 4,000lb (17.8kN) F.2/4 'Beryl' went into the Saunders-Roe SR.A.1 flying boat fighter.

Just to complicate matters there was also the turboprop, which in its early days received several alternative names along the lines of 'airscrew turbine'. Here a jet was used to drive a propeller and one of the first examples of this type of engine was the Rolls-Royce RB.50 Trent. Two were fitted to Gloster Meteor Mk.1 EE227 and, when flown in this form in 1945, it became the first aircraft in the world to fly with a turboprop powerplant. The first generation of turboprops included the Armstrong Siddeley Python and Rolls-Royce Clyde, which featured in a number of post-war projects.

The first time aluminium alloys were used for fuselage and wing skins came in 1919 when the Junkers F.13 airliner employed corrugated sheet for extra strength. The first British all-metal aircraft was the Short Silver Streak of 1920, followed soon afterwards by the Short Springbok fighter, but these machines were

TOP A forged aluminium impeller for the de Havilland Goblin engine. *HDA Forgings*

BOTTOM Old and new technology seen together: a giant American Erie drop hammer made in 1939, of 29 tons (29,466kg) forging weight but really no more than an extension of the blacksmith's art, was used by High Duty Alloys to stamp some of the first aluminium impellers to be produced for jet engines, as seen here. At the time the Erie was the largest of its type in the world. *HDA Forgings*

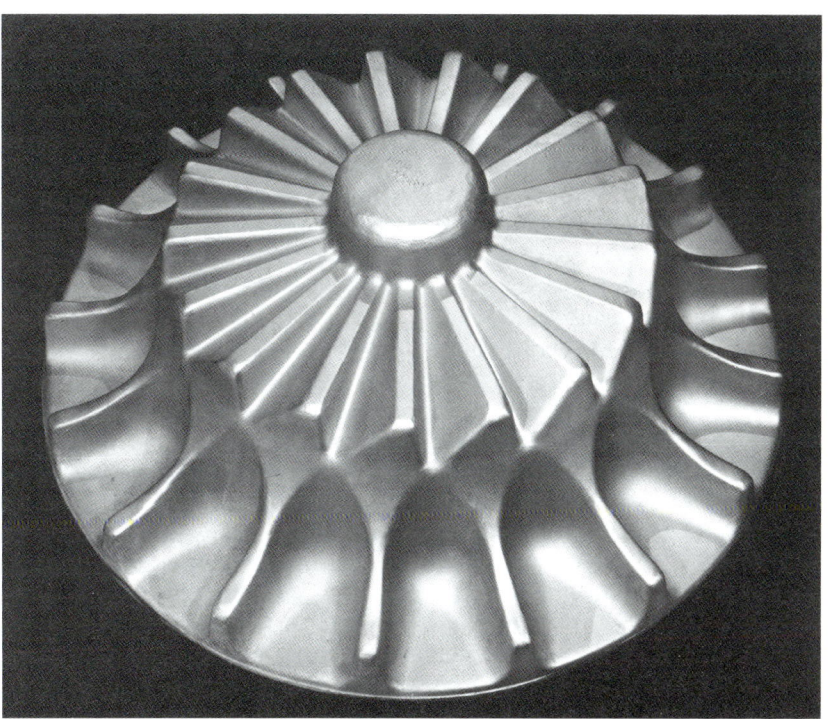

years ahead of their time and it was the 1930s before stressed-skin metal airframes were accepted in types like the Spitfire and Bristol Blenheim bomber. Gradually the old method of metal framing with fabric covering faded away from modern high-performance aircraft but, during the war, one notable exception to metal construction was to be the Mosquito with its all-wood airframe.

The improved design and construction methods that became available after the First World War promoted the development of aeroplanes in which the wing took an appreciable portion of the payload. Metal stressed-skin structures contributed to the aircraft's strength and also, with a smooth exterior and thinner wings, helped to form the correct external shape. This allowed a further advance in speed, and one of the first 'modern' aeroplanes to use these techniques was the American Douglas DC-3 airliner flown in 1935. Most high-performance aircraft were to have stressed skins, but the trend then moved towards shell-like structures where the skin took more of the stress than any inner arrangement of spars and stiffeners, most or all of the material being concentrated in the shell. These monocoque structures were usually employed on the fuselage or engine nacelles.

The development of selected weaponry has been touched on elsewhere, but the Second World War was the conflict where electronics first

TOP The dipole aerial for the Bristol Beaufighter's AI.Mk.IV radar. The aircraft belonged to No 255 Squadron and was photographed in December 1942.

MIDDLE An AI.Mk.VIII radar scanner dish. *Douglas Fisher*

BOTTOM An experimental AI.Mk.VIII nose unit fitted to a Beaufighter in 1941. *Douglas Fisher*

came to prominence. All sorts of 'black boxes' were produced, particularly for navigation and jamming enemy equipment, but the best-known has to be radar. This was used by large bombers for navigation, but specially adapted sets were fitted to night fighters to track down enemy aircraft (Air Interception – AI) and on naval and Coastal Command bombers and patrol aircraft for seeking out enemy shipping and submarines (Anti-Surface Vessel – ASV). The first successful British AI radar was the Mk.IV, which entered production in July 1940 and was fitted in the Bristol Beaufighter as the world's first operational air-to-air radar system. This was followed by the more advanced AI.Mk.VIII based on the cavity magnetron, which introduced a parabolic reflector or dish in the fighter's nose and became the first operational microwave-frequency AI radar. It also equipped the Beaufighter and fighter versions of the Mosquito.

The Second World War was indeed a truly extraordinary period of great technological advance.

Chapter Nine
Stand Alone Projects

ABOVE A manufacturer's artwork dating from 1939 for the ultimate Miles M.22 version, which shows the aircraft in pre-war silver livery. *Miles Aircraft via Peter Amos*

This chapter, new for this second edition, takes a look at some specific projects or groups of projects that either fall outside the mainstream of developments or make interesting subjects as stand-alone studies. In some cases information on these projects has only come to light since the first edition appeared, and there is some crossover with categories covered by other chapters.

Boat Fighters
Blackburn B.44

In 1942 Blackburn drew a single-seat twin-float fighter design called the B.43, which was based on the B.37 Firebrand and powered by a Napier Sabre engine (when work began on the Firebrand part of the initial requirement outlined for that aircraft had to have a capability to change from a land to a water undercarriage). In January 1943 this was followed by an alternative float fighter project called the B.44, which in due course received the luxury of an official Specification, N.2/42. The B.44 was designed by Major J. D. Rennie and embodied a retractable planing bottom or pontoon developed from the B.43 and carried on retractable struts (it also drew on Blackburn's experience with its B.20 flying boat prototype). The B.44 was designed primarily for operations from sheltered waters, but it was also hoped to hoist the aircraft out from escort carriers when out of range of shore bases. After completing a take-off, the

151

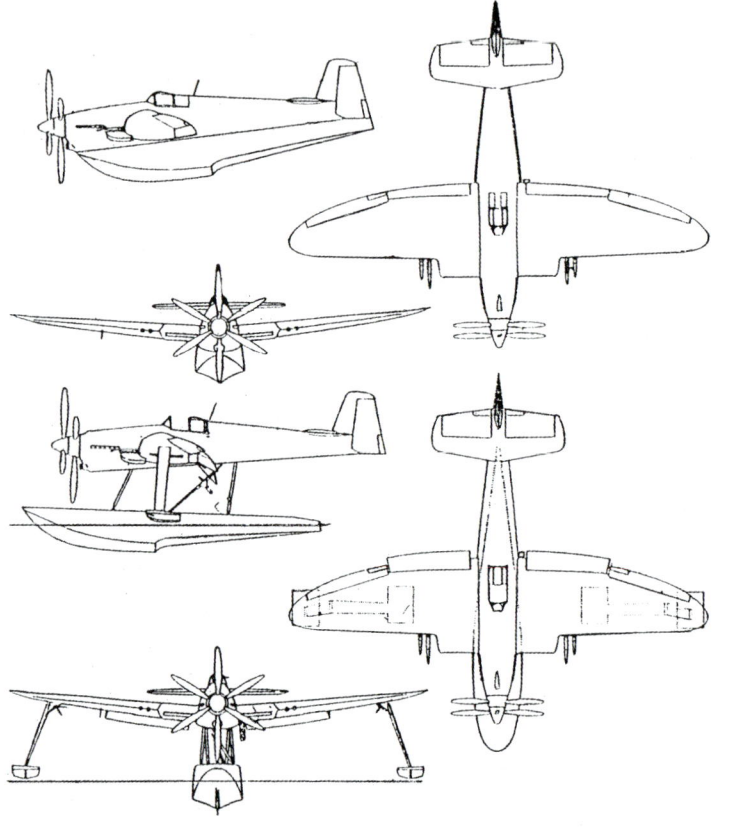

TOP The Blackburn B.44 flying boat fighter had a retractable float (1.43). *BAE Systems Brough Heritage Centre*

MIDDLE A wind tunnel model of the Blackburn B.44 in a photo dated 4 January 1943. *BAE Systems Brough Heritage Centre*

BOTTOM LEFT Supermarine Spitfire W3760 modified as a floatplane in about 1942. Note the fin extension below the lower end fuselage.

BOTTOM RIGHT In 1944 Mk.IX MJ892 was modified to become the final Spitfire floatplane.

B.44 pilot would retract the planing bottom to lie flush with the fuselage while the stabilising floats would retract inwards into the mainplane. This arrangement was intended to remove the extra weight and drag produced by having fixed floats.

The B.44 could be adapted to carry two 500lb (227kg) bombs or two 90-gallon (409-litre) drop tanks, but in other respects it was a standard single-seat fighter powered by a single Sabre Mk.IV and armed with four 20mm Hispano cannon (mounted in the wings outside the leading edge intakes). RAE tested the suitability of the initial proposal to operate from a pontoon at sea, but found that during the take-off it would probably suffer from porpoising, and spray would also damage the propeller. Further calculations indicated that achieving a take-off would be doubtful even with a normal load. A modified pontoon was judged satisfactory in regard to stability, spray formation and water

Blackburn B.44 (8.35)

Span:	50ft (15.24m)
Length:	39ft 4in (11.99m)
Wing area:	381sq ft (35.43sq m)
All-up weight:	?
Powerplant:	1 x Sabre IV
Max speed/height:	360mph (579km/h) at 25,000ft (7,620m)
Armament:	4 x 20mm cannon, 2 x 500lb (227kg) bombs

drag, but it would be necessary to turn the aircraft to clear the spray at low speeds. A B.44 mock-up was built, but the project did not proceed beyond the design stage. The subsequent success achieved in building ground airfields that quickly followed amphibious landings in formerly occupied territory brought to an end any need for a type like the B.44. The design's estimated ceiling was 38,000ft (11,582m) and range 1,000 miles (1,609km).

Spitfire Seaplane

In the end the only British boat or seaplane 'fighters' to be flown during the war were some specially adapted Supermarine Spitfires fitted with floats, together with the Blackburn Roc seaplane prototype L3059, flown in 1939. The Spitfire floatplane conversions first came under consideration in 1940 as part of the plans to undertake an invasion of Norway. Mk.1 R6722 was converted by Folland Aircraft at Hamble, but flotation trials made with this aircraft in June 1940 were unsuccessful, so Supermarine designed its own floats under the Type 344 designation. A modified pair of Supermarine floats, the Type 355, was sent to Folland, which fitted them to Spitfire Mk.VB W3760. Progress was slow, however, and W3760 did not begin its (ultimately successful) official trials until November 1942, by which time the proposed production plans had been dropped. They were revived in 1943, however, with new plans to occupy enemy-held islands in the eastern Mediterranean, and two more Mk.VBs were subsequently converted.

ABOVE The first Miles M.20 prototype, photographed in September 1940. The 'B' mark U9 was eventually replaced by the military serial AX834.

These did make their way out to the Suez Canal Zone, but the type did not enter production. By the end of the war, however, work had begun on the Saunders-Roe SR.A/1 jet boat fighter described in Chapter 11.

Stop Gap Fighters
Miles M.20

The Miles M.20 was an attempt from mid-1940 onwards to address an urgent need for fighters. It had an all-wood airframe and fixed undercarriage, was powered by a Merlin XX, and carried eight machine guns in the wings. Specification F.19/40 was issued to cover the proposal, and prototype AX834 was built and first flown (on 15 September 1940) in just over nine

Miles M.20 (for DR616 - flown)

Span:	34ft 5in (10.49m)
Length:	30ft 9in (9.37m)
Gross Wing Area:	234sq.ft (21.76sq.m)
All-Up-Weight:	8,000lb (3,629kg)
Powerplant:	One Merlin XX 1,300hp (969kW)
Max Speed / Height:	333mph (536km/h) at 20,400ft (6,218m)
Armament:	8 x 0.303in (7.7mm) Browning machine guns

weeks from the start of design work. A second prototype, DR616, was built against naval specification N.1/41. Soon afterwards, however, the RAF's success in the Battle of Britain ended any need for this 'utility' fighter. In addition, some Air Staff members had felt that the M.20's performance was not good enough for day use and that its armament was inadequate for day or night use. The M.20 flew well but failed to ignite any real enthusiasm, so did not reach production.

Westland Mass Production Fighter

In November 1939 Westland also produced a proposal for a fighter that could be manufactured quickly, and which was to have been another all-wood project. The powerplant was one 1,400hp (1,044kW) Hercules (as an alternative to the Merlin if the latter was in short supply) and the design had fixed spatted main wheels. The span was 41ft 0in (12.50m), wing area 240sq ft (22.32sq m), all-up weight 7,200lb (3,266kg), and estimated maximum speed 336mph (541km/h).

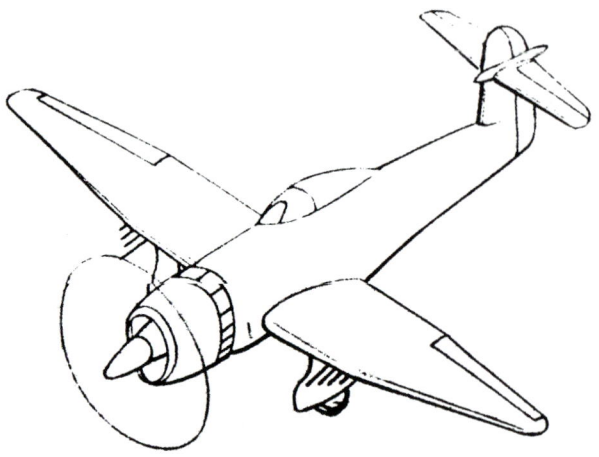

ABOVE The Westland mass-production fighter proposal (11/39).

Miles High Performance Projects

During the first years of the war Miles Aircraft produced two sets of fighter designs, the twin-engine M.22 and M.22A and the single-engine M.23 and M.23A, and in part these were covered by specifications and requirements described elsewhere. Some of these advanced-looking Miles proposals displayed true lines of beauty.

Miles M.22

Work on the Miles M.22, a highly streamlined single-seat fighter with two Griffon engines, was begun possibly as early as 1939 (or even 1938), although it appears that the M.22 label was applied sometime later. An early version was proposed against Specification F.6/39 in 1939 (see Chapter 4), then fully revised in late 1940 as the M.22A against F.18/40

BELOW A two-view drawing of the early M.22 design (1939). *Miles Aircraft via Peter Amos*

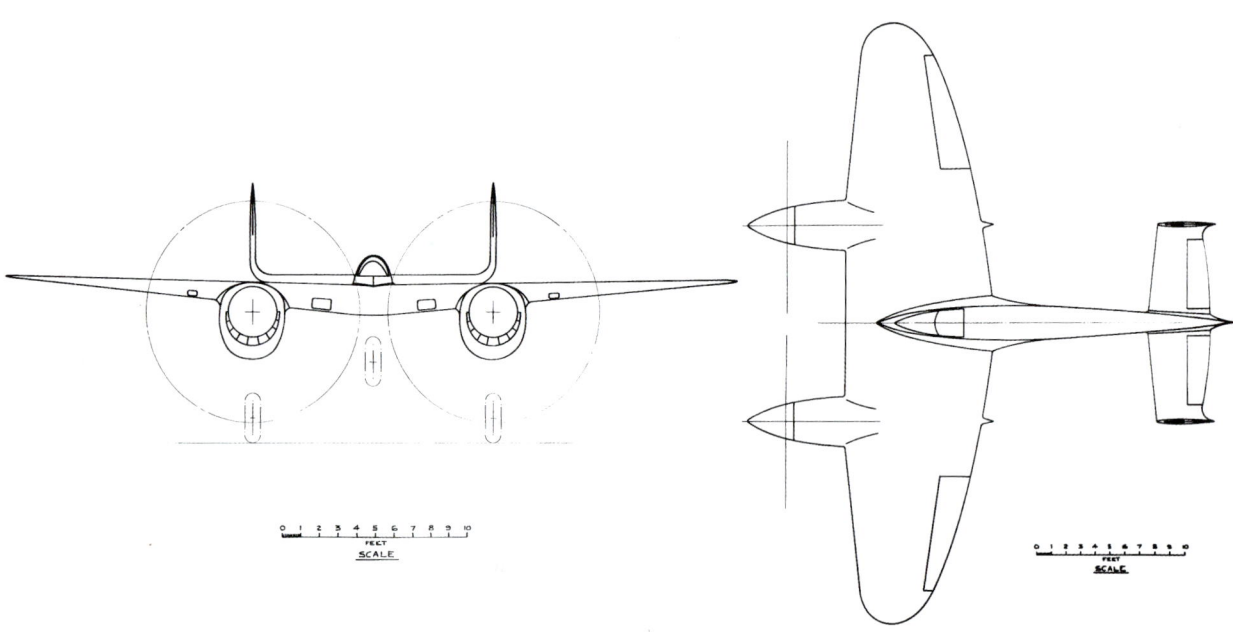

CHAPTER NINE

STAND ALONE PROJECTS

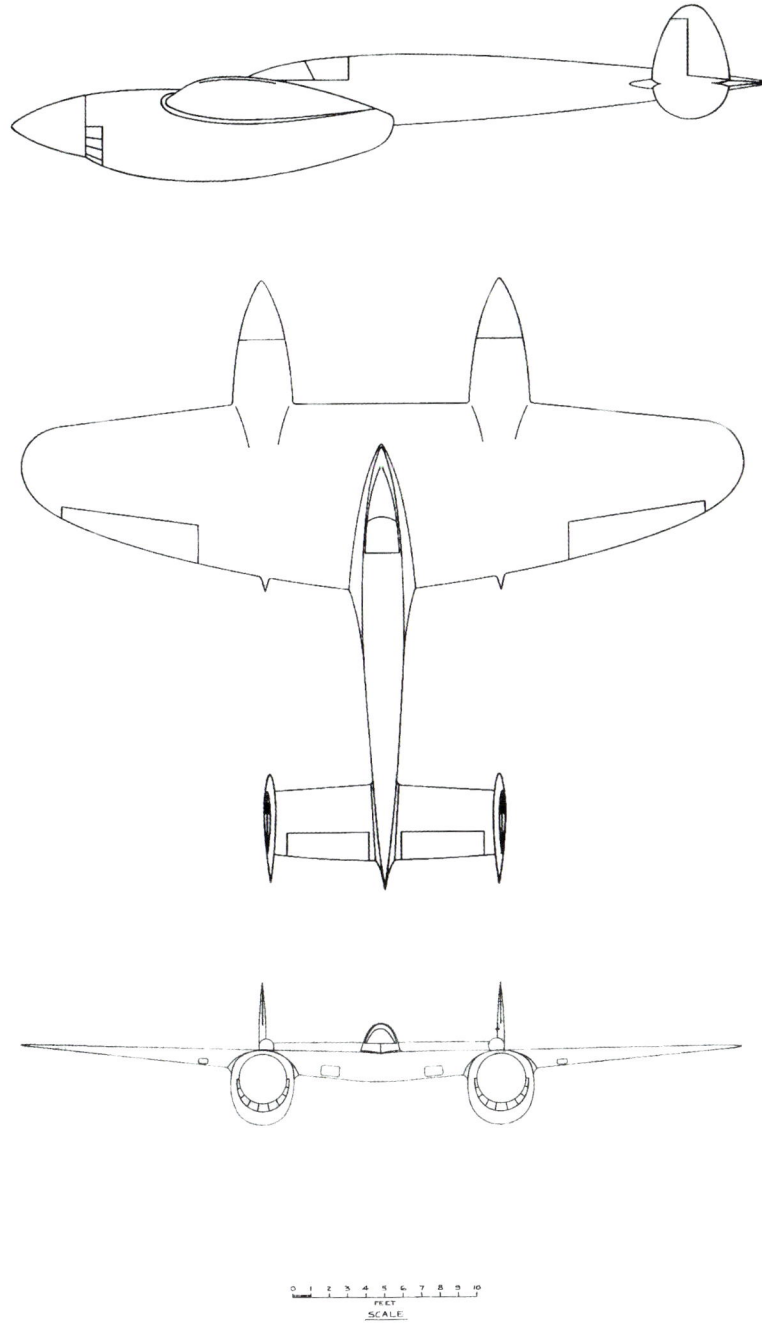

ABOVE **A three-view drawing for the 'ultimate' M.22 layout (1939). Note the different tailplane arrangement.** *Miles Aircraft via Peter Amos*

Miles M.22 (1939)	
Span:	39ft 0in (11.89m)
Length:	33ft 0in (10.06m)
Wing Area:	325sq.ft (30.225sq.m)
All-Up-Weight:	13,000lb (5,897kg)
Powerplant:	2 x Griffon 1,600hp (1,193kW)
Max Speed / Height:	504mph (811km/h) at 15,000ft (4,572m)
Armament:	10 x 0.303in (7.7mm) machine guns

0.303in (7.7mm) machine guns was fitted in the leading edge of the wing centre section ahead of the cockpit. Wing thickness/chord ratio was 18% at the root and 6% at the tip. Performance figures were provided for the full all-up weight with an estimated sea level rate of climb given as 5,180ft/min (1,579m/min), time to 10,000ft (3,048m) 2.4 minutes, and service ceiling 37,000ft (11,278m).

Miles M.22A

The M.22A was a development of Miles's M.22, to be powered by either two Merlin XX or Merlin 60 (RM.6SM) engines mounted in narrow wing nacelles and served by ducted radiators and air intakes in the wing. It was comparable in size to the Mosquito and the fuselage and wing were to be built entirely of wood. The design was prepared against Specification F.18/40 (see Chapter 5) and had four cannon positioned in the upper nose to either side of the cockpit and capable of angular

(see below), but it was never ordered.

What appears to have been the original Miles M.22 had its fins blended into the tailplane, but later this was replaced by a more conventional arrangement where both the fins and rudders were still at the extremities but now had bullet-shaped fairings. Wood construction was used throughout except for the metal wing spars; to reduce frontal area to a minimum the pilot was housed in front of the wing centre section; the engines were housed in underslung nacelles and fitted with airscrews 11ft 6in (3.51m) in diameter; and a 'gun nest' with ten

Miles M.22A (c11.40)	
Span:	51ft 0in (15.54m)
Length:	35ft 0in (10.67m)
Wing Area:	460sq.ft (42.78sq.m)
All-Up-Weight:	16,500lb (7,484kg)
Powerplant:	2 x Merlin XX 1,280hp (954kW) or 2 x Merlin 60 1,390hp (1,037kW)
Max Speed / Height:	Merlin XX 405mph (652km/h) at 22,500ft (6,858m), Merlin 60 425mph (684km/h) at 29,750ft (9,068m)
Armament:	4 x 20mm cannon

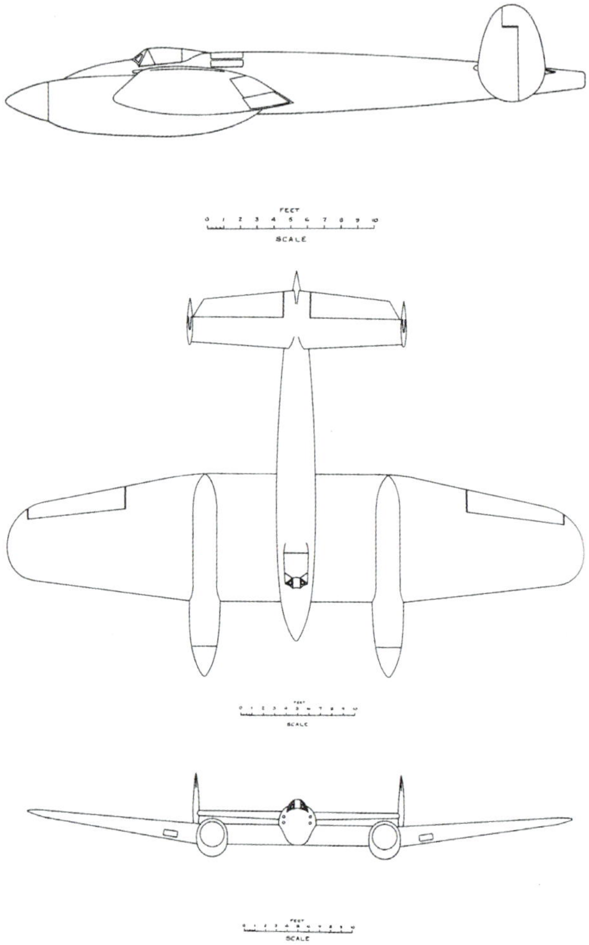

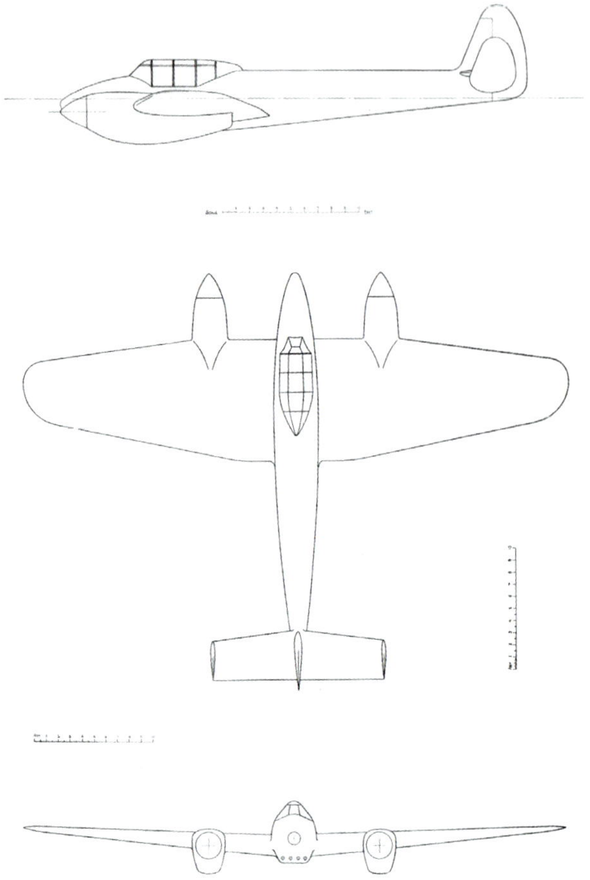

ABOVE LEFT The Miles M.22A (c11.40). *Miles Aircraft via Peter Amos*

ABOVE RIGHT This drawing shows what is thought to be an early version of the M.22A. It has a low wing, three fins with the rudder on the central fin only, a raised canopy, two crew and four guns in the lower nose. *Miles Aircraft via Peter Amos*

settings. In fact, any angle of fire could be obtained between the horizontal and a maximum 7° upward inclination (an alternative version was drawn with a Boulton Paul four-gun turret).

The fuselage used semi-monocoque construction, the wing had been designed as a one-piece structure and was calculated to give satisfactory stiffness criteria at a diving speed of 500mph (805km/h), and the tail plane again carried twin fins and rudders at its extreme ends. M.22A's engine nacelles were of the new drag-less type developed jointly by Miles and Rolls-Royce, and the

LEFT An artist's impression of the M.22A. *Miles Aircraft via Peter Amos*

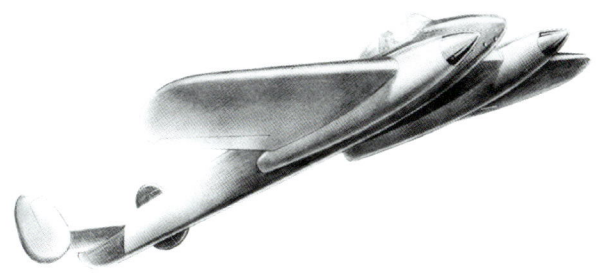

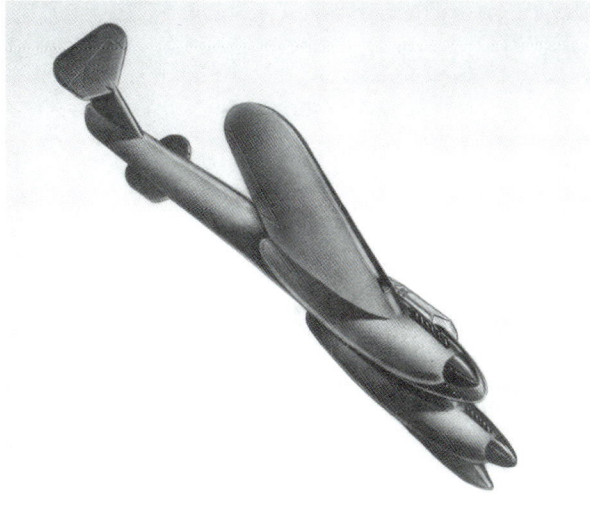

ABOVE & RIGHT Three further artworks showing versions of the Miles M.22A. *Miles Aircraft via Peter Amos*

BOTTOM RIGHT Yet another M.22A layout shows a design with a rather bulkier forward fuselage (1940). *Miles Aircraft via Peter Amos*

BELOW This final M.22A version with twin fins was shown in Miles artworks both with and without wing leading edge radiators. *Miles Aircraft via Peter Amos*

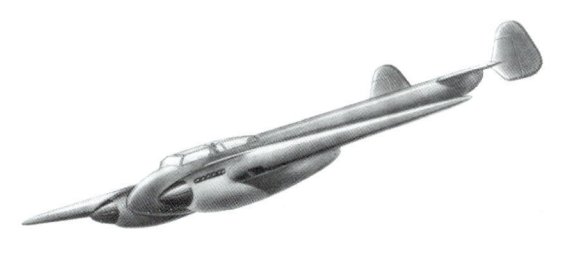

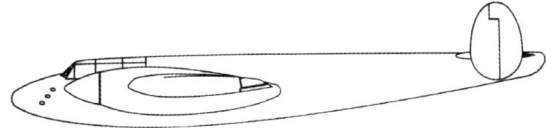

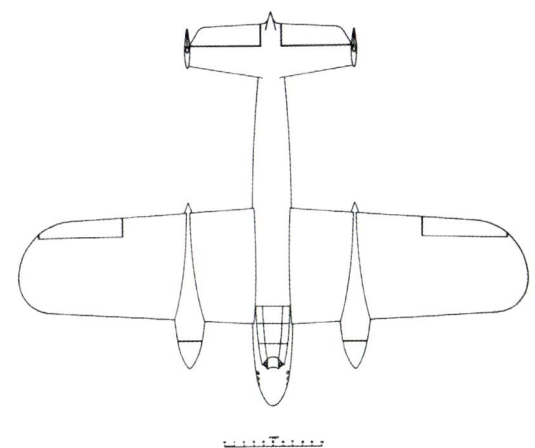

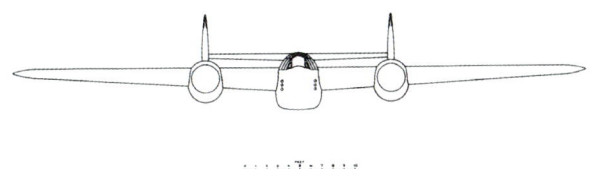

Merlins were to be driven by airscrews 12ft 0in (3.66m) in diameter. The pilot was seated forward of the front spar in a pressure cabin and had an exceptionally good view out 'in all essential directions'. Two Merlin XXs gave an absolute ceiling of 40,000ft (12,192m) while the Merlin 60s would push this up to 43,000ft (13,106m).

Miles M.23

The Miles M.23 of 1941 was to be a high-speed single-seat fighter design powered by a single Rolls-Royce Merlin engine, though it was intended to fit a Griffon later on. Apart from metal wing spars this was another Miles project to use wood construction throughout, there was a low windscreen and canopy to reduce frontal area, and no protrusions to increase drag. The elliptical low-drag wing had a thickness/chord ratio of 20% at the root and 6% at its tip and housed either eight machine guns or two cannon. Its built-up metal spars had spruce and ply ribs and were covered by thick plywood for bracing and to provide a smooth skin. The fuselage was again of semi-monocoque construction with spruce longerons and stringers, plywood frames and covering. An unusual 'special Miles tricycle type' retractable undercarriage was fitted, which had its single wheel positioned aft.

Airscrew diameter was 11ft 0in (3.35m) and the Merlin powerplant

Miles M.23 (1941)	
Span:	31ft 0in (9.45m)
Length:	28ft 8in (8.74m)
Wing Area:	185sq.ft (17.205sq.m)
All-Up-Weight:	(Merlin) 6,200lb (2,812kg), (Griffon) 7,400lb (3,357kg)
Powerplant:	1 x Merlin 1,075hp (802kW) or Griffon 1,600hp (1,193kW)
Max Speed / Height:	Merlin 411mph (661km/h) at 17,750ft (5,410m), Griffon 470mph (756km/h) at 15,000ft (4,572m)
Armament:	2 x 20mm cannon or 8 x 0.303in (7.7mm) machine guns

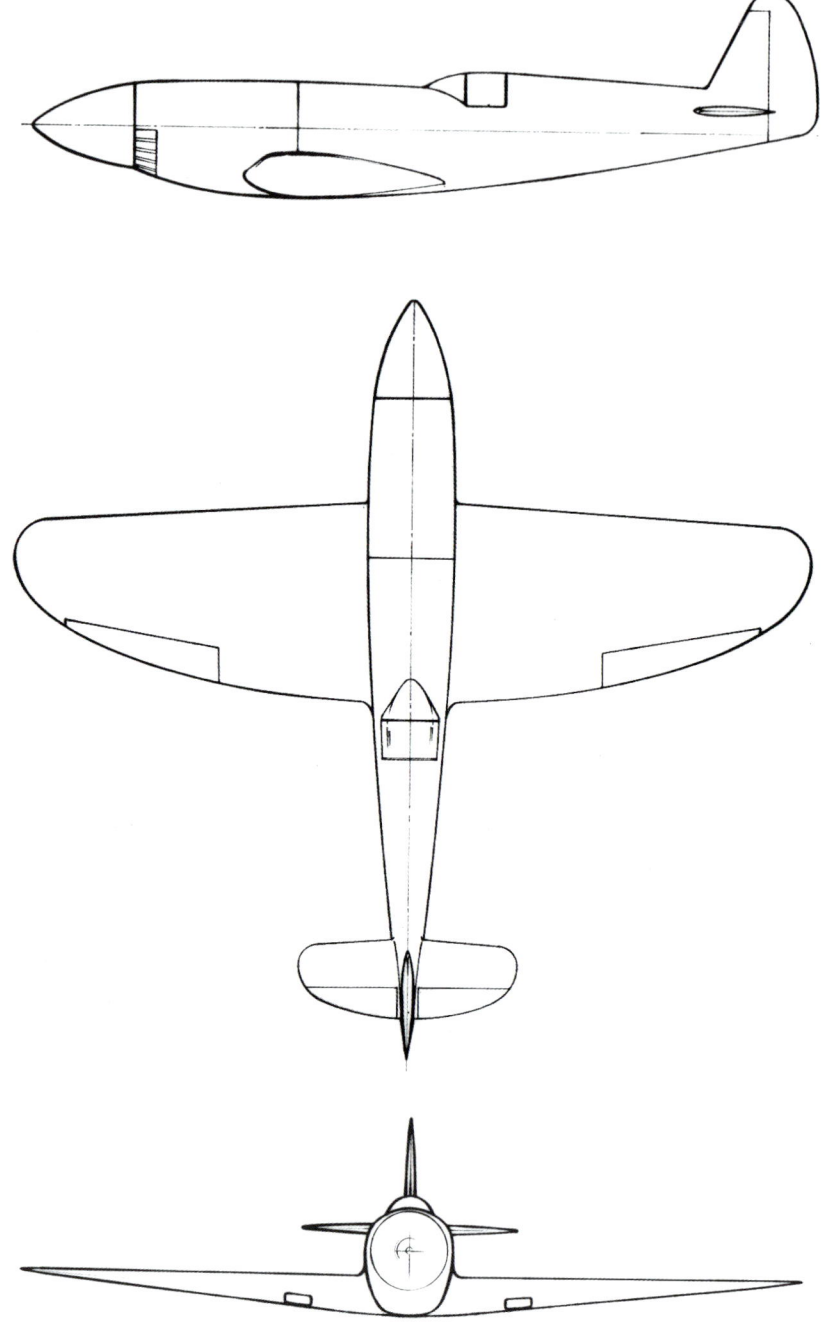

ABOVE This is what is thought to be the initial general arrangement drawing for the Miles M.23 (1941). *Miles Aircraft via Peter Amos*

gave an initial rate of climb of 2,770ft/min (844m/min), a time to 10,000ft (3,048m) of 5.3 minutes, and a service ceiling of 26,000ft (7,925m); the equivalent estimates for the Griffon were 4,680ft/min (1,426m/min), 3 minutes and 38,000ft (11,582m). The M.23 brochure stressed that the design's wing area was 'substantially less than on existing fighters, being only 185sq ft (17.205sq m) compared with 242sq ft (22.51sq m) on the Spitfire and 258sq ft (23.99sq m) on the Hurricane, which gave a higher wing

ABOVE A manufacturer's impression of the M.23. *Miles Aircraft via Peter Amos*

Miles M.23A (9.42)	
Span:	50ft 0in (15.24m) – later reduced to 48ft 0in (14.63m)
Length:	length 31ft 0in (9.45m)
Wing Area:	262sq.ft (24.37sq.m)
All-Up-Weight:	7,440lb (3,375kg) – later reduced to 6,800lb (3,084kg)
Powerplant:	1 x Merlin 61
Max Speed / Height:	440mph (708km/h) at 30,000ft (9,144m)
Armament:	2 x 20mm cannon

loading.' Once again this advanced fighter proposal was not taken up.

Miles M.23A

The M.23A of September 1942 was prepared specifically as a high-altitude fighter; it was powered by a Merlin 60 engine, had a pressurised cockpit, and was the first Miles project to feature a thin high-aspect-ratio wing. In fact, it bore no resemblance at all to the original M.23 and why it was not given a new Miles designation is unknown.

By 1942 German Junkers Ju 86 high-altitude bombers were operating over Britain and could not be intercepted by existing RAF fighters. Some specially adapted versions of the Spitfire were produced in response, but Miles designer Don Brown felt that these could 'only be regarded as a temporary expedient'. It was this situation that prompted him to prepare the M.23A, since it was considered that a high-altitude fighter with cockpit pressurisation should be designed as soon as possible, and it was to have 'a performance hitherto unattained'. In due course a revised design showed a slightly smaller span and reduced weight, which permitted an increase in service ceiling from 45,000ft (13,716m) up to 48,000ft (14,630m). The aircraft's cooling was originally to be provided by two ducted radiators in the wing leading edges, but the second drawing showed

BELOW The Miles M.23A (9.42). *Miles Aircraft via Peter Amos*

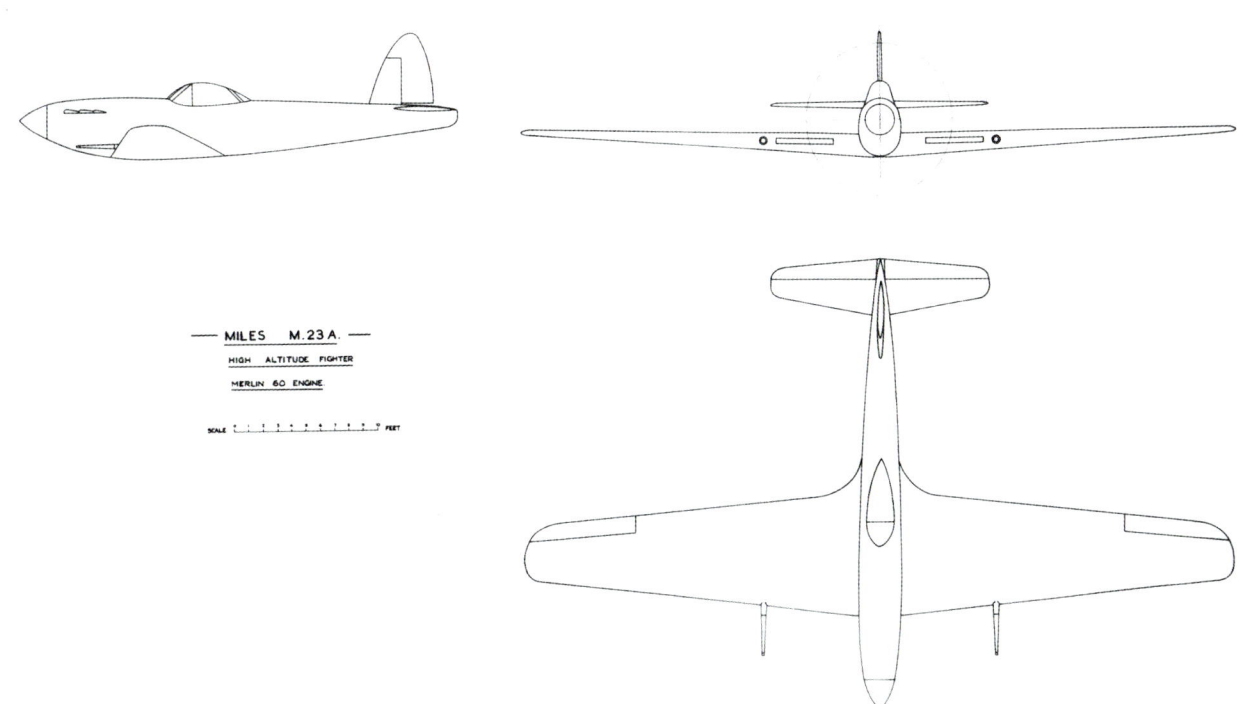

THIS PAGE & NEXT The Malcolm twin-engine fighter brochure included four photos of a project model of the design. Although of poor quality, these images are still sufficient to present a good idea of how the Malcolm fighter would have appeared had it been built.

a central radiator underneath the fuselage. Again this project remained stillborn but for its time it was quite advanced. The Westland Welkin (see Chapter 4) was also designed primarily to deal with the threat of high-flying German bombers.

R. Malcolm Ltd Twin-Engine Fighter

The R. Malcolm Company was founded in December 1936 through the renaming of another firm. In 1940 Marcel Lobelle, former chief designer at Fairey Aviation, joined the company's design office at Slough, which then moved to White Waltham. In October 1946 the White Waltham site became ML Aviation and continued to make a range of aviation products. The following text describes a twin-engined multi-gun day and night fighter aircraft project and is based on the contents of a brochure completed on 27 January 1941, which in fact detailed an improved high-performance development of the firm's previous Specifications completed on 1 October and 15 November 1940 respectively.

The fighter was a mid-wing twin-fuselage monoplane with a nosewheel undercarriage and two centrally placed Napier Sabre engines running in tandem inside a single overwing nacelle. This arrangement permitted a wide choice for both the armament that might be carried and for the roles in which the aircraft might be used. For these reasons the final detail specification would be based upon the requirements of the aircraft's Operational Unit, but particulars were given here for *one* possible arrangement. This had a crew of three, one pilot and two gunners, with the pilot's cockpit in the left-hand

Malcolm Day-and-Night Fighter (27.1.41)	
Span:	66ft 0in (20.12m)
Length:	48ft 0in (14.63m)
Wing Area:	600sq.ft (55.80sq.m)
All-Up-Weight:	21,500lb (9,752kg)
Powerplant:	2 x Sabre
Max Speed / Height:	425mph (684km/h) at 19,000ft (5,791m)
Armament:	4 x 20mm cannon, 6 x 0.303 (7.7mm) machine guns

fuselage and one of the gunners in a turret placed in the nose of the same fuselage immediately in front of and below the pilot. The second gunner was placed in the front of the right-hand fuselage. Armament was four 20mm cannon, two on fixed mountings in the wings and controlled by the pilot and two on a movable mounting in the right-hand cockpit controlled by the gunner, together with six 0.303 (7.7mm) Browning machine guns mounted in the turret in the nose of the left-hand fuselage and controlled by the other gunner.

The performance figures had been calculated on a conservative basis – for instance, no allowance had been made for the increased speed obtained by the use of ejector-type exhaust manifolds, and the engine power had been taken at the then proved rating of the Sabre engine. There would be no difficulty in installing any higher-powered Sabre versions even if these were of a slightly greater weight. Manoeuvrability was expected to be exceptionally good owing to the engine weight being concentrated at the centre of gravity, and as the engines were mounted directly above the wing spars a considerable amount of installation weight had been saved. The tandem arrangement of the engines, with opposite rotating tractor and pusher airscrews, also neutralised the gyroscopic forces, but in the event of an engine failing at slow speeds there would be very little tendency for the aircraft to swing.

No three-view drawing is available for this project, but the performance estimates included a climb to 20,000ft (6,096m) in 6.8 minutes and a ceiling of 38,500ft (11,735m). Besides the central nacelle for the powerplant, another unusual feature was the single fin placed in the centre of the horizontal tailplane – the usual solution for a twin-boom aircraft like this was to have two fins, one per boom. The armament for early 1941 was very powerful indeed and the document stressed that 'no experimental nor doubtful features had been included in this design, for which reason it could be put into production with the minimum of delay.' This innovative design appears to have been an unsolicited proposal made to the Ministry and it was not ordered, but it would surely have been a fascinating type to assess had a prototype been constructed.

Chapter Ten
Jet Fighters from Gloster

ABOVE Meteor F.Mk.IV EE521 is seen at RAF Hullavington in 1946 during a visit for a handling assessment. *Peter Arnold Collection*

The development of the jet engine was to revolutionise the design of both military and civilian aircraft, but it was to be the former, and particularly the fighter, that benefited first. Frank Whittle's achievement in developing the jet is well known, but the task of producing the first aircraft designed to use his engines, principally work by the Gloster Aircraft Company, is not so well documented. By the end of the war Gloster had completed a series of jet fighter designs, and in addition most of the industry's other 'fighter specialists' had also moved into the jet field (as shown in Chapter 11).

Gloster E.28/39

Some Ministry papers refer to Britain's first jet aircraft as the 'Weaver', but in fact this was a security code name. Whittle first visited the Gloster works on 29 April 1939, and spoke to designer George Carter and test pilots Michael Daunt and Gerry Sayer. He had been introduced to both men before and told them 'as much as they could have found out from an examination of patent records'. He also gave Carter some idea of the nature of the jet engine and it was agreed that they should try to get the Air Ministry to make official contact with Gloster. During October it was realised that a specially designed aircraft was essential to test the jet engine because no existing aircraft could be modified to take this new power unit. Fortunately there was a lull in Gloster's design workload, which, coupled with the good relationship that had grown between Whittle and Carter, ensured that the company did get a contract to build some prototypes.

During a meeting held at RAE Farnborough on 13 October 1939 Carter produced drawings of two alternative arrangements for prototype jet aircraft. The basic design was a mid-wing monoplane with the pilot forward of the wing and the engine installation immediately aft of the wing's main spar. One scheme had a normal fuselage with the propelling jet emerging behind the tail; the other had its tail surfaces supported by an extension boom following the lines of the pilot's head fairing, which left the engine bay clear of all structural considerations. In the second case the

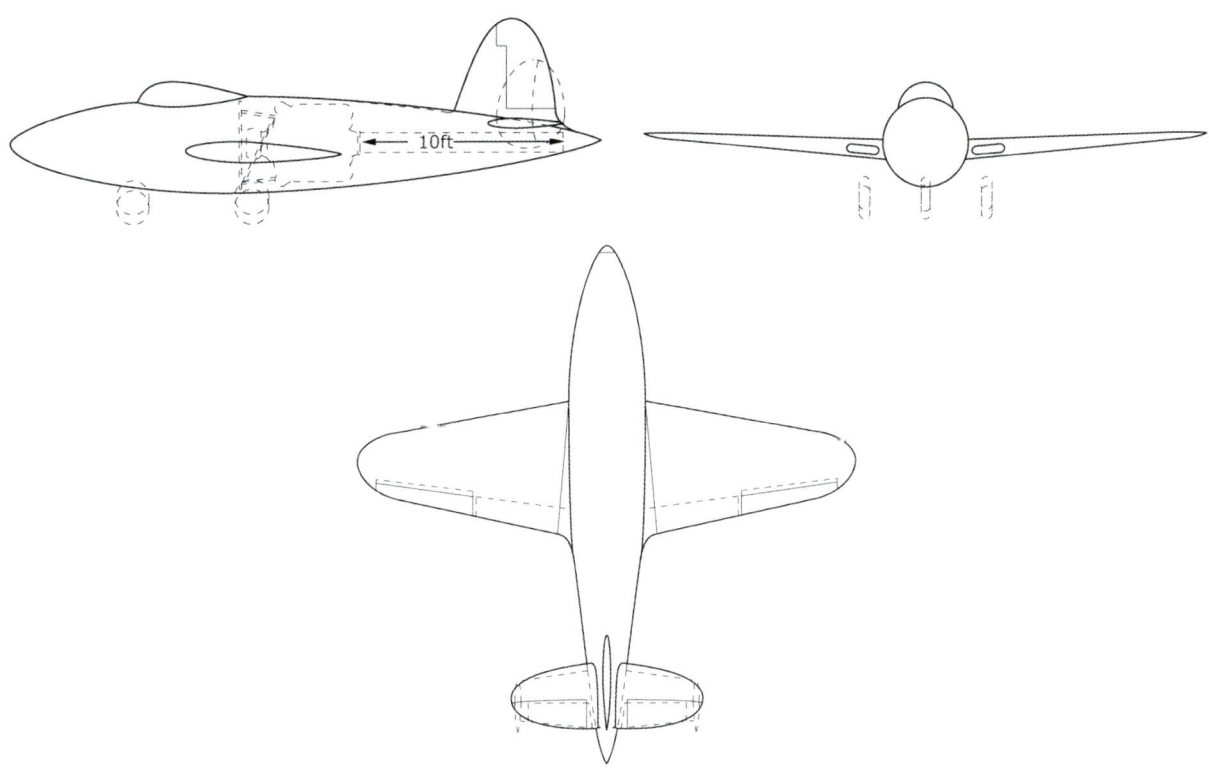

ABOVE This is possibly the earliest known design leading to the pioneering Gloster E.28/39. The date '26.9.39' is scribbled on in pencil, together with the word 'Obsolete'. *Chris Gibson, redrawn from National Archives Avia 30 - 1626*

engine installation was suitably faired into a short exhaust pipe.

The design of an airframe that would fully exploit the unique advantages of jet propulsion had been considered from the points of view of satisfying all strength and structural rigidity requirements together with good control and stability over the speed range. However, to achieve this implied some limitation on the theoretical optimum performance obtainable from the engine; even so, Carter said the performance from every aspect was quite exceptional. One of the biggest problems was to provide a satisfactory method of introducing the air to the 'supercharger' (that is, the compressor). At sea level some 26lb (11.8kg), or 330cu ft (9.3cu m), of air per second was required by the engine and it was not considered desirable to exceed a velocity of 200ft/sec (61m/sec) in the air duct, so this required a pipe of a diameter of about 18in (45.7cm).

A simple form of tricycle undercarriage was adopted and in general the project showed

BELOW The first of two sketches showing George Carter's original ideas for a jet-propelled aircraft as discussed at a meeting held at RAE Farnborough on 13 October 1939 (30.9.39). Made just a few days after the earlier drawing, it shows a number of changes. *Adapted from National Archives AVIA 15 - 3922*

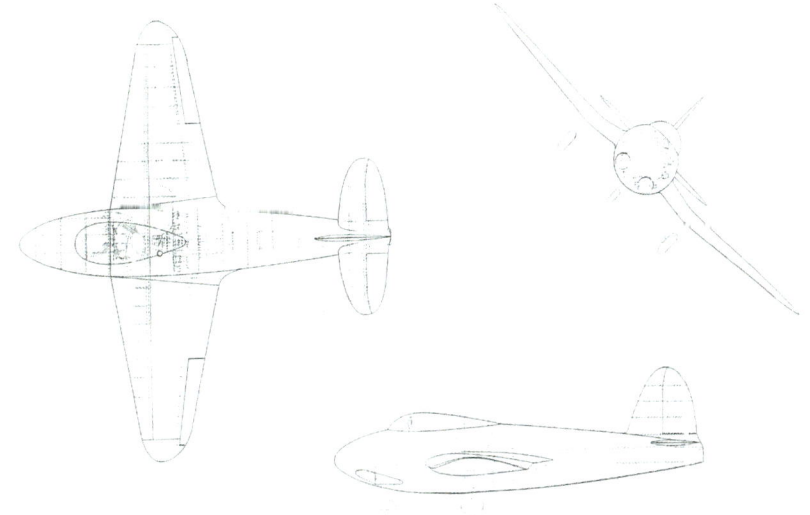

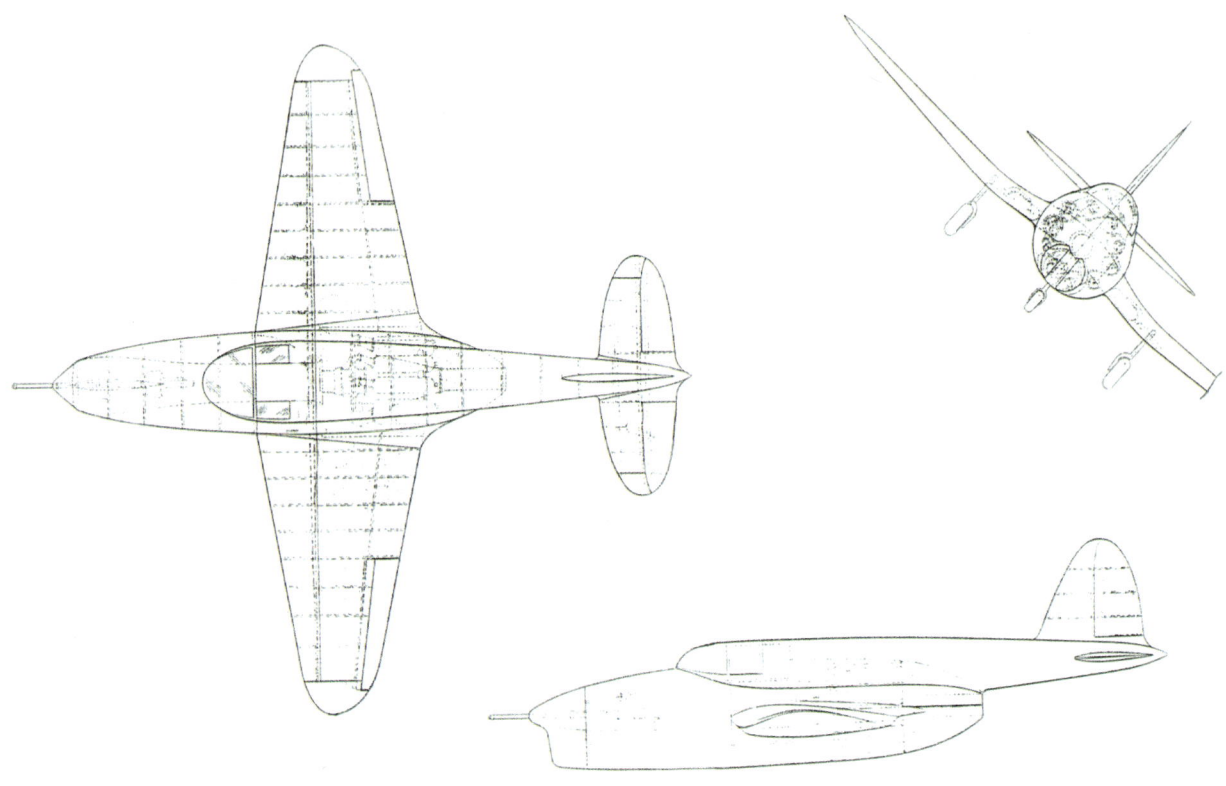

ABOVE How the E.28/39 might have looked: Carter's second jet aircraft scheme for the RAE meeting had a short jet pipe and nose-mounted gun (2.10.39). *Adapted from National Archives AVIA 15 - 3922*

great simplicity; the brochure also speculated on the military advantage of such a type and included possibilities for fitting guns. The estimated top speed was 415mph (668km/h) at sea level, rate of climb at sea level 5,000ft/min (1,524m/min), time to 30,000ft 9.0 minutes, and ceiling 50,000ft (15,240m). The design embodied 12% wing thickness at the root tapering to 9% at the tip, and it was suggested that the maximum thickness should be 0.4 of the chord. RAE's estimated top speed was 470mph (756km/h) at 30,000ft (9,144m), and it was decided to use a model to test the possible influence of the jet on the afterbody design. It was also agreed to recommend building two sets of wings, the second of which would be a special set for high speeds.

On 29 November 1939 a conference was held at the Harrogate Grand Hotel to discuss a covering specification. This was chaired by H. Grinstead and included among others R. W. Walker and G. L. James from Gloster, Perring from RAE Aero Department, R. N. Liptrot and Frank Whittle. Gloster now estimated the weight to be 3,130lb (1,420kg) and, based on a static thrust of 1,200lb (5.33kN), predicted that at sea level the maximum speed would be 401mph (645km/h), and the rate of climb 4,440ft/min (1,353m/min). It was agreed to call for a speed at sea level of 380mph (611km/h) and a rate of climb of 4,000ft/min (1,219m/min), but it was still undecided whether to use a long or short jet pipe. The specification, E.28/39, was approved on 21 January 1940.

Earlier, on 4 January, Richard Walker had told Gloster Hucclecote's RTO that the 'short jet Scheme 2 design is considered an improvement over Scheme 1 as it overcomes the structural, accessibility and maintenance difficulties.' It was felt that the short jet pipe and fuselage would result in an increase of some 14mph (22.5km/h) in maximum speed, but as the jet efflux might give rise to unknown airflow conditions over the boom-mounted tailplane, the Scheme 1 method was ultimately adopted. The small split nose intakes on Scheme 1 were eventually replaced by the larger single orifice that appeared on the completed aircraft.

A contract to build two prototypes, W4041 and W4046, was placed on 3 February 1940 and design work proceeded swiftly. The Mock-Up Conference was held on 22 April and the initial construction work on the two E.28/39s was carried out in the Gloster Experimental Shop at Brockworth. However, the threat of large-scale bombing of aircraft factories sited on aerodromes meant that one of the airframes was moved to Regent Motors Garage in Cheltenham. Work continued in great secrecy and by 8 July the assembly of the fuselage frames was complete, metal covering

Gloster 'Scheme 1' (30.9.39)

Span:	27ft 0in (8.23m)
Length:	23ft 6in (7.16m)
Wing Area:	127sq.ft (11.81sq.m)
All-Up-Weight:	2,800lb (1,270kg)
Powerplant:	1 x Whittle jet engine
Max Speed / Height:	460mph (740km/h) at 30,000ft (9,144m)
Armament:	None fitted

Gloster 'Scheme 2' (2.10.39)

Span:	27ft 0in (8.23m)
Length:	26ft 6in (8.08m)
Wing Area:	127sq.ft (11.81sq.m)
All-Up-Weight:	2,800lb (1,270kg)
Powerplant:	1 x Whittle engine
Max Speed / Height:	460mph (740km/h) at 30,000ft (9,144m)
Armament:	Nose gun on drawing

Gloster E.28/39 (flown)

Span:	29ft 0in (8.84m)
Length:	25ft 4in (7.72m)
Wing Area:	146.5sq.ft (13.62sq.m)
All-Up-Weight:	3,700lb (1,678kg)
Powerplant:	1 x W1 860lb (3.8kN)
Max Speed / Height:	339mph (545km/h) at 20,000ft (6,096m)
Armament:	None fitted

was under way and the first set of wings was coming along well. The tail and fin were tunnel tested and cleared in January 1941, but there was much discussion on the steerable nosewheel unit. This was a new idea because the lack of a propeller meant that there would be no slipstream over the tail surfaces that would reduce the ability of the rudder to keep the undercarriage on a straight course during the take-off run.

On 24 March 1941 Cranwell was chosen as the venue for the first flight because it was desired to reduce the

TOP A nose view of Britain's first jet aircraft to fly, the Gloster E.28/39.

MIDDLE The first E.28/39 W4041 lands at Farnborough with 'A' Shed behind.

BOTTOM W4041 is seen again at RAE Farnborough in 1944 fitted with small auxiliary fins to provide extra directional stability. *Barry Jones*

risk to the early flights by having aerodrome conditions as ideal as possible. It was intended to have a number of official visitors present for the first flight (at least thirty wished to attend), but because of the intention to minimise the interference with other flying and the consequent need for the trip to take place during the early morning or in the evening, there was a need to accommodate them overnight. The number of visitors was not to exceed the amount of available accommodation and this generated quite a bit of correspondence. Those invited to attend were the Secretary of State, the Minister of Aircraft Production (Beaverbrook), Sir Henry Tizard, CAS, Mr Hennessey, DTD, DSR and others, but some had to drop out because the maiden flight was deferred by several days.

The famous first flight of a British jet aircraft took place on 15 May 1941 and W4041 achieved a maximum indicated airspeed of 240mph (386km/h) at 4,000ft (1,219m). Three more flights were made the following day when 280mph (451km/h) ASI was reached at 10,000ft (3,048m). On 20 May Tizard wrote, 'In my opinion we have now reached a stage when the odds against the jet propulsion engine of the Whittle type being developed to a successful issue in the near future have disappeared.' Later, on 12 January 1942, he added that 'consideration must be given to the possible use of the experimental single-engine machine [the E.28/39] as a fighter.' However, it was ultimately decided that the two prototypes would be engaged in Whittle engine flight test work.

Gloster Meteor

Turning to the background to the Meteor, the E.28/39 described above, although nominally a fighter, was not equipped as such and the aircraft was only really intended to test the Whittle engine and to be used for experimental work in general. It was soon realised that a fighter design would have to be started from scratch. When considering aeroplanes powered by current turbine engines, a report from RAE's W. G. A. Perring and Arnold Hall, dated 10 April 1940, confirmed that the following points had to be taken into account:

i. The efficiency of the engine improved with forward speed, so this type of propulsion was therefore best applied to designs in which a high forward speed was essential.

ii. The jet turbine engine offered unique advantages in weight but at the cost of a rather heavy fuel consumption. This consumption decreased with increases in operating altitude, the actual consumption being roughly proportional to the local density of the air.

iii. At a given altitude, the range of aircraft powered by jet turbine engines would be almost independent of the forward speed.

BELOW Gloster drawing ZC.26194 shows an early version of what became the Meteor jet fighter (13.3.40). *National Archives AVIA 30 - 1751. Redrawn by Chris Gibson*

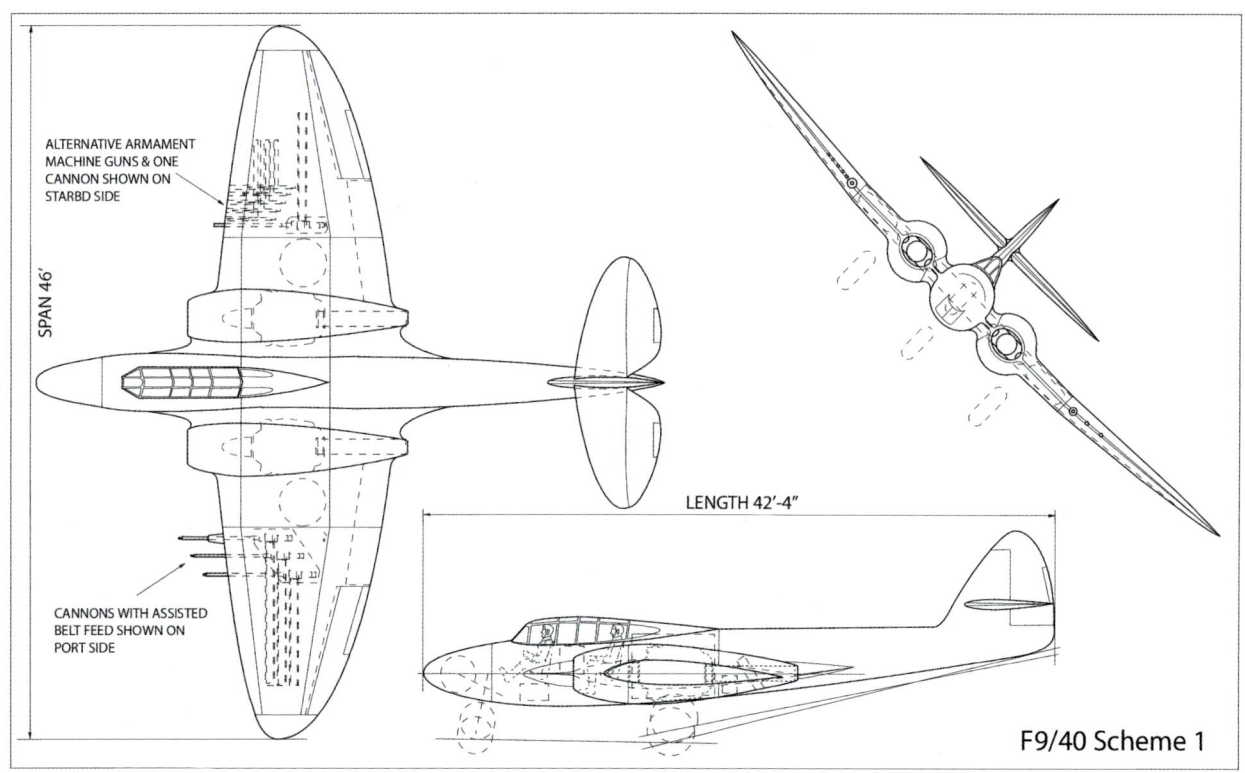

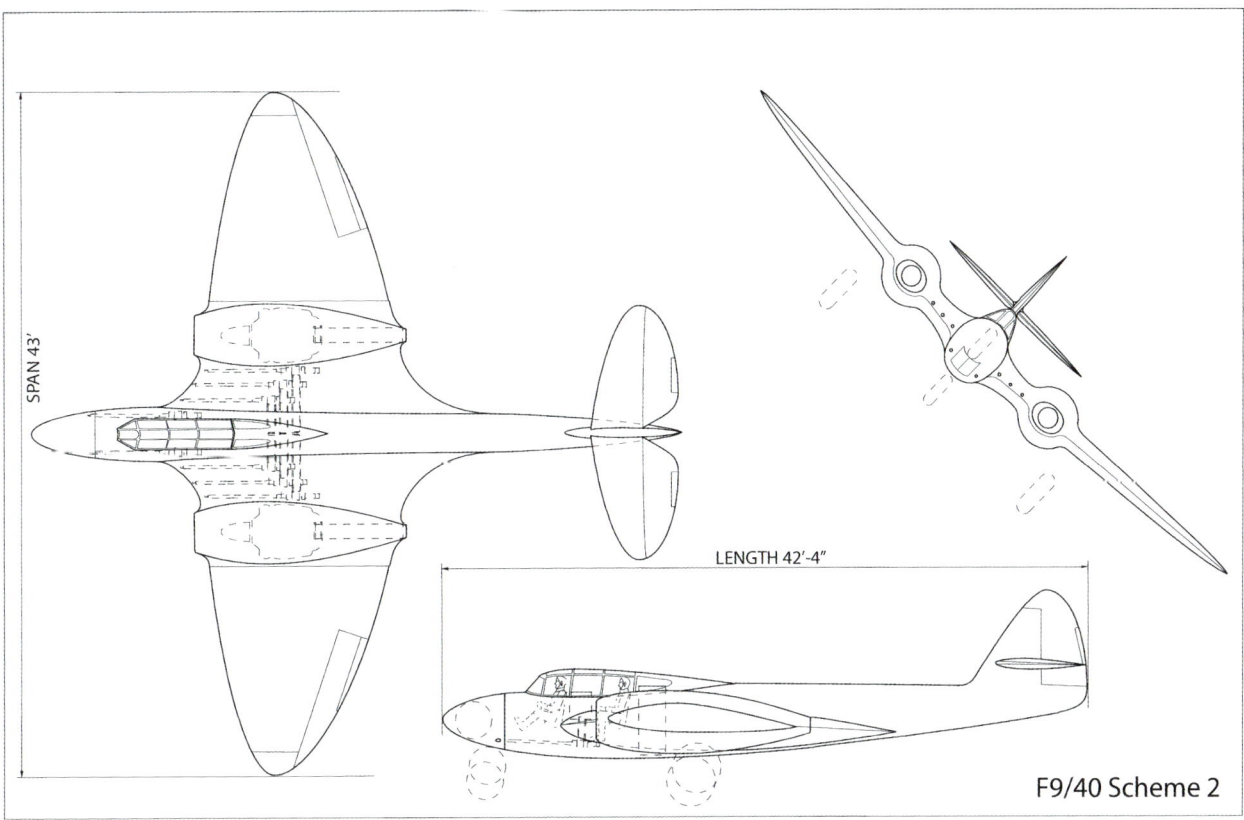

ABOVE Gloster drawing ZC.26728 presents the firm's second twin-jet fighter proposal (8.4.40). *National Archives AVIA 30 - 1752. Redrawn by Chris Gibson*

iv. The maximum forward speed of such an aircraft would not be so greatly affected by altitude as that of a conventional (piston) aeroplane.

The conclusions drawn from these points were that if long range was required a jet-propelled aeroplane should be designed for high altitude, but it would need a pressure cabin. If an efficient cabin was produced and the engine was capable of operating over long distances at high speed, the construction of a high-altitude long-range bomber would then become possible. Finally, because of its high ground speed and high rate of climb, the jet-propelled aeroplane could be adapted to form an excellent interceptor fighter, although in this case it must be recognised that long range was impracticable since attempts to attain long range at low altitudes would involve fuel loads that would completely swamp the weight advantages possessed by the engine.

Provided short range was accepted for fighter work, aircraft of this type should possess excellent characteristics for their roles.

From the viewpoint of aerodynamic efficiency and manoeuvrability, a single-engined type offered advantages over any multi-engined scheme. However, a military load of 1,500lb (680kg) minimum was needed for a fighter and the power ratings expected in the short term from current and new Whittle engines would make a single-engined type unsuitable for this duty. Attention therefore had to be given to the twin-engine arrangement with a total static thrust of some 3,200lb (14.2kN). Perring and Hall recommended that a twin-engined type with an all-up weight of 8,500lb (3,856kg) should be undertaken immediately while the production of an aeroplane of 11,000lb (4,990kg) weight should be borne in mind to use the later Whittle W2 and alternative axial engines. Frequent reference was often made to Whittle's Gyrones, the code name for the Whittle engine. (Test flying eventually revealed that the maximum level speed performance of a jet aircraft was extremely sensitive to changes in air temperature – a 10° rise might cut the speed by 20mph [32km/h], for example from 405mph [652km/h] to 385mph [620km/h].)

On 17 April W. S. Farren told Carter,

'I feel there is a great deal to be said in its favour. If you could manage to include four 20mm combined with a certain amount of 0.303in (7.7mm), it would give us a far higher speed and operational height than any other aircraft we have in view, with an armament which would be fully able to deal with anything for which such a performance would be essential – namely the high speed lightly armed or unarmed bomber.'

Farren saw Carter on 2 May, and the relevant RAE staff four days later, and confirmed that they would proceed immediately with a design on these lines. He also instructed Carter to begin a mock-up immediately, while RAE had the essential wind tunnel work already planned out and was to proceed with it in collaboration with Carter and Whittle. Once the twin-engine fighter had become reality, the problems of its design had to be analysed. The close proximity of the two engine nacelles to the fuselage gave rise to a very poor wing junction, which was likely to result in a breakdown of the flow and an early stall of the wing between the nacelles and fuselage. In addition, the thick section would produce compressibility effects over this part of the wing.

By mid-May 1940, following these initial RAE estimates for a jet fighter and more detailed investigation of them by George Carter, the aircraft was expected to weigh between 8,700lb and 9,000lb (3,946kg and 4,082kg) and carry 1,800lb (816kg) of military load. The armament would comprise two or four 20mm cannon together with six 0.303in (7.7mm) machine guns, and the top speed would fall between 400mph and 431mph (644km/h and 693km/h) at sea level and 450mph to 470mph (724km/h to 756km/h) at 30,000ft (9,144m).

During a meeting held at RAE in September 1940 Lord Cherwell, Churchill's Scientific Advisor, was convinced by Whittle and RAE's Hayne Constant of the importance of jet propulsion. This extension of interest beyond MAP was one of the reasons why, when at last Beaverbrook and Hennessey became aware of the existence of jet propulsion and the aircraft designed for it, the project took such an important place in their discussions for future developments. At this time the tactical ideas of the RAF were being shaped by the massed night attacks of the Luftwaffe and, as a result, two new fighter requirements made their appearance – a night fighter and a high-altitude fighter incorporating a pressure cabin. Designs from Gloster could adequately meet both – the F.18/40 night fighter (see Chapter 5) and the F.9/40 jet fighter – but during December 1940 it became clear that one or other of these designs must give way because the company's design capacity was insufficient to pursue both.

Although existing fighters could be modified to suit the night fighter requirement, the Air Staff was in favour of the specialised Gloster design, and the fact that the E.28/39 experimental aircraft had still not flown with its jet propulsion unit made them hesitate to decide on the F.9/40. Air Staff interest was largely sustained by MAP and it was not until the E.28/39 flew that the Air Staff finally dropped the Gloster night fighter, leaving the firm free to concentrate on its jet fighter. On 9 January 1941 Beaverbrook told Gloster, 'I wish you to concentrate your design strength on the twin-engined Whittle fighter. This will be your main contribution to my development programme. It is of unique importance [and] to assist you on making this effort, work on the night fighter will stop. A pressure cabin must be provided as soon as possible. On this you should collaborate with Westland, who are to design a Merlin-engined fighter with a pressure cabin [the Welkin – see Chapter 4].'

Specification F.9/40 was completed in November 1940 to cover the twin-engined jet fighter, and its top speed at 30,000ft (9,144m) was to be not less than 430mph (692km/h).

Most new civil and military aircraft pass through a series of design configurations before reaching a final and (hopefully) satisfactory layout that will then be selected for construction. The Meteor jet fighter was one type to go down this route, and two drawings uncovered at the British National Archives since the first edition of this book was published reveal configurations considered long before the final prototype design had been established. They are undoubtedly the first twin jet fighter projects to have been drawn in this country.

The first design (drawing ZC.26194 dated 13 March 1940) shows an aircraft with the engine nacelles placed very close to and almost blended into the

BELOW Prototype DG206 powered by de Havilland H.1 engines was the first Gloster Meteor to fly, and as such Britain's first jet fighter to fly. This picture was taken at RAE on 3 March 1944. Note the fat nacelles.

fuselage. The powerplant would have been two Whittle jet engines, but such is the condition of the original drawing that it is no longer possible to tell what type had been specified. Alternative armaments are illustrated – the port wing has three cannon with an assisted belt feed, while the starboard wing has a single cannon inboard, then a battery of five machine guns outboard. This fighter had a span of 46ft 0in (14.02m) and a length of 42ft 4in (12.90m). The drawing has the number F.9/40 written on in crayon, but the specification was not issued until November 1940, so would not have been completed when the drawing was prepared.

The wing on the second design (drawing ZC.26728 of 8 April 1940) has the engine nacelles a little further out, thereby providing space for six of the eight cannon to be mounted in the very thick inner wings. The other pair are in the lower nose and the powerplant is two Whittle Series II engines. Here the span is 43ft 0in (13.11m) and the length 42ft 4in (12.90m).

On each layout the cockpit canopy in particular and some of the fuselage have much in common with the Gloster Reaper twin-piston-engine night fighter project (discussed above and in Chapter 5). Each of these jet fighters has a beautiful elliptical wing shape quite unlike that used subsequently on the Meteor (this is most pronounced on the second type), while the empennage was in due course revised with the horizontal tailplane being moved further up the fin. Both designs also have a modern tricycle undercarriage, but with quite large wheels.

Since there is currently no documentation to go with these projects one is left to speculate what thoughts might have been going through the head of Gloster designer George Carter and the planners. Eight cannon made for a formidable set of weaponry, as did the cannon and machine gun mix, which was far more powerful than contemporary piston

ABOVE DG202 was the first Whittle-powered Meteor prototype.

fighters (it is assumed that the cannon would be the Hispano). Indeed, when it first flew in August 1942 the Martin Baker M.B.3 with its six 20mm Hispanos (see Chapter 3) was at that time considered to be particularly heavily armed. Back in 1940 it is understood that the thinking was that the higher speeds offered by jet engines would allow less time for firing at an opponent, so more guns would provide a greater likelihood of hitting a target a sufficient number of times to bring it down. If the fighter was overtaking a relatively slow bomber target at high speed there would be a very limited time of engagement, so the more shells fired per second the better. In fact, it was calculated that rate of fire was important because a higher overall rate increased the pattern density, and thus at long range the chance of a hit. Most current and forthcoming piston-powered cannon fighters, however, had just four cannon, while the Meteor itself was originally slated to carry six, but two of these were subsequently deleted.

A further question is why did both designs have two crew when the Meteor prototypes were all single-seat? The Hispano cannon on early Bristol Beaufighters had sixty-round drums that could be changed in flight by the radar operator (he could also hopefully clear any stoppages), and in addition Spitfires with the earliest version of the cannon also had a drum feed. So would the second crewman on these aircraft have been required to keep the Hispanos loaded (although on the first design this would not have been possible with the positioning of the guns)? These drawings were made over seventy years ago but they are priceless in filling another gap in the background to Britain's first jet aircraft.

On 24 January 1941 Sir Henry Tizard (who the previous November had replaced Sir Wilfrid Freeman as MAP's Air Member for Development and Production [AMDP]) told the Vice Chief of the Air Staff (VCAS) that the Research Department was now satisfied that the Whittle engine had reached a sufficient stage of development to permit the placing of production orders. Tizard attached great importance to the jet fighter concept, even though it was as yet unproven, but he felt that it should be possible to achieve practical success in time to influence the war. He completed studies of the jet fighter with various levels of engine thrust against the Spitfire Mk.III and showed that, although the F.9/40 with two 1,400lb (6.2kN) engines was estimated to be much faster than the Spitfire III at 38,000ft (11,582m), its role as

TOP Meteor DG204 was powered by two MetroVick F2 jets in underwing nacelles.

MIDDLE The MetroVick F2 axial jet engine. *Jet Age Museum.*

BOTTOM Meteor F.Mk.1 EE214.

an interceptor would be only just as effective as the Spitfire since it had a poorer take-off and rate of climb. In Tizard's view the main production must centre on an engine giving not less than 1,600lb (7.1kN) static thrust at sea level.

A contract for twelve prototypes, DG202 to DG213, was placed on 14 February 1941. Gloster looked at fitting six 20mm cannon, but preferred four, regarding the last pair as overload, and for a fighter fitted with 1,640lb (7.3kN) W2B engines the company's brochure predicted a top speed of 385mph (619km/h) at sea level, a sea level rate of climb of 3,220ft/min (981m/min), and a ceiling of 46,000ft (14,021m). A final Mock-Up Conference was held in February 1941 and it was estimated that the first prototype would be flying by the end of the year. On 21 May, six days after the E.28/39's landmark first flight, Hawker Siddeley's Frank Spriggs told MAP's J. S. Buchanan, 'There is little doubt that the development of the Gloster Whittle project as a military type is absolutely essential and in view of the very satisfactory progress of the [E.28/39] test machine, such development should be regarded as star priority.' An order for 300 F.9/40s was confirmed on 8 August, but the Whittle W2 intended to power them was showing signs of surging and running too hot at high revolutions.

The main security codename given to the F.9/40 was 'Rampage', but by September it was unofficially being called 'Thunderbolt' ('Millet' was also used to screen the F.9/40's first flights from Edgehill and Barford St John). In February 1942 it was agreed that the fighter should be referred to as the 'Gloster F.9/40' rather than using

ABOVE On 20 September 1945 EE227 made its first flight fitted with experimental Rolls-Royce Trent turboprop engines, for which it required small additional finlets.

any unauthorised name, which now included 'Meteor'. Gloster was loath to suggest a name since the company felt that the secrecy of the project would be better safeguarded if it was referred to by the specification number. However, in early summer 1942 Meteor became the agreed choice.

By late 1942 the twelve prototypes had been reduced to seven, but the number was later increased to eight. At the start of 1942 a maiden flight was expected in May, and orders were given forbidding the use of Whittle-type engines on dusty aerodromes. Besides Whittle's engine, developed by his firm Power Jets with assistance from Rover, then Rolls-Royce, two other jets had by now made their appearance. One was designed by Frank Halford and built by de Havilland, and the second came from Metropolitan-Vickers to the general designs of the RAE and featured an axial compressor (all of the others had centrifugal compressors).

It was intended to modify some F.9/40 airframes to fit these engines, but the installation of the MetroVick F.2 (later the Beryl) was difficult; it was found that the simplest solution was to sling the engine under the wing spars, which meant that practically no spar redesign was necessary. The de Havilland H.1 gave fewer problems but, being of somewhat larger diameter than the W2B, it needed longer spars for the centre section and a wider nacelle, which increased the span. When it became clear that the H.1 was proceeding well, a decision was taken on 26 September 1942 to give the engine precedence over the F.2 and push it forward with high priority, a move that ensured that the first Meteor to fly was actually the H.1-powered DG206. A full brochure for an H.1 F.9/40, or Meteor Mk.2, was completed in November 1942. Each engine gave 2,500lb (11.1kN) thrust, so, for what was in all respects a fully operational machine, the predicted top speed of 470mph (756km/h) at sea level was greater than that expected from the W2B version. Fully developed, the H.1 was expected to give 3,000lb (13.3kN) thrust, which suggested speeds in excess of 500mph (805km/h) and that exceptional rates of climb to high altitude would be possible; consequently Gloster declared that this would be a formidable fighter proposition.

However, some Ministry staff felt that the Meteor was a serious waste of effort and that a large number of highly skilled workers could be better employed on alternative types like the Merlin 61-powered Mosquito. On 26 October 1942 R. S. Sorley, ACAS(T), wrote that due to a shortfall in thrust the first Meteor with W2B would be disappointing and it would not be until the 'Stage II' arrived sometime in 1943 that a performance would be available that was comparable with the original requirement. While it would give high speeds at all heights, it was down on climb and unlikely to give the full ceiling that the Air Staff required before 1944. Sorley added that 'by this time we should have the second edition of the Westland Welkin, which shows promise of exceeding the Meteor in climb but is lower in speed' (he also noted that the Mosquito X, the standard fighter, was inferior to both).

Sorley declared that the Meteor 'will do no more than serve as a useful high-speed type for a very short while, but it will provide us with a jet-propelled aircraft on which to gain experience of the new technique, which I think is most necessary.' In fact, the Meteor's future was uncertain because, with the W2B, it would be outclassed, except possibly in speed, by orthodox fighters. However, thanks to a superior rate of climb jet fighters were seen essentially as 'interceptors' and, with no propeller, they could always out-dive a regular type. In addition, building a small batch of W2B-powered machines would, both technically and tactically, be vital because a great deal of development work was ahead, and so much needed to be learned.

It was well into 1943 before suitable W2B flight engines were available, so the first flight-ready prototype did indeed prove to be DG206 with the H.1, two engines having been delivered by 12 January but derated to 2,000lb (8.9kN) for their early runs. DG206 made its maiden flight on 5 March, but keeping the existence of jet aircraft secret was not easy; apart from service personnel seeing aeroplanes with no propellers, there was always that distinct noise for the public to hear. On 6 August 1943 Sorley described to his Minister how, up to now, jets were only allowed to fly from specially cleared airfields, which in practice had amounted to concentrating them at Barford St John (near to Gloster Aircraft) and at Farnborough. This had suited Gloster well, but naturally did not satisfy Rolls-Royce or de Havilland, which were most anxious to fly them from airfields closer to their factories.

The Air Staff had already gone to considerable trouble to obtain security clearance for an airfield nearer to Derby (Balderton), but each time this involved a great deal of work. It often meant that the dismissal of 'doubtful labour' employed at particular airfields led to either a hold-up in construction work or inevitable delays in operating these aircraft from a desired point. With the steady progress being made in both aircraft and engines, it was correct that the contractors should wish to use their own facilities at Hucknall and Hatfield. This would save so much time not only with testing but also if some slight alteration or repair was needed; in addition, once these aircraft were in the air it became impossible to conceal the fact that they were flying. The approaching maiden flight of the de Havilland DH.100 (see Chapter 11) brought matters to a head. It looked as if the aircraft would have to go to Barford St John for its first flight, but then Sorley told Geoffrey de Havilland on 13 August that there had been a change in policy and his jet could fly from Hatfield. He suggested, however, that it should perhaps operate from a hangar on the far side of the airfield that could be securely guarded and that taxiing should be done in the early morning before the airfield was opened.

Also on 13 August 1943 the Minister of Aircraft Production drew attention to the strict necessity for avoiding any reference to jet aircraft in the press – on no account should there be any publication relating to the development, production or flight of jet aircraft (a piece had appeared in the American publication *Esquire* the previous April). There was, however, no objection to articles examining the theory of jet propulsion in general. The first disclosure of Allied jet work was finally released to the national press on 6 January 1944.

A discussion and review of 'Future Gas Turbine Aircraft Projects' was completed on 8 June 1942 and covered two classes – fighters for which engines were likely to be available in a year's time and bombers for which appropriate engines were required two years hence. It was decided to continue the F.9/40 with W2Bs as an operational type, the F.9/40 with H.1 engines was recognised as an experiment of great interest, the de Havilland E.6/41 (the DH.100) was noted as 'an experimental job in which the twin-boom construction needed close attention from the structural point of view' (RAE was to investigate the boom design), and reference was also made to jet fighter schemes from Supermarine and Westland. As a result of discussions on a Gloster fighter scheme known as the 'Ace' (see below), it was decided that

Gloster F.9/40 (early 1941)	
Span:	43ft 0in (13.11m)
Length:	41ft 3in (12.57m)
Wing Area:	374sq.ft (34.78sq.m)
All-Up-Weight:	10,650lb (4,831kg) 4 cannon, 11,020lb (4,999kg) 6 cannon
Powerplant:	2 x Whittle W2B 1,640lb (7.3kN)
Max Speed / Height:	440mph (708km/h) at 30,000ft (9,144m)
Armament:	4 or 6 x 20mm cannon

Gloster Meteor 'Mk.2' (11.42)	
Span:	44ft 4in (13.51m)
Length:	41ft 4in (12.60m)
Wing Area:	387sq.ft (35.99sq.m)
All-Up-Weight:	13,300lb (6,033kg)
Powerplant:	2 x de Havilland (Halford) H.1 2,500lb (11.1kN)
Max Speed / Height:	490mph (788km/h) at 30,000ft (9,144m)
Armament:	4 x 20mm cannon

Gloster Meteor F.Mk.1 (flown)	
Span:	43ft 0in (13.11m)
Length:	41ft 5in (12.62m)
Wing Area:	374sq.ft (34.78sq.m)
All-Up-Weight:	11,775lb (5,341kg)
Powerplant:	2 x W2B/23 1,600lb (7.1kN)
Max Speed / Height:	446mph (718km/h) at 30,000ft (9,144m)
Armament:	4 x 20mm cannon

a second-string fighter with a single engine was required that would have a low-drag wing structurally designed for smoothness.

The fighter engines were the Power Jets W2 (with Rover and British Thomson Houston and including the W2B and W2/500), the Metropolitan Vickers F.2 and F.3, and the de Havilland H.1 (later called the Goblin, while the W2B/23 later became the Welland). These units, further developed, were to be considered as bomber engines and it was decided that manufacturers should be found to produce, in addition to the F.9/40 and E.6/41, one single engined fighter and one tail-first bomber; in fact, Gloster Aircraft was by now working on a single-engined jet fighter. In mid-July 1943 Richard Walker assumed full responsibility for the F.9/40 programme, which gave Carter the freedom to work on new projects.

Alternative Gloster Jet Fighters

Gloster 'Boosted Fighter'

A study made very early in January 1940 as part of Gloster's and George Carter's initiation with jet aircraft was a design to be powered by both a piston and a jet engine, to be known as the 'Boosted Fighter'. This had a conventional piston fighter configuration with a nose propeller, but introduced a jet in the rear fuselage. The Boosted Fighter was prepared in general against the requirements of Specification F.18/37 (see Chapter 1), and was one of the

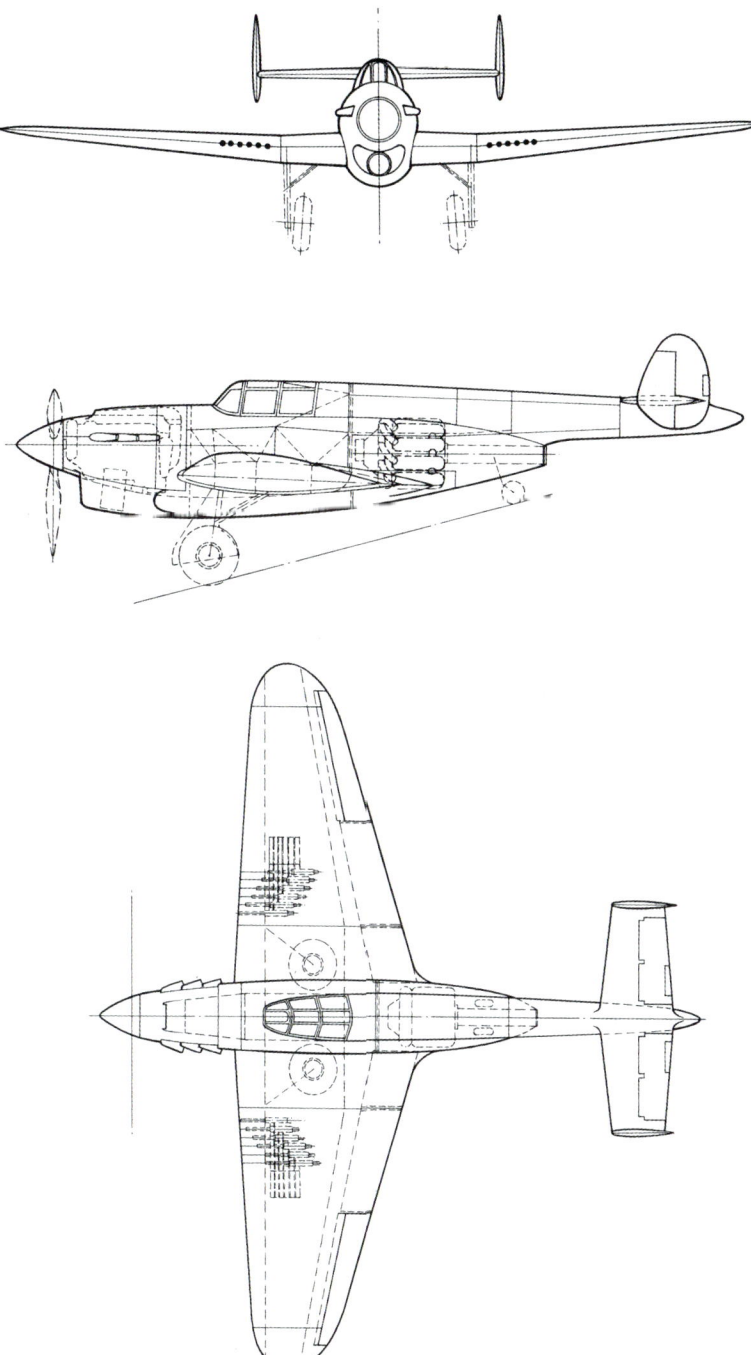

ABOVE The Gloster 'Boosted Fighter' (4.1.40). *The late James Goulding via Jet Age Museum*

Gloster Boosted Fighter (4.1.40)	
Span:	42ft 0in (12.80m)
Length (tail up):	37ft 6in (11.43m)
Wing Area:	?
All-Up-Weight:	?
Powerplant:	1 x Griffon plus 1 x W.1
Max Speed / Height:	Unknown
Armament:	12 x .303in (7.7mm) machine guns

first mixed-powerplant designs ever produced. Its piston unit was to be a Rolls-Royce Griffon with a three-blade propeller 11ft 0in (3.35m) in diameter, and the jet at the rear a Whittle W.1, which would exhaust under a slender rear fuselage; both the piston's cooling air and the jet's bypass air would come through a single large chin intake. There was a tailwheel undercarriage with the main legs retracting inwards into the wings, and small twin tailwheels were positioned in each side of the jet pipe; the fighter had a straight tapered wing and twin fins and rudders, and the armament was twelve 0.303in (7.7mm) Browning machine guns, all housed in the wings. The Boosted Fighter was not built.

Gloster E.5/42 Ace

The extra power now starting to become available from jet engine developments made the single-engined fighter a more practical proposition, and on 31 January 1942, 'because of the possibility of producing engines of bigger output,' Carter suggested such a type to Rowe. He estimated that the fighter would have a span of 40ft (12.19m), a wing area of 285sq ft (26.5sq m) and an all-up weight of 9,000lb (4,082kg), and would carry four 20mm guns. The performance figures included a top speed of 440mph (708km/h) at sea level and 490mph (788km/h) at 30,000ft (9,144m), an operational ceiling of 45,000ft (13,716m), and a time to 30,000ft of 11 minutes. The aircraft was proposed as the Gloster Ace, and Carter said that it merged into one aircraft all of the knowledge and experience that had so far been acquired. It was also clearly associated with the aerodynamic characteristics of the E.28/39 and shared a similar layout, except for a longer fuselage, four cannon housed in the lower portion of a solid nose, wing root intakes, and a T-tail.

The go-ahead for a trial design was given on 20 July 1942 and it was agreed that, because of Gloster's heavy commitment on the F.9/40, the final detail design could be done by 'Jimmy' Lloyd at Armstrong Whitworth Aircraft (a sister company within the Hawker Siddeley Group). The idea of a 'Gloster-Armstrong fighter' was, according to R. S. Sorley, 'a good idea'. The trial design was received by Lloyd by letter on 27 July and he reported that he had already visited Westland and received a copy of Petter's report 'Jet Propelled Aircraft with Special Reference to High Altitude Operation'.

However, on 30 July it was agreed to let Carter, rather than AWA, carry on with the single-engined fighter. A revised drawing was completed in September showing a span of 35ft (10.67m), an all-up weight of 7,750lb (3,515kg), a top speed of 490mph (788km/h) at sea level and 520mph (837km/h) at 30,000ft, and an operational ceiling of 48,000ft (14,630m). The Advisory Design Conference was held on 17 December 1942, but prior to this the military load was increased to 2,500lb (1,134kg) from 2,110lb (957kg), which took the gross weight up to 8,600lb (3,901kg) (this was revised again on 22 January

BELOW **The Gloster E.5/42 fighter project from early 1942.** *Jet Age Museum*

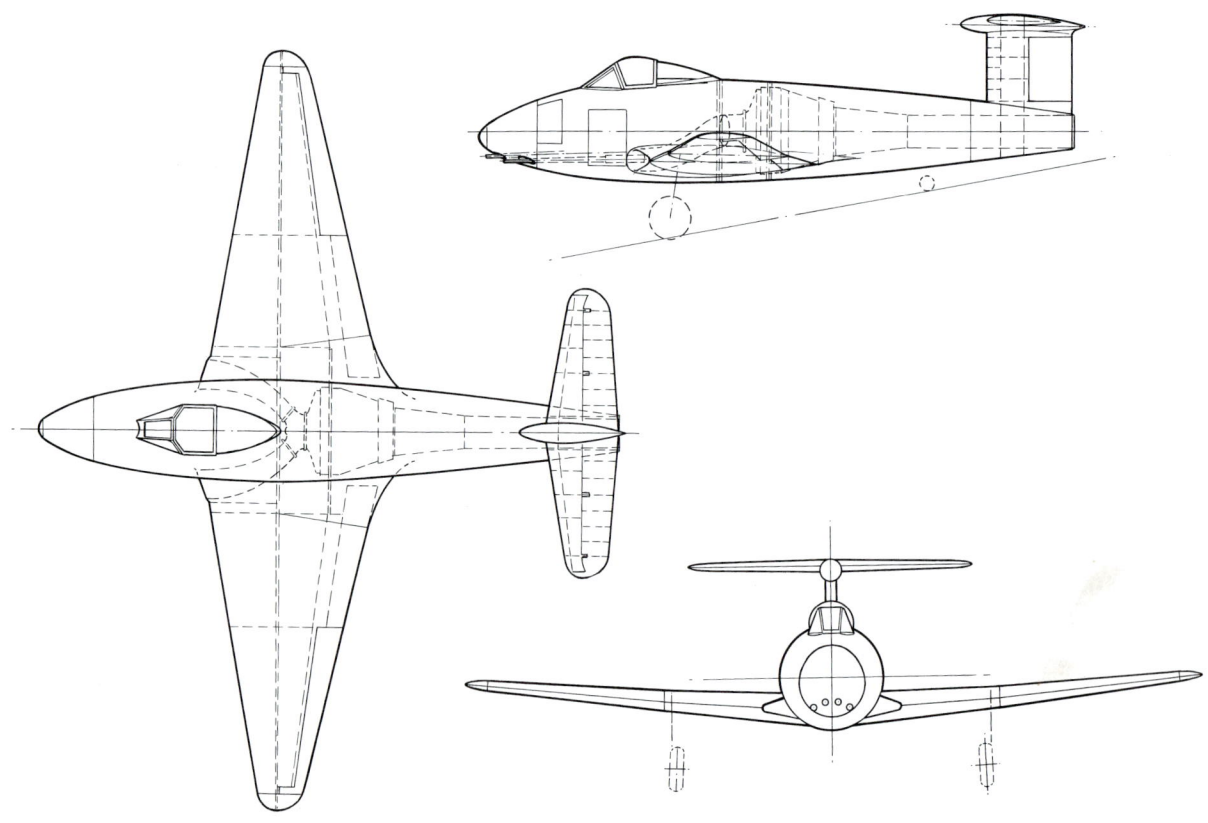

ABOVE A model of the E.5/42. *Joe Cherrie*

1943 to 8,300lb [3,765kg]). The aircraft's wing structure was based on a single main spar running through the fuselage, and several documents called the aircraft the Gloster A.9. Specification E.5/42 was issued to cover the project.

On 29 January 1943 a contract was placed for three E.5/42s, NN648, NN651 and NN655, each with a single 3,000lb (13.3kN) H.1 unit selected ahead of developed W2Bs. On 19 January Rowe had stated that he wanted the E.5/42 to fly 'at the earliest possible moment' and 'in the event of conflict between the Meteor and E.5/42, the latter was to have priority'. The Mock-Up Conference was held at Bentham on 23 and 24 February and the Specification was issued to Gloster on 26 March (some documents refer to it as the F.5/42). This requested a maximum speed of not less than 485mph (780km/h) at 30,000ft (9,144m), and the new type was also known as the Gloster-Halford fighter (the earlier projects had been labelled Gloster-Whittle).

The debate regarding the value of the single-engined fighter was considerable. By 10 February 1943 it was felt that the Meteor and the H.1-powered E.5/42 would have approximately the same top speed and climb performance, but this was with H.1s giving 2,700lb (12.0kN) thrust in the Meteor and 3,000lb (13.3kN) in the E.5/42. However, the former could be in service possibly in early 1944 but, allowing for the development of aircraft and engines, the E.5/42 would probably be in service not less than eighteen months later. It was felt in some quarters that the E.5/42 was a more desirable aircraft all round than the 'larger Meteor' (a variant intended to have Whittle W.2/500 engines), but it could hardly be in service before mid-1945. In addition, the endurance of the H.1 Meteor could be improved quite simply by adding drop tanks.

It appears that the construction of the first 'flying shell' E.5/42 was under way by November 1943 in Gloster's experimental works at Bentham, while a 1:4.5 scale model underwent preliminary testing in RAE's low-speed wind tunnel. In mid-December 1943 studies were also made for alternative engine installations, which RAE reviewed as follows:

i. Standard H.1 with 3,000lb (13.3kN) or 3,300lb (14.7kN) thrust – mean fuselage diameter 5ft 0in (1.52m), all-up weight 8,500lb (3,856kg), maximum speed at 30,000ft (9,144m) 540 or 560mph (869 or 901km/h). At the time the H.1 was only giving 2,300lb (10.2kN), so the chance of getting 3,300lb (14.7kN) seemed remote.

ii. Scaled-up Halford of 3,500 or 4,000lb (15.6 or 17.8kN) thrust – the respective figures were 5ft 7in (1.71m), 9,500lb (4,309kg) and 545mph or 560mph (877km/h or 901km/h). These power units were 'very hypothetical'.

iii. The American 4,000lb (17.8kN) thrust GEC Type I40 – 5ft 9in (1.75m), 9,600lb (4,355kg) and 550mph (885km/h). There were some CofG difficulties that RAE said had been neglected in establishing the weight, etc.

iv. The 4,000lb (17.8kN) MetroVick F.2/4 – a 4ft 6in (1.37m) mean fuselage diameter but CofG difficulties were prohibitive and detail performance estimates had not been made.

v. Whittle 4,000lb (17.8kN) W4/100 – 5ft 8in (1.73m), 10,200lb (4,627kg), and 545mph (877km/h). Here the CofG difficulties were serious and were not taken into account when establishing weights.

vi. Rolls-Royce B.37 of 2,500 or 2,800lb (11.1 or 12.4kN) thrust – 4ft 0in (1.22m), 7,500lb or 7,800lb (3,402kg or 3,539kg), 515mph or 530mph (829km/h or 853km/h). The B.37 was expected to give 2,500lb in its present form and might be developed to 2,800lb (12.4kN). A low rate of climb was the main disadvantage in this version.

Despite being seen as a desirable aircraft, the E.5/42 faded away to be replaced by a larger single-jet fighter,

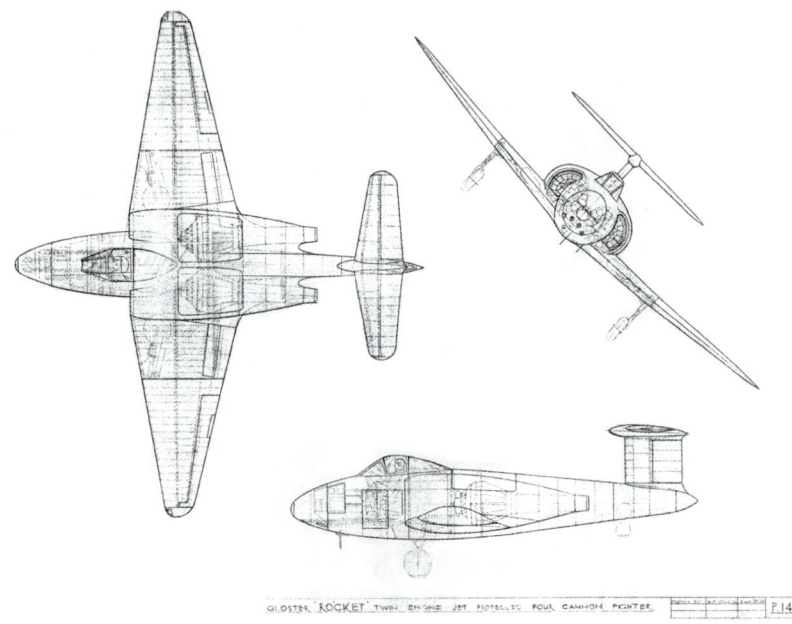

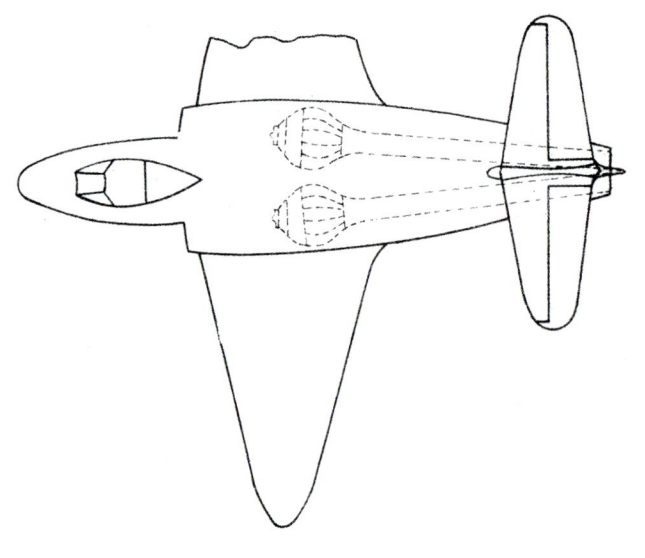

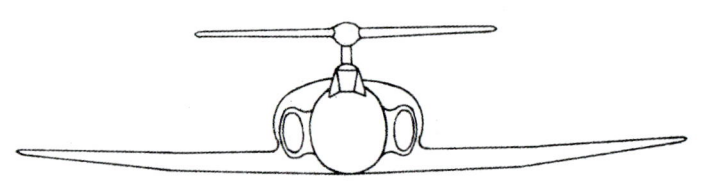

TOP Gloster drawing P.149 shows the original proposal for the Rocket twin-jet fighter (28.6.43). *Jet Age Museum*

BOTTOM A rough RAE sketch of the Gloster Rocket, now with a tail jet pipe, taken from a report that compared wind tunnel tests made on the Meteor, Ace, Rocket and Vampire. This is the only known original drawing of this version.

the E.1/44 Ace, described shortly.

Gloster Rocket

At the end of August 1943 Gloster stated that its twin-engine Rocket proposal

'…marked the introduction of a new design for a fighter and shows the possibility of a further important advance along the road towards ultimate development. It outlines the prospect of achieving a low-level speed of 550mph (885km/h) and a climb rate, commencing at sea level, of about 9,000ft/min (2,743m/min).'

The design was similar to the E.5/42 except that it had a twin side-by-side engine installation that functioned almost as a single unit. Two Rolls-Royce B.37s occupied the same sort of position in the rear fuselage as the Halford engine had occupied in the E.5/42, and the fuselage width was suitably increased in order to accommodate the new format. This extra width was just about the level necessary to duct the air intakes on either side of the front part of the fuselage, and it was expected that the combined thrust of the two units when fully developed would be 5,000lb (22.2kN). Such an increase in power was much more than could be effectively utilised from a single engine in an aircraft of this type; any engine that was large enough for this purpose would be prohibitive in weight and bulk.

There was little fundamental difference between the E.5/42 and the Rocket. What difference there was mostly concerned the fuselage behind the cockpit and to a lesser extent the wing centre section. The front part of the fuselage, outer wings, main undercarriage and tailplane

ABOVE A model of the Gloster Rocket with the tail jet pipe, made by Joe Cherrie. *Joe Cherrie*

Gloster Rocket (28.6.43)	
Span:	38ft 0in (11.58m)
Length:	32ft 3in (9.83m)
Wing Area:	225sq.ft (20.925sq.m)
All-Up-Weight:	9,000lb (4,082kg)
Powerplant:	2 x B.37 2,200lb (9.8kg)
Max Speed / Height:	545mph (877km/h) up to 10,000ft (3,048m), 550mph (885km/h) between 10,000ft (3,048m) and 40,000ft (12,192m)
Armament:	4 x 20mm cannon

were expected to be the same except for some extra strength or stiffness in certain places. The front fuselage was important since it housed the pilot's pressure cockpit and practically all of the military equipment. The basic design was closely allied to the E.5/42, so it was anticipated that, if this proposal was considered acceptable for early development and production, progress in the design and construction of a prototype would be rapid. From a design standpoint Gloster felt that the project was recommended as a type of outstanding technical interest. Both the E.5/42 Ace and the Rocket used an RAE 'high-speed' wing section first developed and fitted to the E.28/39.

On 31 August 1943 Rowe reported on a talk with Whittle about the possible installation of his W4/100 engine in the E.5/42 Ace, but it was thought to be 'not very suitable … the job can be better done by using two of the smaller units as proposed in the Rocket design arrangement.' Whittle was at first somewhat reluctant to accept the close-coupled twin scheme in preference to one larger engine, but later in the discussion agreed that the large engine was generally unsuitable except perhaps for a tail-first or tailless arrangement. Early RAE calculations suggested a top speed for the Rocket of 449mph (722km/h) at sea level and 480mph (772km/h) at 30,000ft (9,144m), but on 22 November RAE reported that it liked the new design, which had 'very much improved aerodynamics over the F.5/42 and less drag.'

However, an earlier meeting held at MAP on 9 October between Rowe, Dr Roxbee Cox, Dr Garner and Frank Whittle had discussed a high-speed project for Miles Aircraft (the M.52 supersonic research aircraft in Chapter 11) and the Rocket. The latter now showed a tricycle undercarriage, but Whittle was not very enthusiastic about the scheme and used the opportunity to point out that if they were going for a super fighter, and with an aeroplane that had not yet gone beyond the drawing stage, they should make a proper job of it and put in the powerplant most suited for the purpose, instead of making it with either B.37s or W2/700s. A full specification needed to be laid down, which Rowe defined as the Meteor military load and endurance but with a top speed of the order of 600mph (965km/h).

The undated rough drawing of the Rocket published in the first edition of this book originated from the Royal Aircraft Establishment (RAE) at Farnborough, and showed a jet pipe at the end of the fuselage; however, an original Gloster brochure has since been discovered that reveals twin jet pipes along the sides of the fuselage. The new brochure also provided some additional information and data.

The original Gloster Rocket drawing (numbered P.149) was dated 28 June 1943 and it appears that a second version called the P.150 was drawn in July (which most probably was the layout represented by the RAE drawing). The P.149's B.37 engines were mounted just ahead of the wing root trailing edge and the jet pipes were faired quite beautifully onto the sides of the rear fuselage. The horizontal tailplane was also tapered and sat on the top of a straight non-tapered fin that had a large rudder. Four 20mm cannon were mounted in the lower nose and (at first) a tailwheel undercarriage was employed. The Rocket's fuel tank capacity was given as 250 gallons (1,138 litres), its sea level rate of climb was 7,650ft/min (2,332m/min) and absolute ceiling 54,000ft (16,459m). The introduction of B.37 engines of 2,500lb (11.1kN) thrust would increase the top speed to 560mph (901km/h) at all heights, sea level rate of climb would rise to 9,150ft/min (2,789m/min) and the absolute ceiling would be 55,000ft (16,764m).

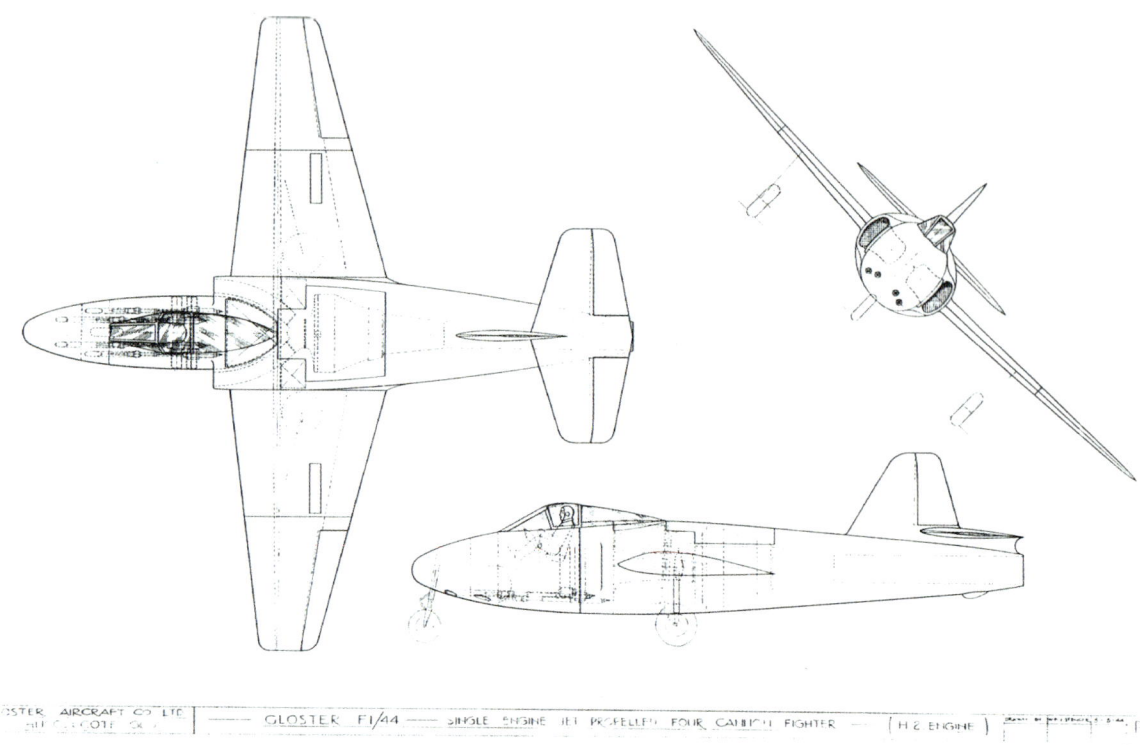

ABOVE Gloster 'F.1/44' with H.2 engine (Drawing P.174 26.1.44). *Jet Age Museum*

BELOW Gloseter 'F.1/44' later configuration (Drawing P.175 3.3.44). *Jet Age Museum*

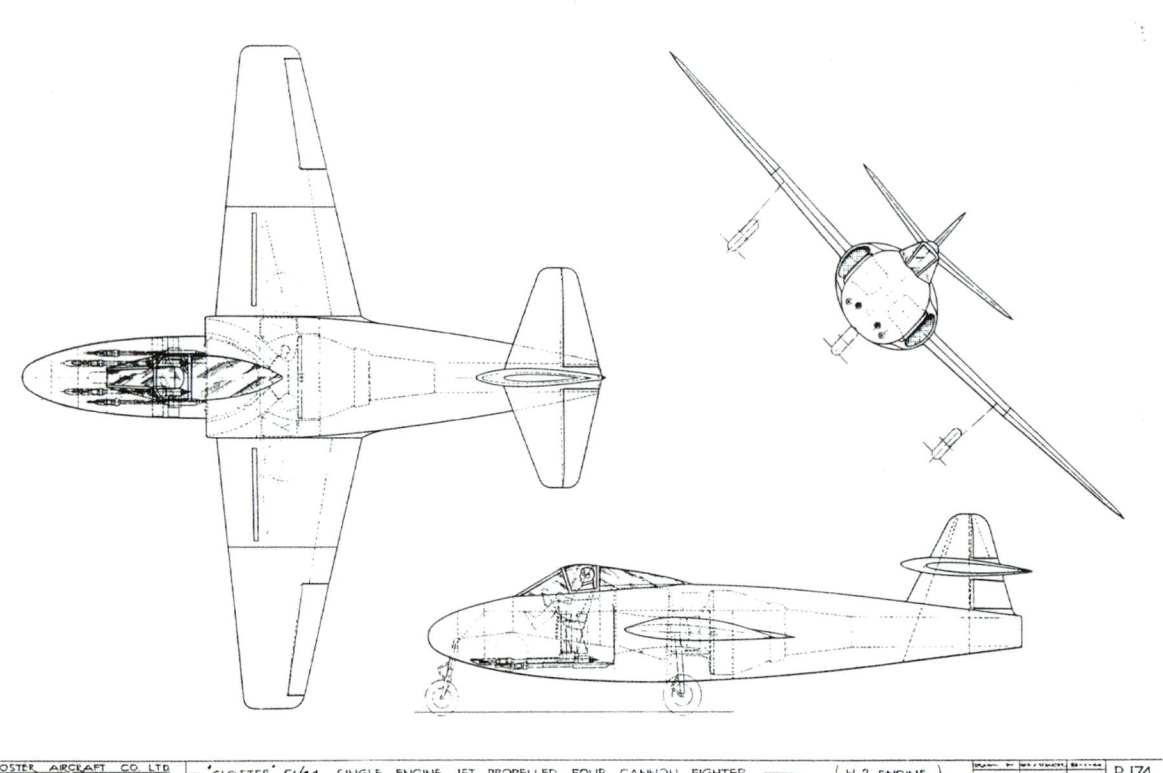

The Rocket was a short-lived project and was never close to being built.

Gloster E.1/44 Ace

The facts are not clear, but in late 1943 and early 1944 the original E.5/42 Ace was either abandoned for a new design or drastically altered. The result was a new project, still called the Ace, and the E.5/42 prototypes were cancelled on 2 February 1944.

The first versions of the modified aircraft – or the bridge between the two (drawings are not available) – appear to have been the P.171 and P.172 projects with variants of the H.1 giving 4,000lb (17.7kN) and 3,300lb (14.7kN) thrust respectively. P.171 had a span of 36ft 0in (10.97m) and a wing area of 230sq ft (21.39sq m), and carried 220 gallons (1,000 litres) of fuel; the P.172's span was 33ft 6in (10.21m), the wing area 200sq ft (18.60sq m), and fuel capacity 195 gallons (887 litres). Their performance with four cannon was summarised as follows: the P.171 had an all-up weight of 10,100lb (4,581kg), a top speed of 600mph (965km/h) at sea level, 595mph (957km/h) at 30,000ft (9,144m), a rate of climb of 6,300ft/min (1,920m/min) at sea level, a time to 30,000ft (9,144m) of 6.5 minutes, a service ceiling of 52,000ft (15,850m), and an absolute ceiling of 54,000ft (16,459m). The P.172's respective figures were 8,800lb (3,992kg), 575mph (925km/h), 585mph (941km/h) (the maximum speed was 595mph [957km/h] between 10,000ft [3,048m] and 20,000ft [6,096m]), 5,700ft/min (1,737m/min), 7.5 minutes, 49,000ft (14,935m), and 52,000ft.

A full brochure was completed in late January 1944 and Gloster felt that the outstanding feature of the design was the very high performance attainable with the de Havilland H.2 series engine (later called the Ghost), which had a declared thrust of 3,600lb (16.0kN) and was expected to give 4,000lb (17.7kN) with full development. Drawing P.174 of 26 January 1944 outlined 'a compact and aerodynamically exceptionally clean machine'. Basic drag had been reduced to a remarkably low figure, about half of that for the Meteor, which Gloster noted was an indication of the progress that had been made. It also emphasised the importance of reducing basic drag as opposed to providing more thrust. It was felt that an engine giving about 4,000lb (17.7kN) of thrust seemed to be as good a compromise as could be expected for a single-engined jet fighter, and there was little gain, if any, from using engines that exceeded the H.2's fully developed 4,000lb (17.7kN). An alternative examination had been made to consider the American General Electric engine as a possible alternative, but this unit was designed to operate in a pressure compartment or nacelle and the air ducts were much larger than those required for the H.2 (where the air ducts were connected directly to the engine compressor casing). Thus it was not regarded as an altogether practical alternative.

The exceptional high-speed performance of the P.174 was such that a reasonable limit in dive conditions would give rise to some very severe strength and stiffness requirements. At sea level a speed of 600mph (965km/h) corresponds to a Mach number of 0.80, and at 40,000ft (12,192m) the speed equivalent to 290mph (467km/h) corresponds to Mach 0.90. To reduce some potentially severe design problems and increases in weight, Gloster stated that it was most desirable to limit the design's diving speed to 600mph (965km/h) Equivalent Airspeed, the corresponding Mach number at this speed being 0.90. This represented a negligible limitation on level speed at sea level and a greater limitation on the diving speed, and made it possible to establish the aircraft's gross weight with two guns (the preferred option) at 10,000lb (4,536kg). The combination of high wing loading and thin wing section (both dictated by performance requirements), together with the proposed symmetrical wing section, had also led to a higher stalling speed than was considered desirable. To offset this, Gloster said that it would be necessary to fit an effective flap system and to consider drooping the ailerons when the flaps were in operation.

The P.174's span was 36ft (10.97m), length 34ft (10.36m), gross wing area 230sq ft (21.39sq m), thickness/chord ratio 10% at the root and 6% at the tip, internal fuel 220 gallons (1,000 litres), and gross weight with four guns 10,550lb (4,785kg). With four guns the top speed figures were the same as the P.171, rate of climb at sea level 6,000ft/min (1,829m/min), time to 30,000ft (9,144m) 7 minutes, operational ceiling 50,000ft (15,240m), and absolute ceiling 52,000ft (15,850m).

In February 1944 Specification F.1/44 was raised to cover the aircraft and by early March, shortly after the Advisory Design Conference, it had been decided to regard the four-gun assembly as the normal load and to provide more fuel. These changes made the aircraft a little larger and the bigger version (drawing P.175 of 3 March) also accommodated an engine of increased diameter, designed to produce 4,400lb (19.6kN) in the fully developed condition rather than the originally planned 4,000lb (17.8kN); gross weight had increased to 11,700lb (5,307kg). As a result of these changes it had been possible to arrange for the air brake to operate clear of the tailplane, and this had made it convenient to bring the tail closer to the fuselage and thus dissociate it from the fin structure. The fin had accordingly been 'stepped' forward of the tailplane, an anticipated advantage in maintaining satisfactory spinning characteristics.

Span was now 38ft (11.58m), length 37ft (11.28m), gross wing area 265sq ft (24.645sq m), and total internal fuel 295 gallons (1,341 litres). With 4,000lb (17.8kN) of thrust, the top speed at sea level was 580mph (933km/h) and at 30,000ft (9,144m) 570mph (917km/h), the sea level rate of climb 5,000ft/min (1,524m/min), the time to

Gloster E.1/44 Ace (flown)	
Span:	36ft 0in (10.97m)
Length:	38ft 0in (11.58m) (serial TX148 38ft 11in [11.86m])
Wing Area:	266sq.ft (24.74sq.m)
All-Up-Weight:	11,470lb (5,203kg)
Powerplant:	1 x Nene RN.2 5,000lb (22.2kN)
Max Speed / Height:	633mph (1,019km/h) at sea level
Armament:	4 x 20mm cannon, bombs or rocket projectiles

30,000ft 9.5 minutes, the operational ceiling 44,000ft (13,411m), and the absolute ceiling 48,000ft (14,630m). With 4,400lb (19.6kN) of thrust these figures became 600mph (965km/h), 590mph (949km/h), 5,700ft/min (1,737m/min), 8.5 minutes, 47,000ft (14,326m) and 49,500ft (15,088m). The specification was soon renumbered E.1/44 and by early July the design was very close to the form that was eventually built; however, Gloster shortly afterwards offered an H.2 variant (drawing P.181) or one with a single Rolls-Royce B.41 Nene engine (P.190 dated 22 September).

The fundamental difference between these engines was that the Halford made use of high-velocity air passing through ducts directly connected to the compressor casing, while the Rolls required that the air should be expanded to a relatively low velocity before entering the engine and a suitable ducting arrangement, because it presented a major problem on account of size in a restricted space. On the Halford-engined aeroplane the air ducts passed through the main wing spar before directly connecting to the compressor casing, and these ducts had their entry areas disposed on either side of the fuselage adjacent

TOP & MIDDLE These views of Gloster E.1/44 Ace prototype TX145, with the fighter's original tail, were taken in 1948.

BOTTOM Gloster Ace TX148 was fitted with an alternative tail arrangement and is seen here taking off from Moreton Valence. *Jet Age Museum*

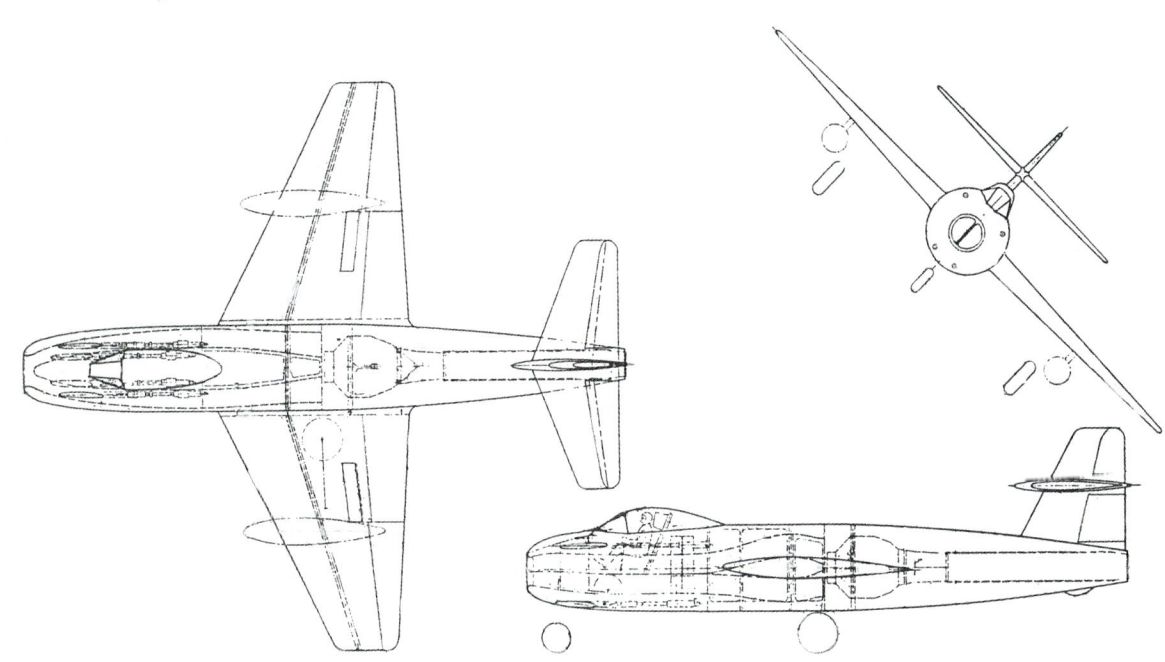

ABOVE The Gloster CXP-1001 China Fighter (1946 onwards).

to the wing roots. When the Rolls engine was installed the ducts, on account of their larger size, passed over and under a straight-through spar before being connected to the plenum chamber surrounding the engine. These differences affected the position of the fuel tanks behind the main spar, there being two for the Halford and one central tank for the Rolls; thus it was impracticable to consider replacing one unit with the other in the same aeroplane.

In early December 1944 Gloster's target date to complete the first aircraft had become August 1945. By May 1945 the aircraft was to be fitted with either a de Havilland Ghost 10 or a Nene, and the prototype line-up had been laid down as SM809, TX145, TX148 and TX150 (the 'strength test' airframe) with Nenes, and SM801 and SM805 with the Ghost; however, when the E.1/44 finally flew it was powered by a Nene. Due to the low priority given to it, progress on the Ace was slow and Gloster's enthusiasm for the project gradually faded; in fact, the aircraft did not fly until 9 March 1948, by which time it was rather out of date. In the end only TX145 and TX148 ever flew, a production order placed on 5 September 1945 and covered by Specification F.23/46 was cancelled, and plans for a Nene II version were dropped in August 1946. The E.1/44 proved to be something of a failure and its nickname, the 'Gloster Gormless', signified just how lowly it was rated. It certainly never came anywhere near matching the achievements of its famous Meteor stablemate, but it did contribute a new tail arrangement to that aircraft, which became the Meteor F.Mk.8.

Gloster CXP-1001 China Fighter

The new rear fuselage and tail were first drawn on 2 September 1946 as the P.212.

The Gloster China Fighter project differs from all others in this book since it was designed purely for an overseas customer – what the Ministry described as an 'offshore' purchase (i.e. an export). It should perhaps have been covered in *British Secret Projects Volume 1: Jet Fighters*, but it was a design based primarily on Second World War technology.

The Chinese Nationalist Government was eager to modernise its Air Force and in mid-1946 sent missions to both the United States and Great Britain. The British Mission was split into three with one section investigating the design and construction of a jet fighter, the second a bomber, and the third a jet engine. Negotiations brought proposals to collaborate with Gloster on the fighter.

An agreement dated 18 July 1946 stated that, as part of a plan to assist the build-up of a Chinese aircraft industry, thirty Chinese personnel were to be given facilities for twelve months instruction at the Design and Drawing Offices at Hucclecote. After six months the Chinese Government could request Gloster to design and build three prototype fighter aircraft to a specification supplied by China and agreed by the firm. The aircraft were to have Rolls-Royce engines and be delivered in thirty months. China then had the option of acquiring the

ABOVE A model of the Gloster China Fighter, made by Joe Cherrie. *Joe Cherrie*

was given but, as a result of misgivings expressed by the Air Ministry, Rolls-Royce was asked to defer completion of the contract for as long as possible. In November the Chinese Government asked Gloster to prepare a contract for the design of a single Nene-powered fighter aircraft to be schemed with the assistance of the Chinese draftsmen.

Gloster asked for Ministry permission to adapt the E.1/44 aircraft already building to Chinese requirements, but not to go into production, and this was agreed (the proposal was called the CXP-102, dated 14 May 1947). But Colonel Ku, who conducted the negotiations with Gloster, wished to secure a more advanced design in view of the length of time needed to get a Chinese factory in operation. The Ministry refused because it objected to an overseas Air Force being equipped with a British design comparable to or in advance of that currently in UK service; also, with available design capacity in the UK limited and the E.1/44 rejected, Gloster was to be invited to prepare a design to one of the fighter specifications (F.43/46 and F.44/46) shortly to be released. The Foreign Office opposed exporting arms to China because of the conflict between the Kuomintang (Nationalists) and the Communists, but it did not object to a manufacturing licence as production was at least two or three years away. In the end the E.1/44 was thoroughly redesigned as the CXP-1001, though at one stage in late 1946 the Meteor and a Nene-powered de Havilland Vampire were considered as alternatives by the Ministry of Supply. The biggest change from the E.1/44 was the nose intake.

In the early design stages the all-up weight was given considerable attention, the target weight having been set at 14,000lb (6,350kg); when the project was brought to a close it had reached 14,250lb (6,464kg). CXP-1001 was considered a fairly efficient design with power coming from a single Nene engine, there were four 20mm Hispano cannon placed in the nose, two above

manufacturing rights to the aeroplane.

The thirty trainees arrived in September 1946 and a section of the Brockworth factory, complete with workshop and offices, was set aside for the visitors. It is thought that each Chinese draftsman received an Austin 8 car. However, during these early days the security aspects presented formidable difficulties. For example, the Gloster Meteor and E.1/44 Ace fighters and Rolls AJ.65 and Nene II engines were all secret, with little likelihood of information on them being cleared for the Chinese. In fact, there would be problems with any document marked Secret. Approval of a manufacturing licence for the Nene I

Gloster CXP-1001 China Fighter (1946 onwards)	
Span:	38ft 0in (11.58m)
Length:	41ft 11in (12.78m)
Wing Area:	360sq.ft (33.48sq.m)
Normal Gross Weight:	13,900lb (6,305kg), overload 18,700lb (5,700kg)
Powerplant:	1 x RR Nene 5,000lb (22.2kN)
Max Speed / Height:	600mph (965km/h) at 10,000ft (3,048m)
Armament:	4 x 20mm cannon

and two below the intake, and the estimated sea level rate of climb was 6,000ft/min (1,829m/min).

Progress was slow and by early 1949, with just two prototypes on order, only a mock-up and some components had been manufactured. By now the Nationalists were suffering at the hands of the Communists, and on 3 February Colonel Lin contacted Air Marshal Coryton to inform him that the contract was to be cancelled and that all work should be cleared up by the end of the month. This at last allowed Gloster to increase its Drawing Office strength on a new design, which would become the Javelin. Gloster received confirmation to discontinue work on 28 February except for the completion and despatch of unfinished drawings, a model and part of the mock-up. In fact, after the Chinese Communist take-over in 1949 the project was continued for the Nationalists in Formosa, but the release of drawings and components was frozen in October 1950 after the Nationalists had attacked a British merchant ship, the *Achises*. On 25 November 1952, and without consulting the Chinese Central People's Government, Gloster decided to dispose of all of the remaining material. The MoS said that this should be acceptable as the aircraft was now an out-of-date design, but also stated that it was not responsible for the firm's actions.

TOP Meteor EE528 was an F.Mk.IV fitted with Rolls-Royce Derwents. This view dates from 1946. *Phil Butler*

ABOVE The final version of the day fighter Meteor was the F.Mk.8, which featured a new tail arrangement. *Phil Butler*

Gloster Meteor Developments
Meteor F.Mk.8

After the war the Meteor went from strength to strength. The first versions lacked performance, but the F.Mk.4 fitted with Rolls-Royce Derwent 5s took the type to maturity and this mark was built in large numbers. However, by 1947 it was clear that the fighter, if it was going to remain competitive with rival products, would need updating, so Gloster began work on a 'second generation' Meteor. Late Mk.4s had a longer nose, but the more forward position of the guns and ammunition, in relation to the whole aircraft, ensured that more pronounced movements in CofG occurred as the ammunition and fuel were used up. The original tail was unsuited to cope with the pitch-up instability this created, but the angular tail fitted to the E.1/44 Ace was, so this was tried on Meteor RA382 and showed good handling. In due course Mk.4 VT150 was converted into a full F.Mk.8 prototype and flew on 12 October 1948. To prove the new tail, the old style was also tried on VT150 in a move that confirmed the superiority of the later version.

This section also looks at a couple of proposed Meteor developments.

Gloster P.263

The object of the P.263 was to increase the Meteor's critical Mach number and to raise the altitude at which effective fighting manoeuvres could be executed. The main proposed design changes included a substantial increase in wing area from 350sq ft to 450sq ft (32.55sq m to 41.85sq m), a reduction of wing thickness/chord ratio from 12% to 10% throughout, an increase in wing span from 37ft to 43ft (11.28m to 13.11m), and the introduction of 20° of sweepback on the wing and tail surfaces. A total of 380 gallons (1,728 litres) of fuel

Gloster P.263 (19.11.47)	
Span:	43ft 0in (13.11m)
Length:	44ft 6in (13.56m)
Wing Area:	450sq.ft (41.85sq.m)
All-Up-Weight:	16,500lb (7,484kg)
Powerplant:	2 x RR Derwent VII 4,500lb (20.0kN)
Max Speed / Height:	565 knots (651mph/1,047km/h) Mach 0.85 at sea level, 540 knots (622mph/1,001km/h) Mach 0.88 at 20,000ft (6,096m)
Armament:	4 x 20mm cannon

BELOW Gloster drawing P.209 showed a proposed Meteor development with a more 'streamlined' fuselage and cockpit canopy and powered by two Rolls-Royce AJ.65 axial jet engines (25.6.46). *Jet Age Museum*

BOTTOM The Gloster P.263 (19.11.47). *Jet Age Museum*

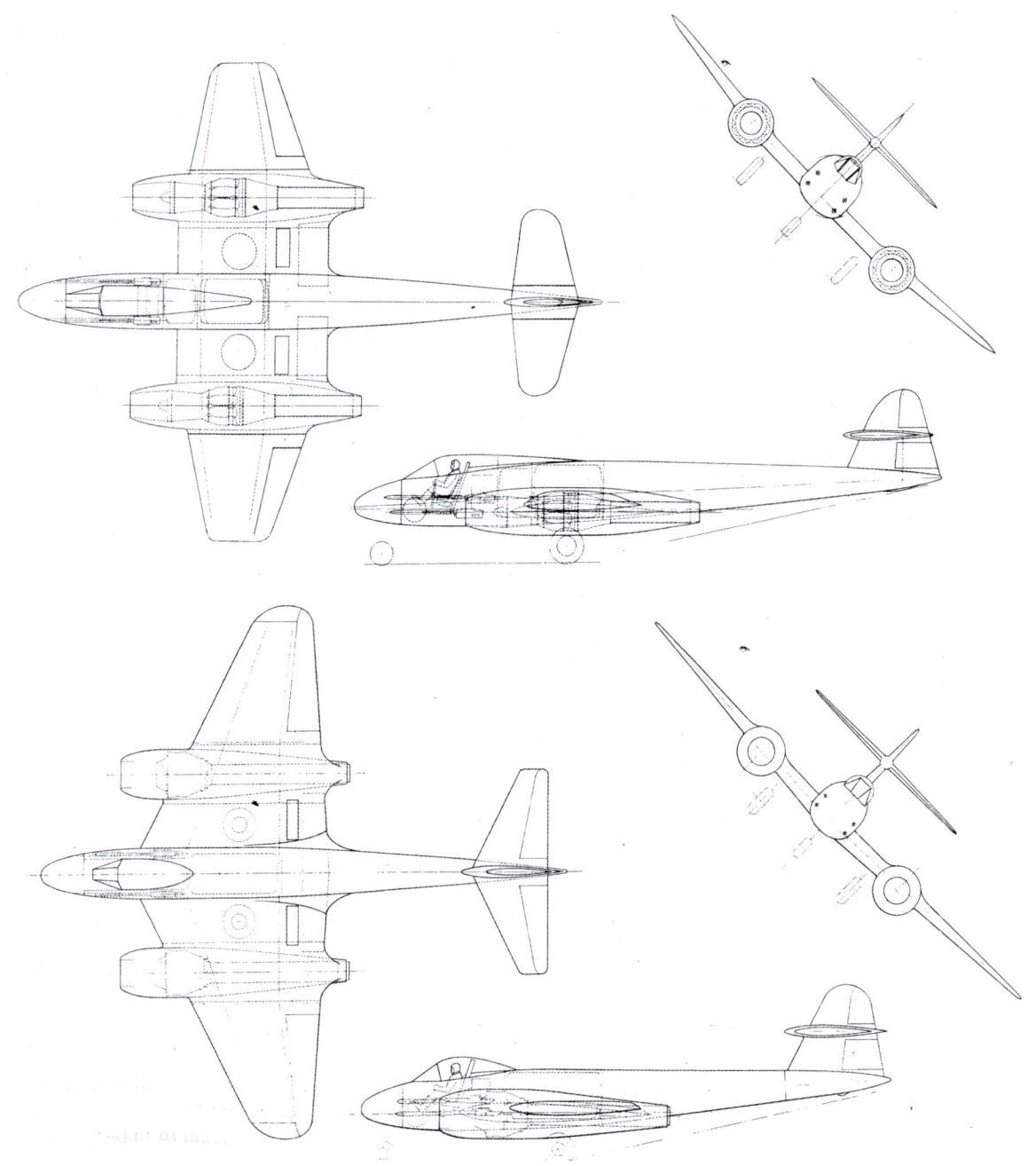

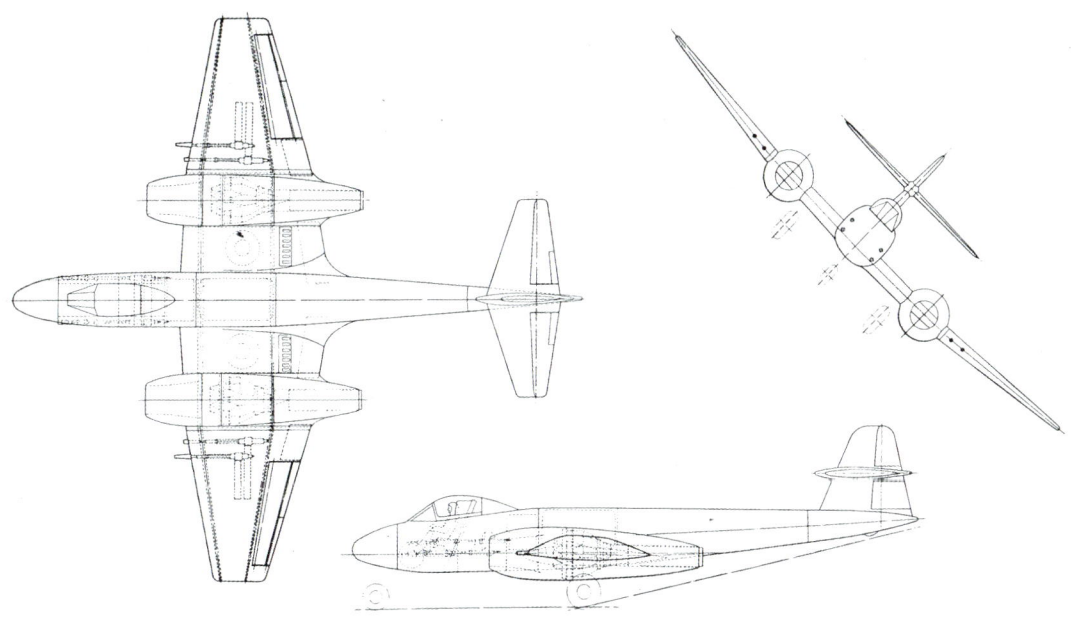

ABOVE Gloster drawing P.309 of February 1950 showed the F.Mk.8 day fighter Meteor combined with the wings of a Mk.11 night fighter. Four 20mm cannon were housed in the nose and four more in the outer wings. *Jet Age Museum*

would be carried internally, sea level rate of climb was given as 11,400ft/min (3,475m/min), and the absolute ceiling was 54,000ft (16,459m).

Gloster P.309 Eight-Gun Meteor

In February 1950 Gloster Aircraft offered a version of the Meteor that brought together within one airframe elements of both of the primary service types, the day and night fighters (see below). The outcome was a powerful jet fighter carrying eight 20mm cannon with four in the nose and four in the wings – the normal Meteor day fighters had their four 20mm armament mounted in the sides of the nose, but on the night fighter the nose radome meant that the guns had to be moved out into the wings.

The eight-gun project brochure explained how this new model would take the standard F.Mk.8 day fighter version's front and rear fuselage and empennage and join them with the wings and fuselage centre section designed for the NF.Mk.11 night fighter. Meteor parts already in production or planned for future production variants were to be used in this latest type, while some undercarriage and type equipment modifications already specified and agreed for the Mk.11 would also appear on this aircraft. Apart from the eight guns, provision was to be made to permit the new aircraft to carry either two 1,000lb (454kg) bombs or eight 95lb (43kg) rocket projectiles under the fuselage, together with wingtip tanks. This would provide a maximum fuel load of 620 gallons (2,819 litres), with 420 gallons (1,910 litres) carried internally. For long-distance operations without any rockets or bombs on board the fuel capacity could be increased again to 995 gallons (4,524 litres) by the carriage of external drop tanks under the wings and fuselage. This brought the maximum fuel load carried externally to 575 gallons (2,614 litres) and the two 100-gallon (455-litre) wingtip tanks could be carried in any flight configuration, something that was not possible on a standard Meteor F.Mk.8.

The design speed and strength factors for this new aircraft at its combat weight were expected to be the same as those for the Meteor Mk.8. However, the brochure added that some local strengthening of the Meteor 8 fuselage and tail, and of the Meteor 11 wings and centre section fuselage, could well be necessary in order to achieve this level of strength, and in consequence the airframe weight would also rise by a small figure. In this connection it was expected that the biggest difficulty in undertaking the project could be to increase the Meteor Mk.11 wing design speed from 500mph to 600mph (805km/h to 965km/h). The eight-gun fighter's span was the same as the standard 'long span' F.Mk.3 and F.Mk.4 day fighter Meteors and all four night fighter versions (the F.Mk.8's wings were shorter); when the tip tanks were in place the span became 46ft 9.5in (14.26m). Thickness/chord ratio over the centre section was 12%, and across the outer wings this fell to 9% at the tips. The powerplant was two Rolls-Royce Derwent engines and at the normal all-up weight these would give the aircraft a rate of climb at sea level of 6,400ft/min (1,951m/min) and an absolute ceiling of 48,000ft (14,630m); it was calculated that the P.309 would take 7.3 minutes to reach 30,000ft (9,144m).

Gloster P.309 (2.50)	
Span:	43ft 0in (13.11m)
Length:	44ft 0in (13.41m)
Wing Area (without tip tanks):	377sq.ft (35.06sq.m)
Normal all-Up-Weight (370gal/1,683lit fuel):	16,900lb (7,666kg)
Powerplant:	2 x RR Derwent 3,500lb (15.6kN)
Max Speed / Height:	515 knots (593mph/954km/h) Mach 0.78 at sea level, 485 knots (558mph/898km/h) Mach 0.82 at 30,000ft (9,144m)
Armament:	8 x 20mm cannon

As a design exercise, the eight-gun Meteor makes fascinating reading, but one assumes that the task of blending elements of the Mks.8 and 11 airframes together would have required rather more effort than is apparent in the covering brochure. For example, one assumes that firing all eight guns together would have had quite an affect on the airframe – or would the pilot have had to be selective as to which guns he fired at any one moment? The style of presentation of the project brochure indicates pretty firmly that this proposed Meteor version was submitted to the Air Ministry for consideration, but obviously it was not taken up. However, had it been built and made to work then one feels that this particular Meteor would surely have been a most formidable weapon.

Armstrong Whitworth Night Fighter Meteor

Soon after the war the need to replace the Mosquito night fighter became critical and F.Mk.3 Meteor EE348 was tested with a nose-mounted AI radar as part of the F.44/46 night fighter programme, which eventually led to the Gloster Javelin (see *British Secret Projects: Jet Fighters since 1950*). But progress was slow and an interim Mosquito replacement with improved performance was required to fill the gap. Gloster's first night fighter Meteor brochure was prepared in October 1948 and showed an adapted two-seat Mk.7 trainer, but the company was fully stretched with its commitments to single-seat Meteors, so the night fighter's development and manufacture was passed to Armstrong Whitworth. Specification F.24/48 was issued on 12 February 1949 to cover the NF.Mk.11 interim night fighter with AI.Mk.10 radar, a mock-up was completed at the end of 1948, and Mk.7 VW413 was converted into a prototype with a nose 4ft (1.2m) longer. It was flown on 28 January 1949 and in March the Mk.8 tail was added, which stretched the length to 48ft 6in (14.8m); to save time the NF.Mk.11 used as much existing Meteor structure as possible. The first full prototype, WA546, first flew on 31 May 1950 and production orders followed for this version and for the later NF.Mks.12, 13 and 14.

ABOVE Two views of WS775, an Armstrong Whitworth NF.Mk.14 Meteor night fighter variant. *Jet Age Museum*

AWA Meteor NF.Mk.11 (flown)	
Span:	43ft 0in (13.11m)
Length:	48ft 6in (14.78m)
Wing Area:	374sq.ft (34.78sq.m)
All-Up-Weight:	16,542lb (7,503kg)
Powerplant:	2 x Derwent 8 3,700lb (16.4kN)
Max Speed / Height:	580mph (933km/h) at sea level
Armament:	4 x 20mm cannon

Chapter Eleven
Jet Fighters from Other Manufacturers

ABOVE **De Havilland Vampire F.Mk.1 TG330.** *Barry Guess, BAE Systems, Farnborough*

Gloster was not the only company to produce jet aircraft designs during and just after the war; others became involved, but the extent of their work varied. Nevertheless, more jet aircraft design was undertaken in Britain at this time than has probably ever previously been acknowledged.

De Havilland Vampire and Venom

Work proceeded fairly quickly on Frank Halford's H.1 Goblin jet engine, which was larger and, with thrusts of up to 3,000lb (13.3kN), more powerful than Whittle's W2B. This additional power made a single-engined fighter a more viable proposition, and at the end of April 1941 negotiations were initiated by Sir Henry Tizard with Halford and de Havilland for a project to build an airframe to accommodate Halford's engine. The suitability of this form of propulsion for high-speed bombing without rear defence was immediately obvious, and the possibilities for this purpose, set out in considerable detail, were communicated to the Ministry in 1942. They were not taken up, but it was finally decided that the alternative fighter application should proceed on the grounds that this would be more important as a national insurance against the enemy sending jet bombers over Britain.

De Havilland DH.99 and DH.100

De Havilland's first jet fighter proposal was called the DH.99 and was detailed in a brochure dated 6 June 1941. This was to be an all-metal twin-tail-boom aircraft with four cannon housed beneath the cockpit (one more 20mm could go in the front of each boom as overload); it had a single wing spar with a D-nose torsion box and was fitted with metal-covered ailerons and slotted flaps. The rudder empennage was carried on tail booms to eliminate any interference from the engine exhaust (which also avoided the necessity for a long tail pipe), and a nosewheel undercarriage was used. There was a large fuel tank holding 178 gallons (809 litres) in the body and one further 26-gallon (118-litre) tank in each wing root, giving 230 gallons (1,045 litres) in all. The estimated performance using 2,700lb (12.0kN) of thrust included a rate of climb at sea level of 4,590ft/min (1,399m/min), a time to 30,000ft (9,144m) of 9.6 minutes, and an operational ceiling of 45,400ft (13,838m).

187

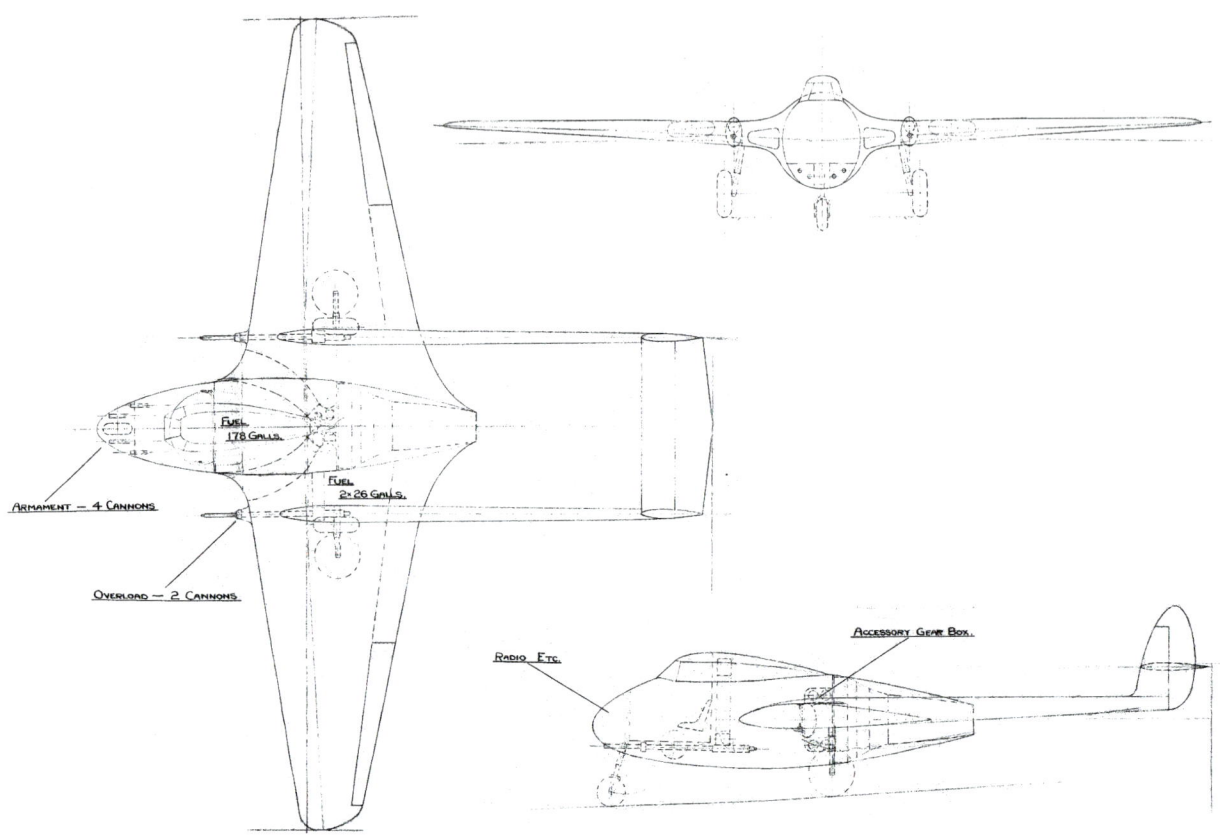

ABOVE The De Havilland DH.99 (23.5.41). The drawing shows a six-cannon overload arrangement, which would have taken the maximum weight to 8,470lb (3,842kg). *Adapted from National Archives AVIA 15-1229 via Phil Butler/Chris Gibson*

de Havilland DH.99 (6.1.41)	
Span:	40ft 0in (12.19m)
Length:	31ft 0in (9.45m)
Wing Area:	260sq.ft (24.18sq.m)
All-Up-Weight:	7,970lb (3,615kg)
Powerplant:	1 x de Havilland H.1 2,900lb (12.9kN)
Max Speed / Height (with 2,700lb/12.0kN thrust):	445mph (716km/h) at sea level, 493mph (793km/h) at 35,000ft (10,668m)
Armament:	4 x 20mm cannon, overload 2 more 20mm

de Havilland Vampire F.Mk.1 (flown)	
Span:	40ft 0in (12.19m)
Length:	30ft 9in (9.37m)
Wing Area:	266sq.ft (24.74sq.m)
All-Up-Weight:	10,480lb (4,754kg)
Powerplant:	1 x Goblin 1 3,100lb (13.8kN)
Max Speed / Height:	540mph (869km/h) at sea level
Armament:	4 x 20mm cannon

The design was criticised by MAP's Capt Liptrot for presenting too little detail, while its structure weights were considered rather optimistic; Liptrot was also doubtful about the performance estimates. However, in late July 1941 Rowe decided to go ahead with the project and on 5 August Sorley confirmed that they were ordering a de Havilland fighter with the Halford engine. In November 1941 the DH.99 designation was allocated briefly to a development of the Mosquito bomber with two Napier Sabre piston engines (which later became the DH.101), and another twin-Merlin project was the DH.102 to be built to Specification B.4/42. However, on 29 December 1942 the Air Staff decided that it did not want the B.4/42 bomber, which relieved the load on de Havilland's design staff (in fact, the company had been working on these lines for some weeks).

By 11 November 1941 the jet fighter had been renumbered DH.100 and was eventually built of mixed wood and metal construction, the pilot essentially being housed in a wooden pod. On 13 February 1942 de Havilland's C. C. Walker, in reply to a suggestion that the fighter should be dropped for a jet bomber, told N. E. Rowe that

'…when we started on this design, the idea was to quickly produce a fully operational jet-propelled fighter in case the enemy had a similar project in hand. We are aware that twin tail booms have sometimes been regarded with suspicion, we cannot, however, see anything in this beyond the purely engineering problem of giving the known and necessary degree of stiffness to the booms. The case, therefore, for our proceeding with the fighter seems to remain as strong as it was six months ago.'

CHAPTER ELEVEN

JET FIGHTERS FROM OTHER MANUFACTURERS

LEFT A model of the original DH.99 with the additional wing cannon, made by Joe Cherrie. *Joe Cherrie*

Two prototypes, LZ548 and LZ551, were authorised on 22 April and Specification E.6/41 was raised to cover the project. On 20 September 1943 the DH.100, Britain's second jet fighter, which for a period was called the 'Spider Crab', made its first flight from Hatfield. A major problem during the flight test phase was 'snaking' (directional instability), which led to a stream of changes to the fin shape and tail arrangement before it was sufficiently cured. Production aircraft entered service as the Vampire and served with both the RAF and overseas air forces.

De Havilland DH.107 and DH.112 Venom

On 9 April 1945 de Havilland completed a preliminary performance, weight and general data assessment of a project called the DH.107, a development of the H.1 Goblin-powered DH.100 Vampire fitted with a more powerful H.2 Ghost engine. This had a span of 35ft (10.67m) as against the Vampire's 40ft (12.19m), wing area 296sq ft (27.53sq m), thickness/chord ratio of 13.5% at the fuselage side and 10% at the booms (Vampire 17.5% and 14%), and 670 gallons (3,046 litres) of internal fuel (Vampire 582 gallons/2,646 litres). The increase in maximum speed over the Vampire was about 70mph (113km/h) at sea level (i.e. 610mph/981km/h), and 50mph (80km/h) at 30,000ft (9,144m) (i.e. 544mph/875km/h). The maximum weight without drop tanks was 11,168lb (5,066kg) and with two 140-gallon (637-litre) drop tanks this rose to 13,668lb (6,200kg). This project was then developed further into the DH.112 Venom.

The de Havilland Venom itself began life as the Vampire FB.Mk.8, but featured a new thin wing and a more powerful Ghost 103 engine. The original 'Thin Wing' Vampire

TOP Serial TG370 was another Vampire F.Mk.1. *Barry Guess, BAE Systems, Farnborough*

ABOVE Night fighter Venom NF.Mk.3 WX868 displays the version's much larger nose radome. *Crown Copyright*

RIGHT These two views from similar angles show the differences between de Havilland Vampire VV217, an FB.Mk.V, and the DH.112 Venom prototype VV612.

BELOW A Venom FB.Mk.1 in RAF service overseas. *Barry Guess, BAE Systems, Farnborough*

de Havilland Venom FB.Mk.1 (flown)	
Span:	41ft 8in (12.70m)
Length:	31ft 10in (9.70m)
Wing Area:	280sq.ft (26.04sq.m)
All-Up-Weight:	15,400lb (6,985kg)
Powerplant:	1 x Ghost 103 4,850lb (21.6kN)
Max Speed / Height:	640mph (1,030km/h)
Armament:	4 x 20mm cannon, 2,000lb (907kg) bombs or rockets

proposal was made on 31 March 1948 and showed 10% larger intakes, about 22° of sweepback on the leading edge, and curved wingtips. After much recent discussion on the subject of high-altitude interception, de Havilland noted that 'present RAF fighters will be in service for five to six years. It will take time to get a new fighter currently at the preliminary stage into service and therefore everything possible should be done to develop current jet fighters as high-altitude interceptors' The Vampire, with its low wing loading, good manoeuvrability and small turning circle, was particularly suited to high-altitude work, and the thin wing improved the Mach performance and made use of the Ghost's extra power. There was nothing experimental about the proposed changes, and the new engine added about 600lb (272kg) of weight.

On 15 July Air Marshal W. A. Coryton wrote that 'it would seem that the rib and spar design and method of attaching the covering will be exactly similar to the Vampire, no new fundamental design principles are introduced. De Havilland may go ahead even without our support as the aircraft will find a ready sale as an interceptor in foreign markets.' Consequently there would be no need to direct any high-grade design staff to the project and risk any detriment to the company's existing RAF commitments (which included the new DH.110 jet fighter). The project went ahead and by early September had been named Venom. The first Venom prototype, VV612, first flew on 2 September 1949 and the type became an interim fighter-bomber to fill the gap between the Meteor and Vampire and the new Hawker Hunter and Supermarine Swift jet fighters. In due course night fighter and naval (Sea Venom) versions were developed, and the type served in numbers throughout the 1950s, both in the UK and overseas.

Hawker P.1040 and Sea Hawk

Hawker's first jet-powered design was the P.1011 project of 1941, which was an exercise in fitting Whittle units into the P.1004 high-altitude fighter. The origin of the Sea Hawk was the P.1035 of 1944, which was described as an F.2/43 Fury with a Rolls B.41 jet installed in the centre fuselage; the piston Fury's elliptical wings were retained, but the project featured air intakes in the wing and a split exhaust pipe. Early in November 1944 Mr Wardle, DOR, and N. E. Rowe visited Claremont House in Esher to discuss jet aircraft (Claremont was the wartime base for Hawker staff involved in the design of new aeroplanes). A single engine was suggested and a few days later Rowe supplied particulars for a 6,000lb (26.7kN) Rolls-Royce unit, and soon after that Hawker sent Rolls details of a bifurcated pipe scheme for investigation. On 22 December a single-seat fighter aircraft with bifurcated (split) jet pipes and a B.41 Nene engine was drawn under the designation P.1040, which was a cleaned-up P.1035 with straight tapered wings and virtually nothing left over from the Fury.

The Nene had a double-sided centrifugal compressor and it was considered sensible to place the intake as close as possible to it because an early criticism of single-engine jet aircraft with nose intakes and long pipes was that the whole fuselage was full of wind and lacked sufficient space for equipment and fuel. A long jet pipe meant large energy losses, a critical aspect because of the low power of early engines, and P.1040's intake and bifurcated pipe arrangement was seen as a way of keeping pipe length and energy loss to a minimum. It also proved to be the optimum aerodynamically, despite Rolls-Royce needing some convincing as to its suitability, and was probably the most important and innovative feature on the P.1040. The elimination of intake and exhaust

BELOW A model of the Hawker P.1040 with 'Tempest' wings. It is possible that this design was similar to the P.1035. *Joe Cherrie*

TOP Hawker P.1040 prototype VP401, photographed in 1948.

ABOVE P.1040 prototype VP401 was rebuilt with an additional rocket motor, becoming the Hawker P.1072. In this form it is seen at the September 1951 Farnborough Air Show. *Terry Panopalis collection*

ducting within the fuselage allowed Hawker to fit large-capacity fuel tanks both ahead of and behind the engine, a most unusual situation that kept the fuselage symmetrical about the CofG. Early jet engines were weighty objects and thus had to be kept as close to the aeroplane's CofG as possible.

The first P.1040 brochure was completed in January 1945 and confirmed that the unique bifurcated pipe (patented the following month in the name of J. V. Stanbury) made room for a large fuel capacity in the tail. The span was 36ft 6in (11.13m) and the length 37ft 2in (11.33m). The project was generally approved by Rowe and Wardle and after seeing it Sir Wilfrid Freeman said 'go right ahead'; the aircraft was sometimes called the 'Fury replacement'. A full tender was submitted to Rowe on 27 February, and he felt justified in accepting the Nene since it offered a good performance and range while lending itself to an experimental rocket boost installation to improve the rate of climb. Design work commenced in March but the air intakes received some criticism. This hold-up was not cleared by RAE until 21 September 1945, when the intakes were declared 90% efficient, but it had already been agreed that the aeroplane was a considerable advance on present types. Early in October a new combined tender was submitted that comprised the P.1040, the P.1047 (a swept-back version with a rocket motor) and the P.1046 (naval swept-wing version with a rocket).

During December Admiral Slattery visited Kingston and expressed great interest in the project, but the company was later advised by Rowe that, at this stage, the P.1040 was not regarded by the Air Staff as one of its new types (allegedly because it offered little improvement in performance over the Meteor). Fortunately the Naval Staff saw it as a support fighter and suggested that the design should be reschemed around the longer but more powerful Rolls-Royce AJ.65 axial jet (later the Avon). However, this second project (the highly swept-wing P.1049 fleet fighter with single AJ.65) was rejected by Hawker in mid-January 1946 as impractical since it would need swept-back wings to balance placing a pilot in the nose, a necessary move to assist with deck landing. Swept wings were considered undesirable for the Fleet when the Nene lent itself to a conventional wing arrangement.

On 21 February 1946 an order was placed for three prototype P.1040 general-purpose and long-range naval fighter and strike support aircraft. Specification N.7/46 was allotted to the project and in June Hawker was advised that the official target date for the first flight of the first machine, without folding wings, was February 1947; the final Mock-Up Conference was held on 10 and 11 October. Metal cutting began during October 1945, but it was November 1946 before the first centre fuselage

Hawker Sea Hawk F.Mk.1 (flown)	
Span:	39ft 0in (11.89m)
Length:	40ft 0in (12.19m)
Wing Area:	278sq.ft (25.85sq.m)
All-Up-Weight:	13,200lb (5,988kg)
Powerplant:	1 x RR Nene 101 5,000lb (22.2kN)
Max Speed / Height:	591mph (951km/h) at sea level
Armament:	4 x 20mm cannon

The P.1040 was never ordered for the RAF, but did enter naval service as the Sea Hawk. In addition, the first of two swept-wing P.1052 conversions flew on 19 November 1948.

Miles M.52

Mentioned under the Gloster Rocket in the previous chapter, the other project discussed at the MAP meeting of 9 October 1943 was a high-speed aircraft, and F. G. Miles of Phillips & Powis was in attendance. In fact, the main purpose of this meeting was to initiate action on a very high-speed experimental aeroplane that was to be built by Phillips & Powis and powered by a Whittle W2/700 'with a No.4 augmenter and bypass heating' (i.e. a form of reheat). Rough dimensions for the power unit and duct sizes were given to Miles and it was decided that the all-up weight should be around 5,000lb to 6,000lb (2,268kg to 2,722kg). The target date was nine months hence and the target speed was to be 1,000mph (1,609km/h). Enough fuel was to be provided for a climb to 40,000ft (12,192m) and a half-hour flight at 700mph (1,126km/h), while the aircraft itself was to be a monoplane with a large tailplane that was wholly moving; in other words, there were no separate elevators. The use of skids was to be considered instead of an undercarriage. Soon afterwards Phillips & Powis became Miles Aircraft.

This was the beginning of the supersonic Miles M.52 research aircraft, and on 8 November Rowe received the first drawings, the firm calling it the Gyrone Project (Gyrone

ABOVE Seahawk F.Mk.1s WF147 and WF159 pose to allow the official cameraman to take pictures that will be used for recognition training. *Phil Butler*

was joined to its front section in the Experimental Department. Work was then interrupted and delayed by the ferociously hard winter of 1947 and the national crisis that this created. The consequent cutting off of heat and light closed the entire works from 10 to 28 February and this, coupled with other problems, delayed the P.1040's first flight; however, the first example, VP401, made a satisfactory maiden sortie on 2 September 1947.

ABOVE & LEFT Views of the Saunders-Roe SR.A/1 prototype TG263. *RAF Museum*

was the name Whittle intended to use to market his engines at Power Jets). The aircraft was ordered in December and Specification E.24/43 was written around it during mid-1944, but during the next two years progress was much slower than had been hoped for. Eventually the M.52 was cancelled in 1946. (The story of this aircraft is described by the author in the companion volume *British Secret Projects: Jet Fighters since 1950* and in depth in his book *Miles M.52: Britain's Top Secret Supersonic Research Aircraft*, published by Crécy in 2016).

Saunders-Roe SR.A/1

A jet-powered flying boat fighter was first suggested by Saunders-Roe (Saro) in a brochure dated 26 July 1943. The estimated top speed of this design, the SR.44 with de Havilland H.1 engines, was 470mph (756km/h) at 20,000ft (6,096m) and 520mph (837km/h) at 40,000ft (12,192m), and the sea level rate of climb was 4,400ft/min (1,341m/min). On 20 August Liptrot wrote that '…the application of jet propulsion to a small boat seaplane fighter would be very attractive since many of the high drag features of the conventional boat are due directly or indirectly to the high engine position which is necessary to give adequate water clearance at the propellers. The N.2/42 [the piston-powered Blackburn B.44 seaplane fighter – see Chapter 9] produced one solution at the expense of the complication and added weight of the retracting hull bottom. Jets would appear to offer the possibility of a better solution and might give a seaplane little inferior to a landplane designed around the same engines and for the same duty. The main difficulty is providing adequate water clearance at the tail unit.'

The chief criticism of Saro's first project was that the wing thickness/chord ratio of 15% was too large for a high-speed high-altitude fighter. However, specification E.6/44 was raised in April 1944 to cover a modified project proposed two months earlier. This design was provided with alternative side jet pipes (which were adopted) or twin jet pipes straight back to the tail, and the span was now 46ft (14.02m), wing area 415sq ft (38.595sq m), and total weight 14,205lb (6,443kg). The estimated top speed was 505mph (813km/h) at sea level and 506mph (814km/h) at 20,000ft (6,096m), and the sea level rate of climb was 6,800ft/min (2,073m/min). Three prototypes, TG263, TG267 and TG271, were ordered in 1944 and the SR.44 was renumbered SR.A/1, but there was never an Air Staff requirement for such a type. The fighter's minimum-drag hull was

Saunders-Roe SR.44 (26.7.43)	
Span:	40ft 0in (12.19m)
Length:	35ft 0in (10.67m)
Wing Area:	270sq.ft (25.11sq.m)
All-Up-Weight:	7,710lb (3,497kg)
Powerplant:	2 x H.1
Max Speed / Height:	520mph (837km/h) at 40,000ft (12,192m)
Armament:	?

Saunders-Roe SR.A/1 (flown)	
Span:	46ft 0in (14.02m)
Length:	50ft 0in (15.24m)
Wing Area:	415sq.ft (38.595sq.m)
All-Up-Weight:	16,255lb (7,373kg)
Powerplant:	2 x MV.B.1 Beryl 3,850lb (17.1kN)
Max Speed / Height:	516mph (830km/h)
Armament:	4 x 20mm cannon plus bombs (never carried)

LEFT Three colour artworks taken from a Saro brochure that had been prepared to illustrate the patrol and interception capabilities of various developments of the firm's SR.A/1 flying boat fighter.

based on that used by the A.37 Shrimp experimental flying boat of 1939, and to cut down air resistance it featured a refined step design both in plan and elevation; this was tested thoroughly by RAE.

By the close of 1945 the hull structure was nearly complete, but since the war had ended Saro had become increasingly occupied with the huge SR.45 Princess flying boat, with the result that the schedules for the jet fighter began to slip. The first SR.A/1 finally flew on 7 July 1947 with MetroVick F.2/4 Beryl axial jets, but there were to be no production orders. Two of the three prototypes eventually crashed and the survivor completed its flying in 1951.

Saunders-Roe P.122

Saro's P.122 project of October 1950 was a proposal for a larger, faster and more heavily armed single-engine version of the SR.A/1, which introduced a small degree of sweep to the wing leading edge and one Armstrong Siddeley Sapphire axial jet engine. It was considered that the advantages in flexibility offered by the twin-engined layout of the original SR.A/1 were outweighed by the advantages in weight, cost and accessibility offered by the single-engine arrangement. The only turbojet engine in current production that would provide the requisite power seemed to be the Armstrong Siddeley Sapphire Mk.3,

Saunders-Roe P.122 (10.50)	
Span:	46ft 5in (14.14m)
Length:	51ft 0in (15.54m)
Wing Area:	?
All-Up-Weight:	16,000lb (7,258kg)
Powerplant:	1 x Sapphire 7,500lb (29.4kg), 9,450lb (37.1kg)
Max Speed / Height:	?
Armament:	4 x 30mm Aden cannon

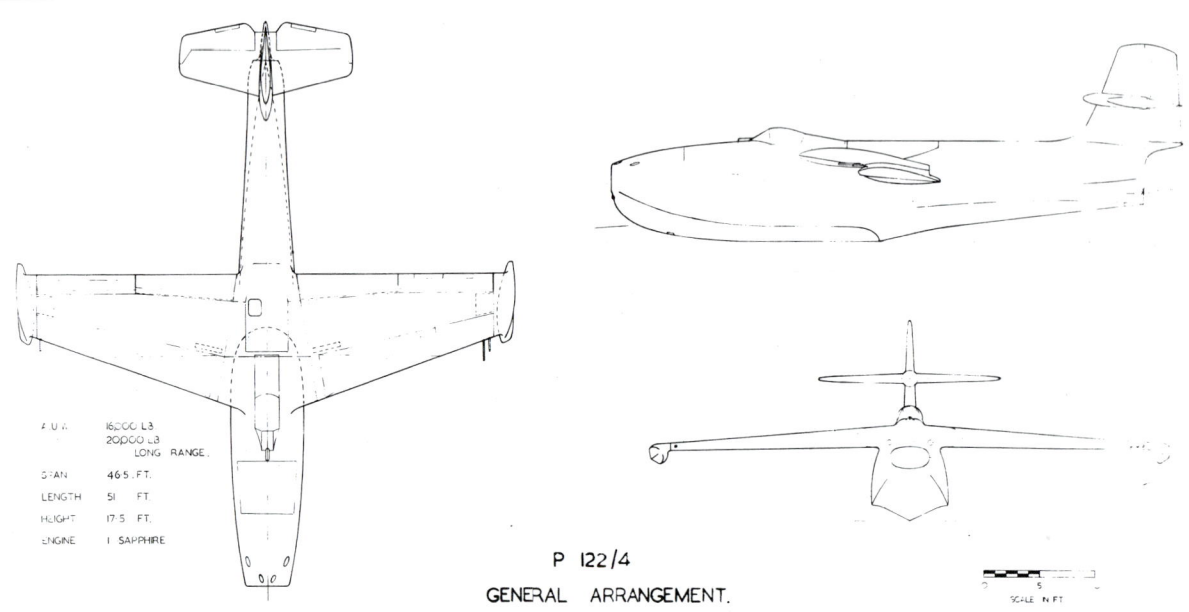

ABOVE The Saunders-Roe P.122-4 (10.50).

an engine that followed closely the design of the original Beryl and produced a maximum static thrust of 7,500lb (29.4kg), but was capable of being boosted to 9,450lb (37.1kg) by the addition of afterburning. It was decided, therefore, to fit one Sapphire in a central position within the hull. This scheme utilised the same air intake duct in the nose of the SR.A/1 but dispensed with the bifurcation that had been necessary with two Beryls, and a single exit pipe was proposed running right aft as opposed to the previous twin exits situated halfway along the afterbody of the hull.

Supermarine Attacker

In a letter dated 19 May 1942 Supermarine Chief Designer Joe Smith wrote to Frank Halford at de Havilland in regard to the H.1 engine, reporting that

'Following upon conversations between the undersigned, DTD and Dr Roxbee-Cox, we have been looking into the possibilities of installing a jet repulsion unit in Spitfires. In this direction we have considered using your H.1 unit, and we have reached a stage in our investigation when a talk between us and your good selves would be most useful.'

(One hopes that the word 'repulsion' was a typing error.) However, at a Future Gas Turbine Aircraft review held on 8 June 1942 it was noted that a scheme from Supermarine, comprising a new fuselage carrying an H.1 engine and fitted with Spitfire wings, was to be discouraged because the company was not in a position to undertake new work. This appears to have been the closest Supermarine ever came to building a 'Jet Spitfire'.

More than two years later, on 6 July 1944, Joe Smith completed Supermarine's Type 392 proposal for a Spiteful-type wing (see Chapter 2) fitted on to a special fuselage for jets. This was described as a 'very natural development of the Spiteful' and had one 4,200lb (18.7kN) Rolls-Royce B.41 (Nene) engine, which gave an estimated top speed of 565mph (909km/h) and a rate of climb at sea level of 6,000ft/min (1,829m/min). J. D. Breakey, ACAS(TR), described the project as 'a very interesting jet-propelled fighter proposal which is capable of rapid development,' while RAE thought the design was 'quite promising'. Three prototypes, TS409, TS413 and TS416, were ordered quickly and for some time the project was called the 'Jet Spiteful', with 'Jet Seafang' describing a proposed carrier version.

The wing (except for the underwing radiators), undercarriage and gun installation were standard Spiteful components currently entering production on the piston fighter, and the only new parts were to be the fuselage to house the B.41 and the tail unit. Since the fuselage on a new aircraft usually took much less time to design and build than the wings, it was felt that the more difficult half of this project had already been designed and would shortly be in production. The idea behind the proposal was to provide a really practical fighter of the highest possible performance for general service use, and provision was made for a pressure cabin, full fighter equipment (including four 20mm guns) and a minimum internal fuel load of 395 gallons (1,796 litres).

The B.41 was considered to be the ideal engine for this project; initially it would have a static thrust of 3,300lb (14.7kN), but was

ABOVE These views of Supermarine E.10/44 prototype TS409 show off the wing that was designed first of all for the piston-powered Spiteful. *Crown Copyright*

capable of development to 4,200lb (18.7kN). Rough estimates for the aircraft's performance included (at 3,300lb thrust) a maximum 522mph (840km/h) at sea level and 551mph (887km/h) at 20,000ft, a sea level rate of climb of 4,390ft/min (1,338m/min), a time to 20,000ft of 5.65 minutes, and a service ceiling of 46,000ft (14,021m). With 4,200lb thrust these figures became 578mph (930km/h), 571mph (919km/h), 6,100ft/min (1,859m/min), 4 minutes, and 51,000ft (15,545m). There was some anxiety that this project should not be 'generally talked about while the present difficult manpower discussions are in progress.'

The Mock-Up Conference was held on 23 November 1944, after which the Central Fighter Establishment pushed for a nosewheel undercarriage and to have the guns moved from the wings to the nose (neither step was adopted). The following January Supermarine was asked to give its jet fighter 'maximum priority' and to suspend work on its concurrent Seagull air-sea rescue amphibian. Specification E.10/44 was issued on 6 February 1945 to cover the aircraft and called for a maximum speed of 550mph (885km/h) at all heights up to 30,000ft (9,144m). In July contracts were placed for twenty-four pre-production aircraft comprising 6 E.10/44 airframes plus eighteen naval variants to Specification E.1/45 (this was cancelled in February 1946 when the Navy switched to eighteen Sea Vampires).

Supermarine Attacker F.Mk.1 (flown)	
Span:	36ft 11in (11.25m)
Length:	37ft 6in (11.43m)
Wing Area:	226sq.ft (21.02sq.m)
All-Up-Weight:	11,500lb (5,216kg)
Powerplant:	1 x Nene 3 5,100kb (22.7kN)
Max Speed / Height:	590mph (949km/h) at sea level
Armament:	4 x 20mm cannon

BRITISH SECRET PROJECTS - FIGHTERS 1935 TO 1950 VOLUME THREE

ABOVE Supermarine Attacker F.Mk.1 WA486 was photographed to provide views for recognition purposes. *Crown Copyright*

BELOW A ground attack version of the Attacker was displayed at Farnborough in 1951. *Terry Panopalis collection*

BELOW The Attacker Mk.2 proposal (14.7.49). *BAE Systems*

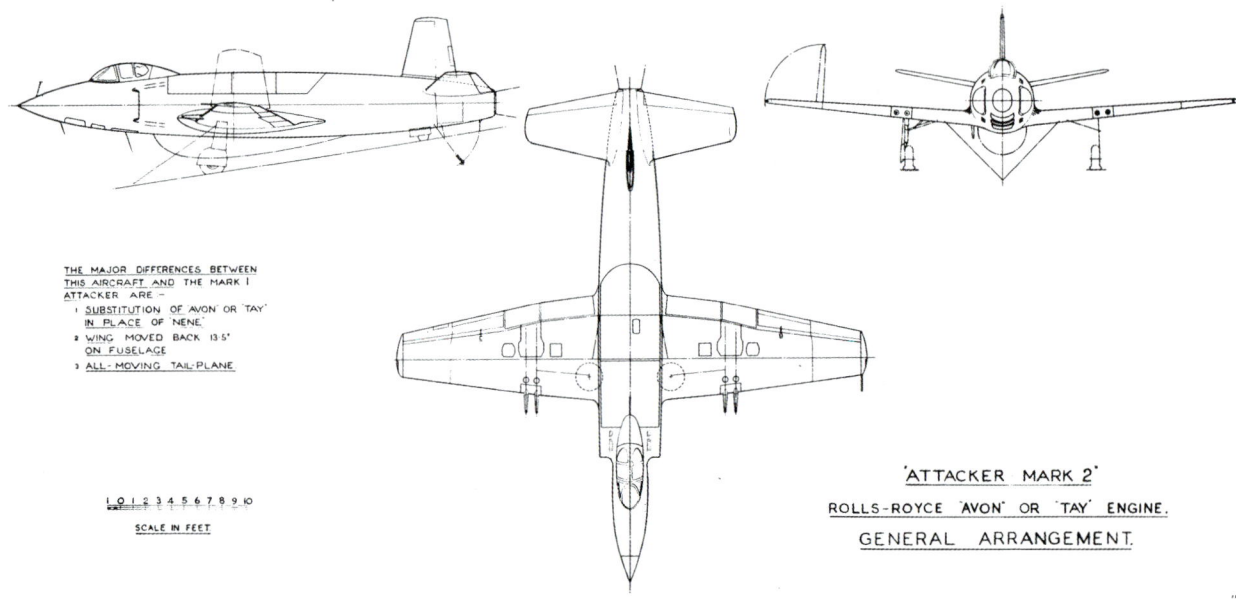

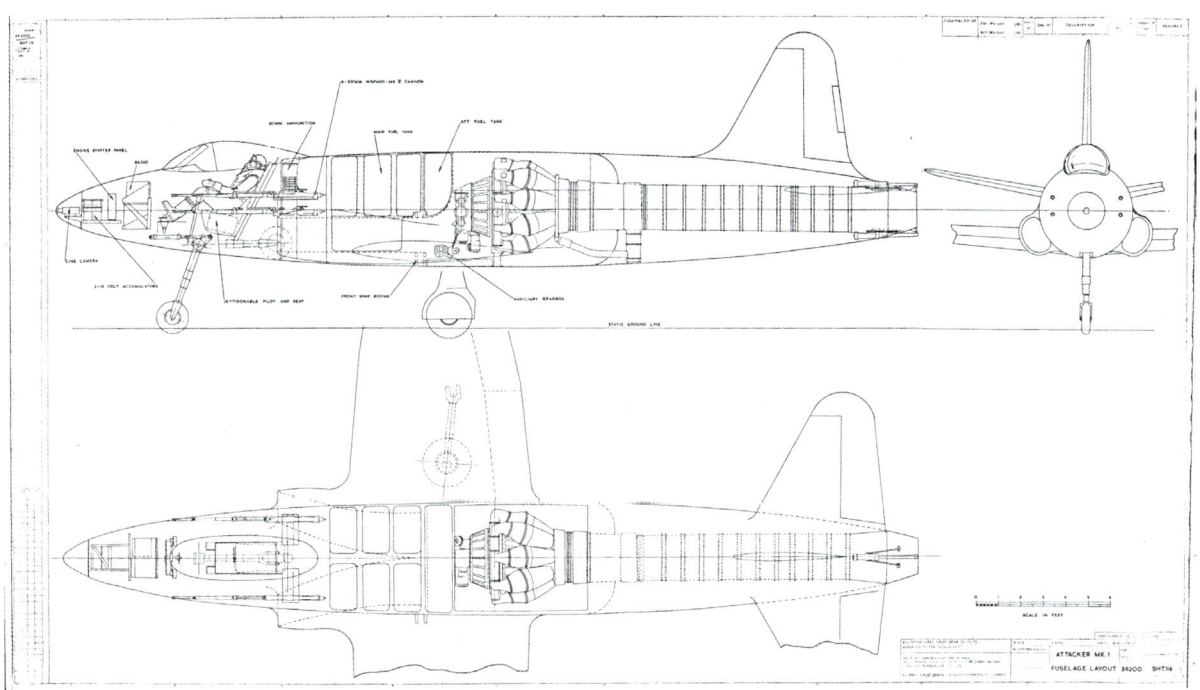

ABOVE Supermarine's studies for further versions of its Attacker included this recently discovered design, which does introduce a tricycle undercarriage. The visible part of the wing suggests that this was to be changed very little, but there was a new tailplane and fin arrangement, the intakes had been revised, and the four 30mm guns moved to the sides of the fuselage. The engine also appears to have reheat and fuel was to be housed in tanks positioned behind the pilot. The drawing is dated 25 July 1945 and it is thought that little further work was done. *RAF Museum via Ralph Pegram*

On 3 February 1945 a member of the Naval Staff wrote that

'...the operation of this aircraft will present the RAF with no new problems. On the other hand, this is the first jet aircraft to be tried in the Navy and we shall be presented with a number of new and serious problems to solve. A comprehensive series of deck trials will have to be provided for.'

The first prototype made its maiden flight on 27 July 1946, but the type was never adopted by the RAF. However, the second and third prototypes became known as 'E.10/44 Hooked Jet Spitefuls' and, after much deliberation, the aircraft did enter service with the Royal Navy as the Attacker. It was the Navy's first jet fighter but was not a great success.

Supermarine Type 527 Attacker Mk.2

Supermarine gave much thought to the possibilities for a Mk.2 Attacker with an improved performance and better flying characteristics, and on 7 February 1950 submitted a brochure for what was called the Type 527 (the drawing with it was dated 14 July 1949). The main features were:

i. Substituting the Nene with a Rolls-Royce Avon axial engine of 6,500lb (28.9kN) thrust, or a 6,250lb (27.8kN) Rolls-Royce Tay centrifugal unit.
ii. The incorporation of an all-moving tail with power assister in the elevator to raise the aircraft's limiting Mach number.
iii. The addition of a power assister in the aileron control system.
iv. Some additional fuel in the aft fuselage – 33 gallons (150 litres) for the Avon, or 63 gallons (286 litres) for the Tay.
v. Drooped ailerons.

Components could be fed into the existing production arrangements with minimal dislocation and consideration was given to including a tricycle undercarriage. However, Supermarine declared that an alteration of that magnitude would defeat the primary object of minimum disruption, so the tailwheel stayed. The more powerful engine required larger intakes and its greater weight required the wing to be moved rearwards by 13.5in (343mm). By this means it was possible to obtain a satisfactory balance with a reduction in the amount of ballast carried in the nose. Normal all-up weight with the Avon was 12,975lb (5,885kg), maximum speed 599mph (964km/h) at sea level and 552mph (888km/h) at 30,000ft (9,144m), limiting Mach number 0.86, and sea level rate of climb 9,250ft/min (2,819m/min). With the Tay these figures were 13,025lb (5,908kg), 598mph (962km/h), 552mph (888km/h), 0.86, and 7,900ft/min (2,408m/min).

Both the larger intakes and the new wing position were already embodied in the third prototype, so were relatively minor modifications. The all-moving tail was now being designed for the Swift jet fighter and the Attacker unit would be similar but of course without sweepback. This alteration would also allow the entire stern, including the tail, elevator, fin and rudder, to be built as a separate unit. The power-assisted ailerons had been thoroughly tested on the Seafang, and RAE and other pilots had reported on them very favourably. Fitting a trimming tailplane with a power-operated small-chord elevator was expected to extend the upper Mach number limit – although Mach 0.825 had been reached on the prototype Attacker, this was not the limit for longitudinal control. However, on 12 April 1950 Mr F. Holroyd, working for the Director of Military Aircraft R&D at the Ministry, told Supermarine, 'You will appreciate that further developments of naval aircraft must proceed along the lines of swept-back wings which your proposals for the Attacker do not include.' That brought the short existence of this Mk.2 Attacker project to an end.

Westland Jet Fighters

In January 1941 the first technical contact was made between Westland and Power Jets, and details of the jet engine were revealed to the aircraft company. There was an immediate proposal by Westland to try two Whittle W2B engines of 1,800lb (8.0kN) thrust in its Whirlwind piston fighter, but this project was subsequently abandoned (the project's estimated all-up weight was 10,000lb [4,536kg], span 45ft [13.72m], wing area 250sq ft [23.25sq m] and maximum speed 420mph [676km/h] at 30,000ft).

Another early jet fighter project from Westland's designer W. E. W. Petter was the J.8, a long-span Delanne tandem-wing type with a high 'tail' proposed in June 1942 (the first drawing was apparently dated 10 April of that year). It is understood that this was to be a competitor to the high-altitude long-span Meteor, but no reports survive, though the project was apparently tested in the wind tunnel during November and December 1942. Its wing owed much to the Welkin high-altitude piston fighter (see Chapter 4) and this project was in the tunnel just a few days after the Welkin's maiden flight. In fact, it was designed to the Welkin specification F.4/40 and was to be powered by two Whittle W2B/700 units; the span was 60ft (18.29m), main wing area 380sq ft (35.34sq m), Delanne wing area 180sq ft (16.74sq m), all-up weight 16,500lb (7,484kg), and estimated top speed

ABOVE A wind tunnel model of the Westland J.8 Delanne high-altitude fighter of June 1942. *The late Fred Ballam, Westland Archive*

Westland J.15 (10.42)	
Span:	46ft 0in (14.02m)
Length:	?
Wing Area:	240sq.ft (22.32sq.m)
All-Up-Weight:	9,600lb (4,355kg)
Powerplant:	1 x H.1 3,000lb (13.3kN)
Max Speed / Height:	490mph (788km/h) at 35,000ft (10,668m)
Armament:	4 x 20mm cannon

420mph (676km/h). The J.8 was later abandoned.

By the time of the Jet Aircraft review of 8 June 1942 mentioned under the Attacker, Petter was trying a Delanne high-altitude fighter scheme called the J.14, which had a low position 'tail' – the version with a high position surface, though offering sufficient stability, had produced too much drag and was structurally uneconomical (note: if this refers to the J.8, the official document conflicts with Westland sources). This new design used two 3,000lb (13.3kN) H.1s, had a span of 51ft (15.54m), its wing area was 290sq ft (26.97sq m), all up weight was 13,000lb (5,897kg), maximum speed was 480mph (772km/h) at 40,000ft (12,192m), and the operational ceiling was 52,000ft (15,850m); four guns were mounted in the lower nose. This too was abandoned.

Next, the J.15 was begun in October 1942 and closely resembled the DH.100 with a twin-boom configuration, short jet pipe and four nose guns; there is strong evidence to suggest that it was prepared to Specification E.5/42. In May 1943 a heavier navalised version was proposed to Specification N.7/43 (see Chapter 7), but neither of these designs was to be built. Finally a study was made in January 1945 for a straight-wing fighter designed to exceed 500mph (805km/h), which looked similar to the Supermarine Attacker but had a nose intake.

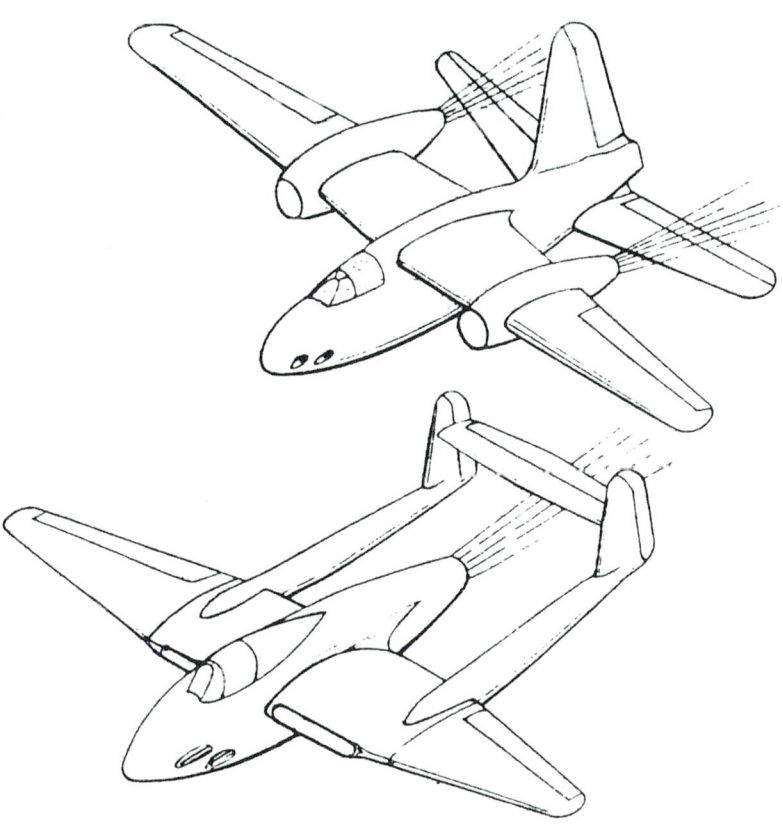

ABOVE **Rough sketches made in 1945 by Rab Page of Westland showing the firm's J.14 Delanne high-altitude fighter and J.15 jet fighter. They are the only known illustrations of these designs.** *The late Fred Ballam, Westland Archive*

The development of the jet is a great story, but its arrival must have been something of a shock to many in the aircraft industry. The earlier chapters have described what were in fact to be the last major developments in piston combat aircraft, and types such as the Sea Fury and Hornet represent the zenith of piston fighter design. These aircraft had immensely powerful and complex engines and, due to the limits of the 'Sound Barrier', gave just about the maximum performance that could ever be expected from their form of propulsion. Then along came this chap Whittle who, with a relatively crude jet engine stuffed into a very basic airframe (the Meteor), produced a performance that nearly matched the 'ultimate' piston fighters; in fact, after the war the Meteor regained the World Air Speed Record for Britain. There were many problems to solve of course – for example the early jets guzzled fuel at a rapid rate – but when all of this sank in the realisation of the near limitless potential of the jet, coupled with more advanced aerodynamics, must have been an astonishing and thrilling moment for the industry's aircraft designers.

Appendix One
British Fighter Projects Summary

During their years of independence many of Britain's aircraft firms became wedded to certain types of aeroplane or areas of manufacture. Hawker, for example, was always a fighter specialist while Avro, Handley Page and Vickers usually built or designed heavy bombers. Blackburn and Fairey were regular suppliers of aircraft to the Fleet Air Arm, and this often influenced their lines of development.

The following list contains all known fighter designs and projects produced by the companies between 1935 until the mid to late 1940s (until they roughly overlap with the project list in *British Secret Projects Volume 1*). Selected earlier types that were still in production are also included, together with research types that were developed essentially to advance the fighter designer's art. In theory, all projects are 'official', despite some schemes having such a brief life that they really have no right to be here but sneak in as one cannot always determine which they are; in fact, some of the designs that are here can really only be considered as draft or provisional layouts. Information for a good number of Second World War projects does not appear to have survived and has probably been lost forever. In addition, with so many firms and specifications (to which many projects were prepared without project numbers) it is impossible to say how complete this list might be. Finally, some wartime jet fighter projects are listed here only briefly because they were covered in more depth by the previous volumes in this series, where they essentially formed part of the post-war story.

AIRSPEED (taken over by de Havilland in 1940)

AS.31   High-speed project to 35/35, 1936. Most unusual layout with twin booms, egg-shaped cabin nacelle in centre of tailplane, one 880hp (656kW) Rolls-Royce Merlin E engine and eight Browning machine guns in wings outboard of booms (when first drawn engine was apparently Rolls-Royce Kestrel). No rudder or fin (except for nacelle itself) but split flaps across wing trailing edge between booms. Wide-span ailerons outboard of booms, fuel in wing, wide-track tailwheel undercarriage. Philosophy behind this strange design: pilot had good field of view, and having cockpit in this position reduced turbulence and drag over wing. Project not proceeded with. Span 33ft 0in (10.06m), length 26ft 6in (8.08m), wing area 195sq ft (18.14sq m).

AS.48   Projected single-seat night fighter with 2,150hp (1,603kW) Napier Sabre and six 20mm cannon (possibly six in each wing), 1939/40. Span 40ft (12.19m), length 40ft (12.19m), top speed 425mph

BELOW The Airspeed AS.31 (early 1936).

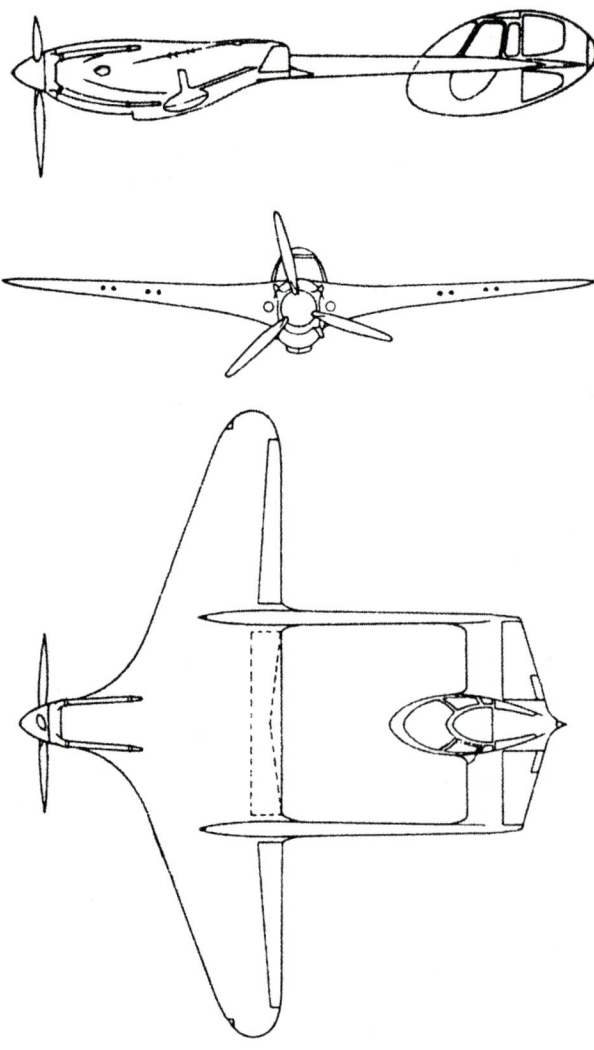

APPENDICES

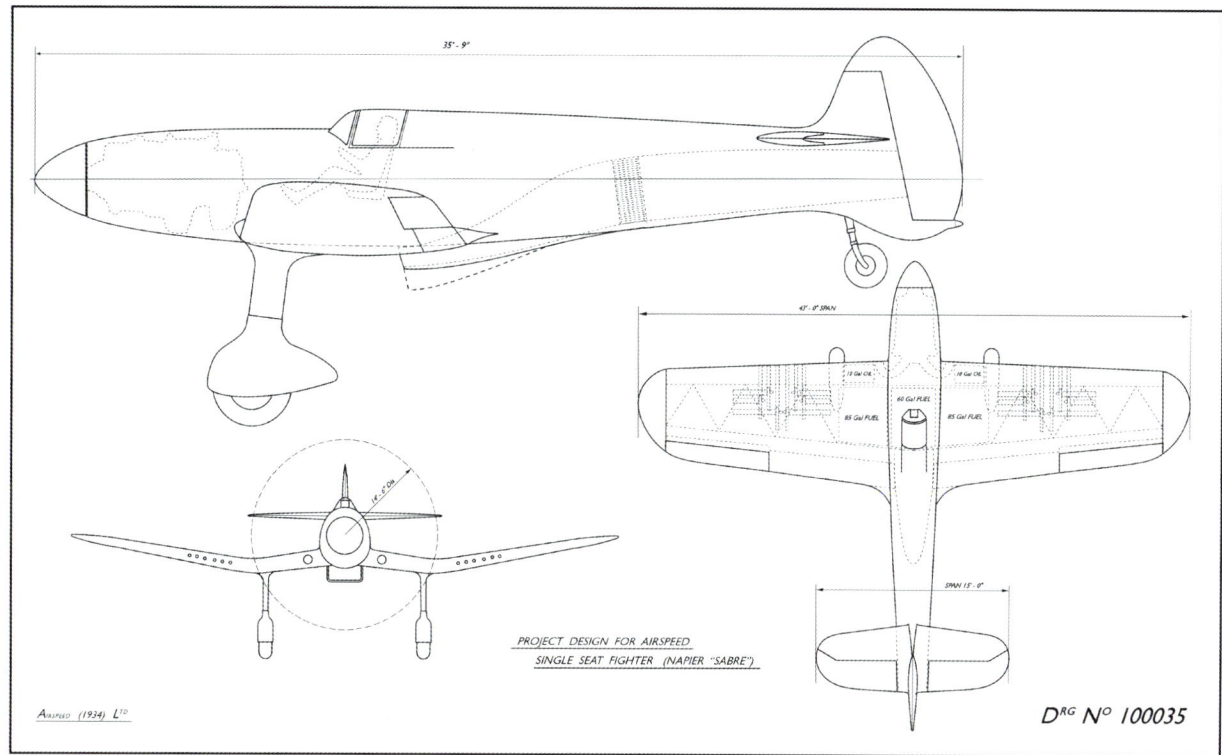

ABOVE This is the Airspeed single-seat 'Napier Sabre' Fighter with fixed undercarriage. The date on the original could not be discerned but is assumed to be mid-1940. *RAF Museum, redrawn by Ralph Pegram*

BELOW The Airspeed 'Napier Sabre' Fighter with retractable undercarriage was similar to the fixed-undercarriage version but appeared a little sleeker (11.6.40). *RAF Museum, redrawn by Ralph Pegram*

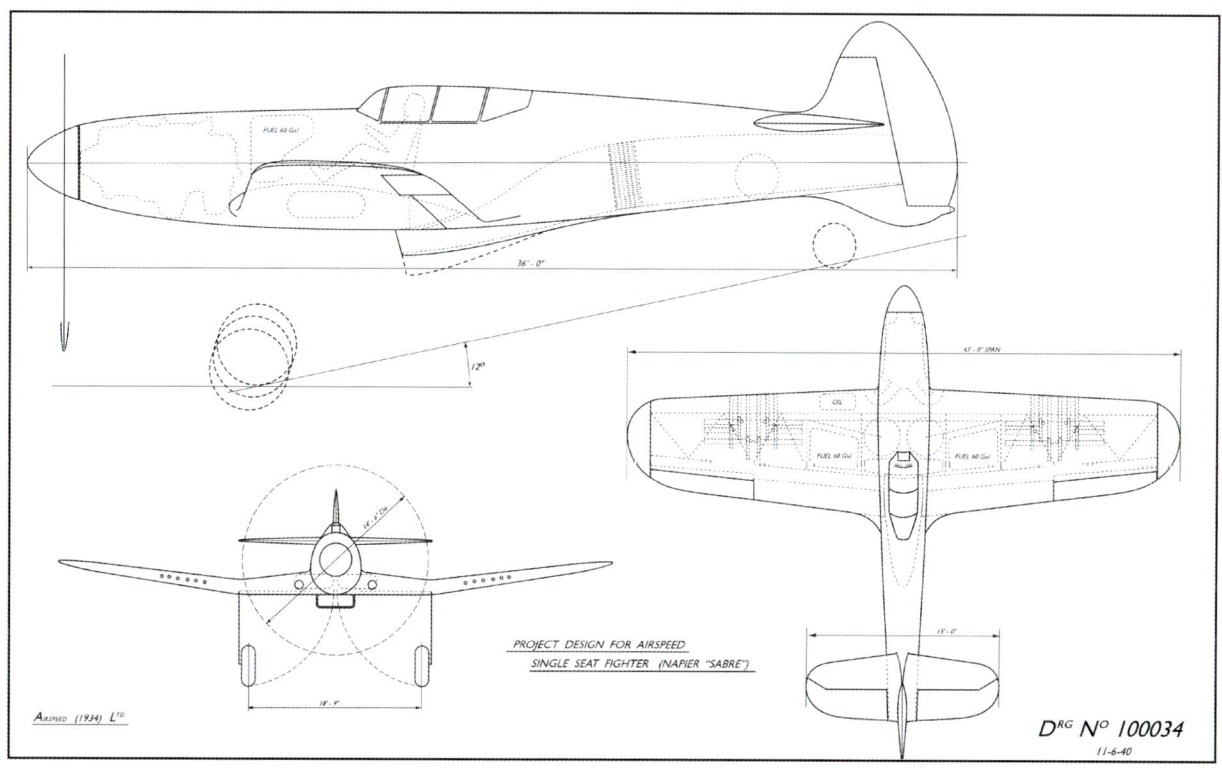

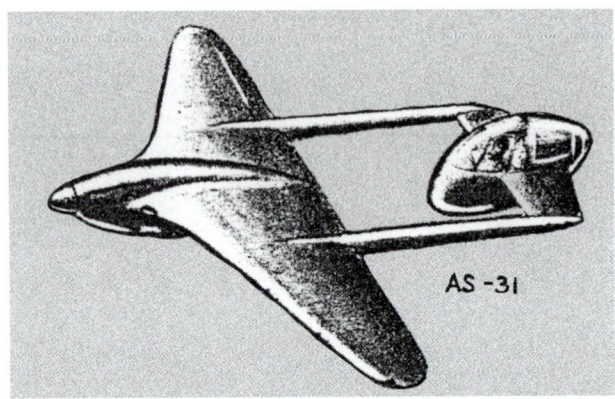

ABOVE Manufacturer's artwork for the Airspeed AS.31.

(684km/h) at 21,500ft (6,553m), time to 20,000ft (6,096m) 6 minutes, service ceiling 36,000ft (10,973m). Provisional drawings prepared 1939, mock-up built at Hatfield, but drawings, data and mock-up destroyed in bombing raid on Hatfield 3.10.40. Project cancelled.

'Napier Sabre' Fighter   Two similar designs with fixed and retractable undercarriage – former no date, latter 11.6.40. Possibly related to or part of AS.48 project. Both had span of 43ft 0in (13.11m) and propeller diameter of 14ft 6in (4.42m), and armed with twelve machine guns housed in wings, six per side. Retractable undercarriage version's length 36ft 0in (10.97m), with three 60gal (273lit) fuel tanks, one in each wing and one in forward fuselage between engine and cockpit. Fixed undercarriage version's length 35ft 9in (10.90m) and wing tanks each contained 85gal (386lit) fuel, reflecting extra space available when no wheel wells. Forward fuselage tank still 60gal (273lit).

AS.56   Projected single-seat fighter to F.6/42, 8.9.42.

ARMSTRONG WHITWORTH

Two-seat fighter   Unnumbered development of AW.34 fighter project of 1934 prepared to F.9/35, 8.35. Prototype serial allocated but never built.

Turret fighter   Unnumbered twin-engine turret fighter to F.11/37, 8.37.

AVRO

678   Unconventional fighter design powered by single Rolls-Royce Merlin driving twin two-blade airscrews, 8.36. Span 34ft 0in (10.36m), length 30ft 6in (9.30m).

BLACKBURN

B.24   Two-seat dive bomber and fighter, first flown 9.2.37.

B.25   Roc two seat fleet turret fighter to O.30/35, first flown 23.12.38.
B.31   Naval fighter fitted with rear turret to N.9/39, 8.39.
B.33   Naval fighter to N.8/39, 9.39. Follow-on single-seater (to NAD.925/39), possibly the B.37, late 12.39.
B.37   Single-seat fighter, 1940. Became Firebrand Mk.I, first flown 27.2.42.
B.41   Single-seat RAF fighter based on B.37 Firebrand I, 1940.
B.42   Firebrand design study with high-lift wing, 1942.
B.43   Single-seat twin-float fighter with Napier Sabre, 1942. Based on B.37 Firebrand.
B.44   Alternative float fighter to B.43 twin-float Firebrand designed to N.2/42, 1.43.
B.45   Firebrand TF.Mk.III fitted with Bristol Centaurus VII to S.8/43. Flown 21.12.43.
B.46   Firebrand variants TF.Mks.4, 5 and 5A.

BELOW The Avro 678 (8.36). *Avro Heritage*

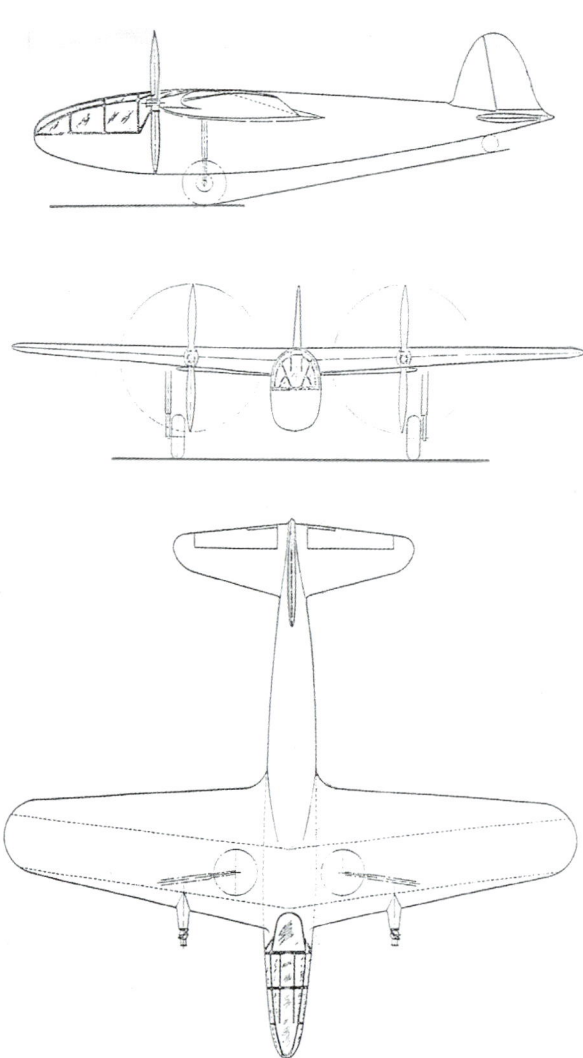

APPENDICES

ABOVE Blackburn Roc naval turret fighter serial L3084.

B.48 'Firecrest' development of Firebrand to S.28/43. First flown 1.4.47 as Y.A.1. Version planned with Sabre to S.10/45.

B.50 Designs for Fleet Air Arm 'fighter striker' study. Brochure submitted to Air Ministry 17.2.45. Rolls-Royce Nene jet-powered versions covered in *British Secret Projects Volume 1*, but artwork found for mixed-powerplant striker that might have been in response to Fairey Strike Fighter.

BOULTON PAUL

P.82 Two-seat day and night fighter to F.9/35, 8.35. Became Defiant, first flown 11.8.37.

P.85 Two-seat fleet fighter to O.30/35, late 1935. Navalised Defiant with one Bristol Hercules HE.1.SM but lost competition to Blackburn Roc. Production Rocs built by Boulton Paul as P.93.

P.88 Single-seat fighter to F.37/35 with alternative Hercules HE.1.SM or Rolls-Royce Vulture, 5.36. L6591 and L6592 allocated to prototypes but never built.

P.89 Two-seat fighter with four 20mm cannon and twin modified Rolls-Royce Kestrel XVI engines, first raised early 1936. No drawings or data known to have survived. Not related to any issued Air Ministry Specification but possibly start of F.11/37 studies.

P.92 Twin-engine two-seat turret fighter to F.11/37, 30.7.37. Prototypes ordered but never completed. Scale model P.92/2 built by Heston Aircraft as J.A.8 and flown spring 1941.

P.93 Designation covering Blackburn Roc detail design, prototypes and production.

P.94 Single-seat Defiant development with 1,280hp (954kW) Merlin XX, mid-1940.

P.96 Single Napier Sabre-engined two-seat two-cannon

BELOW The Bristol Type 151 high-speed research aircraft to 35/35 (early 1936). Specification 35/35 appears to have been an attempt to produce an aeroplane in which all other qualities were to some extent sacrificed for speed, probably for the first time since the end of the Schneider Trophy Races. However, eight forward-firing machine guns were also part of the requirement.

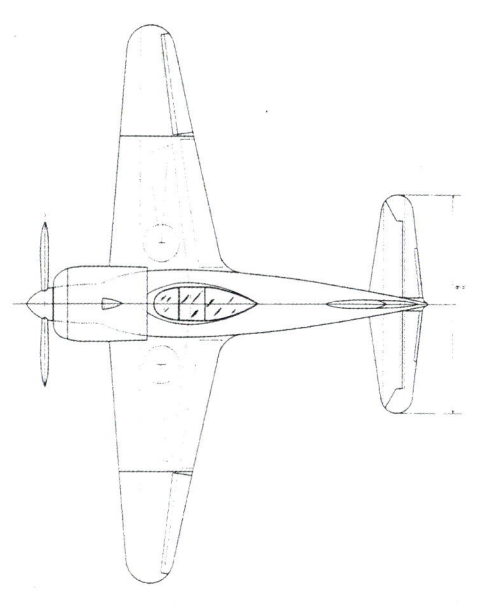
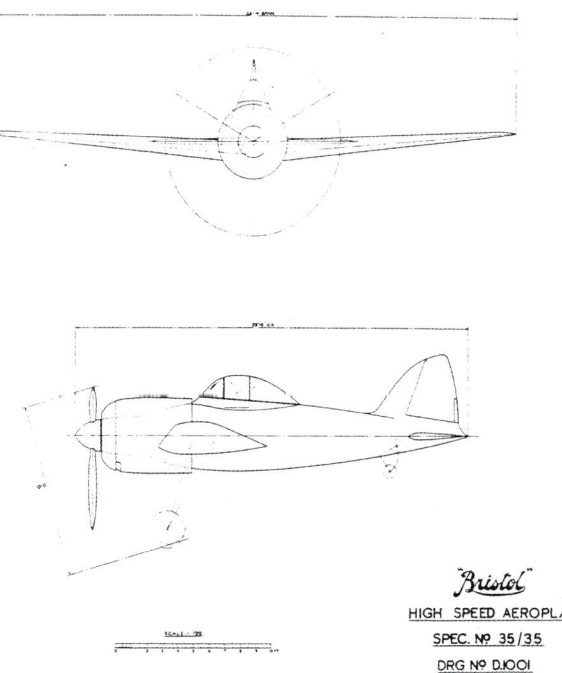

turret fighter to F.18/40, c11.40. Five versions proposed.

P.97 Twin Sabre two-seat night fighter to F.18/40, c11.40. Two versions, P.97A and B.

P.98 Single-seat tail-first pusher fighter with single engine and contra-rotating propellers to F.6/42, 5.9.42. Three versions, P.98A, B and C, with alternative engines.

P.102 Single-seat naval fighter driven by Whittle W2B jet, early 1943. No details survive but not linked to Jet Barracuda.

P.103 Single-seat naval fighter with Griffon or Centaurus to N.7/43, 4.43. Two versions, P.103A and B.

P.104 Single-seat naval tail-first pusher fighter with one Griffon to N.7/43, 4.43.

P.105 Single-engine naval aircraft with one Centaurus, 1.44.

P.107 Two-seat land-based escort fighter with one Centaurus, 4.44.

BRISTOL

146 Single-seat fighter to F.5/34, first flown 11.2.38.

147 Two-seat turret fighter to F.9/35 with Bristol Perseus engine, 17.8.35. Type 147A (9.35) had more powerful Hercules.

151 High-speed experimental aircraft to 35/35, early 1936. Powered by Bristol Hercules radial engine, very small aircraft of span 33ft 4in (10.16m) and overall length 25ft 0in (7.62m). Two tanks held 50gal and 30gal (227lit and 136lit) of fuel respectively. Estimated maximum speed 400mph (644km/h).

153 Cannon-armed fighter, single engine, to F.37/35, 30.4.36.

153A Cannon-armed fighter, twin engine, to F.37/35, 30.4.36.

Turret Fighter 'Small' and 'Large' versions of design to F.11/37, 8.37.

Single-Seat Fighter Unnumbered projects with alternative engines to F.18/37, 2.5.38.

156 Beaufighter two-seat fighter, first flown 17.7.39.

158 Slim-fuselage Beaufighter Mk.III, 1.39. Prototype never completed.

DE HAVILLAND

DH.98 Unarmed bomber proposal of 9.39 onwards that became Mosquito. First flown 25.11.40 and built in many versions including fighters.

DH.99 High-speed bomber development of Mosquito, early 1941. Soon renumbered DH.101. Designation DH.99 reallocated to jet fighter, then to civil design.

DH.100 Vampire jet fighter, first flown 20.9.43 (project begun as DH.99).

DH.103 Hornet and Sea Hornet high-speed twin-engine fighter, first flown 28.7.44.

DH.107 Proposed Vampire development that eventually became Venom, 4.45.

DH.112 Venom thin-wing development of Vampire, first flown 2.9.49. Sea Venom developed for Fleet Air Arm.

FAIREY

Fairey did not make full use of project numbers and consequently this list only contains projects known to have existed. There will almost certainly have been more, particularly for the late 1930s, but details are lacking.

Turret Fighter Project to F.9/35, 4.8.35.

Naval Fighters Designs proposed to N.8/39 and N.9/39, 8.39. Single-seater (to NAD.925/39) late 12.39. Work eventually resulted in Firefly, first flown 22.12.41.

Fulmar Two-seat FAA fighter to O.8/38, first flown 4.1.40.

Night Fighter Project proposed to F.18/40, late 1940.

Fighter/Bomber Single-seat design studied in 1940.

Cannon Fighter Single-seat design with Fairey P.24 pusher engine, 1941.

Firefly Development Single-seat Firefly for FAA with 1,850bhp (1,380kW) Centaurus CE.3.SM and alternative single or contra-rotating propellers. Brochure dated 26.7.41 added 750lb (3.3kN) jet for all-up weight 12,400lb (5,625kg), top speed 343mph (552km/h) at 10,000ft (3,048m), 4.4 minutes to 10,000ft, and 590 miles (949km) range.

Naval Fighter Design studies to N.7/43, 24.4.43 onwards.

Firefly Development Single-seat fighter with 1,640bhp (1,223kW) RR Griffon 71 and 780lb (3.5kN) jet, 18.8.43. All-up weight 13,250lb (6,010kg), maximum speed (using jet) 428mph (689km/h) at 20,000ft (6,096m), 3.2 minutes to 10,000ft (3,048m), 162nm (261km) range.

BELOW A view of the Folland Fo.108 'Frightful' engine test bed after a Bristol Centaurus IV had been fitted. *Phil Butler*

Single-Seat Fighter Preliminary studies into machine using Firefly components, early 1944. Alternative RR Pennine or Griffon engine.

Strike Fighter Twin tandem engine studies from 8.44. Turboprop developments from mid-1945. Three prototypes ordered to N.16/45 but not built. Programme replaced by Gannet.

FOLLAND

Fo.101 Fighter with twin Alvis Pelides engines, 4.37.

Fo.102 Vulture-powered interceptor, 4.37.

Fo.107 Sabre-powered interceptor, 4.38.

Fo.108 Test bed aircraft to 43/37 (Folland 'Frightful') first flown 1940. Used to test different versions of Bristol Hercules and Centaurus, Napier Sabre and RR Griffon, plus various propellers.

Fo.117 Single-seat fighter to F.6/42, 4.9.42.

Fo.117A Revised Fo.117 with laminar flow wing, 2,500hp (1,864kW) Centaurus 12 and contra-rotating propeller. To be built by English Electric. Six examples, RD104, RD107, RD108, RD113, RD115 and RD118, ordered 10.9.43 but never built. Variant fitted with single jet engine not given project number, 12.43.

Fo.118 Single-seat naval fighter to N.7/43, 5.43.

GENERAL AIRCRAFT

GAL.28 High-speed aircraft to 35/35, 1936. Had variable area wings and single Hercules engine.

GAL.43 Designation given to two engine test bed projects, GAL.43a and b, to 43/37, mid-1938.

GAL.46 High-altitude fighter to F.4/40, 18.10.39. Revised c9.40.

GAL.52 Folding-wing version of Supermarine Seafire, c1942. Proposal to fold wings backwards rather than upwards as preferred by Supermarine and Admiralty. General Aircraft mechanism simpler than Supermarine proposal but heavier, so rejected.

BELOW The General Aircraft GAL.53 jet fighter project (c1942).

GAL.53 Single-engine naval jet fighter, 1942. One 1,600lb (7.1kN) Power Jets W.2B engine, four 20 mm cannon in nose.

GLOSTER

The P numbers here list drawings, not projects, and many of the 'gaps' belong to drawings of the same aircraft showing internal detail, etc, not different designs.

Gladiator RAF's last biplane fighter, built to 14/35. Prototype first flown 12.9.34.

Single-seat Fighter Prototype to F.5/34, first flown 5.36.

Turret fighter design work to F.5/33 and F.9/35 culminated in order to F.34/35 (serial K8625) in 1935. Work replaced by design to F.9/37, became single-seat (no turret) and first flown 3.4.39.

High-Speed Aircraft Design to 35/35, 1936. Powered by eighteen-cylinder twin-row radial engine. Only known drawing shows just nose detail – is quite similar to F.5/34 fighter.

Turret Fighter Design to F.11/37, mid-1937. Bomber F.11/37 also proposed with Hercules engines, 1937.

High-Speed Fighters Single-engine twin-boom and twin-engine designs to F.18/37, 27.4.38 and 14.5.38 respectively. Both armed with twelve machine guns. Twin-boom design revised 15.10.38 with same armament, and again 7.11.38 but with five cannon.

Naval Fighters FAA fighter to N.8/39 and turret fighter to N.9/39, 8.39. Single-seat development (presumed to NAD.925/39) 22.11.39.

Pioneer Research aircraft to E.28/39 and Britain's first jet, flown on 15.5.41. Three known pre-design drawings dated 26.9.39, 30.9.39 and 2.10.39.

Gloster Boosted Fighter Design with combined powerplant of Griffon piston engine and Whittle jet, 4.1.40.

Reaper Heavy fighter development of F.9/37, 23.7.40.

Night Fighter Development of F.9/37 to F.18/40, c11.40.

G.A.1 Jet fighter to E.5/42, early 1942 onwards. Mock-up and components produced before abandoned 1944 and replaced by G.A.2.

Drawing ZC26194 Early F.9/40 fighter design (27.3.40).

Drawing ZC26728 Early F.9/40 fighter layout (8.4.40).

P.146 Thought to be F.9/40 with Whittle engines (c5.43).

Meteor Britain's first jet fighter to F.9/40, first flown 5.3.43.

P.147 Gloster F.9/40 with de Havilland Halford engine, c7.43.

P.148 Gloster F.9/40 with MetroVick jet engine, c7.43.

P.149 Original Gloster Rocket (E.5/42 development) proposal with side fuselage jet pipes for RR B.37 Derwent I engines (28.6.43).

P.150 Rocket with two B.37 or B.38 engines in fuselage behind pilot, plus end-fuselage jet pipe, 7.43.

P.171 & P.172 Single Halford engine projects bridging gap between E.5/42 and E.1/44 fighters, late 1943.

P.173 Meteor Mk.I with RR W2B/37 propeller combination installation, 13.1.44. Became 'Trent Meteor' powered by Trent turboprop and first flown 20.9.45.

P.174 P.171/P.172 development with H.2 engine, 26.1.44.

P.175 Further development of P.174, 3.3.44.

P.181 Development of G.A.1 to E.1/44, Halford H.2 engine, 2.7.44.

P.187 Meteor IV with RR Derwent (28.4.44).

P.190/G.A.2 Ace P.181 with B.41 (Nene) engine, flown 9.3.48. Name little used.

P.199 AJ.65 (Avon)-powered version of E.1/44, 1945.

P.202 Gloster twin jet fighter with RR AJ.65 engines (29.1.46).

P.203 Meteor high-altitude aircraft with RR Derwent 5, 30.1.46. Greater span wings with square tips.

P.209 Twin-jet fighter with two RR AJ.65 (Avon) engines, 25.6.46.

CXP-1001 Collaboration with Chinese Nationalist Government for single-seat fighter, agreed 7.46. Work frozen 10.50 and surviving material disposed of 11.52.

P.212 G.A.2 Ace third prototype fitted with tail high on fin, 2.9.46, flown 1949. Tail later adopted for Meteor F.Mk.8.

P.213 F.23/46/P jet fighter with one Nene, 30.8.46. Shorter wingspan than P.212.

Meteor Night Fighter Full prototype to F.24/48, first flown 31.5.50. Design and production assumed by Armstrong Whitworth.

P.263 Meteor modified with delta wing, slab tail and two RR Derwent 5 or 7 engines, 19.11.47.

P.309 Eight-gun version of Meteor, 2.50.

HAWKER

One of the most famous of fighter manufacturers, Hawker rarely forayed into bomber development. The P.1000-series of project numbers was introduced in 1940 but, at the time of writing, drawings for most of the projects listed up to P.1050 have not been traced and may no longer exist. Even into the war, not every project received a number.

Hurricane Single-seat fighter to F.36/34, first flown 6.11.35.

Hotspur Day and night turret fighter to F.9/35, 9.8.35, first flown 14.6.38.

Research Aircraft Single-seat high-speed project based on Hurricane to 35/35, tendered 21.2.36. Merlin engine coolant radiator duct in line with mainplane leading edge.

Day and Night Fighter Hurricane with four Oerlikon cannon to F.37/35, 23.4.36.

Turret Fighter Two-seat twin-engine fighter to F.11/37, tendered mid-1937.

Tornado Single-seat high-speed fighter with Vulture to F.18/37, first flown 6.10.39.

Typhoon Single-seat fighter with Sabre to F.18/37, first flown 24.2.40.

Fleet Fighters Fixed-gun naval fighter to N.8/39 and turret fighter to N.9/39, 8.39. Single-seat project (NAD.925/39) late 12.39.

Fighter Single-seat fighter with Griffon and two 40mm guns, schemed 1939.

Tornado Test Beds Preliminary schemes to fit alternative engines to Tornado – Bristol Centaurus (1939), Duplex Wright Cyclone (1940/41) and Fairey Monarch (1940). Tornado prototype flown with Centaurus 23.10.41.

P.1000 Single-seat fighter with single shaft-drive Sabre and contra-rotating propellers, 1940.

Typhoon Development Proposal to fit wing with six cannon, 1940. Set of wings built.

P.1002 20mm cannon installation for Hurricane Mk.IIc, 1940.

Long-Range Fighter Development of Henley light bomber with two seats, 1940.

P.1003 Escort fighter conversion of Henley, 1940.

P.1004 Two-seat high-altitude fighter (Typhoon scaled up by 25%) to F.4/40, c9.40.

P.1007 Single-seat high-altitude fighter, 1940.

P.1008 Night fighter to F.18/40, 1940.

Hurricane Floatplane Proposed conversion, 1940. Cancelled.

Hurricane Development Variant with Griffon engine, 1940. Abandoned 1941.

P.1009 Fleet fighter based on Typhoon to N.11/40, c2.41.

P.1010 Typhoon with turbocharged engines, 1941.

P.1011 P.1004 fitted with Power Jets engine, 1941.

P.1012 Typhoon Mk.2 fitted with leading edge radiators to F.10/41, 1941. Became Tempest Mk.I, flown 24.2.43. Tempest Mk.V with Sabre and chin radiators first flown 2.9.42.

P.1014 Single-seat fighter with one Power Jets engine, 1941.

P.1016 Typhoon Mk.II with Griffon, 10.4.42. Became Tempests III and IV but not built.

P.1017 Single-seat fighter with Griffon and Typhoon wings, 1942.

P.1018 Light fighter with Sabre 43 to F.6/42, 14.9.42.

P.1019 Light fighter with Griffon 61 to F.6/42, 14.9.42.

P.1020 Light fighter with Centaurus to F.6/42, 14.9.42. Formed basis of Fury Mk.I, flown 1.9.44.

Tempest Variant Scheme to fit 0.5in (12.7mm) machine guns, 1942.

P.1021 Tempest with Centaurus to F.6/42, 1942. As Tempest Mk.II, first flown 28.6.43.

RIGHT **Martin-Baker's proposal to 35/35 (1936).** *Martin-Baker*

BELOW **An unnumbered Martin-Baker twin-boom fighter (c1944/45).** *Martin-Baker*

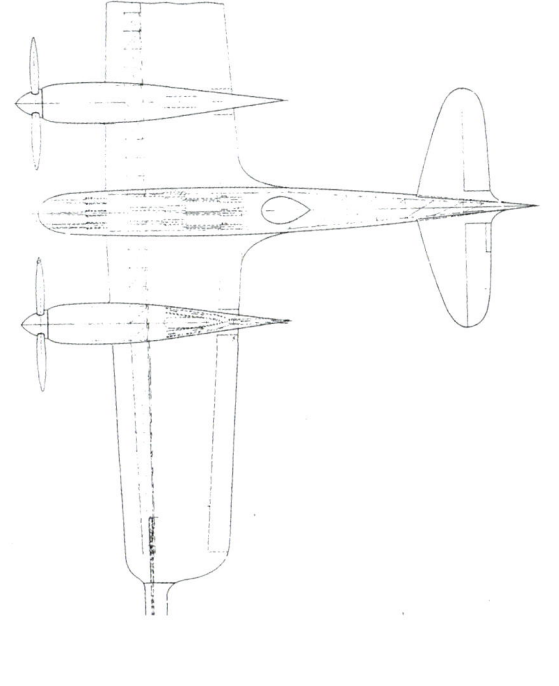

P.1022 Naval fighter to N.7/43, 1943. Became Sea Fury Mk.X, first flown 21.2.45.
P.1023 Tempest I with Sabre IV, tendered 1943.
P.1024 Tempest development with Sabre V, 1943. Not tendered.
P.1025 Light fighter with Griffon, tendered 1943.
P.1026 Fighter to F.2/43 with Griffon, 1943. Built as LA610 and flown with Griffon 85 27.11.44. Later fitted with Sabre VII and flown 3.4.46.
P.1027 Tempest with RR.46 Eagle engine, 1.7.43. Not tendered.
P.1028 Tailless fighter, 1943. Scheme only, not tendered.
P.1029 Tail-first fighter, 1943. Scheme only, not tendered.
P.1030 Fighter with '4,000hp' (2,983kW) Eagle, 11.9.43. Basic design and data completed but not tendered.
P.1031 Fighter based on Fury with Rolls-Royce B.40 jet in nose, 1944.
P.1032 P.1026 fitted with Eagle to F.2/43, 1944.
P.1035 P.1026 fitted with B.41 (Nene) jet amidships to F.2/43, 1944. Air intakes in wing and split jet exhaust pipe.
P.1036 Private venture scheme for P.1026 fitted with Sabre V, 1944.
P.1037 Twin-boom fighter with two Griffons, 1944. Not tendered.
P.1040 Variant of P.1035 with 'Tempest' wing replaced by new design, 12.44. Prototype first flown 2.9.47 and became Sea Hawk.
P.1042 Variant of P.1040, 1945.
P.1043 P.1040 with undercarriage removed for landing on flexible decks, 1945.

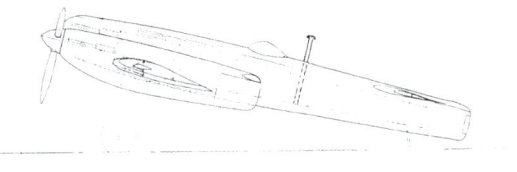

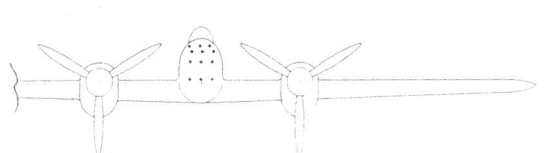

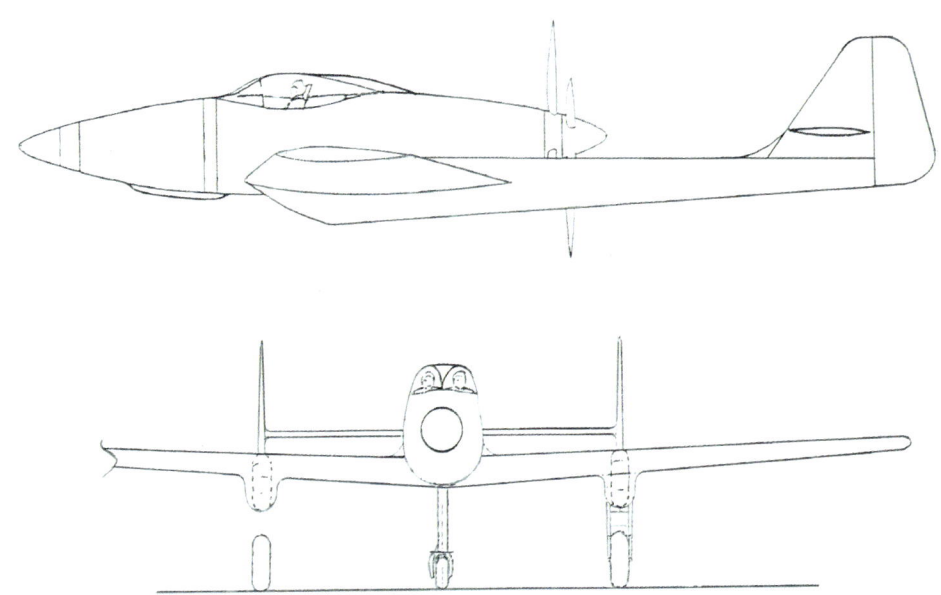

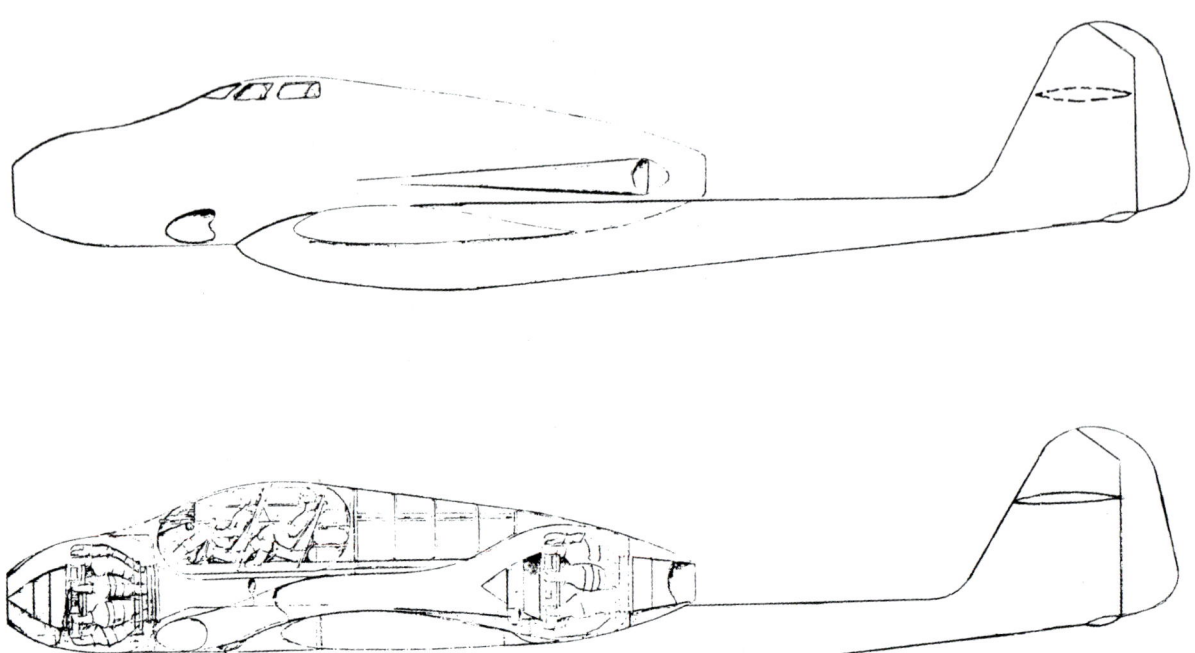

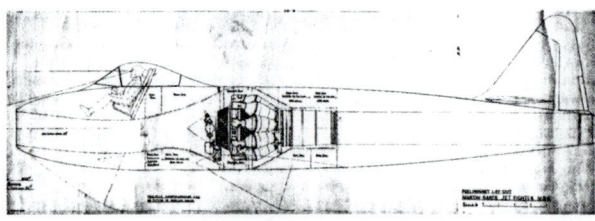

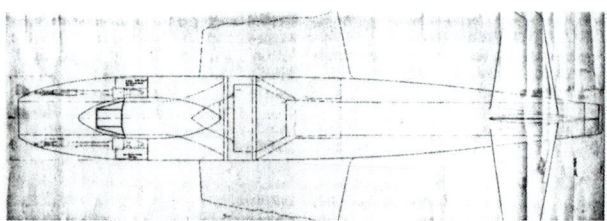

ABOVE The experimental Martin-Baker jet fighter design with twin booms, a Rolls-Royce Derwent jet in its nose and a second in the rear fuselage (c1945). *Martin-Baker*

LEFT The only known drawings of the Martin-Baker MB.6 (c1945). *Martin-Baker*

MARTIN-BAKER

MB.2   Single-seat fighter to F.5/34, flown 3.8.38.

Twin-engine Fighter   Unnumbered single-seat private venture project to 35/35, 1936. Two RR Merlins with exhaust manifolds fitted flush with cowlings and finned to assist heat dispersion. Wing of all-metal tube construction had tip ailerons, fuselage simple tubular steel construction, no fin, rudder formed by extension of slab-sided fuselage. Twelve Browning machine guns in nose in four banks of three, retractable undercarriage with both main wheels retracting into nacelles behind each engine, three-blade air screws. Three fuel tanks in fuselage each of 56gal (255lit) capacity. Span 50ft (15.24m), length 36ft (10.97m), weight 8,500lb (3,856kg).

MB.3   Single-seat fighter to F.18/39, flown 3.8.42.

MB.4   Unbuilt development of MB.3 with Centaurus, 1942. One drawing shows possible version with Griffon.

MB.5   Single-seat fighter to F.18/39, final development of MB.4, flown 23.5.44.

Twin-Boom Fighter   Two-seat low-wing monoplane, c1944/45. Two Griffons mounted in nose

P.1044   Scheme for naval fighter bomber, 1945.

P.1045   Fighter version of P.1040 with Rolls-Royce AJ.54 engine, 7.45.

P.1046   P.1045 project fitted with rocket boost, 1944/45. P.1040's straight wing replaced by alternative with moderate sweep and high taper.

P.1047   P.1046 fitted with highly swept wings, rocket boost and one B.41 engine, 1945.

P.1052   Swept-wing experimental development of Sea Hawk, first flown 19.11.48.

APPENDICES

and rear fuselage, each with two three-blade contra-rotating airscrews. Fuselage and wing structure probably identical to Martin-Baker steel tube structure skinned with stressed light alloy, as used on MB.5. Fixed incidence tailplane and elevator, main wheel housed in wing booms, side-by-side seating. Span 53ft 0in (16.15m), length 51ft 8in (15.75m), fuselage length 33ft 2in (10.11m), no performance data available.

MB.6 Single-engine low-wing fighter with four 20mm Hispano cannon, c1945. Cigar-shaped fuselage with nose intake, straight wing and tail, all-metal stressed skin construction, tailplane and elevator positioned on top of aft fuselage. Two skids fitted in lieu of optional tricycle undercarriage. Engine unspecified and no performance figures available. Length 36ft 3in (11.05m), wing area 263sq ft (24.46sq m).

Jet Fighter Experimental twin-boom design with one RR Derwent in nose and another in rear fuselage, c1945. All-metal stressed skin wing structure with all-metal fins and rudders, cigar-shaped fuselage with nose intake for forward engine plus side intakes to rear fuselage unit, tandem seating. Length 51ft 0in (15.54m), fuselage length 30ft 0in (9.14m), no data.

ABOVE The Miles M.58 naval patrol fighter with composite power plant. *Peter Amos*

MILES (Phillips & Powis until October 1943)

M.20 Fighter prototype to Specification F.19/40, first flown 14.9.40. Designed to be built in quick time to supplement supply of standard fighters. Several more advanced developments proposed but not proceeded with.

M.22 Designs for highly streamlined single-seat fighter with two Griffons, 1939 onwards. One version to F.6/39.

BELOW The Parnall Type 381 heavy gun research aircraft and test bed (5.9.38). *Air-Britain, restored by Chris Gibson*

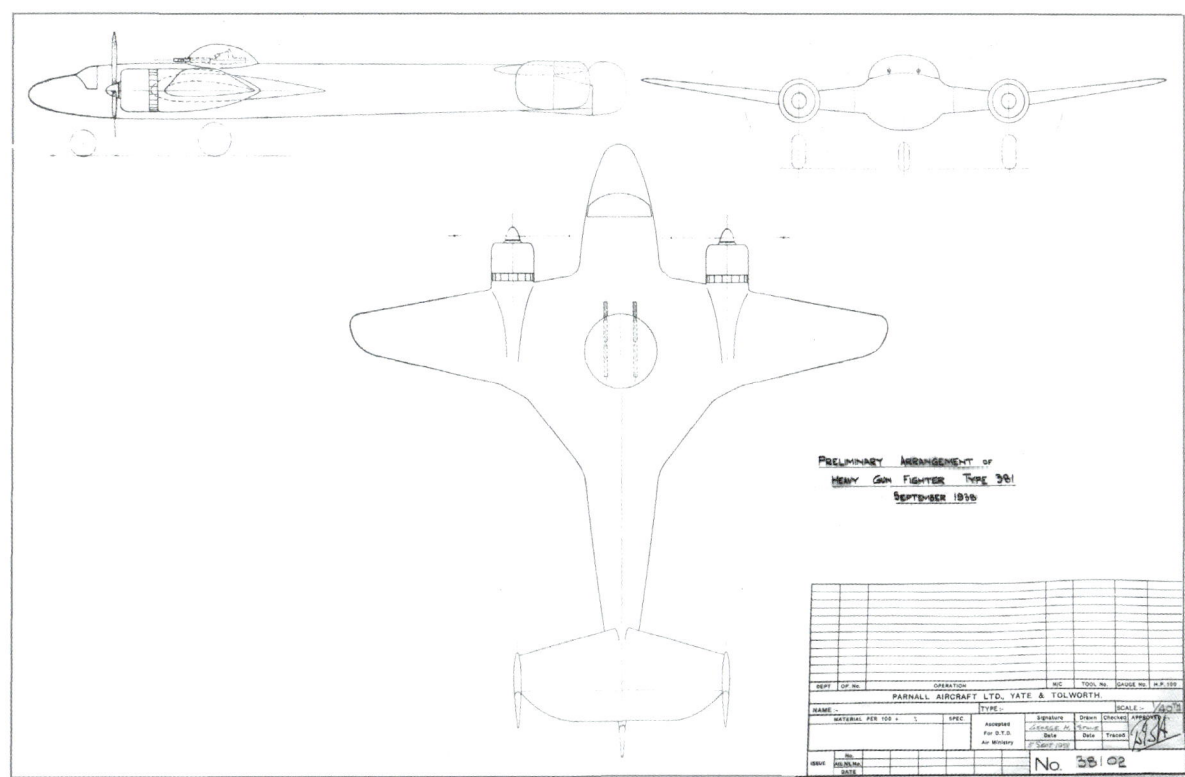

211

M.22A   Two-seat night fighter development of M.22 to F.18/40, c11.40.

M.23   High-speed single-seat fighter with single Merlin or Griffon, 1941.

M.23A   Pressurised high-altitude fighter, 9.42.

M.35   Libellula aerodynamic research aircraft fitted with de Havilland Gipsy Major I pusher engine. Flown 1.5.42 with Class B serial U0235.

M.42   Single-seat attack fighter with Libellula wing arrangement and twin tractor engines, probably to F.6/42, 8.42. Also torpedo bomber version.

M.43   Single-seat attack fighter project and single pusher engine, probably to F.6/42, 8.42. Also naval fighter version.

M.44   Single-seat twin-engine attack fighter with orthodox wing arrangement, probably to F.6/42, 9.42. Possibly several versions. (M.42, M.43 and M.44 are described in *British Secret Projects: Bombers 1935 to 1950*.)

M.52   High-speed experimental aircraft to E.24/43. First attempt to build aircraft to fly faster than sound. First flight planned 1947, project cancelled 3.46.

M.58   Very small naval patrol fighter with mixed piston/jet powerplant, c1945. Possible 7-hour patrol at low speed with jet shut down, top speed with both engines running 463mph (745km/h) at 27,000ft (8,230m). Piston engine 500hp (373kW), Power Jets W.2/700 2,000lb (8.9kN) thrust. Two forward-firing Hispano Suiza cannon, one each in forward ends of tail booms.

NAPIER-HESTON

Racer   Aircraft designed specifically to break World Air Speed Record. First and only flight 12.6.40; damaged beyond repair. Second example never completed.

PARNALL

Type 381   Proposal for heavy gun research aircraft and test bed, 5.9.38. Blended wing and fuselage, large 'mid-upper' turret on top of centre fuselage with two 20mm, 37mm or 40mm cannon and predictor sighting system (alternative turret position underneath fuselage). Twin fins plus third rudder on end of fuselage, tricycle undercarriage, light alloy main structure with plywood outer wing sections. Seriously considered by Air Ministry but turned down 4.39 because official speed estimates fell below brochure figures. Also Parnall inexperienced in manufacture of such large aircraft and would take too long to build it. Data at c11.38: span 63ft 6in (19.35m), length 61ft 3in (18.69m), gross wing area 735sq ft (68.355sq m), gross weight 20,700lb (9,390kg), 2 x 1,550hp (1,156kW) Hercules HE.6.SM engines, maximum 297mph (478km/h) at sea level, 341mph (549km/h) at 30,000ft (9,144m).

PERCIVAL

P.26   Two projects, P.26 and P.26a, proposed as engine test beds to 43/37, mid-1938.

BELOW The Supermarine 319 two-seat fighter (8.37).

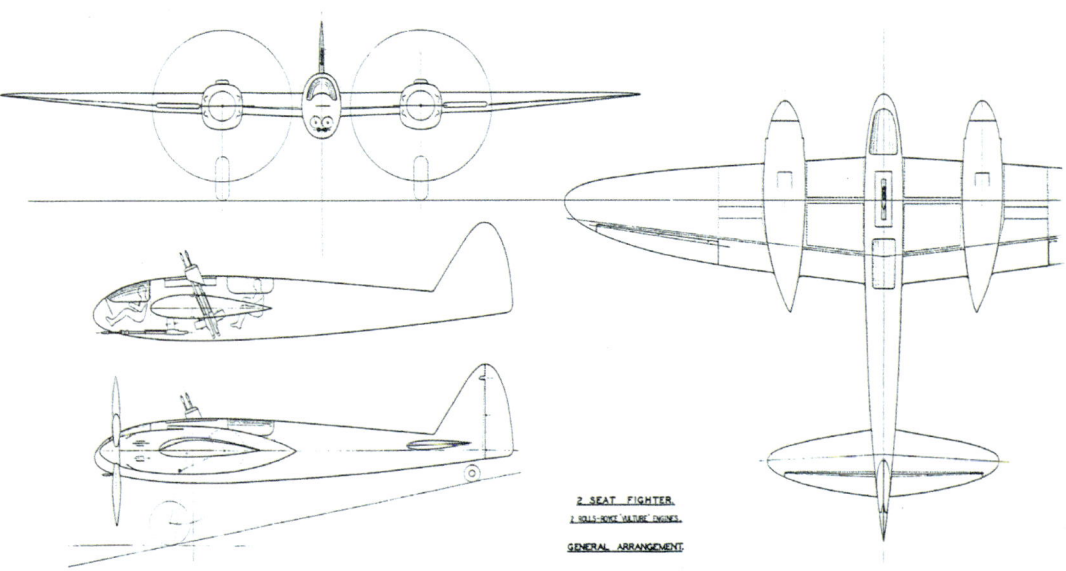

R. MALCOLM

Day and Night Fighter Twin-Sabre-engine proposal, 10.40 and 27.1.41.

SAUNDERS-ROE

Saro was a flying boat specialist.

- *P.103* Swept-wing variant of SR.A/1 boat fighter, c1947. Nose intakes flanked radome.
- *P.113/SR.44/SR.A/1* Experimental flying boat fighter to E.6/44, flown 16.7.47.
- *P.114/SR.44* Long jet pipe version of P.113 rejected in favour of that project's twin pipes, 1.44.
- *P.122* Larger, faster and more heavily armed SR.A/1, 10.50.

SHORT BROTHERS (from 1943 Short Brothers & Harland)

Shorts had a big reputation for building flying boats.

- *S.41* S.A.3 jet fighter, possibly produced to N.7/46, c1946. Possibility is 'Jet Sturgeon' night fighter, c1945.

VICKERS-ARMSTRONG

Vickers allocated project numbers to individual prototypes, to production versions and to unbuilt projects and designs.

- 249 Not allocated to a specific type. The '249' series of Vickers drawings (24901 to 24999) embraced most of the company's unbuilt projects from the early 1930s to towards the end of Second World War and included fighters (F.9/35, F.22/39, etc), bombers and other types. Separate project numbers were still allocated to some designs.
- *Turret Fighter* Design to F.9/35, 9.8.35.
- 279 Single-seat Venom fighter, first flown 17.6.36.
- 414 Fighter project to F.6/39, 6.39. Specification replaced by F.22/39 and project modified with different armament and different tail arrangements. Also night fighter developments to F.18/40, 10.40 and 1.41.
- 420 Fighter project to F.16/40, 1940.
- 432 Cannon fighter to F.7/41, first flown 24.12.42.
- 446 Cannon fighter to F.7/41. Second prototype serial DZ223, never completed.
- *Single-seat Fighter* Unnumbered project to F.6/42, 11.9.42.

VICKERS SUPERMARINE

Following Vickers practice, many of the following relate to prototypes and production aircraft rather than projects.

- 300 Projects leading to Spitfire prototype K5054 (first flown 5.3.36), and initial production aircraft.
- 305 Two-seat fighter with one Merlin to F.9/35, 16.8.35.
- 311 Fighter (Spitfire) to F.37/34, 4.36.
- 312 Spitfire development to F.37/35, 23.4.36.
- 313 Single-seat fighter with two RR Goshawk B engines to F.37/35, 25.4.36.
- 319 Two-seat development of F.11/37 fighter with two Vultures, 8.37. Four 20mm cannon, two in lower nose firing forward, two in dorsal position mounted at approximately 65° to fire at target above. Span 56ft 6in (17.22m), length 37ft 6in (11.43m).
- 324 Single-seat fighter with twin Bristol Taurus or Merlin tractor engines to F.18/37, 21.4.38.
- 325 Single-seat fighter with twin Taurus or Merlin pusher engines to F.18/37, 26.4.38.
- 327 Six-20mm-cannon fighter development of F.18/37 project, 26.8.38.
- 329 Spitfire F.Mk.II production (design 9.38).
- 330 Spitfire F.Mk.III N3927 and W3237 only.
- 331 Spitfire F.Mk.VB.
- 332 Spitfire with FN gun installation in wings, 4.39.
- 333 Two-seat fleet fighters with Merlin or Griffon to N.8/39, 6.9.39. Single-seat developments of Spitfire with Griffon and Sabre (to NAD.925/39) 16.12.39.
- 334 Fighter to F.6/39, mid-1939. Mock-up only.
- 337 Spitfire F.Mk.IV (serial DP845 only). Original Griffon Spitfire design brochure dated 4.12.39.
- 338 Spitfire Mk.I design for Fleet Air Arm, 11.39.
- 339 Single-seat FAA fighter projects, 12.39.
- 340 Seafire F.Mk.IB prototype and production.
- 342 Spitfire Mk.I fitted with Blackburn Roc floats.
- 343 Long-range Spitfire design, 5.40.
- 344 Spitfire Mk.I with floats.
- 345 Spitfire Mk.I design with 13.2mm guns, 5.40.
- 346 Spitfire Mk.I with 'C' wing and 20mm guns.
- 348 Spitfire F.Mk.III second prototype W3237.
- 349 Spitfire F.Mk.VC production aircraft.
- 350 Spitfire F.Mk.VI production.
- 351 Spitfire F.Mk.VII production.
- 352 Spitfire F.Mk.VB tropical variant production.
- 354 Spitfire development, design 9.41.
- 355 Spitfire Mk.V Special with floats (W3760).
- 356 Spitfire F.Mks.21, 22 and 24 production.
- 357 Seafire F.Mk.IIC production.
- 358 Seafire F.Mk.III production.
- 359 Spitfire F.Mk.VIII design, 3.42, and prototype JF299.
- 360 Spitfire F.Mk.VIID and VIII design, 3.42, and production.
- *Navy Fighter* Unnumbered proposal for naval version of Spitfire with Griffon engine and V-tail, 26.3.42.
- 361 Spitfire F.Mk.IX/XVI.
- 363 Tropical Spitfire design, 5.42.
- 364 Tropical Spitfire design, 5.42.
- *Lightweight Fighter* Unnumbered project for Navy fighter with Sabre engine, 3.9.42.
- *Single-seat Fighter* Unnumbered Spitfire Mk.21 development to F.6/42, 10.9.42.
- *Jet Spitfire* Jet fighter with new fuselage, H.1 engine and Spitfire wings, 1942. No drawing available.
- 366 Spitfire F.Mk.XII prototype and production.

368	Heston project for Spitfire F.Mk.VIII with Malinowski wing.
369	Spitfire F.Mk.XIV (JF316 converted from Mk.VIII).
371	Spiteful with laminar flow wing to F.1/43, 11.42, first flown 30.6.44.
372	Spitfire F.Mk.VIII (or Mk.21) design with semi-laminar wing, 1.43.
373	Spitfire F.Mk.XIV DP851 with contra-rotating propeller.
375	Seafire LF.Mk.IIC design (2.43) and production.
376	Spitfire Mk.VIII with contra-rotating propeller, 2.43.
377	Seafire F.Mk.XV, 3.43. Prototype NS487.
378	Spitfire F.Mk.IX design for tropical conditions, 4.43.
379	Spitfire F.Mk.XIV (= Mk.VIII with Griffon). Original design brochure dated 5.43.
382	Seafang F.Mks.31 and 32 design, 10.43; first flown early 1946.
383	Spiteful design, 11.43.
384	Seafire F.Mk.XVII design (11.43) and production.
385	Spitfire F.Mk.IX seaplane MJ892.
386	Seafire F.Mk.XV design (11.43).
388	Seafire F.Mks.45, 46 and 47 design (11.43).
391	High-performance fighter with single RR 46H Eagle, 20.3.44.
392	Jet fighter with single B.41 Nene to E.10/44. Prototype first flew 27.7.46. Naval development to E.1/45. Entered service as Attacker.
393	Spiteful F.Mk.XIV design, 11.44.
394	Spiteful F. and PR.Mk.XVIII design (11.44) and production.
395	Seafire F.Mk.XVIII design, 11.44.
396	Seafang F.Mk.32 (development of Seafire Mk.XVII) design, 11.44.
397	Attacker with folding wings for overseas sales.
398	Attacker F.Mk.1 and FB.Mk.2 naval prototype and production. Prototype first flown 17.6.47.
500	Revised version of Type 392, c1946.
501	Experimental Spitfire intended for powerplant development.
510	Swept-wing experimental development of Attacker to E.41/46, first flown 29.12.48.
515	Projected Attacker F.Mk.2 with DH Ghost II engine, 1947.
516	Attacker variant, c1947.
519	Attacker fitted with jet deflection, c1948/49.
527	Proposed Attacker Mk.2 variants with RR Avon or Tay engine, 7.49 onwards.

WESTLAND

It is known that most of Westland's wartime project and design study brochures were still in existence after the war, but it appears that many have now been destroyed. Fortunately a large 'chart' exists that outlines many of these projects together with some brief details and a basic sketch.

Fighter	Single-seat low/mid-wing fighter with one Bristol Perseus to F.5/34, 1935/36. Span 37ft 6in (11.43m).
P.9 Whirlwind	Day fighter to F.37/35, first flown 11.10.38. Proposed development 11.39 with single Hercules in nose and 'controllable' guns in wing nacelles. Mk.II Whirlwind with more powerful Peregrines suggested 5.40.
Long-Range Fighter	Alternative designs to F.6/39 with Griffon tractor or pusher engines, both 5.39.
Fleet Fighter	Design studies to N.8/39 and N.9/39, 7.39 and 12.39.
Mass Production Fighter	All-wood project to F.19/40, 11.39. Same spec as Miles M.20.
P.13	High-altitude fighter to F.4/40, c9.40.
P.14	High-altitude fighter to F.4/40, c9.40. Resulted in Welkin, first flown 1.11.42.
Jet Whirlwind	Design study for development of P.9 with two 1,800lb (8.0kN) Power Jets W2Bs, 1.41. Same wings and fuselage.
High-Altitude Fighter	Delanne type with 1,415hp (1,055kW) Griffon pusher engine, shaft drive and contraprops, 7.41. Span 50ft (15.24m), wing area 245sq ft (22.79sq m), all-up weight 11,000lb (4,990kg), maximum speed 400mph (644km/h) at 32,000ft (9,754m).
High-Altitude Jet Fighter	Delanne type with two 1,800lb (8kN) Whittle W2B jets, 10.41. Span 42ft 6in (12.82m), wing area 180sq ft (16.74sq m), all-up weight 7,600lb (3,447kg), max speed 440mph (708km/h) at 35,000ft (10,668m).
J.8	Jet fighter based on Welkin with two Power Jets W2B/700, 10.4.42. Tunnel tested 11 and 12.42. Abandoned.
J.14	High-altitude jet fighter, 6.42.
Fighter	Lightweight project to F.6/42, 2.9.42.
J.15	Twin-boom jet fighter (to E.5/42?), 10.42.
Naval Fighter	Two twin-boom designs to N.7/43, 5.43. First was development of J.15 jet project with single de Havilland H.1; second was piston variant with one Griffon pusher engine.
Fighter Bomber	Twin tandem Merlin-powered study possibly to F.12/43, 5.44.
W.34	Wyvern long-range naval strike fighter to N.11/44. RR 24.H46 Eagle piston engine, first flew 12.12.46. De-navalised variant prepared to F.13/44 but discontinued.
Jet Fighter	Designs with Avon engine to F.11/45, 1.45.
W.35	Wyvern with RR Clyde or AS Python turboprop to N.12/45, first flew 18.1.49.
Wyvern S.Mk.5E	Proposed Wyvern development with Napier E.141 Double Eland, 3.54.
W.36	Wyvern development with RR AJ.65 or MV F.9 jet, 1946.

Appendix Two
British 'wartime' fighter project specifications

The Air Ministry traditionally signalled to the British aircraft industry its expected future requirements via a series of specifications, against which tenders were usually invited.

Until the end of 1949 the sequential system used in issuing these specifications was a letter/number/year arrangement. A typical example is F.4/40, which described a high-altitude fighter (in fact, what became the Westland Welkin): F stood for fighter; '4' indicated it was the 4th specification issued in that year, and the year was 1940. Alternative prefix letters included B (bomber), E (experimental), G (general purpose), M (torpedo bomber), N (naval) and P (light bomber); from about 1936 the lettering became complex but the above description will suffice for this book. The reader should also note that specifications were not always put out to tender – for example there were a number of military types developed 'independently' during the period covered by this book, such as the Spitfire and the first jets, and each would have had a specification written around them.

Specifications for an aircraft required for military service were usually accompanied by an Operational Requirement with its own 'OR' number, for example OR.81 for F.4/40. Further details of pre-1950 specifications can be found in *The British Aircraft Specifications File* by Meekcoms and Morgan, while details of ORs appeared in *Aeromilitaria* issues 4/96 and 1/97 – all published by Air-Britain.

F.36/34 (OR.16)   Fighter: Hawker Hurricane.
F.37/34 (OR.17)   Fighter: Supermarine 300 Spitfire.
F.9/35 (OR.20)   Turret Fighter: Boulton Paul P.82 Defiant, Hawker Hotspur, Bristol 147, Supermarine 305, Armstrong Whitworth AW.34 development, Fairey project, Gloster project, Vickers Project.
O.30/35   Fleet Fighter: Blackburn B.25 Roc, Boulton Paul P.85.
F.34/35   Turret Fighter: Gloster project.
35/35   Experimental Single-Seat High Speed Aircraft: Airspeed AS.31, Bristol 151, General Aircraft GAL.28, Gloster project, Hawker Hurricane variant, Martin-Baker project (Specification not proceeded with).
F.37/35 (OR.31)   Fighter: Bristol 153 and 153A, Boulton Paul P.88, Hawker Hurricane development, Supermarine 312 and 313, Westland P.9 Whirlwind.

F.9/37 (OR.49)   Fighter: Boulton Paul P.89, Gloster design.
F.11/37 (OR.50)   Turret Fighter: Armstrong Whitworth project, Boulton Paul P.92, Bristol project, Gloster project.
F.18/37 (OR.51)   Fighter: Bristol Projects, Gloster projects, Hawker Tornado and Typhoon, Supermarine 324 and 325.
43/37 (OR.55)   Engine Test-Bed: Folland 'Frightful', General GAL.43a, Percival P.26.
O.8/38 (OR.56)   Fleet Fighter: Fairey Fulmar.
F.6/39   Fighter: Supermarine 334, Vickers 414, Westland projects.
N.8/39   Fleet Fighter: N.9/39 Fleet Turret Fighter and designs to NAD925/39 Projects from Blackburn (B.31 and B.33), Fairey, Gloster, Hawker, Supermarine (including Type 333), Westland.
F.17/39 (OR.72)   Fighter: Bristol 156 Beaufighter.
F.18/39 (OR.73)   Fighter: Martin-Baker MB.3, MB.4 and MB.5.
F.22/39 (OR.76)   Fighter: Vickers 414.
E.28/39 (OR.77)   Jet-Powered Research Aircraft: Gloster Pioneer.
F.4/40 (OR.81)   High-Altitude Fighter: General Aircraft GAL.46, Hawker P.1004, Westland P.13 and P.14 (Welkin).
5/40 (OR.82)   Fleet Fighter: Fairey Firefly.
F.9/40 (OR.86)   Jet Fighter: Gloster Meteor.
N.11/40 (OR.88)   Fleet Fighter: Blackburn B.37 Firebrand, Hawker P.1009.
F.16/40   Fighter: Vickers 420.
F.18/40 (OR.95)   Night Fighter: Boulton Paul P.96 and P.97, Fairey project, Gloster F.9/37 variant, Hawker P.1008, Miles M.22A, Vickers project.
F.19/40   Basic Fighter: Miles M.20, Westland project.
F.21/40 (OR.96)   Fighter: De Havilland DH.98 Mosquito.
E.6/41 (OR.107)   Jet Fighter: De Havilland DH.100 Vampire.
F.7/41 (OR.108)   Fighter: Vickers 432.
F.10/41 (OR.109)   Fighter: Hawker P.1012 Tempest I.
N.2/42 (OR.114)   Boat Fighter: Blackburn B.44.
E.5/42   Jet Fighter: Gloster G.A.1, Westland project.
F.6/42   Fighter: Airspeed AS.56, Boulton Paul P.98, Folland Fo.117, Hawker P.1018, P.1019, P.1020 and P.1021 Tempest II, Miles M.42, M.43 and M.44 (probably), Supermarine project, Vickers project, Westland project.

F.1/43 (OR.120)   Fighter: Supermarine 371 Spiteful.
F.2/43 (OR.121)   Fighter: Hawker P.1026 Fury.
N.7/43   Naval Fighter: Boulton Paul P.103 and P.104, Fairey project, Folland Fo.118, Hawker P.1022, Westland projects.
S.8/43 (OR.124)   Torpedo Fighter: Blackburn B.45 Firebrand Mk.III.
F.12/43 (OR.126)   Fighter: De Havilland DH.103 Hornet, Westland project.
F.19/43   Fighter: Folland Fo.117A.
N.22/43 (OR.155) Naval Fighter: Hawker Sea Fury.
S.28/43 (OR.150)   Torpedo Fighter: Blackburn B.48 Firecrest.
E.1/44 (OR.157)   Jet Fighter: Gloster G.A.2 Ace.
N.5/44 (OR.162)   Naval Fighter; De Havilland DH.103 Sea Hornet.
E.6/44 (OR.170)   Jet-Powered Boat Fighter: Saro P.113/SR.44/SR.A/1.
E.10/44 (OR.182) Jet Fighter: Supermarine 392.
N.11/44 (OR.174) Naval Fighter: Westland W.34 Wyvern.

E.1/45 (OR.195)   Naval Jet Fighter: Supermarine 392 Attacker.
N.5/45   Naval Fighter: Supermarine 382 Seafang.
S.10/45   Torpedo Fighter: Blackburn B.48 Firecrest (Sabre engine).
F.11/45   Naval Jet Fighter: De Havilland Sea Vampire, Westland project.
N.12/45 (OR.213) Naval Fighter: Westland W.35 Wyvern.
N.21/45 (OR.226) Naval Night Fighter: De Havilland Sea Hornet Mk.21.
N.7/46 (OR.218)   Naval Jet Fighter: Hawker P.1040 Sea Hawk, Short S.41/SA.3(?).
E.38/46 (OR.243)   Research Aircraft; Hawker P.1052.
E.41/46   Research Aircraft: Supermarine 510.
F.24/48 (OR.265)   Night Fighter: Armstrong Whitworth Meteor Mk.11.
15/49 (OR.277)   Strike Fighter: De Havilland DH.112 Venom.

Appendix Three
British 'wartime' prototype fighter contracts

This list covers prototypes and unbuilt designs only; there are no production aircraft. The dates give the point where serials were allocated and come from the Ministry's serial ledger. It should fall very close to the date of an Instruction to Proceed (ITP), which was the official authority to spend money, but some of the dates given above come after the start of work on a particular project. In such cases the firm concerned may have begun work as a private venture, or short-term contracts may have preceded the ITP.

Serial(s)	Type	Contract	Date	Comments
K5054	Supermarine F.37/34	361140/34	Spitfire	
K5061	Armstrong Whitworth F.5/33	356293/34	4.1.35	Two-seat fighter, see K8624
K5083	Hawker F.36/34	357483/34	21.2.35	Hurricane
K5119	Bristol F.5/34	395998/35	25.3.35	Bristol 146
K5200	Gloster SS.37 (F.7/30)	395996/35	25.3.35	Gladiator
K5604	Gloster F.5/34	395999/35	14.5.35	
K8088	Bristol F.5/34	395998/35		Not completed
K8089	Gloster F.5/34	395999/35		Second prototype
K8309	Hawker F.9/35	453461/35	7.11.35	Hotspur
K8310	Boulton Paul F.9/35	453462/35	7.11.35	Defiant
K8620	Boulton Paul F.9/35	453462/35	13.1.36	
K8621	Hawker F.9/35	453461/35	24.1.36	
K8622/K8623	Fairey F.9/35	453463/35	1.2.36	
K8624	Armstrong Whitworth F.9/35	490715/35	12.2.36	AW.34 (K5061 cancelled same day)
K8625	Gloster F.5/33	450108/35	8.2.36	Some sources say F.34/35
L6591/6592	Boulton Paul F.37/35	556966/36	7.12.36	Cancelled 6.1.37
L6593	Supermarine F.37/35	556964/36	7.12.36	Cancelled 28.1.37
L6844/6845	Westland F.37/35	556965/36	11.2.37	Whirlwind
L7999/L8001	Gloster F.9/37	697972/37	4.2.38?	
L9629/L9632	Boulton Paul F.11/37	708600/37	2.3.38	P.92
P5212/P5216/P5219/P5224	Hawker F.18/37	815124/38		Typhoon and Tornado
P9594	Martin Baker MB.2	982598/39		Stated to be 'F.5/34'
R2492/R2496/R2500	Martin Baker F.18/39	1165/39		
R4236/R4239	Vickers F.22/39	17894/39		
V3142	Heston model of B. Paul P.92	B.19037/39		
V9258	Boulton Paul F.11/37 (P.92)	498571/36		See L9629 etc
W4041/W4046	Gloster E.28/39	SB.3229		
AX834	Miles M.20/2	B.140247/40		N.1/41
DD804/DD810/DD815	Blackburn N.11/40	B.156337/40	27.1.41	Firebrand
DG202-DG213	Gloster F.9/40	SB.21179		Meteor
DG558/DG562	Westland F.4/40	C/Acft/633		Welkin
DP845/DP851	Supermarine F.4/41	C/Acft/821	26.5.41?	
DX160/DX165	Folland E.28/40	C/Acft/741	15.8.41	
DZ217/DZ223	Vickers F.7/41	C/Acft/1346		Vickers 432
HG641	Hawker Tornado	SB.21392		
HM595/HM599	Hawker F.10/41	SB.32483		Tempest

LA594/LA597/LA602/LA607/LA610/LA614	Hawker Tempest	C/Acft/1986		
LZ548/LZ551	De Havilland E.6/41	SB.24539		Vampire
MP838	De Havilland E.6/41	SB.24539		
MZ275/MZ277	Blackburn N.2/42	C/Acft/2542		Blackburn B.44 (originally C/Acft/2189, 19.5.42)
NN648/NN651/NN655	Gloster E.5/42	SB.26236	29.1.43	Cancelled 7.2.44
NN660/NN664/ NN667	Supermarine F.1/43	C/Acft/2329	1.2.43	Spiteful
NS487/NS490/NS493	Supermarine Seafire XV	C/Acft/2901	8.3.43	
NV636	Blackburn Firebrand	no contract number		Ledger states 'Ref. DD810'
NX798/NX802	Hawker F.2/43	No number	22.3.43	Fury
PF370/PF376	Westland F.9/43	SB.26569	29.4.43	Welkin II
PK240/PK243/PK245	Supermarine N.4/43	C/Acft/2901	24.5.43	Griffon Seafire
PP139	Supermarine Spitfire 21	C/Acft/821	5.7.43	
RD104/RD107/RD108/RD113/RD115/RD118	English Electric F.6/42	SB.26924	10.9.43	Folland Fo.117A
RR915/RR919	De Havilland F.12/43	SB.26873	12.11.43	Hornet
RT133/RT136	Miles E.24/43	SB.27157	15.12.43	Miles M.52
RT646	Supermarine 'Spitfire VIII'	C/Acft/2329	24.12.43	Seafang
RT651/RT656	Blackburn S.28/43	SB.27216	1.1.44	'Firecrest'; ledger gives Fairey S.28/43
RT661	Westland F.9/43	SB.26569	6.1.44	Welkin II
SM801/SM805/SM809	Gloster E.1/44	SB.27324	7.2.44	Ace
SR661/SR666	Hawker N.22/43	SB.27022	24.2.44	Sea Fury
SX549	Supermarine	SB.27489	6.4.44	'Spitfire F.21 2nd version'
TG263/TG267/TG271	Saro E.6/44	C/Acft/4122		
TM379/TM383/TM389	Supermarine Spitfire F.21	B.981687/39		'To be navalised'
TS371/TS375/TS378/TS380/TS384/TS387	Westland N.11/44	C/Acft/4522	26.8.44	Wyvern
TS409/TS413/TS416	Supermarine E.10/44	C/Acft/4562	30.8.44	Attacker
TX145/TX148/TX150	Gloster E.1/44	SB.27324	26.1.45	Ace
VB847	Hawker N.22/43	SB.27022		Sea Fury
VB893/VB895	Supermarine N.5/45	C/Acft/5176	12.3.45	Seafang
VF172	Blackburn S.28/43	SB.27216		'Firecrest'
VF254/VF257/VF262	Blackburn S.10/45	SB.84896		Sabre 'Firecrest'
VP109/VP113/VP120	Westland N.12/45	C/Acft/5982	7.2.46	Wyvern turboprop
VP401/VP413/VP422	Hawker P.1040	C/Acft/6115	30.3.46	Sea Hawk
VV106/VV109	Supermarine 510 (E.41/46)	6/Acft/1031	4.3.47	Swept Attacker
VX272/VX279	Hawker P.1052 (E.38/46)	6/Acft/1156	23.3.48	Swept P.1040
WA546	AWA Meteor (F.24/48)	6/Acft/3437	31.5.49	Night fighter

Select bibliography and source notes

During research for this book a great deal of primary source material has been consulted, including original documents held by the Public Record Office (AVIA 15, AVIA 53, AVIA 54, AIR 2 and AIR 20) and by museums, heritage centres, groups and individuals, as noted in the Acknowledgements. Drawings and photographs are credited individually unless they came from the author's collection. Important secondary source material helped to get things started and to fill gaps:

Armstrong Whitworth Aircraft since 1913: Oliver Tapper (Putnam, 1973)
Armstrong Whitworth Paper Planes: Ray Williams (*Air Enthusiast* No 43, 1991)
Avro Aircraft since 1908: A. J. Jackson (Putnam, 1965)
The Best Fighter the Navy Never Had – Boulton Paul's 'Sea Defiant': Alec Brew (*Air Enthusiast* No 106, 2003)
Blackburn Aircraft since 1909: A. J. Jackson (Putnam, 1968)
Boulton Paul Aircraft since 1915: Alec Brew (Putnam, 1993)
Bristol Aircraft since 1910: C. H. Barnes (Putnam, 1964)
Bristol – An Aircraft Album: James D. Oughton (Ian Allan, 1973)
The British Aircraft Specifications File: K. J. Meekcoms and E. B. Morgan (Air-Britain, 1994)
De Havilland Aircraft since 1909: A. J. Jackson (Putnam, 1962)
Design and Development of Weapons – Studies in Government and Industrial Organisation: M. M. Postan, D. Hay and J. D. Scott (HMSO, 1964)
Fairey Aircraft since 1915: H. A. Taylor (Putnam, 1974)
Fairey Firefly: W. A. Harrison (Airlife, 1992)
From Sea to Air – The Heritage of Sam Saunders: A. E. Tagg and R. L. Wheeler (Crossprint, 1989)
General Aircraft Ltd: Potted History (*The Aeroplane Spotter*, 26 June 1948)
Gloster Aircraft since 1917: Derek James (Putnam, 1971)
Hawker Aircraft since 1920: Francis K. Mason (Putnam, 1971)
Industry and Air Power – The Expansion of British Aircraft Production 1935-1941: Sebastian Ritchie (Frank Cass, 1997)
Interceptor: James Goulding (Ian Allan, 1986)
Interceptor Fighters for the Royal Air Force 1939-45: Michael J. F. Bowyer (Patrick Stephens, 1984)
The Lion has Wings – The Race to Prepare the RAF for World War II 1935-1940: L. F. E. Coombs (Airlife, 1997)
Miles Aircraft since 1925: Don L. Brown (Putnam, 1970)
Miles Aircraft – the Wartime Years: Production, Research and Development During WWII: Peter Amos (Air-Britain, 2012)

Operational Requirements: Ray Sturtivant (*Aeromilitaria* No 4, 1996, and No 1, 1997)
Parnall's Final Fling: The Parnall Type 381 Gunnery Research Aircraft: Philip Jarrett (*Air Enthusiast* No 55, Autumn 1994)
Planemakers 2 – Westland: David Mondey (Janes, 1982)
Reap the Whirlwind – Britain's Pioneer Cannon Fighter: Tony Buttler (*Air Enthusiast* No 99, 2002)
The Royal Air Force and Aircraft Design 1923-1939: Colin Sinnott (Frank Cass, 2001)
The Search for Fighter Performance: James Goulding (*Aviation News,* August 2002)
Saunders and Saro Aircraft since 1917: Peter London (Putnam, 1988)
Shorts Aircraft since 1900: C. H. Barnes (Putnam, 1967)
Sir James Martin: Sarah Sharman (Patrick Stephens, 1996)
Spirit of Hamble: Folland Aircraft: Derek N. James (Tempus, 2000)
Spitfire – the History: E. B. Morgan and E. Shacklady (Key Publishing, 1987)
Supermarine Aircraft since 1914: C. F. Andrews and E. B. Morgan (Putnam, 1981)
The 'Super' Twin – Supermarine F.18/37 (*Twenty-First Profile Magazine* No 7)
Sydney Camm and the Hurricane: John Fozard (ed) (Airlife, 1991)
UK Jet Pioneers: Tony Buttler (*Air Enthusiast* Nos 105 and 106, 2003)
Vickers Aircraft since 1908: C. F. Andrews and E. B. Morgan (Putnam)
Vickers' Last Fighter: Tony Buttler (*Air Enthusiast* No 67, 1997)
Westland Aircraft since 1915: D. James (Putnam, 1991)
Westland P.9 Whirlwind (*Twenty-First Profile Magazine* No 14)
Wilfrid Freeman: Anthony Furse (Spellmount, 2000)

Glossary

A&AEE	Aircraft and Armament Experimental Establishment, Martlesham Heath (pre-9.9.39), Boscombe Down (post-9.9.39).
ACAS(OR)	Assistant Chief of the Air Staff (Operational Requirements) [Air Ministry post].
ACAS(TR)	Assistant Chief of the Air Staff (Technical Requirements) [Air Ministry post].
ACM	Air Chief Marshal.
AMDP	Air Member for Development and Production.
AMRD	Air Member for Research and Development.
anhedral	Downward slope of wing from root to tip.
AoA	Angle of attack, the angle at which the wing is inclined relative to the airflow.
AI	Air interception (radar).
AP	Armour piercing.
AS	Armstrong Siddeley.
A/S	Anti-submarine.
aspect ratio	Ratio of wingspan to mean chord, calculated by dividing the square of the span by the wing area.
ASV	Anti-surface vessel (radar).
AVM	Air Vice Marshal.
AWA	Armstrong Whitworth Aircraft Ltd.
BP	Boulton Paul Aircraft.
CAS	Chief of the Air Staff [Air Ministry post].
CinC	Commander-in-Chief.
chord	Distance between centres of curvature of wing leading and trailing edges when measured parallel to the longitudinal axis.
CNR	Chief Naval Representative (to MAP).
CofG	Centre of gravity.
CRD	Controller of Research and Development [MAP post].
DAMDP	Deputy Air Member for Development and Production.
DCAS	Deputy Chief of the Air Staff [Air Ministry post].
DDOR	Deputy Director of Operational Requirements.
DD/RDT	Deputy Director/Research and Development (Technical).
DDTD	Deputy Director of Technical Development [MAP post].
DGRD	Director General of Research and Development.
DH	de Havilland.
dihedral	Upward slope of wing from root to tip.
DOR(A)	Director of Operational Requirements (Air).
DSR	Director of Scientific Research
DTD	Director of Technical Development [MAP post].
FAA	Fleet Air Arm.
HAL	Hawker Aircraft Limited.
HMG	His/Her Majesty's Government.
HP	Handley Page.
HSG	Hawker Siddeley Group.
IAS	Indicated airspeed.
incidence	Angle at which the wing (or tail) is set relative to the fuselage.
ITP	Instruction to Proceed.
Laminar Flow Wing	Specifically designed to ensure a smooth flow of air over its surfaces with uniform separation between the layers of air.
MAEE	Marine Aircraft Experimental Establishment.
MAP	Ministry of Aircraft Production – created in May 1940 to relieve the Air Ministry of its role of procuring aircraft and the equipment and supplies associated with them. Functions transferred to the Ministry of Supply in 1946.

MoS	Ministry of Supply – created August 1939 to provide stores used by the RAF (and Army and Navy).
nm	Nautical mile.
OR	Operational Requirement.
OTU	Operational Training Unit
PR	Photo reconnaissance.
R & D	Research and Development.
RAAF	Royal Australian Air Force.
RAE	Royal Aircraft Establishment, Farnborough.
RDT	Research and Development (Technical).
RN	Royal Navy.
RP	Unguided rocket projectile.
RR	Rolls-Royce.
RTO	Resident Technical Officer.
SBAC	Society of British Aircraft Constructors, the UK's national trade association which represented companies that supplied military and civil aircraft and their equipment. It later became the Society of British Aerospace Companies.
TAS	True airspeed.
t/c	Thickness/chord ratio.
TRE	Telecommunications Research Establishment, Malvern.
TT	Torpedo.
USAAF	United States Army Air Force.
USN	United States Navy.
VCAS	Vice Chief of the Air Staff.

Useful conversion factors:

x 0.093	square feet (sq.ft) to square metres (sq.m)
x 0.3048	feet (ft) to metres (m)
x 0.4539	pounds (lb) to kilograms (kg)
x 1.2	Imperial (UK) gallons to US gallons
x 1.609	miles to kilometres (km) (also for mph to km/h)
x 1.853	knots to kilometres/hour (km/h)
x 2.54	inches (in) to centimetres (cm)
x 4.5469	Imperial/UK gallons (gal) to litres (lit)
÷ 225	pounds (lb) to kilonewton (kN)

Index

INDEX OF HARDWARE

Airspeed
- AS.56 — 35, 38, 39

Armstrong Whitworth
- AW.34 — 86
- F.9/35 — 86, 89
- F.11/37 — 92, 93
- Meteor NF Mk.11 — 185, 186

Avro
- Lancaster — 65, 146, 147
- Manchester — 146

BAC Concorde — 8

Blackburn
- B.20 — 151
- B.24 Skua — 90, 109
- B.25 Roc — 90, 153
- B.31 — 109, 110
- B.33 — 106
- B.37 Firebrand — 105, 106, 110, 112, 114-117, 131, 151
- B.43 — 151
- B.44 — 151-153, 194
- B.48 Firecrest — 130-133
- B.50 — 131

Boulton Paul
- B.1/35 — 87
- Overstrand — 85
- P.82 Defiant — 61, 85-87, 89-91, 96, 98, 104, 122
- P.85 — 90
- P.88 — 52, 53, 59
- P.92 & P.92/2 — 25, 27, 89, 92, 93, 96, 97
- P.93 — 90
- P.94 — 91
- P.96 — 36, 98, 99, 104
- P.97 — 99, 100, 104
- P.98 — 35, 36, 39
- P.100 — 35
- P.103 — 36, 120-122
- P.104 — 122
- P.105 — 129, 130
- P.107 — 130

Bristol
- 146 — 9, 10, 87
- 147 — 87, 89
- 148 — 87
- 151 — 53
- 153 & 153A — 53-55
- 156 Beaufighter — 27, 28, 63-65, 97, 103, 104, 147, 150, 169
- 157 — 65
- 158 — 65
- 163 Buckingham — 65
- Beaufort — 27, 63, 64
- Blenheim — 65, 97, 149
- F.11/37 — 93-95
- F.18/37 — 16-18, 27

De Havilland
- DH.98 Mosquito — 66, 82, 83, 97, 103, 104, 146, 149, 150, 172
- DH.99/DH.100 Vampire — 82, 147, 172, 173, 182, 187-191, 197
- DH.102 — 82
- DH.103 Hornet/Sea Hornet — 51, 67, 82-84, 126-128, 146, 147, 201
- DH.107/DH.112 Venom/Sea Venom — 147, 187, 189-191
- DH.110 — 191

Douglas
- DC-3 — 149
- Havoc — 97

Fairey
- F.6/39 — 68
- F.9/35 — 87-89
- F.18/40 — 100, 101, 104
- Firefly — 100, 113, 114, 127
- Fulmar — 105, 106
- Gannet — 137
- N.7/43 — 122, 123
- N.8/39 — 106, 107, 109
- N.9/39 — 106, 107, 109, 110
- NAD.925/39 — 110-112
- P.4/34 — 105
- Spearfish — 135
- Strike Fighter — 133-137

Focke Wulf
- Fw190 — 34, 36

Folland
- Fo.116 — 40
- Fo.117 — 36, 37, 39, 40, 124
- Fo.118 — 124-126

General Aircraft
- GAL.46 — 74-76, 79, 80
- Monospar — 74, 75

Gloster
- Boosted Fighter — 173, 174
- CXP-1001 China Fighter — 181-183
- E.1/44 Ace — 178-183
- E.5/42 Ace — 172, 174-177
- E.28/39 — 148, 162-166, 168, 174
- F.5/34 — 9, 10, 36
- F.9/35 — 88, 89, 92
- F.9/37 — 19, 27, 61-63, 102
- F.11/37 — 63, 92, 95, 96
- F.18/37 — 18, 19, 28, 62
- F.18/40 Reaper — 63, 101-103, 168, 169
- F.34/35 — 61

222

INDEX

	Gamecock	36
	Gauntlet	36
	Gladiator	9, 36
	Grebe	36
	Javelin	183, 186
	Meteor	84, 147, 148, 162, 166-173, 175, 181-186, 191, 200, 201
	N.8/39	107
	N.9/39	109, 110
	NAD.925/39	111, 112
	P.209	184
	P.263	184, 185
	P.309	185, 186
	Rocket	176, 177, 179, 193
	Twin Boom Studies	28

Grumman

	F4F Wildcat	119
	XF5F-1 Skyrocket	54

Handley Page

	Hampden	65

Hawker

	F.11/37	96
	F.37/35	55
	Fury Biplane	10
	Fury Monoplane	10
	Fury/Sea Fury	16, 29, 32, 40-44, 46, 48, 51, 105, 125, 126, 143, 201
	Harrier	8
	Henley	70
	Hotspur	85, 88, 89, 91, 92
	Hunter	46, 191
	Hurricane	8, 10-12, 16, 29, 31, 32, 40, 46, 55, 60, 85, 92, 146, 158
	N.8/39	107, 108
	N.9/39	109, 110
	NAD.925/39	111
	P.1004	76, 79, 80, 191
	P.1008	102
	P.1009	116
	P.1011	191
	P.1012	29
	P.1016	31
	P.1018/P.1019/P.1020	37, 38
	P.1022	125, 126
	P.1027	46, 47
	P.1030	47, 48
	P.1032	48
	P.1035	191
	P.1040/Sea Hawk	46, 128, 191-193
	P.1046	192
	P.1047	192
	P.1049	192
	P.1072	192
	Tempest	16, 25, 29-34, 39-43, 46, 47, 117, 131, 146, 191
	Tornado	13, 19, 23-25, 30, 40
	Typhoon	8, 13, 16, 19, 20, 23-25, 28-30, 32, 34, 37, 40, 76, 116, 117, 145, 146

Heston

	J.A.8	96

Junkers

	F-13	148
	Ju 86	159

Martin-Baker

	MB.2	10, 49
	MB.3	49, 50, 169
	MB.4	49, 51
	MB.5	49-51

Miles

	M.20	153, 154
	M.22/M.22A	67, 68, 102, 151, 154-158
	M.23/M.23A	154, 158-160
	M.42	35
	M.43	35
	M.44	35
	M.52	177, 193, 194

North American

	P.51 Mustang	46

R. Malcolm

	Fighter	160-161

Saunders-Roe

	A.37 Shrimp	195
	P.122	195, 196
	SR.44/SR.A.1	153, 194-196
	SR.45 Princess	195

Short

	Jet Sturgeon/Night Fighter	127, 128
	Silver Streak	148
	Sturgeon	127, 146

Sopwith Snipe 42

Vickers-Armstrongs

	279 Venom	10
	414	68-70, 72
	420	70, 71, 102
	432	67, 72, 73
	F.6/42	37, 39
	F.9/35	89
	F.18/40	102, 103
	Twin-Boom Fighter	71
	Wellington	70

Vickers Supermarine

	224	16, 21, 57
	300 Spitfire	8, 11-16, 21, 26, 27, 29, 34, 37, 44-46, 56, 60, 85, 88, 108, 112, 117, 119, 146, 149, 152, 153, 158, 169, 196
	305	88, 89
	312	55-57
	313	56-59
	324	20-22, 26
	325	21-23
	327	25-28
	333	108-110
	334	68
	371 Spiteful	13, 43-46, 84, 196
	382 Seafang	44-46, 105, 144
	391	48, 49, 105
	392 Attacker	45, 46, 196-199, 201
	527 Attacker Mk.2	198-200

	B.12/36	21
	F.6/42	37, 39
	NAD.925/39	111, 112
	Naval Fighter Proposal	118, 119
	Seafire	12, 46, 117-119
	Seagull	197
	Swift	46, 191
Westland		
	F.6/42	37-39
	F.6/39	68
	F.12/43	82
	J.8	200, 201
	J.14	204
	J.15	125, 200, 201
	Mass Production Fighter	154
	N.7/43	125
	N.8/39 & N.9/39	109
	NAD.925/39	112
	P.9 Whirlwind	25, 27, 28, 52, 57-61, 63, 64, 78, 80, 146
	P.13	76-78
	P.14	76-79
	W.34 Wyvern	48, 115, 120, 132-135, 137-142, 147
	W.36 'Jet Wyvern'	142
	Welkin	67, 73, 74, 80-82, 160, 168, 172, 200
	Wyvern Mk.5	141, 142

INDEX OF PEOPLE

Alexander, A V	116
Baker, Capt Val	49, 50
Barnwell, Capt Frank	54
Beaverbrook, Lord	63, 80, 116, 166, 168
Breakey, J D	137, 196
Buchanan, Major J S	10, 11, 170
Camm, Sydney	10, 13, 16, 19, 20, 28-31, 34, 40-43, 80
Campbell, Lt Cdr	117
Carter, George	103, 162, 163, 167-169, 173, 174
Cherwell, Lord	168
Constant, Hayne	168
Coryton, Air Marshal W A	183, 191
Daunt, Michael	162
Davenport, Arthur	139
de Havilland, Sir Geoffrey	83, 103, 172, 187
Digby, John	139
Douglas, Air Vice Marshal W Sholto	26, 63, 65, 97
Dunbar, Mr	68
Farren, W S	72, 75, 79, 80, 103, 167, 168
Fedden, Sir Roy	34
Folland, Henry	36, 39
Freeman, Sir Wilfrid	39, 65, 68, 169, 192
Frise, Leslie	54, 63
Garner, Dr	177
Grinstead, H	11, 27, 75, 164
Halford, Maj Frank	171, 187, 196
Hall, Arnold	166, 167
Hennessy, Mr	166, 168
Higgins, Sir John	9
Hill, Air Vice Marshal Roderick	11, 27, 75
Hives, E W	138
Hollis-Williams, D L	135
Holroyd, F	200
James, G L	164
John, Capt Casper	117
Joubert, Air Marshal Sir Philip	97, 103
Kilner, Maj	73
Ku, Colonel	182
Leatheart, Sqn Ldr	98
Lin, Colonel	183
Linnell, Air Marshal F J	31, 39, 40, 65, 130
Liptrot, Capt R N	10, 26, 38, 39, 75, 82, 104, 164, 188, 194
Lloyd, John 'Jimmy'	174
Lobelle, Marcel	160
Lucas, Philip	47
Martin, Sir James	49, 50
McClean, Sir Robert	26
Miles, F G	193
Mitchell, Reginald J	11-13, 55, 58
Newell, Air Vice Marshal Cyril	9
North, J D	41, 129
Page, Rab	201
Perring, W G A	164, 166, 167
Petter, W E W	137, 139, 200, 201
Petty, George	130
Pierson, Rex	68, 70-73
Portal, Marshal of the Royal Air Force Sir Charles	39
Rennie, Maj J D	151
Ross, Major A A	79
Rowe, N E	29-31, 39, 40-42, 73, 82, 104, 126, 132, 134, 135, 174, 175, 177, 188, 191, 192
Rowley, Wg Cdr H	70
Roxbee Cox, Harold Dr	177, 196
Sayer, Flg Off Gerry	162
Saundby, Air Marshal Sir Robert	75
Scott-Hall, Stuart	132
Serby, J E	42
Sinnott, Colin	9
Slattery, Adm M S	112, 192
Smith, Joe	196
Sorley, Sqn Ldr Ralph	8, 9, 11, 32, 65, 135, 171, 172, 174
Spriggs, Sir Frank	40, 170
Thompson, Maj H S V	27
Tizard, Sir Henry	72, 80, 103, 166, 169, 170, 187
Trenchard, Lord	9
Verney, Air Cdr R H	19
Walker, C C	188
Walker, R W	164
Wallis, Barnes	73
Wardle, Mr	191, 192
Westbrook, Mr	72
Whittle, Frank	147, 164, 167, 177, 193, 201